Psychedelic Capitalism

Psychedelic Capitalism

Jamie Brownlee
Kevin Walby

Fernwood Publishing
Halifax & Winnipeg

Copyright 2025 © Jamie Brownlee and Kevin Walby.

All rights reserved. No part of this book may be reproduced or transmitted in any form by any means without permission in writing from the publisher, except by a reviewer, who may quote brief passages in a review.

Development editor: Wayne Antony
Copyediting: Jessica Antony
Text design: Lauren Jeanneau
Cover design: Evan Marnoch
Printed and bound in the UK

Published by Fernwood Publishing
Halifax and Winnipeg
2970 Oxford Street, Halifax, Nova Scotia, B3L 2W4
www.fernwoodpublishing.ca

Fernwood Publishing Company Limited gratefully acknowledges the financial support of the Government of Canada through the Canada Book Fund and the Canada Council for the Arts. We acknowledge the Province of Manitoba for support through the Manitoba Publishers Marketing Assistance Program and the Book Publishing Tax Credit. We acknowledge the Nova Scotia Department of Communities, Culture and Heritage for support through the Publishers Assistance Fund.

Library and Archives Canada Cataloguing in Publication
Title: Psychedelic capitalism / Jamie Brownlee, Kevin Walby.
Names: Brownlee, Jamie, author | Walby, Kevin, 1981- author
Description: Includes bibliographical references and index.
Identifiers: Canadiana 20250112345 | ISBN 9781773637310 (softcover)
Subjects: LCSH: Hallucinogenic drugs—Economic aspects. | LCSH: Hallucinogenic drugs—Therapeutic use. | LCSH: Hallucinogenic drugs—Social aspects.
Classification: LCC RM324.8 .B76 2025 | DDC 615.7/883—dc23

CONTENTS

ACKNOWLEDGEMENTS VIII

1 – A JUST FUTURE FOR PSYCHEDELICS..1

2 – THE PSYCHEDELIC RENAISSANCE 6
    Classifying Psychedelics.. 8
    A History of the Psychedelic Renaissance 10
        From Counterculture to Pop Culture 10
        The Role of the Media 13
        Greater Acceptance and Enduring Stigma....................................... 15
        Psychedelics Outside of the Lab.. 18
        Research and Medicalization 20
        Politics and Legalities... 22
        The Big Business of Psychedelics.. 24
    A Political Economy of Psychedelia 26
        The Pitfalls of Corporatization and Medicalization 27
        Avoiding Psychedelic Exceptionalism 29
        The Case for Decriminalization and Legal, Safe Access................32

3 – THE ENDLESS WAR ON DRUGS..34
    The Early Days of Drug Prohibition 35
    The Rise of Psychedelic Science... 39
    The Modern War on Drugs Begins.. 42
    Enter Harm Reduction.. 53
    Decriminalization and Legalization.. 58

4 – MYSTICAL EXPERIENCES AND THE PROCESS OF BELIEF 61
    Mystical Experiences, Religion and Psychedelics................................... 62
    Mystical Experiences and Psychedelic Science......................................65
    Can Psychedelics Change Your Beliefs?... 71

5 – POWER, POLITICS AND SOCIAL CHANGE 77
    Left-Wing Psychedelia 79
        Empathy, Openness and Political Beliefs 80
        Ecology and Nature Relatedness 82
        The Allure of Tripping Elites 86
        Anti-Capitalist Perspectives 89

Right-Wing Psychedelia 92
    Authoritarianism and the Far Right 93
    The CIA and US Military 95
    US Republicans and the Military-Industrial Complex 98
    Transhumanism and the Hallucinogenic Elite 102
Psychedelics and Social Change 106

6 – PSYCHEDELIC MEDICALIZATION 110
Knowledge Claims and the Medical Model 111
Clinical Trials and Methodological Challenges 116
    Today's Clinical Research 122
Medicalization and Mental Health 125
    Psychedelics and the "Mental Health Crisis" 126
    Questions about Efficacy 129
    Is the Trip Necessary? 134
    The Microdosing Debate 138
    Don't Believe the Hype? 142
    The FDA Rejects MDMA-Assisted Therapy 145
Safety and Risks 148
    Ranking of Harms 149
    Bad Trips and "Challenging Experiences" 154
    The Issue of Therapist Abuse and Related Risks 159

7 – PSYCHEDELIC CAPITALISM 163
The Psychedelic Industry 166
    Are Psychedelics Like the Cannabis Industry? 168
    The Rise and Fall of the Psychedelic Stock Market 170
    An Uncertain Future and the Question of Big Pharma 172
The Corporadelic Set and Setting 175
    A Unique Industry? 175
    Psychedelic Capitalists and Decriminalization 177
    Following the Money: From MAPS PBC to Lykos Therapeutics ... 180
Psychedelics and the Corporate "Wellness" Industry 184
    Big Tech, Wellness Apps and Surveillance Capitalism 186
    The Cautionary Tale of Ketamine Clinics 190
    Psychedelic Tourism 194
Intellectual Property and Patent Wars 200
    Next-Generation Psychedelics 202
    Psychedelics in a Broken IP System 205
    "Bad Patents" and the Challenge of Prior Art 210
    Compass Pathways 214
    Psychedelic Enclosure 218

8 – LEGAL CHANGE AND PSYCHEDELIC FUTURES 220
- Legal Access to Psychedelics in Canada 221
- Australia: Medical Model Par Excellence 224
- The US: Each State is a Piece of the Puzzle 225
  - Oregon and Measures 109 and 110 227
  - Colorado and Proposition 122 232
  - California, Bill 58 and TREAT 235
  - Other US Initiatives at the Local, State and Federal Levels 238
- Law, Religion and Culture: A Back Door for Access? 240
- The Drug War Continues 244
- The Legal Landscape and the Future of Access 251

9 – TURN ON, TUNE IN, CASH OUT? 253
- The Threat of Corporate Capture 255
- The Importance of Psychedelic Activism 258
- Ending the War on Drugs 259

REFERENCES 262

INDEX 311

ACKNOWLEDGEMENTS

AS SOCIAL SCIENCE RESEARCHERS who have studied the impacts of capitalism and corporate power in other domains, the mysterious world of psychedelics was unchartered territory for us. Fortunately, we had a lot of support and assistance that helped make this project a reality. We are incredibly grateful to Salena Brickey for taking countless hours out of her weekends to skillfully edit every chapter. We are also indebted to our production editor, Wayne Antony, for his project advocacy and his vision in helping to craft the manuscript. We would also like to thank the rest of the Fernwood team for their enthusiasm and hard work, as well as our research assistants for their valuable contributions. Finally, we would like to acknowledge the many independent journalists, researchers, harm reduction advocates and social activists who inspired our work. Psychedelics are a remarkable class of substances that are too important to be appropriated and commodified by institutional power structures. We hope this book makes a small contribution to a more just psychedelic future.

A JUST FUTURE FOR PSYCHEDELICS

IN JUNE 2023, the Multidisciplinary Association for Psychedelic Studies (MAPS) held its fourth Psychedelic Science conference in Denver, Colorado. The conference was advertised as the largest of its kind in history, with roughly 12,000 healthcare professionals, scientists, investors, politicians, journalists and celebrities taking part. It was hailed as a celebration of the steady growth of psychedelic science, medicine and advocacy in the twenty-first century. In the conference's final session, MAPS founder Rick Doblin appeared on stage for his closing remarks. Doblin has spent over thirty-five years arguing for the benefits of psychedelics. He is also among the players in the psychedelic field credited with helping to restore the legitimacy of psychedelic research and therapy in the face of the deadly war on drugs. However, Doblin's talk was quickly interrupted by Indigenous rights activists who criticized MAPS and the broader psychedelic community for commodifying plant medicines and tokenizing Indigenous voices. "You have been deceived by this movement," one protestor proclaimed, "this is not a collective liberation movement. This is capitalization." Critics also asserted that processes of commodification have led to abuses against Indigenous peoples in the past (for example, with tobacco and coca) and that the same would happen again if the corporate-medical establishment was allowed to appropriate psychedelic medicines.

The 2023 MAPS conference and the critical commentary that ensued is important for several reasons. The fact that a huge psychedelic conference could happen at all might have seemed like an impossibility during the height of the drug war just a few decades ago. The war on drugs was instrumental in shuttering psychedelic research and pushing the movement underground. But here it was, a reputable scientific conference much like any other. In his remarks, Doblin noted that MAPS had taken its research on MDMA for the treatment of post-traumatic stress disorder (PTSD) into Phase 3 clinical trials and that other organizations were approaching a similar position with respect to different psychedelic substances and treatments. The protest at the conference's close, however, revealed deep divisions among psychedelic supporters over if and how psychedelics should be integrated into the mainstream.

The MAPS event was by no means the first time this type of controversy has played out publicly. During the 2022 Wonderland Miami conference, members of Psymposia — a non-profit organization that provides critical perspectives on psychedelic politics and culture — were banned from attending by the event organizers (Kent 2022a). Psymposia has sharply criticized "corporadelic" culture in recent years, exposing contradictions and problems associated with psychedelic capitalism, while drawing attention to fraud and abuse in psychedelic science and therapy. Hamilton Morris, another prominent figure in the psychedelic field and creator of the popular television series "Hamilton's Pharmacopeia," was one of the conference's speakers. With a distinct air of condescension, Morris attacked critics of the "psychedelic-industrial complex." He mocked Psymposia members Brian Pace and Neşe Devenot's work on right-wing psychedelia and the "moralizing, hand-wringing" critiques of intellectual property in the psychedelic sector, like Shayla Love's award-winning series in *VICE*.

Across the psychedelic landscape, the competing visions of actors with divergent interests have become a breeding ground for ethical and political tensions, referred to by some as a "psychedelic turf war" or the "psychedelic infighting Olympics" (Beiner 2021; Ferriss 2022a). The events in Miami, like those in Denver, highlight this divide and the growing intolerance of views that fall outside the corporate-medical paradigm of psychedelic advocacy. Today, these divisions are most pronounced between business leaders, governments and many scientists on the one hand, who believe psychedelics should follow the customary route of medicalized approvals and corporate development, and policy experts, drug researchers and activists on the other, who argue for a more democratic model centred around decriminalization. In some spheres, the divisions run even deeper. Some psychedelic advocates, including many on the left, do not welcome any critical reflection or criticism of this movement at all. As psychedelic researcher and journalist David Nickles explains, "within psychedelic spaces, there seem to be people who worry that any critique or dissent ... will somehow jeopardize their imagined end goal (such as destigmatization, decriminalization or legalization), and they've been largely successful in quashing dissenting voices" (cited in Hausfeld 2023a).

These debates have been part of the recent "psychedelic renaissance," an upsurge of scientific, economic and cultural interest in the therapeutic, intellectual and spiritual dimensions of psychedelics. Following decades of stigma and prohibition, this movement is changing how psychedelics are featured in culture, politics, the law and scientific study. The mass media now regularly features stories on the potential benefits of psychedelic drugs. Politicians of all stripes are embracing psychedelic research and its potential for treating at-risk populations. The legal landscape is shifting as decriminalization and legalization initiatives begin to take hold. In the academic and scientific fields, psychedelic research is revitalizing a number of disciplines, including neuroscience, pharmacology and consciousness studies. Psychedelics are also becoming big business, as biotechnology start-ups raise capital and run clinical trials on psychedelic medicines, while investors and venture capitalists eye the possibilities of a multi-billion-dollar mass market.

The large amount of reporting, discussion and debate around the psychedelic renaissance contains little critical analysis of how the political economy of modern capitalism and other relations of power are impacting these developments. We are interested in psychedelics at a personal level, both as an intellectual pursuit and as an issue for advocacy. Our perspective on the psychedelic renaissance has changed considerably since we started this work. Like many who have been excited by the pace of change, we began with a sense of enthusiasm. Yet as we learned more about the trajectory of the field and its various actors and interests, we came to a far more critical and nuanced position. While we remain convinced that psychedelics hold enormous potential for people and communities around the world, we are also concerned that the psychedelic renaissance is advancing in ways that could not only limit this potential but cause significant harm and entrench systems of social and economic inequality.

In fact, our concerns are wide and growing. They include: the likelihood that psychedelic medicalization will result in hyper-controlled clinical access; the preponderance of over-hyped research results saturating the media landscape; the appropriation and commodification of Indigenous knowledge; the encroachment of right-wing psychedelia and its ties to the military-industrial complex; the silencing of documented abuse in psychedelic therapy; the commercialization of psychedelics by venture capitalists and for-profit companies; conflicts of interest among researchers and their ties to the psychedelic industry; and the enclosure of the psychedelic commons by corporations and their intellectual property schemes.

Some of the key questions to ask about the psychedelic renaissance include: Which views of psychedelics are being promoted and which are being marginalized? Who benefits from the psychedelic renaissance and who is subjugated? Who will have access? Who will be treated as an expert? What do Indigenous communities think of the worldwide proliferation of their medicines and sacraments? Should psychedelics be viewed as new psychiatric drugs, tools of spiritual enlightenment, agents of social change, or all of the above? How has the media participated in selling psychedelics to new consumer markets and creating hype around psychedelic medicines? How are issues of equity and diversity being addressed, as well as harm and abuse? Are psychiatrists, pharmaceutical companies and the medical establishment suited to steward the mainstreaming of psychedelics? How do we create legal and ethical frameworks for psychedelic-related health services? How will processes of medicalization and corporatization affect the decriminalization movement and harm reduction services? And how is the mainstreaming of psychedelics connected to larger issues of capitalism, militarism and ecological destruction?

Unlike many advocates, we do not believe the overriding goal of this movement should be to restore the legitimacy of psychedelics in the eyes of the dominant culture or that we need to fight for change in ways that powerful actors will accept. Indeed, many people are drawn to psychedelics precisely because they find themselves alienated from the dominant culture and its institutions. Shaping psychedelics to fit existing power structures could mean they become little more than maintenance therapies or tools of the corporate wellness industry that help people cope with and adapt to unjust social conditions — a vision very much in line with Aldous Huxley's dystopian novel, *Brave New World* (1932). On the other hand, a class of substances that can alter our perceptions of the world and what needs to be done to improve it could breathe new life into a culture seemingly bent on self-destruction. If we can mitigate and avoid some of these threats, the psychedelic renaissance may not simply entrench Western power structures but instead be a force for positive social change. We believe it is incumbent on those who care about this movement to prioritize social equality and justice.

It remains unclear what the future of the psychedelic renaissance will look like. What is clear, however, is that the future of psychedelics should not be left up to governments, the pharmaceutical industry, venture capitalists and medical professionals. It should be centred in and integrate a wide set of public constituencies and stakeholders, including underground therapists and researchers, Indigenous practitioners, policy experts, harm reduction advocates and drug reform activists. Our focus is on drawing out what may be lost if the psychedelic renaissance continues toward medicalization and corporatization, and what is to be gained from a just and equitable psychedelic future rooted in the public interest.

02

THE PSYCHEDELIC RENAISSANCE

PSYCHEDELICS ARE A UNIQUE AND LOOSELY GROUPED CLASS of psychoactive substances that can induce extraordinary changes in sensory perception, profound alterations of thought, mood and behaviour, transcendent states of consciousness and intense emotional reactions ranging from rapture to terror and despair. Psychedelic experiences can be destabilizing but also unifying, challenging the subjective character of conscious experience while promoting a strong sense of interconnectedness. They can also induce transformative changes in attitudes and beliefs, with the impacts often being ineffable or difficult to put into words. Psychedelic researcher Daniel Freedman wrote in 1968 that psychedelics allow the mind "to see more than it can tell, to experience more than it can explicate, to believe in and be impressed with more than it can rationally justify" (cited in Nichols 2016, 269).

These substances have a long history of human use. Many Indigenous and other early civilizations ingested psychedelic plants and fungi for hundreds and, in some cases, thousands of years (Samorini 2019; Spiers et al. 2024). The historical motivations and traditions surrounding psychedelic use are wide-ranging. The picture that emerges is not one of random consumption or spontaneous experimentation, but managed traditions and rituals that defined cultural boundaries, supported religious practices, strengthened social bonds and socialized individuals into communities (Stein, Costello and Foster 2021). Psychedelics were also used for specific purposes such as hunting, war preparation, rites of passage and celebration and healing ceremonies. They have even played a role in resisting political oppression. As Indigenous communities in the US faced the destruction of their cultures, the prevalence of peyote ceremonies increased as a way to process trauma and preserve cultural identity (Schultes, Hofmann and Rätsch 2001). Ayahuasca rituals among Indigenous peoples in the Amazon also played a part in resisting violence and exploitation at the hands of colonial settlers (May 2017a).

Some argue that psychedelics have shaped human history in profound and enduring ways. For example, these substances occupy a central place in the history of religion and have been integrated into sacred ceremonies for much of human history (Muraresku 2020; Winkelman 2019). Some root Western philosophy in the psychedelic experience because of Plato's use of *kykeon*, the Ancient Greek beverage that is believed to have contained psychedelic compounds (Wasson, Hofmann and Ruck 2008). There are even those who contend that psychedelics may have expedited the process of human evolution (Khamsehzadeh 2022; Macedo-Bedoya and Calvo-Bellido 2024). This proposition, famously advanced by well-known ethnobotanist and psychedelic enthusiast Terence McKenna (1999), became known as the "Stoned Ape Hypothesis." The consumption of psilocybin mushrooms by early hominids, he said, served as a catalyst for the development of human consciousness.

The breadth of influence that psychedelics have had on creative human endeavours is extraordinary and well-documented. They have impacted psychiatry, neuroscience, pharmacology, medicine, psychology, anthropology, ethics, philosophy, art, technology, music, ecology, religion, spirituality and politics. Psychiatrist Stanislav Grof (1973: 18) once famously compared the significance of psychedelics for psychiatry and psychology "to that of the microscope for medicine or of the telescope for astronomy." Philosopher Peter Sjöstedt-Hughes uses similar language to describe their impact on philosophy and metaphysics. The esteemed mathematician Ralph Abraham (2008) claims that psychedelics had a profound impact on his career and played a pivotal role in the development of chaos theory and fractal geometry. Nobel Prize-winning chemist Kary Mullis, the inventor of the Polymerase Chain Reaction (PCR) process, says he likely would never have invented PCR if not for the insights he attributed to LSD.

One of the most important features of the psychedelic experience is that it is heavily dependent on "set and setting." The principle of set and setting maintains that the effects of psychedelics are non-specific and fundamentally shaped by contextual or extra-pharmacological factors. These include psychological factors such as the user's personality, intentions, expectations, mood and beliefs (set), as well as the physical, social and cultural environment within which the experience takes place (setting). Set and setting play an important role in academic and scientific efforts to untangle the various effects of psychedelics, in the work of therapists trying to improve their patients' experiences and outcomes and in the narratives of individuals who use psychedelics in recreational venues. The pharmacological properties of psychedelics and the way they interact with the brain's serotonergic system are part of what renders the psychedelic experience particularly sensitive to context (Carhart-Harris et al. 2018).

How these substances are framed in our imaginations is also an important part of set and setting. Psychedelics have been variously framed as illicit drugs, plant medicines, religious sacraments, cognitive tools, psychiatric medications, recreational pleasures and/or catalysts for political action. This framing impacts how they affect us and how they are positioned within law, politics and culture. In the 1960s, for example, psychedelics were immersed in the counterculture and political movements for change, which affected how many users interpreted their experiences. Today, a new "corporadelic" set and setting — marked by a corporate structure, ethos and logic — is threatening to fundamentally transform the meanings attached to the psychedelic experience (Hartogsohn 2023).

CLASSIFYING PSYCHEDELICS

While humans have used psychedelic plants and fungi for thousands of years, the name for them only emerged in the twentieth century. In the early 1950s they were often called "psychotomimetics" — psychoactive drugs that mimicked psychosis. Others preferred the term "psycholytic," which means "mind loosening." The term "psychedelic" was first used by psychiatrist Humphry Osmond in 1956 during a discussion with author Aldous Huxley, who wrote the classic psychedelic work *The Doors of Perception* (1954). Osmond felt the term psychedelic was devoid of the negative connotations that other concepts carried. The etymology of the word is derived from the Greek meaning "mind-manifesting" — compounds that help to reveal or disclose those parts of the mind that are not normally accessible.

Today, the terms psychedelic and "hallucinogen" are often used interchangeably in popular culture and the scientific literature. Yet, as psychedelic researcher Rick Strassman (2022, 26) points out, there continue to be negative connotations associated with the term hallucinogen as it suggests an experience that is "unreal, imaginary, somehow pathological or deranged." These pejorative connotations may explain why hallucinogen is still frequently used by conservative politicians and criminal justice policymakers. Others use the term "entheogen," which was coined in the late 1970s as an alternative to hallucinogen to counter any association to psychosis or insanity, and to move away from the term psychedelic, which was stigmatized because of its connection with the counterculture. Entheogen is used to designate the spiritual dimensions of the psychedelic experience — plants that provoke ecstasy and produce visions often associated with religious or shamanic rites (Ott 1996; Ruck et al. 1979). Today, entheogen is the preferred terminology of the activist group Decriminalize Nature because it stresses the close spiritual relationship between humans and the natural world. The words we use are important as they both reflect and shape set and setting.

Scientists tend to categorize psychedelic compounds based on their neurobiological mechanisms of action. Others categorize psychedelics by comparing the effects of a drug to what are typically considered to be psychedelic effects. "Classical" psychedelics refer to substances that work on similar serotonin receptors in the brain, though the nature, intensity and duration of "the trip" can vary widely. These include some of the most recognizable and historically significant psychedelics, including LSD, psilocybin, mescaline, DMT, ayahuasca (which contains DMT) and 5-MeO-DMT. Classical and other psychedelics can be broken down further based on their structure. Most psychedelics are considered to be either tryptamines or phenethylamines. Tryptamines selectively bind to serotonin receptors and include many of the well-known naturally occurring psychedelics, including psilocybin and psilocin, DMT, 5-MeO-DMT and ibogaine (Araújo et al. 2015; Strassman 2022). LSD is a synthetic compound but is usually included with tryptamines as well. Phenethylamines have a different chemical structure and mechanism of action within the brain. Mescaline is the only common naturally occurring phenylethylamine (including mescaline-containing cacti like peyote and San Pedro). This class also includes several well-known synthetic compounds such as MDMA (also known as ecstasy or molly) and 2C-B.

Another familiar classification method distinguishes indolamines (such as psilocybin, LSD, DMT) from phenylalkylamines (such as MDMA, mescaline) based on their selectivity for different serotonin receptors. In addition, some psychedelics have an especially complex mechanism of action and more distinct subjective effects. For this reason, some researchers assert that substances like ibogaine and salvia divinorum are best classified as "oneirogens" because of their capacity to induce waking dream-like states (Toro, Thomas and Ott 2007).

It is important to note that some psychoactive substances that figure prominently in the psychedelic renaissance are often not considered to be psychedelics at all. One of these is MDMA. MDMA is sometimes referred to as an "empathogen" or "entactogen," denoting its capacity to trigger deep feelings of empathy and emotional openness (Nichols 2022). Its biological mechanism of action is different than classical psychedelics and it does not yield typical psychedelic effects, leading some to question its designation as a psychedelic. Another outlier is ketamine. In contrast to classical psychedelics, ketamine primarily interacts with the glutamatergic system as opposed to the serotonergic system. It has a history of being used as an anesthetic. But ketamine can also produce psychedelic-like effects, such as a sense of awe, distorted sensory perceptions, out-of-body experiences and sometimes hallucinations. Like MDMA, some consider so-called "dissociatives" like ketamine and PCP to be psychedelics while others do not. Nevertheless, given their well-entrenched position in today's psychedelic renaissance, MDMA and ketamine are included as psychedelics for the purposes of this book.

A HISTORY OF THE PSYCHEDELIC RENAISSANCE

From Counterculture to Pop Culture

Experimentation with psychedelics was a major component of the counterculture and anti-establishment ethos of the 1960s and 1970s. It influenced art, music, fashion, politics and activism. In the middle of the twentieth century, dozens of Hollywood actors began taking LSD as part of psychotherapy, including Cary Grant, who was so taken with the drug that he took the unusual step of going public with his experiences, claiming it improved his acting and allowed him to make peace with his past (Balaban and Beauchamp 2010). Today, Grant's disclosures would be considered commonplace as hardly a month goes by without a celebrity, actor, artist or professional athlete trumpeting the benefits of their encounters with psychedelics. Examples include musicians Harry Styles, Lil Nas X and A$AP Rocky, who claim that psychedelic use inspired recent albums and allowed them to tap into creative flow states (Mohr 2021; Sheffield 2019). Another is Prince Harry, who revealed he used psychedelics to cope with the death of his mother, Princess Diana.

No psychedelic has captured celebrity attention quite the way ayahuasca has. This traditional Indigenous medicine has been dubbed "Hollywood's Hip, Heavy Hallucinogen," as entertainers from Sting to Megan Fox to Lindsay Lohan publicly endorse its healing potential (Ginsberg 2015). Actor Will Smith disclosed that he took part in more than a dozen ayahuasca ceremonies in Peru, which he variously described as the "unparalleled greatest feeling" he ever had to the "most hellish psychological experience" of his life (Lowery 2021; Nolfi 2022).

A quick search on the streaming service Netflix helps to illustrate how psychedelics have penetrated mainstream culture. In the 2020 documentary *Have a Good Trip*, celebrities such as Ben Stiller, Natasha Lyonne and Sarah Silverman, along with the late Anthony Bourdain and Carrie Fisher, recount their mind-altering and life-changing experiences with psychedelics. In her documentary series *Chelsea Does*, Chelsea Handler ingests ayahuasca with a group of friends and takes viewers on a journey, including as she vomits into a bowl on camera. Gwyneth Paltrow and her team at *The Goop Lab* find themselves on a magic mushroom retreat, while Leonardo DiCaprio serves as executive director for the psychedelic documentary *The Last Shaman*. As well, Michael Pollan's 2022 series *How to Change Your Mind*, named after his best-selling book of the same name, explores the history and uses of LSD, psilocybin, MDMA and mescaline.

Psychedelics have also become a mainstay in the high-tech culture of Silicon Valley. The late Steve Jobs, best known as the co-founder of Apple, was open about his psychedelic use: "Taking LSD was a profound experience, one of the most important things in my life ... It reinforced my sense of what was important — creating great things instead of making money, putting things back into the stream of history and of human consciousness as much as I could" (cited in Baer 2015). Jobs once criticized Bill Gates, best known for founding Microsoft, for not experimenting more seriously with these substances. Today, psychedelics are mainstreamed in the tech industry's culture and identity, including through the development and testing of psychedelic applications in virtual reality, artificial intelligence and blockchain technology. High-profile executives are touted as engaging in "expensive mystical Esalen Institute retreats, Burning Man visits, and ayahuasca tourism" (Tvorun-Dunn 2022, 2). According to *The Wall Street Journal*, tech executives view psychedelics, such as psilocybin, LSD and ketamine, as "gateways to business breakthroughs" (Grind and Bindley 2023).

The list of wealthy individuals with pseudo-celebrity status who have donated, invested in or publicly endorsed psychedelics is long and growing. It includes Tesla CEO Elon Musk, billionaire investor and former Goldman Sachs partner Mike Novogratz, GoDaddy founder Bob Parsons, WordPress co-founder Matt Mullenweg, OpenAI CEO Sam Altman, hedge fund manager and New York Mets owner Steve Cohen and Canadian pundit and *Shark Tank* host Kevin O'Leary. Members of the Rockefeller family in the US have been major donors and public advocates for psychedelic research (Lattin 2017). According to psychedelic philanthropist and podcast host Tim Ferriss, "the billionaires I know, almost without exception, use hallucinogens on a regular basis" (cited in Tvorun-Dunn 2022, 3).

Psychedelics are similarly popular in the world of professional sports, where athletes publicly endorse them in a therapeutic context and as potential performance enhancers. The seemingly impossible "no-hitter" pulled off by Pittsburgh Pirates pitcher Dock Ellis while "high as a Georgia pine" on LSD in 1970 is one of the earliest examples (Graham 2020). Former NHL superstar Marc Messier, winner of six Stanley Cups and two Hart Trophies, revealed that a transcendent mushroom experience helped to advance his career by allowing him to harness the mental aspects of the sport (Srinivasan 2022). NFL quarterback Aaron Rogers, who won back-to-back league most valuable player (MVP) awards in 2020 and 2021, has also attributed some of his success to psychedelics. Speaking at the 2023 Psychedelic Science conference, Rogers described his 2020 MVP season this way: "Ayahuasca — 48 touchdowns, five interceptions, MVP. What are you gonna say?" (cited in Ramsay 2023).

Former heavyweight boxer Mike Tyson has been one of the most vocal psychedelic advocates in recent years. He claims that psilocybin mushrooms helped him overcome drug addiction and depression, while 5-MeO-DMT profoundly improved his interpersonal relationships. It was like "dying and being reborn," Tyson told podcaster Joe Rogan.

NFL player Kerry Rhodes, NHL player Daniel Carcillo and Ultimate Fighting Championship (UFC) fighters Dean Lister and Ian McCall are just a few of the retired athletes who have been vocal in their support of psychedelics to manage brain trauma, including chronic traumatic encephalopathy (CTE).

These kinds of celebrity endorsements are on a completely different scale and scope than the activities of the psychedelic torchbearers who kept the movement alive during prohibition, but they illustrate the extent to which psychedelics have moved from the counterculture to the mainstream. Although psychedelics remain a part of underground and dissident circles today, they have been co-opted by the wellness industry and promoted within popular culture.

The Role of the Media

For many decades, the mainstream media in North America served up fear-based, anti-drug propaganda and regularly put forward horror stories about psychedelics. As such, one might have expected at least some media pushback during the current resurgence. Yet, the opposite has been true. Positive media coverage is omnipresent, including in the pages of *The New York Times*, *The Washington Post*, *The Wall Street Journal*, *The Economist*, *Forbes* and the *Financial Times* of London.

Over the past few years alone, the influential CBS news show *60 Minutes* has run an episode exploring the potential of psychedelics to treat addiction and anxiety, talk show host John Oliver devoted an entire episode of *Last Week Tonight* to psychedelics, CNN's Anderson Cooper hosted a documentary special on magic mushrooms and Oprah Winfrey discussed psychedelic medicine with the late Roland Griffiths, founder of the Center for Psychedelic and Consciousness Research. Popular podcasts like *The Joe Rogan Experience* and *The Tim Ferriss Show* regularly feature high-profile advocates, and both hosts are psychedelic advocates themselves. There have even been feature articles in unlikely venues such as *Cosmopolitan* and *Good Housekeeping* (Landau 2021; Williams 2021). A *Fox News* host having welcomed Matthew Johnson — one of the world's most reputable psychedelic scientists — onto the airwaves to discuss these issues without censure or derision speaks volumes about the recent political and cultural shift (Chenevey 2022). Indeed, some psychedelic researchers have arguably reached the status of intellectual celebrities, such as Robin Carhart-Harris who notched a position in the

TIME100 Next list in 2021. Unsurprisingly, this increased media attention has also gone hand in hand with growing public interest. By virtually every popularity metric available, it is clear that interest in psychedelics has exploded over the past decade. These include Google Trends that show online search interest over time, Google Books Ngram that charts the frequency of terms in printed texts, News on the Web that examines information in online magazines and newspapers, as well as the Corpus of Contemporary American English covering a representative body of English language works (Hardman 2024a).

While there are obvious reasons to be wary of the context behind this media groundswell, the growth in media coverage has brought attention to breakthroughs in the field and contributed to destigmatizing psychedelic use. However, the pendulum may have swung too far. We have gone from sanctioning and demonizing these substances to hailing them as wonder drugs and magic bullets that are set to "revolutionize" mental health. We are told that psychedelics can do everything from solving the climate crisis to fighting fascism to saving the planet (Ratner 2018; Schmidt 2021). Even corporate leaders in the nascent psychedelic industry are embracing these narratives, in part to stave off criticism of their for-profit ventures and intellectual property schemes.

Researchers at the Johns Hopkins Center for Psychedelic and Consciousness Research argue that psychedelics are trapped in a hype bubble. They point out that "a disturbingly large number of articles have touted psychedelics as a cure or miracle drug" (Yaden, Potash and Griffiths 2022, 943). Media outlets often do little vetting, re-publishing unfounded claims and corporate press releases (Nickles 2020a). As well, many media companies that have been established to promote psychedelics are owned by venture capital funds that do not necessarily have an interest in providing balanced coverage. Celebrities, media pundits, researchers and scientists all play a role by exaggerating research results in the popular press. The result has been an over-emphasis on the potential benefits of psychedelics and an under-emphasis on their potential risks. One of the biggest dangers of psychedelic hype is that it can lead to unrealistic expectations in potential patients and inadequate mitigation of harm. These expectations are part of what has been called the "Pollan effect" — the dramatically heightened expectations many people have after reading the powerful testimonies in Michael Pollan's influential book, *How to Change Your Mind* (Noorani 2020a). However, it appears that the hype cycle has likely peaked. Many journalists and commentators are now reacting against uncritical publicity and embracing a more circumspect approach to psychedelic research and therapy. Sober and critical scrutiny will be important in the coming years to bring a wider set of stakeholders into the discussion and draw out a more accurate account of how psychedelic use fits with the public interest.

In many ways, what is happening with psychedelics today is ostensibly a framing contest over how to think about what psychedelics are and what they do. The interesting (or scary) aspect of framing is that even things that appear to be empirical facts (such as the dangers of climate change) are subject to this process. Some groups might present contrary or counter-frames to mainstream and scientific ideas, contesting the knowledge claims of authorities and experts. This can be useful at times when authorities are being secretive, deceitful or oppressive, but it can be problematic when groups making counterclaims deny basic aspects of history, science or politics. Framing contests are not simply debates, as the results end up shaping policy and real-world material conditions (Wozniak, Wessler and Lück 2017).

In today's psychedelic renaissance, the biomedical and psychotherapeutic frames currently dominate discussion and debate around what psychedelics can and should be used for. Young people today are far more likely to have heard about MDMA for PTSD or psilocybin for depression than they are to have read *The Doors of Perception*. These biomedical and psychotherapeutic frames are influenced by pharmaceutical companies as well as researchers and medical experts whose jobs and livelihoods are invested in this line of thinking. Moreover, the host of problems and injustices associated with the corporatization and medicalization of psychedelics generally go unrecognized or are ignored within this dominant frame.

Greater Acceptance and Enduring Stigma

Positive media coverage and advances in medical research have had an impact on public opinion, especially around the therapeutic potential of psychedelics. Canadians, for one, appear to be highly supportive of the use of psilocybin for therapeutic purposes. A 2021 poll commissioned by the Canadian Psychedelic Association found that 82 percent of those surveyed approve of the use of psilocybin-assisted psychotherapy for end-of-life illness (just 4 percent disapproved) and nearly two-thirds believe Canada should expand legal access for those who qualify for Medical Assistance in Dying (Psychedelic Alpha 2021). Likewise, a 2022 poll by TheraPsil, a non-profit organization dedicated to helping Canadians access psilocybin-assisted therapy, found a large majority of respondents offer tacit approval or acceptance of legalizing it for patients suffering from a terminal illness (84 percent), depression, anxiety and PTSD (81 percent) and chronic pain (82 percent) (TheraPsil 2022). Polls in the UK, Brazil and Norway indicate similar public attitudes (Drug Science 2021; Hardman 2024a).

Opinions in the US are more divided. A 2021 study found that less than half of Americans (47 percent) approve of the use of psychedelics for therapeutic purposes (Riley 2021). Compared with marijuana, most psychedelics were considered to have lower overall benefits and significantly higher risks to users. However, a more recent cross-national survey by the UC Berkeley Center for the Science of Psychedelics (2023) suggests that US public support is growing. It found that 61 percent of respondents support legalizing therapeutic access to psychedelics, 78 percent support actions to make it easier for researchers to study them and 49 percent support removing criminal penalties for personal use and possession. Research has also found that younger Americans tend to be more tolerant of psychedelics than older generations. One 2023 survey found that millennials are far more willing than baby boomers to try psychedelics as a medical treatment for mental health issues, representing a stark generational divide (MorningConsult 2023).

Support for psychedelic therapy is also growing among those suffering from mental health conditions. A survey of US adults suffering from anxiety, depression and/or PTSD found that 65 percent believe psychedelic medicine should be made available to patients with these conditions and 83 percent would be open to pursuing alternative treatment options shown to be more effective than current prescription medications (Gilman 2022). A 2023 survey of individuals with alcohol and other substance use disorders revealed that 70 percent believe MDMA-assisted therapy might be a useful treatment and 59 percent said they would be willing to try MDMA-assisted therapy (Jones 2023c). Once again, higher levels of support were found among younger age cohorts. These kinds of results suggest that existing laws and regulations, which largely prohibit the use of psychedelics, are wildly out of sync with public opinion.

There can be significant risks associated with using psychedelics, risks that are amplified in some ways by processes of corporatization and medicalization. Yet, it is also true that most psychedelics have strong social and pharmacological safety profiles compared with other legal and illegal drugs, a conclusion supported by academic research as well as decades of underground use and experimentation. Nevertheless, misinformation and criminalization have allowed myths and stereotypes to persist among healthcare practitioners and the public at large.

Some career paths remain closed to individuals based solely on their past psychedelic use. US Customs and Border Protection, for example, denies applicants who have used classical psychedelics in the past three years, while the Federal Bureau of Investigation (FBI) denies applicants who have used classical psychedelics in the past ten years. Benjamin Korman (2022) has noted the irony here, given that lifetime psychedelic use is associated with lower workplace absenteeism and a reduced likelihood of engaging in criminal behaviour (unlike the use of most other drugs, including marijuana). In the UK, a 2018 YouGov survey found that 43 percent of respondents thought it was unacceptable for politicians or business leaders to have *ever* taken magic mushrooms and reside in their current job. For MDMA and LSD, these figures were 51 percent and 52 percent respectively (Smith 2018a). Another study found that admitting to the personal use of psychedelics (or being linked to the psychedelic subculture) negatively influenced the public's views of a researcher's work, including the validity of the research and the integrity of the researcher in question (Forstmann and Sagioglou 2021).

Among healthcare professionals, there is both support and skepticism concerning the benefits of psychedelic use. One survey of physicians in multiple countries found that two-thirds believe psilocybin therapy has potential benefits for patients with treatment-resistant depression and half would prescribe the therapy if it was approved (Compass Pathways 2022). A survey of 145 US addiction specialists also found generally positive attitudes toward psychedelic therapies, with 63 percent believing they show promise in treating substance use disorders and 82 percent seeing promise for the treatment of psychiatric disorders (Kim and Suzuki 2023). Similarly, a US survey of over 1,100 nurses revealed that more than 70 percent agreed that psychedelics showed promise in treating psychiatric disorders while nearly half were in favour of psychedelic decriminalization (Porta et al. 2024).

Other professionals have shown greater resistance, though this appears to be changing. A 2016 survey of US psychiatrists by Dr. Brian Barnett and his colleagues found that less than half (43 percent) agreed that psychedelics showed promise in treating psychiatric disorders and fewer than a third (29 percent) agreed they can improve therapeutic outcomes (Barnett, Siu and Pope 2018). A more recent study revealed similar attitudes among US psychologists (Davis et al. 2022). Less than half (47 percent) agreed that psychedelics showed promise in treating psychiatric disorders and nearly one in five (17 percent) believed psychedelics to be unsafe under medical supervision. Remarkably, these psychologists tended to judge psychedelics and alcohol to be comparable in terms of safety, followed by opioids and cocaine, indicating a stunning lack of knowledge regarding comparative risk profiles. However, in a follow-up to their earlier research on US psychiatrists, Barnett and colleagues (2024) found that over 80 percent agreed that psychedelics show promise in treating psychiatric disorders, nearly double the percentage of their previous study (43 percent).

Psychedelics Outside of the Lab

Most psychedelic use occurs in social and recreational settings, yet recreational consumption has largely been ignored in contemporary scholarship and in the psychedelic renaissance more broadly. From the evidence available, the non-medical use of psychedelics is on the rise. According to the Global Drugs Survey (2020), the consumption of many common psychedelics including LSD, psilocybin, DMT, ketamine and MDMA has increased in recent years. The survey also highlights the growing popularity of microdosing — the practice of taking small doses of psychedelics that do not yield subjective effects — which is consistent with anecdotal evidence (Landau 2022).

The 2019 Canadian Alcohol and Drugs Survey found that psychedelic use among Canadians aged fifteen and older steadily increased from 2013 to 2019 (Health Canada 2019). In the US, between 2002 and 2019, the lifetime use of psilocybin, LSD, ketamine, DMT and salvia increased significantly, though peyote and mescaline use did not (Killion et al. 2021; Walsh et al. 2022). The US Monitoring the Future survey, which provides annual data on self-reported drug use across different time periods, notes an especially large jump in usage among adults aged thirty-five to fifty in recent years, which is significant for a population that has stereotypically passed its "experimenting with drugs" phase of life (Patrick et al. 2023).

What is behind the recent increase in psychedelic use? Nora Volkow, director of the US National Institute on Drug Abuse (NIDA), offers a simple explanation: "with all the attention that the psychedelic drugs have attracted, the train has left the station" (cited in Jaeger 2022a). Psychiatrist Ofir Livne and his colleagues (2022) attribute the increases to popular media reports of a "psychedelic revolution" that is altering the public's perception of risk. Matt Zemon, author of *Psychedelics for Everyone* (2022), suggests several factors, including greater acceptance and understanding of the therapeutic value of psychedelics, more awareness of their relative safety and a rise in depression and anxiety among young adults who are using these substances to self-medicate. The growing recognition of and respect for traditional Indigenous knowledge may also help to explain the rising interest and participation in entheogenic healing practices.

The Global Drugs Survey (2020) suggests self-medication is at play. While the most commonly cited reason for psychedelic use was to enhance general well-being, nearly a third of respondents reported using them to address emotional distress or psychiatric conditions — in other words, as a DIY mental health treatment. This trend is not surprising given the failure of the medical establishment and the pharmaceutical industry to adequately treat these conditions. The Global Drugs Survey (2021) also found that among psychedelic microdosers who also took prescribed medications, around half reported that microdosing led them to stop or reduce their other medications. These results are in keeping with recent surveys of Canadians (Boehnke, Kruger and Lucas 2024; Lake and Lucas 2023).

Different drugs are associated with unique motivational patterns. People who microdose with psychedelics are typically motivated by cognitive, self-improvement and performance-enhancement purposes (Hutten et al. 2019; Lea, Amada and Jungaberle 2020; Liokaftos 2021). A more complex set of motivations is associated with higher doses of classical psychedelics, where studies often point to the enhancement of "self-knowledge" as a primary motivator (Kavenská and Simonová 2015; Móró et al. 2011). In contrast to alcohol and cannabis, classical psychedelic users are also more likely to be motivated by a desire to experience nature, expand their consciousness and have a "spiritual" experience

(Kettner, Mason and Kuypers 2019). These findings are supported by the 2022 Canadian Psychedelic Survey, which found that nearly three-quarters of respondents reported using psychedelics for spiritual, psychological or personal self-exploration (Lake and Lucas 2023). Interview data from a 2021 survey reveal similar patterns, including the desire for experiential growth and psycho-spiritual evolution (Dollar 2021). Some users also highlight a desire to experience the "deeper emancipatory potential" of psychedelics as well as the importance of "respecting" these substances, a narrative that is unusual among other substance users. This respect is tied to both positive experiences and an acknowledgment of the internal confrontations that psychedelics can generate.

Research and Medicalization

In the 1950s, many psychiatrists and other health professionals regarded psychedelics as effective mental health treatments coinciding with the sharp growth in psychedelic research. Beginning in the 1960s, however, a combination of moral panic, social stigma, punitive criminal justice policies and changing scientific protocols stunted clinical inquiry, with a small, vibrant network of scientists, practitioners and therapists continuing the work underground. Psychedelic research in the 1980s and 1990s was largely supported by non-profit organizations that were heavily dependent on philanthropy, such as MAPS and the Heffter Institute in the US and the Beckley Foundation in the UK. Underground venues and organizations, such as Erowid, Bluelight and the DMT-Nexus, also played an important role in advancing the state of knowledge around psychoactive plants and harm reduction.

After a lengthy hiatus, hundreds of universities around the world are now engaged in research on psychedelics, with a wide range of partners including for-profit companies, non-profit organizations, hospitals and government agencies. Major research programs have opened at some of the most prestigious universities in the world, including the Center for Psychedelic and Consciousness Research at Johns Hopkins University and others at Imperial College London, the University of California, New York University and the Icahn School of Medicine at Mount Sinai. Meanwhile, Massachusetts General Hospital, the largest teaching affiliate of Harvard Medical School, launched the Center for the Neuroscience of Psychedelics and Harvard Law School created the Project on Psychedelics Law and Regulation (POPLAR). These Harvard initiatives are particularly interesting as the university was once home to renowned psychologist Timothy Leary, who conducted studies on LSD and led the Harvard Psilocybin Project before being fired over the controversy surrounding his research practices and informal dispensary (the official reason for his firing was that he failed to show up for classes). Not only are leading universities studying psychedelics, but the results are also being published in top medical journals such as *The New England Journal of Medicine*, *Nature Medicine* and the *Journal of the American Medical Association*.

Universities in Canada have also embraced psychedelic research. The University of Ottawa established programs in both Psychedelic Science and Psychedelics and Spirituality Studies. The Nikean Psychedelic Psychotherapy Research Centre is now operating at the Toronto-based University Health Network, while Canada's first research chair in psychedelics was created at the University of Calgary. A psychedelic research centre at Vancouver Island University — the Naut sa mawt Center for Psychedelic Research — combines Western biomedical approaches with Indigenous knowledge to co-develop its research and programming. In 2024, Providence Care Hospital partnered with Queen's University in Kingston to launch the Centre for Psychedelics Health and Research. In addition, Canadian researchers can now apply for federal funding through the Canadian Institutes of Health Research to study psychedelics as mental health treatments.

International psychedelic research alliances are expanding as well, including the Psychae Institute and Psychedelic Access and Research European Alliance, and a growing number of non-profits — like the Usona Institute in the US and Psychedelic Research in Science and Medicine in Australia — are expanding their research and therapeutic initiatives. New psychedelic companies are also a key node in the burgeoning research landscape, with firms such as Mind Medicine, Cybin, Compass Pathways and Atai Life Sciences conducting clinical trials on psychedelic medicines. Even organizations like the US Department of Defense are getting involved, investing tens of millions of dollars in psychedelic research to help veterans.

The psychedelic research output in the current wave appears to have eclipsed that of the previous century. PubMed — a search engine devoted to life sciences and biomedical topics — shows that 2020–2022 were the three years with the highest number of published records since

1957 (Brandt 2023). Some of this research takes the form of clinical trials for mental health conditions such as depression, addiction and post-traumatic stress. Physical health conditions are also being investigated, including chronic pain, inflammation, traumatic brain injury, autism, Parkinson's disease and Alzheimer's disease. As well, a growing number of research labs and private companies are exploring so-called next generation psychedelics to condense the psychedelic trip or retain their purported beneficial properties without the hallucinogenic or psychoactive effects. Psychedelic neuroscience informed by functional magnetic resonance imaging (fMRI) and other technologies is another evolving field that is advancing the understanding of molecular pharmacology, the serotonergic system and the neurobiological mechanisms of therapeutic action (Carhart-Harris et al. 2011; Daws et al. 2022).

Current research into psychedelics is broad and multi-dimensional with many potential benefits and applications. However, the resurgence is largely driven by the medical establishment and rooted in medicalization, in part because current drug laws continue to criminalize most non-clinical activities. Legalized medical use has been touted as a strategic response to criminalization and the most viable model to destigmatize psychedelics and provide therapeutic access to patients. The configuration of social actors and institutions currently driving medicalization — including psychiatry, governments, billionaire investors, venture firms and the pharmaceutical industry — represents a formidable constellation of power.

Politics and Legalities

The stereotypical psychedelic advocates were countercultural leftists of the anti-war and environmental movements of the 1960s. Although psychedelics have never had a purely left-wing base, psychedelic policy reform is now being championed by some unlikely political actors. Consider the United States. Texas legalized psychedelic research in 2021, a move backed by Rick Perry, the state's arch-conservative former governor. Perry is now a regular speaker at psychedelic conferences across the country. Republican politicians in Missouri, Pennsylvania, Virginia, New Hampshire, Massachusetts and Washington, DC have introduced proposals to broaden access and relax restrictions on research (Gifford 2023). While most Republican support for psychedelics centres around treatment for military veterans, some members have also been calling for legalization and decriminalization. For example, Massachusetts lawmaker Nicholas Boldyga, who describes himself as the "most conservative" member of the legislature, filed three psychedelics reform bills in 2023, including proposals to legalize psilocybin and reschedule MDMA pending federal approval (Jaeger 2023a).

In addition to the GOP, today's psychedelic renaissance is attracting a growing number of other reactionary supporters. They include billionaire Peter Thiel and Christian Angermayer, founder and chairman of the psychedelic drug development company Atai Life Sciences and board member of the market-fundamentalist Hayek Institute. "First Lady of the Alt-Right" Rebekah Mercer provides financial support for psychedelic research. Popular media pundits like Jordan Peterson, Dave Rubin and Sam Harris have also embraced psychedelics. In observing the changing face of psychedelic advocates, writer Bett Williams (2020) has asserted that the "apolitical hippie has been replaced by the anti-woke podcaster as the poster child of the psychedelic mainstream." According to journalist Shayla Love (2023a), psychedelic culture now includes "tech bros, venture capitalists, billionaires, Burning Man aficionados, suburban moms, Erewhon shoppers, and QAnon shamans." Clearly, psychedelics are undergoing a political rebranding. While the countercultural aspects of psychedelics are alive and well, they are also being undermined by a vanguard of financiers, Silicon Valley elites and corporate opportunists.

In addition to these changes in the political sphere, there have also been changes in the legal landscape. In a groundbreaking series of moves, Australia legalized MDMA and psilocybin for medical use in 2023. In January 2024, an Australian woman became the first person to receive a legal prescription for MDMA therapy under the new rules. Federal policy and regulations in Canada continue to be more restrictive. In Canada, psychedelics are regulated by Health Canada under the *Controlled Drugs and Substances Act* (CDSA), in compliance with United Nations (UN) drug conventions. Most psychedelics are scheduled as controlled substances. In the US, most psychedelics are not only illegal but classified as Schedule 1 by the Drug Enforcement Administration (DEA), the most restrictive category. In both Canada and the US, these policies translate into a general prohibition on the sale, export, import, possession and production of these substances.

Although US federal law continues to restrict the use and sale of psychedelics, the decriminalization movement is advancing at both municipal and state levels. Some of this progress is a result of social activism, such as the work of Decriminalize Nature, an organization fighting for the decriminalized use of naturally occurring psychedelics for non-clinical purposes in cities across North America. Starting with Denver and Oakland in 2019, many US cities including Detroit, Minneapolis, Seattle, San Francisco, Berkeley, Santa Cruz and Washington, DC have partially decriminalized psilocybin and other plant-based psychedelics. At the state level, Oregon officially legalized psilocybin at the beginning of 2023. Around the same time, Colorado decriminalized the possession, cultivation and sharing of some psychedelic plants and fungi. Many other state legislatures have undertaken initiatives to legalize psychedelics, downgrade criminal penalties and expand access to research and therapy.

Federal law in North America remains obstructive but there are signs of change. Politicians as ideologically opposed as Alexandria Ocasio-Cortez and former Navy SEAL Dan Crenshaw have been working together to pass House amendments on psychedelics (Terris 2023). In 2023, a bipartisan group of congressional lawmakers filed a bill to clarify that federal right-to-try laws allow terminally ill patients access to Schedule 1 drugs like psilocybin and MDMA. Bipartisan efforts also resulted in the 2024 *National Defense Authorization Act* containing provisions to fund clinical trials on the therapeutic potential of psychedelics for military service members. In Canada, psychedelics remain banned at the federal level, but some progress has been made in the area of medicinal use. In 2020, patient advocates gained a legal foothold with the limited authorization of psilocybin-assisted therapy for end-of-life cancer treatment. These rules have since been broadened to include patients with mental health diagnoses. There has also been movement at the provincial level. In 2022, Alberta became the first province to regulate the use of psychedelic therapies for the treatment of mental health disorders, while Quebec became the first province to cover the cost of psilocybin-assisted psychotherapy.

The Big Business of Psychedelics

In May 2022, a Bloomberg News headline declared: "Forget Burning Man, Psychedelic Shamans are Heading to Davos" (Kary 2022). The article discussed the Psychedelic House of Davos, one of several satellite events that was happening in conjunction with the World Economic Forum (WEF) meetings that year. Though not officially associated with the core WEF program, it occupied a space along the town's main promenade that traditionally showcases high-powered and emerging businesses to the global elite. The event was an important indication that the world of psychedelics, long considered antithetical to the world of profit and materialism, was changing its stripes.

Put simply, we have entered the era of "psychedelic capitalism." Just as private capital flooded the cannabis sector years ago, a psychedelic gold rush is now underway. The battle is being waged on many fronts. Large companies are clamouring to find new molecules to monetize, while smaller biotech start-ups raise capital to secure a foothold in the market. Wealthy entrepreneurs and venture capitalists are pouring billions into the sector, assigning valuations to for-profit companies based on how much intellectual property (IP) they can generate. There are now dozens of publicly traded companies whose shares trade freely on major stock exchanges and hundreds of psychedelic companies overall. The psychedelics drug industry is projected to be worth nearly US$12 billion by 2029 and some analysts speculate it may eventually exceed US$100 billion globally (Grind and Bindley 2023; Psychedelic News Wire 2020).

These projections have companies racing to capture psychedelic IP, walling off information about the efficacy of certain molecules from scientists, competitors, non-profit organizations and the public in the process. These companies are attempting to erect legal barriers around new chemicals, as well as new formulations and applications of existing chemicals. In recent years, psychedelic companies and researchers have applied for hundreds of patents involving substances such as psilocybin, MDMA, LSD and DMT, with dozens of these applications being granted. Many of these IP claims involve "low-quality" patents where companies claim ownership over natural substances that in some cases have been in the public domain for thousands of years.

Other for-profit ventures are thriving as well. The lucrative ayahuasca tourism industry has expanded enormously and is now targeting elite clients from every corner of the world. A plethora of luxury psilocybin and DMT retreat centres are being rolled out, whether or not their founders have the experience or expertise to do so. Psychedelic treatment clinics, rehabilitation centres and hospices, as well as "designer" psychedelics with specific effects or treatment durations are just a few of the other for-profit initiatives underway. Ancillary services in the psychedelic industry are also growing in anticipation of commercialization. This includes companies that provide psychedelic therapy training and certification and the infrastructure to support safe usage, as well as tech firms on the periphery of drug development positioning themselves to assist in the administration of psychedelic therapy. According to one estimate, 19 percent of funded psychedelics start-ups in 2020 went to companies that were not specifically drug related (Vedantam 2022a). A year later, that proportion had doubled to 38 percent.

A Political Economy of Psychedelia

There are sharp disagreements in the field of psychedelics, especially between those who call for mainstream acceptance through legalized medical provision and corporate involvement and those who advocate for a more decentralized model less constrained by institutional gatekeepers. Medically approved psychedelic use could soon be a reality on a broad scale. At the same time, many jurisdictions are currently passing or considering passing psychedelic decriminalization initiatives. According to Shayla Love (2021a), "how these two paths will intersect, interact, or interfere with each other is an open question, but proponents of both worry that one might somehow harm, or even preclude the existence of, the other."

Some commentators contend that decriminalization could create an unfortunate political backlash that will derail the psychedelic renaissance. Michael Pollan (2019, 2021a), for example, has suggested that grassroots decriminalization campaigns risk jeopardizing the work of institutional researchers. Pollan is certainly no fan of the drug war, but he stops short of advocating for the kinds of policies that would directly challenge it, preferring "safe and sane" models of psychedelic use that will be less disruptive to the dominant culture. He advises his readers not to politicize psychedelics and let disinterested science do its work.

However, prohibition and the cultural stigma it perpetuates are far more dangerous than the reputational risks posed by decriminalization. Criminal justice policies surrounding psychedelics and other drugs continue to cause untold suffering, especially to vulnerable populations. Moreover, by preventing education and stifling public discourse around responsible use and support for harm reduction services, prohibition produces morally punitive cultural settings that can lead to exactly the negative outcomes that Pollan and others foresee. Many advocates that defend medicalization while opposing decriminalization appear to be operating with an elitist mindset; scientists, medical professionals and corporate executives can be counted on to deliver psychedelics through carefully guarded access, but left to its own devices, the public will inevitably mess things up. This is hardly an apolitical stance.

Some proponents of medicalization claim it will increase access. For example, psychiatrist Ben Sessa, author of *The Psychedelic Renaissance* (2012), states: "some parts of the psychedelic community are saying, 'It's going to become exclusive' … That's nuts. It's the current situation that's exclusive … The majority of people don't use these drugs because they're illegal and they're banned. By medicalizing them or corporatizing them or whatever you want to call it, we are increasing accessibility" (cited in Love 2021a). Similarly, business executive and psychedelic activist David Bronner (2020a) argues that medical and decriminalized access does not necessitate a pick-or-choose situation. Both tracks are making progress and serving different populations in need. In theory, this may be correct — these two paths could coexist to serve a diverse population. "This will require good faith behavior on all sides," writes Shayla Love (2021a), "from people accepting that others will access psychedelics in ways that may not resonate with them (like in a doctor's office), to companies staking claim in a new industry accepting that their profit margins might be smaller when there's a diversity of places to take psychedelics."

Whether these two paths will co-exist is another question entirely. Psychedelic companies have an interest in limiting legal access to anything outside of the medical-pharma frame. Broad access centred around decriminalization is not in their interests and the new industry accepting reduced profit margins seems contrary to everything we know about the workings of for-profit systems. It is also doubtful that most governments would accept the co-existence of medicalization and decriminalization. What is more likely is a system of bifurcated scheduling, where a drug "product" is placed in a schedule different from the active ingredient or substance. This provides organizations like the US Food and Drug Administration (FDA) with a legal mechanism to create markets for regulating lawful use while avoiding concerns and blowback over broader drug rescheduling.

The Pitfalls of Corporatization and Medicalization

Medicalization in the absence of decriminalization is the likely — but problematic — scenario in most of North America. The seeds of psychedelic capitalism were sown in the establishment of a legal and corporate model of medical science that reflects the legacy of the war on drugs. This approach will continue to limit access to psychedelics while enabling corporate control over the sector. Venture capitalists and for-profit psychedelic companies are moving quickly and beginning to employ many of the same practices as mainstream pharmaceutical companies (like baseless hype and deceptive advertising). Companies like Compass Pathways are filing broad patent claims to prevent competition and monopolize the psilocybin supply chain (Hausfeld and Nickles 2021). The profit-driven focus on patenting psychedelic applications is a threat to the psychedelic commons and runs contrary to longstanding consciousness-raising practices by Indigenous and underground communities.

A capitalist model of psychedelic knowledge production conflicts with the principles of open access and collaboration held by most practitioners, scientists and researchers in the field, and is incompatible with the purported altruistic narratives these psychedelic companies are peddling to the public. The big winners in such a system are likely to be pharmaceutical companies, venture capitalists and patent holders. Under existing regulations, well-capitalized firms are in a privileged position to fund psychedelics research and, in the process, shape and control the research agenda. Their lack of interest in investigative neuroscience and other research exploring the complexity of the psychedelic experience is indicative of the broader trajectory of the psychedelic renaissance. Mason Marks of Harvard's Project on Psychedelics Law and Regulation (POPLAR) explains the implications:

> When wealthy private companies fund most research on psychedelics, have special permission from the DEA to handle them, and hold associated patent rights, they are shielded by several layers of government-granted monopolies. They can use that privileged position to shape the narratives surrounding psychedelics, influence government officials, buy the loyalty of scientists, and charge whatever prices they want for psychedelic therapies. The restricted Schedule I status of psychedelics serves their interests, because it helps maintain their dominant positions. (cited in Reichel 2021)

Many psychedelic advocates are hopeful that once medicalized, there will be a diverse ecology of equitable psychedelic-assisted therapies and these substances will be introduced to a wider population than ever before, inspiring larger social benefits. Broad public access in the interests of social change has always been part of the strategy behind the pharmacological model — something akin to a "psychedelic Trojan horse." In other words, we can sneak psychedelics into the mainstream through a container of medicalization and watch as they change the world. In some respects, this has been a successful strategy to gain mainstream credibility. But it has meant that biomedical science and pharmaceutical firms have been able to dictate the rules and assert control over what could be a potentially life-changing experience.

The medical system taking control over the promise of psychedelics also disregards the long history of Indigenous healing practices as well as underground researchers, therapists and guides. The medical route, therefore, risks appropriating Indigenous medicines and excluding traditional practitioners. Millions of people have consumed psychedelics for therapeutic and other purposes for centuries, with only a tiny fraction having done so under the guidance of Western medicine. Medicalization, while potentially opening up access in some ways, could also put boundaries around it that ostensibly turn psychedelics into little more than maintenance therapies in support of capitalist productivity.

Confining psychedelic use to a Western medicalized framework is also problematic for those who view psychedelics as more than simply a conduit to personal healing. Framing psychedelics as solutions to individual problems feeds into self-improvement logic. It reinforces the prohibitionist narrative that these substances are unsuitable for use outside of the medical paradigm. This framing also directs attention away from how medicalized therapy might perpetuate a neoliberal ideology that locates "disorder" within an individual mental state, rather than addressing systemic causes such as poverty, inequality and social exclusion. A system of expensive individualized therapy, medically trained clinicians and hyper-controlled clinical access is not the model of "mainstreaming" that most advocates have envisioned.

Avoiding Psychedelic Exceptionalism

Psychedelic exceptionalism refers to viewing certain psychedelics as inherently superior to other substances or deserving of special legal protection ("good drugs"), while other "hard drugs" are seen as dangerous and deserving of continued prohibition. It is true that psychedelics are different than other classes of drugs. For example, people often rate their psychedelic experiences as among the most meaningful experiences of their lives. We rarely hear such grand endorsements about alcohol, methamphetamine or cocaine. The psychedelic experience also raises profound questions about the meaning of life, the nature of reality, the capacities of human consciousness and how human beings relate to each other and the natural world. Classical psychedelics are also less addictive and toxic than the vast majority of other legal and illegal drugs. At least in terms of the breadth of their potential uses and applications, psychedelic exceptionalism does have some merit.

On the other hand, there are many problems associated with psychedelic exceptionalism and the broader moralizing mindset that demonizes some drugs but not others. Contrary to popular wisdom, the vast majority of people who try or use any drug do so without issue, and most drugs that are classified as highly detrimental are at least partially misunderstood. The commodified products of Western tobacco companies kill millions of people each year, yet tobacco has been used in a medical context and Indigenous ceremonies for centuries. Cocaine is associated with addiction and the extreme violence of nation-states and drug cartels, while coca has long been a respected part of Andean traditions from both a cultural and medicinal perspective. Strychnine and arsenic are poisons that can be deadly at certain doses but were at one time active ingredients in medicinal "nerve tonics" (strychnine was also used as a performance enhancer by athletes). Morphine is highly addictive but an incredibly effective painkiller. Even a drug like heroin, which is widely considered to be dangerous and addictive, is used safely by large numbers of people throughout their lives. The opioid epidemic is tragic and deadly, but this has more to do with criminalization, stigma and the social and economic conditions underlying drug use than the properties of the drugs themselves.

Psychologist and neuroscientist Carl Hart has spoken extensively about psychedelic exceptionalism. He notes that some of the psychedelic substances celebrated by researchers today have similar chemical and pharmacological properties to the "hard drugs" that are vilified. Some of these so-called hard drugs even include select psychedelics that are ignored or dismissed by medical professionals and advocates. PCP, for example, is a psychedelic with a history of therapeutic use. Unlike ketamine, which is widely embraced by the psychedelic community, PCP is often viewed differently because of its connections to urban zones of crime and poverty. "Ketamine is a derivative of PCP, and PCP is a psychedelic," Hart says. "But it's one we disown in this community. We love ketamine for its therapeutic and recreational effects, while we have been silent about the vilification of PCP. We are told PCP causes violence and agitation, which is simply not true" (cited in Lekhtman 2019). There is nothing about PCP that makes it inherently more dangerous than other dissociatives like ketamine. Nevertheless, narratives associating PCP with violence have circulated in the media and entertainment industry for decades and have long been used as a justification for police brutality (Farah 2021).

Hart also calls attention to how MDMA and the "street drug" methamphetamine are treated very differently by psychedelic advocates: "MDMA is an amphetamine … they have a lot of overlapping effects, while some obvious differential effects. Yet methamphetamine is also vilified, and the community has been silent" (cited in Lekhtman 2019). It is worth noting that the chemical and clinical differences between methamphetamine and prescription drugs like Adderall and Ritalin are minimal, but one substance is criminalized while the others are commonly prescribed to children. According to authors Steven Kotler and Jamie Wheal (2017, 64), "the 1.2 million Americans who tried meth last year were breaking bad, while the 4.4 million *children* who took ADHD drugs were striving to become better students. Same drugs, different contexts. One is manufactured by major pharmaceutical companies and enthusiastically dispensed by suburban doctors; the other is cooked up in trailers and sold on street corners" (emphasis in original). None of this is to say that methamphetamine use is not a serious problem for some people, but again the current framing is largely a product of social and economic conditions underlying drug use.

Viewing some psychedelic substances as superior and therefore deserving of special legal protection risks glorifying them while continuing to stigmatize other substances and the people who use them. It also legitimizes the classification scheme behind drug criminalization and the drug war it perpetuates. One of the key problems with this narrative is that it runs along socioeconomic and racial lines. The use of "hard drugs" occurs disproportionately within lower class communities marked by poverty and homelessness, which also tend to include a greater proportion of people of colour. By contrast, psychedelics tend to be used disproportionately by highly educated white people and those with higher-than-average incomes (Orth 2022; YouGov 2022).

We see these dynamics at play in how some psychedelic users view themselves. People who microdose with psychedelics, for example, tend to see themselves as "conventional citizens" who use drugs for rational and instrumental purposes (Liokaftos 2021; Webb, Copes and Hendricks 2019). They describe their use within the context of embracing traditional middle-class values such as "healthy lifestyles" and "self-improvement." In the process, they create boundaries between themselves and other recreational users whose motives and behaviours are deemed more suspect (that is, "crackheads" and "junkies"). As decriminalization initiatives continue to gather momentum, it is vital to not create further disparities by regarding psychoactive substances primarily used by affluent white people as worthy of decriminalization while keeping other substances illegal.

The Case for Decriminalization and Legal, Safe Access

If psychedelics have a wide range of personal, health and social benefits, why should those benefits be limited to people who are dying or dealing with an acute health crisis? A growing body of evidence suggests that psychedelics can improve the well-being and quality of life for people without diagnosed medical conditions, or what researchers sometimes call "healthy normals." Psychedelics should be substances or tools that people can access with few restrictions (Walsh 2016). Safe and equitable access should be a human right, and no one should be criminalized for choosing to alter their consciousness.

Yet, we already see law trending in contradictory directions. New laws surrounding the medicalization of psychedelics do not necessarily open up science and research or make these substances more accessible to people. This is especially true when legalization is narrow in scope, limited to acute medical conditions and/or designed to advance corporate interests. In contrast, decriminalization holds more promise for people, communities and social justice. Decriminalization initiatives are starting to advance at the municipal and state levels in the US. Part of what is holding these efforts back is that the war on drugs remains deeply entrenched in our culture. To confront it, we need sensible drug policy, not only the decriminalization of psychedelics but of all drugs, with funding and resources for harm reduction. Conservative politicians may claim that we need to step up the battle against drugs and that harm reduction is part of the problem, but this rhetoric only contributes to ineffective law and policy and the deaths of countless numbers of people.

The Coca Leaf Café in Vancouver is an interesting example of pushing the envelope when it comes to creating a different kind of psychedelic future, one where access to psychedelics is open and safe, adulterated drugs are less of a threat and there is no stigmatization of other drug use. As Joshua Davis (2015) points out, a parallel in the 1960s was "head shops," which strove for a balance between economic development and the counterculture. Head shops were a space that persisted in a way that eventually contributed to cannabis becoming legalized, first for medical use and then for recreational use. Head shops were the tip of the spear in terms of creating a future for cannabis where it was less stigmatized and access was more open. The Coca Leaf Café and dozens of other psychedelic suppliers in Canada and the US are doing similar things. They are creating the kind of psychedelic future they want to see, one where mutual aid, community support and activism take centre stage, and one in which the safe supply of all drugs is part of the conversation.

The medicalization and corporatization of psychedelics is not only helping to sustain the drug war, but it may also provide new targets for surveillance and criminalization. The broad-based legalization of psychedelics is not feasible in the near future. It does not have anywhere close to broad public support. It is also not a panacea. In Canada, for example, corporate players are reaping massive profits from the legalization of cannabis, while thousands of people are still being arrested for petty cannabis infractions (Devillaer 2024). Black people in North America continue to be marginalized not only in terms of being excluded from the cannabis market but also lack of reparations or cannabis amnesty (Owusu-Bempah and Rehmatullah 2023). Other futures that are more practical, more open and more aware of the harms and benefits of drug use need to be fostered. Community-controlled decriminalization is, in our view, a far better path to mainstreaming psychedelics and ending the war on drugs than relinquishing power to the medical industry and pharmaceutical cartels that provide monopolized services to primarily affluent customers.

03

THE ENDLESS WAR ON DRUGS

THE WIDESPREAD PROHIBITION OF DRUGS is a peculiarity of modern times. From the mid-seventeenth century to the late nineteenth century, drug taxation and revenues were a fiscal cornerstone of the state, and a key financial instrument used to sustain European colonial empires. During this period, the trade of psychoactive substances was not only commonplace but of great financial benefit to mercantile and imperial elites. Stringent prohibition of any kind would have been seen as wasteful and futile. Since the late nineteenth century, however, most governments around the world have largely abandoned policies of taxed, legal drug commerce in favour of introducing restrictions and, in some cases, prohibition. For historian David Courtwright (2001), this shift represents one of the greatest about-faces in human history. It can be explained, in part, by the advancement of industrialization, where widespread drug use threatened to interfere with factory labour and workplace productivity. Seen in this way, prohibition was effectively class legislation designed to support owners and discipline workers in the emerging capitalist system.

Beginning in this period and beyond, changes in elite priorities are reflected in the use and representation of the word "drugs." In his book *Psychonauts* (2023), Mike Jay shows that as recently as the late 1800s the word was used as a label for medications and remedies provided by doctors. Many of today's illicit substances, such as cannabis, cocaine and heroin, were originally introduced as medicines in the nineteenth century and were freely available for purchase as part of the broader supply of sedatives, stimulants and painkillers. In the spirit of cognitive libertarianism that characterized this period, scientists and physicians regularly experimented with drugs themselves. Self-experimentation was a respected practice and seen as the best method for investigating substances that altered mood, perception and consciousness. It was also viewed as a marker of professional dedication and ethical practice in the medical field (Altman 1998). It was not until the early twentieth century that the term drugs became widely associated with pejorative connotations, such as danger, abuse, pathology, depravity, criminality and disease. It became a shorthand for substances that, outside of medical frameworks, carried the risk of addiction, mental illness and death. As a result, people who used drugs, especially groups such as workers, immigrants or those from "inferior races," were stigmatized and imbued with low social status.

The distinction between what is considered medical use versus recreational abuse has long been embedded in prohibitionist discourse. Yet, there are no intrinsic properties of any substance that naturally lend themselves to the designation of "medicine." The ancient Greek word *pharmakon* captures this ambiguity, as it denotes drugs as both medicines and poisons under the same terminology, each one capable of good and evil, healing and harming. The labels we apply and the statuses we afford different substances today have as much or more to do with the economic and political interests of industry and government authorities as they do with scientifically informed evidence of therapeutic value or social harm (Tupper 2012). This is reflected in the fact that these distinctions are constantly changing. LSD, for example, was seen as a promising medicine in the 1950s and 1960s, only to be demonized and scheduled as a dangerous drug with no medical utility shortly thereafter. Today, LSD is again starting to regain its medicinal status. The following provides some historical background regarding drug prohibition in Canada and the US, including why it emerged, the forms it took and some of the implications for psychedelic and drug policy reform today.

THE EARLY DAYS OF DRUG PROHIBITION

Historically, Canada's drug laws have been prohibitionist (Boyd 2017; Erickson 1992). Some of the earliest forms took place in the context of religious temperance movements and the bans on opium and alcohol. The religious temperance movement was the main force fighting against opium and alcohol use in the nineteenth century before official prohibitionist laws and policies. This era championed puritanism and abstinence from drugs as an issue of morality (Mackay 2018). The temperance movement against alcohol, ironically, led to Canada becoming a major hub for the production of bootleg alcohol and its distribution throughout North America (Bruno and Csiernik 2018). Bootleg alcohol poisoned and killed large numbers of people, which was one reason authorities felt compelled to legalize and regulate it.

In the US, the motivations behind alcohol prohibition included controlling particular groups, such as immigrants, and advancing corporate interests. For example, prohibition laws were intended to close down the saloons in New York City, not to stop the consumption of alcohol in more affluent areas of the state such as Westchester County. According to Kathleen Auerhahn (1999, 430), "for the immigrant working class in the northern cities ... saloons offered a place where the community could gather and make business deals, plan political strategies, and generally develop as a community." Business leaders argued that alcohol consumption by the working class interfered with the rhythms of factory work. Worse still, saloons were sites where unions were organized and where socialist and anarchist groups found recruits. For the elite, then, targeting drinking among these "dangerous" classes — groups who could threaten the rights and privileges of dominant minorities — was part of a strategy of social control (Reinarman and Levine 1989). Meanwhile, prescription or "medicinal" alcohol was expensive, which meant this loophole was a luxury reserved for the wealthy. The prescription power of physicians and the less overt practice of selling prescription forms to bootleggers allowed doctors and pharmacies to line their pockets during this period (Okrent 2011).

Drug control in Canada began in earnest as part of policing Chinese communities on the west coast. In the media, "opium dens" were described as vile places where Chinese men lured innocent young white women into lives of addiction and prostitution. In this way, opium use was often associated, in Canada and the US, with this population. The first major federal drug law in Canada was the 1908 *Opium Act*. The *Opium Act* carried penalties such as fines and prison time for the importation, manufacturing, possession and selling of opium for recreational purposes. It primarily targeted Chinese labourers in British Columbia (BC) and elsewhere along the construction of the Trans Canada Railway (Bruno and Csiernik 2018). The *Opium Act* was an anti-Asian drug law.

Amid growing anti-Chinese sentiment, there was significant racism and vigilante violence directed against Chinese-owned businesses in downtown Vancouver. At the federal level in the US, the 1909 *Smoking Opium Exclusion Act* prohibited importing and smoking opium. Like Canada, US opium laws largely reflected anti-Chinese sentiment rather than health or other problems associated with opium use (Reinarman and Levine 1989).

These early forms of narcotic control were tied up with attempts at regulating and even deporting Chinese people. These drug laws overlapped with other racist laws in Canada (and elsewhere), such as the Chinese Head Tax and the Continuous Journey Regulation, which deterred Asian people from settling in Canada or elsewhere in the British Empire. There is also evidence of blatant hypocrisy and racism, as many other substances at the time were not regulated in the same way because they were not associated with efforts to control a vilified minority. Key elements of drug law during this period shaped subsequent drug laws in North America.

In Canada, the 1911 *Opium and Drug Act* added cocaine and derivatives of opium to federal drug law and imposed severe penalties for legal violations. In the US, the *Harrison Narcotics Act* of 1914 featured a similar prohibitionist approach, primarily targeting opium and coca. It also formalized the language of "narcotics" as a medical-legal term for controlled drugs. Its proponents were motivated by a desire to assert power and control over Black Americans. Media coverage at the time described cocaine as giving Black men superhuman strength and making them more belligerent and violent, a narrative that was exploited by physicians and politicians. The myth of the "negro cocaine fiend" helped to shape early US drug policy (Hart 2014). There were also concerns in Britain and France that drug problems from the US and Canada would trickle into Europe, hence the focus on drugs in Britain's *Defence of the Realm Act* in 1916, which banned drugs, including cocaine.

Drug control in the 1920s and 1930s broadened to include other substances. Canada's *Opium and Narcotic Drug Act* of 1920 added the language of "narcotics" and increased the minimum fines for drug-related activities. The Opium and Narcotic Drug Branch was renamed the Narcotic Division in 1921, and the Royal Canadian Mounted Police (RCMP) took charge of regulating drugs across the country. In the 1930s, Canada, like many other countries, was facing an economic depression.

There was inflation, food price gouging, food shortages and a lack of work. In response to this pervasive social anxiety, moral entrepreneurs started to demonize drug use and drug users, including drugs like cannabis. For example, while fighting for the right of women's suffrage, moral entrepreneurs like Nellie McClung and Emily Murphy also rallied against drug use.

In the US, there were similar, though more aggressive, changes in drug policy and regulation. The US Federal Bureau of Narcotics (FBN) was created in 1930, with Harry Anslinger at the helm. It is difficult to overstate the effect Anslinger had on drug law and policy in the US and at the global level. Anslinger was the head of the FBN between 1930 and 1962, which became the DEA in 1973. Under Anslinger, the US (as well as Canada and other countries) adopted even harsher prohibitionist laws, with the FBN instructing its agents to focus on illicit drug use in poor communities rather than the misuse of prescription drugs like barbiturates and amphetamines, drugs that were largely used by white women and other more affluent populations (Foster 2023). Anslinger was not only anti-communist but anti-Asian, anti-Black and anti-immigrant as well (Boldt 2010). His fervour for drug prohibition was shaped by his conservative social and political views. During this time, marijuana became a prime target of campaigns by the FBN. Canadian Prime Minister William Lyon McKenzie King met with Anslinger to coordinate marijuana control in 1938.

In the case of the increased focus on marijuana, once again drug-control policies were directed against dangerous or "undesirable" classes. Policymakers had no reason to believe that marijuana was dangerous, from a health or social perspective. Rather, marijuana prohibition in southwestern US states began as a mechanism for disciplining and criminalizing Mexican immigrants (Bonnie and Whitebread 1974). Explicit references were made to the drug's Mexican origins and to the criminal conduct that followed when Mexicans used marijuana. According to Alexander Cockburn and Jeffrey St. Clair (1998, 71–72), "Anslinger's first major campaign was to criminalize the drug commonly known at the time as hemp. But Anslinger renamed it 'marijuana' to associate it with Mexican laborers who, like the Chinese before them, were unwelcome competitors for scarce jobs in the Depression." Anslinger also claimed that marijuana could arouse a state of fury or homicidal attack in both Blacks and Hispanics, and he linked marijuana with jazz music to persecute Black musicians. In the US Congress, Anslinger testified that "coloreds with big lips lure white women with jazz and marijuana."

In Canada, the notion of drug addiction and drug addicts as social problems became more prominent as the Narcotic Division sought to criminalize more drugs and drug users. In 1946, Constable Harry Price of the RCMP wrote about what he called "criminal addicts," suggesting that drug use was a pathway to sex work and moral depravity. This point of view reflected popular cultural depictions of drugs and drug addiction found in novels and movies of the time, such as *Marihuana: The Weed with Roots in Hell* (1936), *Reefer Madness* (1936), *Drug Addict* (1948) and *Monkey on the Back* (1956). As the Narcotic Division and the RCMP pushed forward with attempts to control drugs and as popular culture touted this notion of the drug addict, drug use became stigmatized and public drug use was no longer deemed acceptable. In 1955, the Proceedings of the Special Committee on the Traffic in Narcotic Drugs entrenched the prohibitionist position of Canada's federal government, with an emphasis on punitive drug laws.

THE RISE OF PSYCHEDELIC SCIENCE

Despite the entrenched stance on prohibition and the increased coordination of Canadian and US authorities regarding drug use during this time, some substances were starting to be used in mental health and addiction treatment, and in the unlikeliest of places. For example, there was a period in the history of psychedelics when LSD therapy was practiced in Canada. In the 1950s and 1960s, LSD was used at the Saskatchewan Mental Hospital in Weyburn, Saskatchewan and the Hollywood Hospital in BC. Psychiatrist Humphry Osmond worked together with the Co-operative Commonwealth Federation (CCF) government in Saskatchewan to bring LSD to the Saskatchewan Mental Hospital (Dyck 2012, 2008). The CCF gave Osmond approval to use LSD for the treatment of schizophrenia and alcoholism. Another key player in Saskatchewan was Abram Hoffer. Hoffer and Osmond engaged in LSD experiments, pioneering an approach to treating a variety of mental health and substance use issues. Part of the approach involved having therapists use LSD to gain insight into what people with schizophrenia, for instance, might be experiencing in terms of hallucinations. It also involved talk therapy during LSD trips, a precursor to psychedelic-assisted psychotherapy today.

Hoffer and Osmond regularly treated people with LSD for alcoholism. Between 1954 and 1960, they treated approximately two thousand alcoholics with LSD-assisted therapy, finding that 40 to 45 percent of them did not return to drinking after a year (Tanne 2004). Other researchers replicated their results. For instance, the first controlled trial on using LSD to treat alcoholism by Sven Jensen at Weyburn found that more than 65 percent of patients continued to abstain from alcohol up to eighteen months later (Dyck 2006). This is compared to the abstinence level of roughly 18 percent for alcoholics receiving only group therapy. In Prague, prominent psychedelic therapist Stanislav Grof was using LSD to treat heroin addiction in a similar way and with similar results (Grof 1980). Additionally, Dutch psychiatrist Jan Bastiaans was also using LSD therapy to treat "concentration camp syndrome," a type of PTSD affecting Holocaust survivors (Sharir 2020).

Hoffer and Osmond were equally interested in mescaline (peyotism). The use of peyote has a long history with Indigenous peoples in North America. The Native American Church, whose members were using peyote for healing and as part of their religious ceremonies, was subject to intense surveillance and control by the RCMP and Indian Agents (Canadian government representatives on First Nations reserves). The RCMP, the Narcotic Division and other regulatory agencies tried to ban peyote, but advocacy by the Native American Church prevented it. Hoffer and Osmond thought that peyote might have transformative effects for people suffering from mental health issues given its potential to transport people into mystical realms (Barber 2018). Osmond was so interested in mescaline that he planned a project called Outsight where prominent authors and cultural figures would report on their mescaline experiences, though the project never came to fruition.

Like Hoffer and Osmond, the Hollywood Hospital in New Westminster, BC was also using LSD to treat people suffering from alcoholism and other ailments, under the direction of figures like Dr. Ross Maclean and psychedelic pioneer Al Hubbard. The enthusiastic Hubbard, who somehow had unfettered access to LSD through the 1950s and introduced many early advocates to the drug, had ties to the Weyburn group in Saskatchewan. More than six thousand therapeutic LSD sessions were conducted at Hollywood Hospital for the treatment of alcoholism, anxiety and depression. The biggest improvements were noted for alcoholism. Even after fifty-five months, more than half of the patients treated reportedly showed sustained levels of abstinence (Donaldson and Dyck 2022; MacLean et al. 1961). Other "conditions" fell under the rubric of these treatments too, such as sexual deviancy (Donaldson 2019; Ens 2019). LSD and mescaline-assisted "conversion therapy" were not only practiced in Canada but in the US and UK as well (Kingsland 2019). LSD was also being researched and tested on vulnerable populations in correctional facilities across North America and Europe, including in Canadian prisons as a potential "correctional tool" (Jones 2023a). Many in Canada's psychiatric community did not approve of LSD therapy or the theories underlying it and began to question what was happening at Hollywood Hospital. Between 1962 and 1967, politicians were also urging the BC government to ban LSD. Only a few treatments took place after 1967, and Hollywood Hospital was eventually bulldozed in 1975.

While LSD therapy was the most common form of psychedelic therapy at the time, other psychedelics were being used in a therapeutic context in Canada, the US and elsewhere. The scale of the practice and level of academic output were significant. Between 1950 and the mid-1960s, there were more than a thousand published clinical papers involving approximately 40,000 patients, as well as several dozen books and six international conferences on psychedelic therapy (Grinspoon and Bakalar 1979). According to Michael Pollan (2015), between 1953 and 1973, the US federal government funded 116 studies of LSD involving more than 1,700 research subjects. Pollan notes that psychedelics were tested on "alcoholics, people struggling with obsessive-compulsive disorder, depressives, autistic children, schizophrenics, terminal cancer patients, and convicts, as well as on perfectly healthy artists and scientists (to study creativity) and divinity students (to study spirituality)." Despite the methodological limitations of this early research, it was deeply influential. According to pharmacologist and chemist David Nichols (2016), the entire field of serotonin neuroscience was catalyzed by the discovery of LSD (see also Healy 2002). Psychedelic researcher Sam Gandy (2015) posits that the scientific field of psychopharmacology was largely founded on research into psychedelics. The discovery that chemicals "could profoundly alter consciousness, and by extension were intimately tied to consciousness" altered the field's trajectory. It is important to note that psychedelic research did not begin with the discovery of LSD. Rather, LSD research was building upon underground, academic and clinical investigations of other psychedelics like psilocybin and mescaline. Psilocybin, for instance, was already being studied in disciplines like chemistry and anthropology, while mescaline was widely researched by scientists in the early twentieth century who were interested in its ability to induce "hallucinations" and its potential uses in psychotherapy (Aday, Bloesch and Davoli 2019).

THE MODERN WAR ON DRUGS BEGINS

Despite the positive findings emerging from psychedelic-assisted therapy, the 1960s saw the control of and moral panic about psychedelics intensify. Hoffer and Osmond feared these developments and tried to intervene. For example, they contacted Timothy Leary and asked him to tone down his proselytizing approach. They were worried about Leary's activities and the growing interest in LSD in the counterculture, which they believed would lead to a dismantling of medical authority. Osmond even wrote to US Senator Robert F. Kennedy asking him to reflect on their therapeutic findings and those of other researchers. The Canadian federal government, partly in response to these larger conversations, began debating the merits and ills of LSD in 1966 and 1967 (Dyck 2011). The debates initially focused on placing LSD on the banned narcotics list and eliminating psychedelic research. The following year, Bill S-60 came before the Senate, proposing penalties for the distribution and sale of LSD. During these debates, the doctors in Weyburn and Vancouver were not able to contest the framing of LSD as a dangerous substance by the Canadian Parliament. In 1968, LSD was banned but not by adding it to the *Narcotic Control Act*; it was restricted under the *Food and Drugs Act* under the same classification as DMT.

Psilocybin was also banned under the *Food and Drugs Act* in Canada but not until 1974. There have been a few interesting pieces of case law regarding psilocybin. The 1979 case *R. v. Parnell* in the British Columbia Court of Appeal found that simply possessing psilocybin mushrooms did not violate the *Food and Drugs Act* if the mushrooms were naturally occurring and kept in a natural state. The case was referred to the Court of Appeal of Alberta as *R. v. Cartier* in 1980, which came to the same conclusion. However, this precedent was ultimately struck down in 1982 by the Supreme Court of Canada in *R. v. Dunn*. Thus, from 1979 to 1982, there was a precedent for legal access to psilocybin (or at least there was legal ambiguity as long as psilocybin was kept in a natural state). The

Supreme Court of Canada later struck down those appeal decisions based on Schedule H of the *Food and Drugs Act* and the *Criminal Code of Canada* sections on possession and trafficking.

At the international level, the UN introduced the Single Convention on Narcotic Drugs in 1961. It is often simply called the "Single Convention" as this treaty created one global drug policy that countries were pressured to adopt and follow as they would any other international treaty. The Single Convention, which explicitly described drugs as "evil" and harmful to individuals and society, replaced all other previous treaties on narcotics. It was adopted and came into effect in 1964, meaning all signatories had to change their laws to reflect it. The Single Convention entrenched a prohibitionist approach to drugs that encouraged criminalization and policing of supply, recommending that all offences should be met with "adequate punishment particularly by imprisonment or other penalties of deprivation of liberty" (cited in Jay 2023, 273). It also codified the schedules of drugs, schedules that are still used by the UN today. As part of these international efforts, the Canadian *Narcotic Control Act* of 1961 replaced the former *Opium and Narcotic Drug Act*.

Despite the efforts of activists at the time to counter the criminalization agenda, such as Professor Marie-Andrée Bertrand, an anti-prohibitionist and penal abolitionist, Canadian drug policy continued down a prohibitionist path. This includes when Canada became a party to the 1971 UN Convention on Psychotropic Substances. The 1971 Convention banned the sale, possession and transport of a wider range of drugs covered by the Single Convention, including psychedelics. Guided by the 1971 Convention, Canada further criminalized synthetic drugs such as amphetamines, benzodiazepines, barbiturates and what the 1971 Convention labelled "hallucinogens." LSD and DMT were already banned in Canada as of 1968 under the *Food and Drugs Act*; however, when the 1971 Convention was adopted, Canada introduced harsher penalties for the trafficking of restricted drugs, especially synthetics. As of 2025, 182 of 193 UN member states remain party to the 1971 Convention, which ostensibly created a universal policy against psychedelics and other drugs (McAllister 2000).

Through the Single Convention and the Convention on Psychotropic Substances, nearly every known drug was a target of the international prohibitionist regime. Canadian public health professor Kenneth Tupper (2012, 475) notes that the primary metaphor implicit in the discourses of these conventions is that of "drugs as malevolent agents," where substances are understood as a kind of "intrinsically evil force, like a demon or wild creature, possessing its own nefarious volition and the capacity to subjugate or override the free will of 'weak' or 'immoral' individuals." In other words, the very existence of drugs is the root of the problem, with little consideration of how socioeconomic factors might influence drug use patterns and outcomes.

While Canada was a party to the 1971 Convention, Canada also adopted a position of "partial non-acceptance" (Kos-Rabcewicz-Zubkowski 1975). Canada nuanced its position in this way because it already had some of the toughest drug laws in the world by 1968, having scheduled most known drugs. Canada also articulated on the floor of the 1971 Convention an intention to undertake a medical, educational and sociological research program on drugs. The US also had some reservations about the 1971 Convention. Most psychotropic drugs at the time were manufactured by US and German pharmaceutical companies, so US representatives demanded it be crafted in a way that allowed the industry to continue unfettered. The result was that the treaty effectively gave pharmaceutical companies free rein to develop new drugs and evade convention restrictions.

Like in Canada, psychedelics had come under legal scrutiny in the US well before the 1971 Convention. The Drug Abuse Control Amendments of 1965 made the sale and manufacture of hallucinogens illegal. The possession of popular psychedelics like LSD and psilocybin was banned federally through the 1968 Staggers-Dodd Bill and then the *Controlled Substances Act* in 1970. The *Controlled Substances Act* classified drugs into five schedules, ranked by medical benefits and abuse potential. LSD, psilocybin and other psychedelics were put under Schedule 1, the most restrictive category, indicating they had "no currently accepted medical use and a high potential for abuse." There were also local precursors to federal prohibition in the US and Canada. By the end of 1967, several US states had banned psychedelics, with the State of California making LSD possession illegal in May 1966. In 1967, the public health officer of Vancouver and the Narcotics Association of British Columbia began a concerted campaign against LSD, arguing that it shrank the brain and led to suicide.

While there was never an explicit ban on psychedelic research in North America, the legal restrictions on psychedelics led to a major decline in academic inquiry. While many commentators were (and still are) quick to blame the counterculture for provoking a conservative backlash, the reality is that psychedelic research had already been scaled back significantly by 1966-67. The 1965 Drug Abuse Control Amendments in the US, for example, forced LSD suppliers like Sandoz to stop marketing the drug, which meant it was less available for research purposes. Growing stigma and self-censorship within the academy on the part of researchers, professors, university departments and granting agencies also played a role, as did the difficulties that psychedelic researchers had in aligning their treatment models with new scientific and clinical methodologies (Oram 2018). The subsequent institutional shutdown of psychedelic research is perhaps unprecedented in the history of modern science. In the view of neuropsychopharmacologist David Nutt, the political decision to ban psychedelics represented "the worst censorship of research in the history of the world" (cited in Sants 2022). Of course, the scheduling of LSD and other compounds did not mean that psychedelic science and research ended. Rather, it moved underground and into some capable hands, such as renowned chemist Alexander "Sasha" Shulgin, ethnobotanist Jonathan Ott and "the garage botanists who haunted the great Entheogen Review" (Davis 2022).

A key element of the history of prohibitionist drug laws in North America is that they often targeted particular groups of people, such as racialized minorities. US President Nixon expanded this to include another "dangerous group" — individuals and organizations who were protesting the Vietnam War. The Nixon administration realized they could not openly target individuals for their political views, but they could jail them for breaking drug laws. Some years later, former Nixon advisor John Erlichman openly stated the true aims of Nixon's drug war:

> The Nixon campaign in 1968, and the Nixon White House after that, had two enemies: the antiwar left and black people ... We knew we couldn't make it illegal to be either against the war or blacks, but by getting the public to associate the hippies with marijuana and blacks with heroin, and then criminalizing both heavily, we could disrupt those communities. We could arrest their leaders, raid their homes, break up their meetings, and vilify them night after night on the evening news. Did we know we were lying about the drugs? Of course we did. (cited in Baum 2016)

The prohibition of psychedelics was part of this campaign as these substances played a significant role in many social movements of the period, including the organizing efforts of student groups and anti-war activists. As Michael Pollan (2018, 58) puts it, "the Nixon administration sought to blunt the counterculture by attacking its chemical infrastructure." The FBI was also involved in strategies to target political and cultural dissent, including a "concerted campaign to make political arrests by charging radicals with possession of small amounts of marijuana" (Lee and Shlain 1985, 225). Black student leader and anti-war activist Lee Otis Johnson, for example, received a thirty-year sentence for giving a joint to an undercover police officer. The goals of these campaigns had almost nothing to do with public health or the dangers of drugs, and everything to do with criminalizing what were seen as politically troublesome populations. Building on the *Controlled Substances Act* of 1970, Nixon claimed that drugs were "public enemy number one" and that the country needed to wage an all-out offensive to combat them. In 1973, the DEA was created and given vast powers to undertake the anti-drug offensive.

One psychedelic that was not on Nixon's radar was MDMA. MDMA was officially banned in Canada in 1976 under the *Food and Drugs Act*. In the US, however, the recreational use of MDMA spread across the country in the 1970s and early 1980s (Passie and Benzenhöfer 2016). Like other psychedelics before it, MDMA found its way into the hands of therapists. According to some estimates, over this time period approximately half a million doses of MDMA would be administered by psychiatrists, psychotherapists and lay therapists for the treatment of relationship issues, anxiety, PTSD and other conditions (Nuwer 2021). The popularity of the drug in the underground and a deluge of studies falsely claiming that MDMA was a dangerous neurotoxin led the DEA to step in. In 1985, MDMA was placed in Schedule 1 of the *Controlled Substances Act* by emergency ruling.

While Nixon was responsible for entrenching prohibition in the bureaucracy of the US government, it was Ronald and Nancy Reagan who were primarily responsible for instilling prohibitionism in the collective psyche of Americans (and many Canadians as well). In the 1980s and 1990s, virtually every young person in the US who watched Saturday morning cartoons was exposed to a large dose of "this is your brain on drugs" commercials. The "Just Say No" messaging was also part and parcel of the activities of the main arm of the war on drugs:

the police. Los Angeles Police Chief Daryl Gates helped found the DARE (Drug Abuse Resistance Education) program in 1983, which was subsequently adopted nationwide. The program involved police officers lecturing children about the dangers of drugs and aggressively promoting an abstinence-only approach. Gates is on record stating in a US Senate hearing that casual drug users "ought to be taken out and shot." "We're in a war," Gates proclaimed, and even casual drug use amounts to "treason" (cited in Ostrow 1990). DARE was not only ineffective but may have actually been counterproductive in reducing drug use (Felker-Kantor 2024). Mandatory minimums for drug possession were also strengthened during this period at both the federal and state levels, while funding for education and prevention declined dramatically (Provine 2008). Federal expenditures on anti-drug law enforcement more than tripled between 1981 and 1987, from less than $1 billion per year to roughly $3 billion (Nadelmann 1989).

Under the Reagan administration, the war on drugs continued with a disproportionate focus on crack cocaine, further criminalizing Black Americans (Reinarman and Levine 2004). Despite there being no real chemical difference between crack cocaine and powder cocaine, powder cocaine was seen as a symbol of luxury and associated with white middle-class communities, while crack was purported to be uniquely addictive and associated with poor, inner-city Black communities. Crack users were described as criminal, violent and psychotic, as well as morally repugnant, as reflected in terms like "crackwhore" (Hart 2013; Kerr 1987). It has since been well-established that the linkages between crack use and a greater propensity toward violence were a complete myth (Reinarman and Levine 1997). The criminal justice system participated directly in this structural racism. As part of the *Anti-Drug Abuse Act* of 1986, which ratcheted up penalties for many drug crimes, the sentencing provisions for possessing one gram of crack cocaine were equivalent to that of possessing 100 grams of powder cocaine (Alexander 2012). Under federal law, the possession of five grams of crack became a felony that also carried a mandatory minimum sentence of five years for a first offence, while possession of the same amount of powder cocaine remained a misdemeanor, punishable by a maximum of one year in prison. Both before and after these legal changes were made, approximately 75 percent of arrests for powder cocaine involved white people, while around 90 percent of crack arrests involved Black people, even though the majority of crack users were white (Donziger 1996). These provisions helped to fuel huge racial disparities in incarceration.

The role of the media in hardening public attitudes toward drugs during this period was pivotal. Shortly after the 1988 US federal election, for example, one poll found that 34 percent of US respondents selected the budget deficit as George Bush Sr.'s top priority once he took office. Just 3 percent selected drugs as the top priority. Following an anti-drug media blitz the next year, 43 percent of Americans said that drugs were the nation's most important issue, followed by the budget deficit at 6 percent (Chomsky 1991). By the early 1990s, drug arrests were the third most frequent category of arrests in the US, behind larceny and drunk driving. In 1992, 58 percent of federal inmates and over 30 percent of state prisoners were locked up for drug offenses (Chambliss 1994).

The drug policies of Reagan and George Bush Sr. were motivated by social control at home and used as pretexts for intervention abroad. A study by the Organization for Economic Cooperation and Development (OECD) in the early 1990s estimated that half a trillion dollars of drug money gets laundered internationally each year, more than half of it through US banks (Chomsky 2002). This money was not traced, but it easily could have been if the federal government was interested, as the Federal Reserve required that banks provide notification of all cash deposits over $10,000. In fact, when George Bush Sr. oversaw running the drug war under Reagan, he dismantled the one program — "Operation Greenback" — that targeted money laundering connected to drug trafficking. Likewise, when the Central Intelligence Agency (CIA) discovered that most of the exports from US chemical corporations to Latin America were being used for drug production, the US government looked the other way. If the concern was drugs, drug production and money laundering would have been at the top of the list of federal priorities, and banking and chemical executives would have been a target of federal prosecution. Instead, both the Reagan and Bush administrations were using public fears about drugs, which were largely created through anti-drug government propaganda, as a pretext for counterinsurgency activities in Latin America and a cover for intervention. One of the justifications used for the invasion of Panama, for example, was that the US population needed to be protected from foreign narco-traffickers (Chomsky 1991). At the same time, international drug traffickers that towed an anti-communist line were dutifully ignored by intelligence agencies.

In 1994, under President Bill Clinton, the *Violent Crime Control and Law Enforcement Act* was passed, which continues to represent the single largest crime bill in US history. It escalated the drug war by imposing additional mandatory minimum sentences, contributing to the further mass incarceration of Black men and backing grant programs that encouraged police officers to carry out more drug-related arrests in inner-city communities. The 1990s also marked the beginning of the opioid crisis, another indicator of the injustices in how the drug war was framed and executed. At the same time as the DEA was targeting individuals and small-time dealers for growing and selling opium, Purdue Pharma was introducing and falsely marketing OxyContin to legal authorities and the medical establishment as a safe, non-addictive pain reliever. Other pharmaceutical companies were also bringing new opioids to market, such as fentanyl patches and lollipops. The number of OxyContin and other opioid prescriptions would sharply increase over the next few decades; by 2012, these prescriptions numbered 255 million amongst a US population of 309 million (Foster 2023). Many people who began using these legal opiates later transitioned to tainted illegal street drugs, with dire consequences.

Clinton's "tough on crime" drug policies also served a convenient purpose in the context of neoliberalism and the attack on social welfare systems. The drug war was ramped up in the 1980s and 1990s at the same time as inequality was increasing, US cities were being de-industrialized, social safety nets were scaled back and insecure forms of employment were on the rise. Within this context, the US turned to mass incarceration, bolstered by the war on drugs, as a mechanism of social control. Mass incarceration became an instrument for managing and neutralizing the impacts of poverty, unemployment and inequality to control these increasingly disenfranchised populations.

Canadian law followed a similar trend over this period but was not associated with quite the same level of propaganda or extreme use of the penal arm of the criminal justice system. Through the 1970s and 1980s, waves of moral panic about drugs swept the country, animated by narratives of racialized drug traffickers luring young people into drug use and addiction (Michaud et al. 2024). These moral panics culminated in the declaration of a "drug epidemic" in 1986 by Conservative Prime

Minister Brian Mulroney, leading to the intensification of policing and punitive law enforcement practices. In the years that followed, the number of Black people charged for drug trafficking offences in Canada skyrocketed (Gordon 2006).

In 1997, the *Controlled Drugs and Substances Act* (CDSA) became the new federal drug law under the Jean Chrétien Liberals. This created a single, uniform drug law in Canada. The CDSA replaced the *Narcotic Control Act* and parts of the *Food and Drugs Act*. LSD and DMT as well as psilocybin and mescaline were classified as Schedule 3 drugs, while MDA/MDMA and ketamine were placed under Schedule 1, the most restrictive category. Compared with US and international systems of drug scheduling, Canada's CDSA uses a more opaque system of classification. Its designations are based on a number of factors, including the chemical properties of molecules, toxicity, dependency potential, interaction and availability. There appears to be little scientific basis for such decisions and no rational relationship between the harms posed by different drugs and the punishments imposed for possessing and distributing them (Boyd, Carter and MacPherson 2016).

Prohibitionist tendencies have remained prominent in North America in recent years and can be seen, for example, in the reaction of the DEA and FDA to the substance kratom. Kratom is a tree leaf with psychoactive properties that grows in Southeast Asia. It shares properties similar to those of coca leaves and coffee insofar as it gives people endurance and has long been used in Southeast Asia as a stimulant and pain reliever. Many people in North America also use it for pain relief and to deal with symptoms of addiction, including opioid addiction. The DEA and FDA have attempted to schedule kratom several times and have pushed states to make it illegal, with little knowledge or consideration of its risks and benefits. Ultimately, these efforts have failed at the federal level because of pushback from advocacy groups such as the American Kratom Association, but the DEA and FDA are still considering a federal ban (Adlin 2023). In Canada, we have seen some substances, such as the psychedelic salvia divinorum, subjected to rolling bans. Bowing to the pressure of conservative and police advocacy groups, the Conservative government of Stephen Harper made salvia illegal to sell, export and produce in 2016, despite the government knowing little about its uses or properties (Yaremko and Walby 2023). Canadian federal agencies continue to try to deter the use of some psychedelics that are not banned outright under the CDSA. For example, in 2017, Health Canada added ibogaine to its Prescription Drug List, a regulation that allows the agency to restrict access to certain substances and provides law enforcement agents with increased authority to seize them.

In general terms, criminalizing drug use still relies on discourses of addiction, harm and social disorder as justifications. Drug prohibition is anchored in social control, creating a crisis of unsafe supply. Drug prohibition efforts have also been riddled with paradoxes and hypocrisy. Banning drugs on the premise that they are addictive and harmful is absurd and everywhere contradicted by the social and health-related harms caused by legal drugs such as alcohol and tobacco, as well as the tendency of Western governments to export these harmful substances to other parts of the world via international trade agreements. Going back decades, the US has forced countries in Asia and elsewhere to accept US tobacco shipments (and even advertising for tobacco) under the threat of punitive trade sanctions (Chomsky 2002). Today, tobacco and alcohol are often not even considered to be "drugs," evidenced by the common phrase "drugs and alcohol" and the separation of the two in the workings of government departments and agencies.

Politicians and criminal justice personnel have justified the excessive sentences for drug use and possession by blaming people who use drugs for a variety of social problems, such as underage pregnancy, violence and crime. Though police executives in Canada have rhetorically gestured toward the decriminalization of personal use as a policy and legal option (Bronskill 2020), police and conservative politicians still generally balk at the idea of harm reduction. Despite the rhetoric, arrests for all forms of drug possession continue daily as part of the drug war. The policing of drugs does not increase public safety or the well-being of people who use them. In fact, a growing body of evidence suggests that overdoses and deaths increase following police interventions such as arrests and drug seizures (Cano et al. 2024; Ray et al. 2023; Zibbell et al. 2022).

The criminalization and prohibition of drugs have inflicted major collateral damage, destroying families and even generations of people who are largely engaged in victimless activities. Psychedelics were swept up in this zeal, with their prohibition leading to severe consequences for many caught possessing or selling these substances. An example is Timothy Tyler, who was convicted in 1994 of selling LSD to a police informant. Tyler received a life sentence and was only released twenty-six years later when President Barack Obama commuted his sentence (Lekhtman 2018).

Like in the US, the drug war in Canada has long been racialized in its design and implementation. Indigenous and Black people bear the brunt of discriminatory policies, sentencing disparities and harsh and dangerous policing practices (Khenti 2014). Although the rate of drug possession charges and arrests has declined in Canada, Indigenous and Black people are still far more likely to be arrested for drug possession (Global Commission on Drug Policy 2024). In one major Canadian city, Indigenous people were eight times more likely to be arrested than white people (Browne 2022). The racialized intensity of the drug war is ongoing, including for drugs such as cannabis. There are differences in arrest data by race/ethnicity leading up to changes in cannabis laws, as well as in how cannabis is policed in areas where it has been legalized (Owusu-Bempah and Luscombe 2021). Although adults can now legally possess specified quantities of cannabis in Canada, there are more (and in some cases harsher) laws surrounding the drug than there were under prohibition, such as trafficking to underage users and underage possession. Likewise, in many US states that have legalized cannabis, it remains illegal to grow the plant, and the wealthy have disproportionate access to legal growing and dispensing facilities because of the large capital investment required.

Despite some notable changes in drug policy, the global war on drugs continues. In 2019, over 1.5 million people were arrested for drug offenses in the US, far more than any other type of crime (Pew Charitable Trusts 2022). The vast majority of these arrests were for possession. In 2022, approximately 45 percent of people in US federal prisons were serving time for a drug crime. At the global level, more than one in five people currently in prison are incarcerated for a drug offence and upwards of half a million are estimated to be subject to compulsory drug detention (International Drug Policy Consortium 2023). In 2023, executions for drug convictions surged to new global highs, accounting for 42 percent of all confirmed executions globally (Girelli, Jofré and Larasati 2023). There is little question that the war on drugs and prohibitionist policies have wrought far more social harm than drugs themselves. Moreover, the criminalization of drugs continues to foster new kinds of substances, including more dangerous synthetic alternatives (Taylor 2015). There is also little evidence that policies aimed at the eradication of drugs have been effective in reducing illegal drug markets or addressing their connections with violence, insecurity and organized crime. On the contrary, prohibition continues to fuel violence and conflict (International Drug Policy Consortium 2023). The drug war has long been used as a pretext, particularly by the US, to render new territories available for extraction (oil and gas, mining) and to establish police and military training centres that function as staging grounds to repress organized resistance and social movements across the Global South (Paley 2014).

In the context of the ongoing war on drugs, there are various complexities in introducing new psychedelic substances into the public sphere and having them accepted as medicines or recreational substances. Although there are serious problems associated with the medicalization of psychedelics today, one can at least understand why proponents like Rick Doblin and researchers like Roland Griffiths have advocated for careful attention to legal and medical protocols in any attempt to mainstream. The combination of criminal justice policymakers, conservative politicians and moral entrepreneurs is a powerful trifecta, and when they turn on a drug it is difficult to counter the aura of panic, harm and danger they can spawn. Yet, there are initiatives that have and continue to challenge the drug war in Canada and elsewhere. In particular, harm reduction is one major development that offers some hope for more just and sensible drug policies.

ENTER HARM REDUCTION

The Downtown Eastside is an inner-city neighbourhood in Vancouver, BC. It is a complex place with intersecting challenges including poverty, mental health issues and drug use. The *Opium Act* of 1908 focused on downtown Vancouver and especially on Chinese and other Asian communities. Since that time, the Downtown Eastside has been the focus of intense drug policing and criminalization. The Downtown Eastside is also important because it has been at the forefront of harm reduction activism. Drug researchers and activists Susan Boyd and Donald MacPherson (2018) assert that grassroots harm reduction is a form of resistance to the state-led drug war. Harm reduction acknowledges and indicts the harms of drug prohibition and offers a practical way to provide safer practices and safer access to drugs, ultimately informing changes in policy. While harm reduction as a discourse can be co-opted by state agencies and the police, the core of harm reduction is centred around resisting criminalization and the policing of drugs.

Groups like the Vancouver Area Network of Drug Users (VANDU) engage in harm reduction activism to keep people alive in the face of adulterated drugs and HIV infection. The Vancouver approach to harm reduction is partly based on the 2001 report, "A Framework for Action: The Four Pillar Approach to Drug Problems in Vancouver," authored by Donald McPherson. This policy framework became influential as a national model for harm reduction and was also exported globally. As a result of VANDU's and other activism, a supervised injection site called INSITE opened in the Downtown Eastside in 2003. It was the first supervised injection site in Canada at the time, and it would be the only supervised injection site in Canada for many years. Conservative politicians in Canada have continued to agitate against supervised drug use and safe injection sites, even contesting their legality, despite the sharp increase in deaths due to tainted substances. They advocate instead for a moralistic abstinence-based approach to drug use. In contrast, people engaging in harm reduction work understand that people will not stop using drugs, and the only choice is to make the substances, equipment and environment safer. Harm reduction can also go further to include the provision of social services, community and social development, as well as employment and education opportunities for users.

VANDU argues that in the name of the right to life, liberty and security of the person (section 7 of the *Canadian Charter of Rights and Freedoms*), the federal Minister of Health should decriminalize the possession of all drugs under the CDSA. They view this as the only way to keep people from dying and to protect the basic human rights of users. They argue that full decriminalization would allow people to use more safely, access harm reduction services more frequently and protect themselves from the harms of policing. VANDU, the Drug User Liberation Front and other groups in Vancouver situate themselves as part of a drug user liberation movement. Other approaches to normalizing psychedelics are also taking shape in Vancouver's Downtown Eastside, such as the Coca Leaf Café, which sells psychedelics and other substances with an emphasis on safety and harm reduction.

Perspectives vary on the extent to which law enforcement should have any involvement in harm reduction. Carl Hart, in his book *Drug Use for Grown-Ups* (2022), suggests that harm reduction is a limited measure because it still validates or endorses current drug laws and relations with police. Other researchers argue that the continued involvement of law enforcement in harm reduction practices will hinder the movement because policing institutions are inherently conservative and reactionary (Cohen and Csete 2006). The decriminalization of drugs and harm reduction threaten the jobs of public police, so police will generally fight against sensible drug policy. In most cities, police seek more and more resources at the expense of community development and public health (Lippert and Walby 2022). And public police have a history of undermining harm reduction through intimidating and arresting people around needle exchange and safe injection sites, even in the Downtown Eastside.

Much of the discourse around harm reduction in recent years has focused on safe supply and safe use. Safe supply includes efforts that are taken to ensure drugs are free of adulterants. This could include establishing testing sites where people can have their drugs checked or government agencies providing drugs that are already tested to mitigate levels of fentanyl and other dangerous substances. Safe supply also includes providing alternative substances that may be safer and less addictive (for instance, tested hydromorphone as opposed to street-bought heroin). The term safe use refers to any other practices that increase the safety or reduce the harms of drug use. This includes sanitizing implements used to consume drugs (like needles) and using drugs in the presence of others in case something goes wrong. Safe use also refers to safe injection and safe use sites, most often funded and operated by government agencies.

Debates about safe supply in North America are unfolding across a backdrop of heightened anxieties around decriminalization, homelessness and public drug use. In 2023, public criticism of safe supply programs in Canada began to converge around several narratives put forward by critics of harm reduction and the media (Michaud et al. 2024). The biggest source of moral panic has involved the threat of "diversion," or the unauthorized distribution of regulated drugs beyond the individuals to whom they are intended. Media narratives suggest that opioid medications provided by safe supply programs are being diverted and sold to youth, which is leading to an increase in substance use disorders and overdose deaths. According to Health Canada (2023), however, the vast majority of drug-related deaths among young people in Canada stem from unregulated fentanyl. There is currently no evidence that prescribed safe supply is leading to a rash of new diagnoses of opioid use disorder or contributing to unregulated drug deaths. That being said, one of the challenges of making a known quantity of opioid products available as an alternative to the impure and risky street supply is to not increase the overall quantity of opioids at the population level, which has the potential to increase the number of new and dependent users. Safe supply drugs should not simply be handed out; "unwitnessed safe supply" has the potential to cause social harm (Mallet 2023). This is one reason why safe and regulated use spaces are so important.

Fueled by the moral panic around decriminalization and harm reduction, most conservative politicians have adopted an anti-harm reduction approach to drugs. The most recent iteration of this sentiment is in Alberta, where Premier Danielle Smith has formally rejected decriminalization and harm reduction models in favour of addiction treatment. Harm reduction advocates note that focusing on individualized addiction treatment exacerbates the costs of healthcare and policing when it comes to criminalized substances. It is also likely to come at a great cost to individual health and well-being. The problem is that a one-month treatment for substance use disorders, which might be compelled or coerced, may not be long enough to change habits. It is usually long enough, however, to alter tolerance. Someone may get out of addictions treatment and then seek to use again, but because their tolerance is lower and there is no safe supply or use space, they may use adulterated substances or die from an overdose using the same substances at the same dose (or even a lesser dose) than they used before treatment. The retiring chief coroner of BC, Lisa Lapointe, points out that since BC declared a public health emergency in response to drug-related deaths in 2016, roughly two hundred people per month have died from unregulated, adulterated drugs in the province (BC Coroners Service 2024). People are dying at similar rates in Alberta. Lapointe suggests that abstinence-based programs may be contributing to the death rate.

Moreover, building up the capacity of the healthcare system to provide addictions treatment is lengthy and time-consuming. People can suffer serious health consequences or overdose before they can be admitted. It is also true that the vast majority of people with a substance use disorder do not want or believe they need treatment (Substance Abuse and Mental Health Services Administration 2022). Some suggest these users are simply "in denial," when the reality is usually more complicated. In spite of these challenges, many experts argue that addictions treatment can and should exist as an option alongside safe supply and safe use spaces, as treatment can work when people want it and are ready for it.

Conservative politicians continue to base their policies around the perceived morality of drug use. They have long been among the most vocal proponents of problematic narratives surrounding drug addiction, dating back nearly a century in Canada (Boyd 2017). The myth of drug addiction as something that can be "cured" was largely created by politicians and criminal justice policymakers, along with the idea that drug use is fundamentally linked to depravity and that social policy can and should be used to wipe out drug use altogether. These moralistic positions make little sense in terms of health outcomes or even economic outcomes; when exacerbated healthcare and policing costs are factored in, individualized addictions treatment is the far more expensive option.

One Canadian politician pushing hard for drug prohibition and criminalization is federal Conservative Party leader Pierre Poilievre. He espouses the disingenuous and wholly ideological position that safe supply programs are one of the primary causes of increasing opioid deaths. In reality, most people who use drugs or know people who use drugs understand that safe supply programs are saving lives. Interviews with people who use drugs in BC show that they believe decriminalization initiatives are important, but they are primarily concerned with the "severity of drug toxicity and the imminent threat of death" (Xavier et al. 2024). This position is not surprising given that toxic drugs are a central factor in four out of five overdose deaths (Zimonjic 2023). In 2016, the rate of opioid-related deaths was 7.8 per 100,000 Canadians; by 2021, the rate was 20.9 per 100,000. Journalist Brishti Basu (2023) tells the story of a young woman in Alberta who is suing the province over policies that restrict her access to a safe supply of drugs to manage her opioid use. For her, these drugs allow for a healthy life while simultaneously managing drug use. While most safe supply programs are still in their early stages, evidence is emerging of their effectiveness in reducing hospital admissions, healthcare costs and overdose mortality (Atkinson 2023; Ledlie et al. 2024; Rammohan et al. 2024; Slaunwhite et al. 2024). Currently, however, countries around the world spend 750 times more money on punitive drug law enforcement than they do on harm reduction (Harm Reduction International 2024).

DECRIMINALIZATION AND LEGALIZATION

There are many varieties of psychedelic and other drug decriminalization. These range from what is often called "deprioritization," or *de facto* decriminalization, which involves reducing law enforcement engagement for the purposes of arrest and prosecution (but no explicit change in criminal law), to abolishing criminal penalties across the board. Legalization typically permits the possession, use and sale of a substance, but may still impose some limits on these activities. Here the state decides how a substance is produced and circulated in society by regulating private manufacturers and distributors and implementing rules around safety and access.

Portugal is one country that has decriminalized all drug use. Much of the research on the Portugal model suggests that decriminalization has led to reductions in problematic drug use and drug-related harms (Hughes and Stevens 2010). The proportion of prisoners sentenced for drugs has fallen dramatically, reducing prison overcrowding, while both the rates of drug use and drug-related deaths have remained below the European Union (EU) average (Slade 2021). Many advocates argue that the Portuguese model of drug decriminalization should be extended to other countries (Whitelaw 2017). Others, however, underscore that decriminalization alone does not solve some of the interconnected issues, such as tainted drugs, and its success depends on the concurrent establishment of social and community development initiatives to support users (Laqueur 2015). For these reasons, the Portugal model started to falter in 2017-18 when the social development aspects of its policies were hollowed out.

Medical marijuana is an example of a legal reform path. The prohibitionist approach in Canada began to change with the movement for medical marijuana in the early 2000s. In 2013, regulations for medical marijuana were published by Health Canada and the department began to provide some licensing for it. By October 2018, recreational and medicinal cannabis was legal in Canada under the *Cannabis Act*, albeit regulated unevenly across provinces and territories. As the legalization of recreational cannabis shows, it is possible to go from prohibition to much more open access. However, Canada's example also shows how the process of legalization can become intertwined with the interests of corporate-dominated industries. As Michael Devillaer documents in his book *Buzz Kill* (2024), Canada's cannabis industry has been rife with corruption, crime and conflicts of interest. It has focused on profit maximization, product promotion and increased consumption at the expense of public health concerns. This example can and should serve as a warning about what may come to pass with the establishment of a legal psychedelic industry in the absence of decriminalization. As Devillaer (2024, 161) puts it, history has shown that we "have more to fear from the legal industries that produce drugs than we do from the drugs themselves."

In Canada, there have also been strategic policy changes regarding other drugs. The 2020 *Guideline of the Prosecution Service of Canada Director on the Controlled Drugs and Substances Act in Canada* suggests that prosecutors should resort to criminal prosecution for possession of a controlled substance only for the most serious offenses. As well, prosecutors must take into account whether or not people have access to supervised use or other safety provisions, and they must assess whether people are involved in Indigenous culture-based programming and deserve restorative justice. In January 2023, BC received a federal exemption to decriminalize the possession of some illegal drugs (opioids, cocaine, methamphetamine and MDMA) for personal use. The province's overriding goal was to reduce overdoses and prevent fatalities. While a step forward, a successful decriminalization model requires further investments in social services and social and community support for people who use drugs. The small legal limit in BC (2.5 grams combined) has also been critiqued as arbitrary, and more attention is needed in the areas of safe supply and safe use. In 2022, the City of Toronto also requested a federal exemption similar to the one granted in BC. The request was supported by harm reduction experts and advocates, and even the Toronto Police Service. However, the application was rejected in 2024 citing safety concerns.

There is no single point in time when all drugs or psychedelics became illegal in the US or Canada. Drug laws may appear coherent, but they tend to represent a hodgepodge of political and criminal justice ideas that have been assembled and amended in line with the objectives of the day. A limited number of laws and policies are being undone, which may reverse some of the harms they have created. In the US there are many cities and a few states that have partially decriminalized psychedelics. In addition, no fewer than twenty states are now introducing legislation on psychedelic access. There is also considerable movement toward medical legalization. However, these kinds of initiatives are limited and often tied up in corporate interests. The future of psychedelics is not just economic or cultural or medical. It is also political. Beyond conservative politicians and the carceral state, scientists, researchers, academics, corporations, venture capitalists, activists and recreational users all have a lot at stake in debates over whether psychedelics should be decriminalized, legalized and/or medicalized.

04

MYSTICAL EXPERIENCES AND THE PROCESS OF BELIEF

HUMANS HAVE USED PSYCHEDELIC PLANTS, fungi and other mind-altering substances for thousands of years (Merlin 2003; Spiers et al. 2024). Rock art in northern Australia and Tanzania dating to 10,000 BCE contains mushroom iconography with distinct psychedelic themes (Pettigrew 2011). Archeological evidence in Europe points to the ritual use of psilocybin mushrooms as far back as eight thousand years ago (Akers et al. 2011). The use of psychedelic plants was also common in pre-Columbian Mesoamerican societies, including Maya, Aztec, Zapotec and Toltec cultures (Carod-Artal 2015). Peyote has been used by Indigenous communities in Mexico and the Southwestern US for at least 5,700 years (Bruhn et al. 2002; El-Seedi et al. 2005); the use of San Pedro, another mescaline-containing cactus, dates back no less than ten thousand years (Samorini 2019); and ayahuasca has been consumed for spiritual and therapeutic purposes among Indigenous peoples in the Amazon for centuries.

Early Romans, Greeks and Egyptians also used psychoactive plants and substances (Emboden 1981). In Ancient Greece, prominent philosophers like Plato experimented with altered states of consciousness at secretive ceremonies known as the Eleusinian Mysteries. These secretive rituals involved the consumption of a drink known as *kykeon*, which is thought to have contained potent psychedelic compounds (Wasson, Hofmann and Ruck 2008). Communities in ancient India regularly consumed a beverage called *soma*, which is also believed to have had powerful psychedelic properties (Wasson 1968). Indigenous peoples in Siberia have ritualized the well-known red and white spotted *Amanita muscaria* hallucinogenic mushroom since at least the 1600s (Nyberg 1992), while practitioners of the Bwiti religion in West Africa have incorporated the psychedelic plant iboga into their traditions for hundreds of years. According to Michael Pollan, "probably 95 percent of cultures around the world have some plant or fungus they use to change consciousness, to achieve transcendent experience" (cited in Ferriss 2021a).

Clearly, psychedelics have been part of human culture for much of recorded history. However, in the push toward medicalization and corporatization in today's psychedelic renaissance, the discourse surrounding psychedelics has become increasingly narrow. We should not lose sight of the broader psychedelic landscape, including important questions that arise about the nature of human consciousness, philosophy and belief systems. Notions of the sacred, of spiritual meaning and significance, and psychedelic use as a bridge to what is often referred to as "mystical" experiences, are an important part of this history.

MYSTICAL EXPERIENCES, RELIGION AND PSYCHEDELICS

Mystical experiences encompass a profound sense of reverence or awe, deeply felt positive mood, a sense of sacredness, feelings of ineffability (difficulty putting an experience into words), the transcendence of time and space, a strong sense of unity and interconnectedness, as well as a "noetic" quality (the intuitive belief that the experience is a valid source of objective truth about the nature of reality) (MacLean, Johnson and Griffiths 2011; Richards 2015). Mystical experiences are also associated with "ego dissolution," sometimes referred to as ego loss or ego death, which has been described as the loss of one's sense of self, the suspension of self-awareness and feelings of unity with one's surroundings or the breakdown of the basic subjective character of conscious experience (Millière 2017). Some have likened mystical experiences to near-death experiences (Sweeney et al. 2022). According to Sam Gandy (2021, 32), researcher collaborator with the Centre for Psychedelic Research at Imperial College London, "these experiences are associated with eliciting 'quantum change,' or change that is sudden, robust, benevolent, deeply meaningful and enduring to personal emotion, cognition and behaviour."

People can "achieve" mystical experiences in a variety of ways, including practicing advanced yoga and meditation, certain forms of dance, fasting and holotropic breathwork. However, they are also associated with high-dose consumption of classical psychedelics. Based on his clinical research on DMT trips, Rick Strassman (2001, 234) describes the psychedelic mystical experience this way:

> The three pillars of self, time, and space all undergo profound transfiguration ... There no longer is any separation between the self and what is not the self. Personal identity and all of existence become one and the same. In fact, there is no 'personal' identity because we understand at the most basic level the underlying unit and interdependence of all existence. Past, present, and future merge together into a timeless movement ... like time, space is no longer here or there but everywhere, limitless, without edges.

British philosopher Alan Watts (1968) argues that the state induced by psychedelics should not be seen as an escape from reality. Assuming otherwise is based on the false supposition that mystical experiences are themselves unreal. For Watts, there is something important about these experiences for understanding human consciousness and the human condition. Laws that prohibit these substances are therefore "a barbarous restriction of spiritual and intellectual freedom" (1968, 85).

While some remain skeptical of the authenticity of psychedelic-induced mystical experiences, research suggests they are not qualitatively different from those produced in other ways and may even be more powerful. Johns Hopkins University researcher David Yaden and his colleagues (2017a) surveyed over seven hundred people who claimed to have had a mystical experience in their lives. They found that psychedelic-induced experiences were rated as more intense and more "spiritual" compared to those triggered in other ways, including religious practice. This may explain, in part, why many are turning to psychedelics as a way of enhancing their already-established religious practices and beliefs. Some religious leaders are training to become "psychedelic chaplains" to provide spiritual guidance and to work alongside mental health professionals administering these drugs in the context of therapy (Cole-Turner 2022).

Mystical experiences are at the root of religious traditions. In *The Varieties of Religious Experience* (1902), renowned philosopher William James identifies commonalities in religious experiences across different faiths and cultures. Every religion, James argues, has a mystical strain at its core, which is ultimately more important than the theological formulas or sacred texts passed down through the generations. Some years later, British philosopher Walter Stace (1960) examined firsthand accounts of mystical experiences across numerous religious texts. Like James, Stace points to a common set of qualities that define mystical experiences independent of culture or origin. The different forms of religion throughout history, he suggests, are the cultural expressions of these altered states of consciousness.

In more recent years, researchers have continued to assert that psychedelics — and the mystical experiences they can generate — occupy a central place in the history of religion. Psychedelic plants and fungi have been used across diverse forms of cultural and religious life and integrated into sacred ceremonies throughout much of human history (Furst 1976; Harner 1973; Winkelman 2019). Some claim to have documented the presence of psychedelics in the Bible and their use by early Christians and Jews as part of religious rites (Brown and Brown 2016; Merkur 2000; Nemu 2019). Others point to the likely use of psychedelic plants and mushrooms in early Buddhist traditions (Crowley 2019). The consumption of *soma* in ancient India was also interlaced with religious traditions and was known for imparting mystical visions (Smith 2000). Indigenous Central American artwork suggests psychedelic mushrooms were a means of communicating with the gods. Many have claimed that the Nahuatl language of the Maya and Aztec peoples named psychedelic mushrooms *teonanácatl*, meaning "flesh of the gods" (Schultes 1940), though this has been challenged by some Indigenous researchers (Williams and Brant 2023). Psychedelic ceremonies in religious contexts continue to occur around the world, including the use of peyote in the Native American Church in North America.

Some researchers go further, implicating psychedelics in the origins of religion itself (La Barre 1972). Ethnomycologist R. Gordon Wasson (1986) proposes that the religious impulse may have originated with psychedelic substances as a reaction to ingesting psychedelic plants. In *The Immortality Key* (2020), Brian Muraresku posits that early rituals involving psychedelic brews were the origins of the Christian Eucharist. He sees Western civilization as partially rooted in the psychedelic experience. The connectedness of psychedelic experiences and ancient religious practices is no doubt highly speculative, but it underscores the importance and longstanding influence of psychedelics in human history. The fact that some of these researchers have at times overinterpreted the strength of their evidence does not mean that the evidence should be rejected altogether.

William James believed mind-altering substances provided a way to induce mystical experiences and he used drugs himself to try to generate them (Tymoczko 1996). This made his work alluring to psychedelic researchers and enthusiasts in the 1960s. According to Travis Kitchens (2022):

> Explicitly singling out drugs as being useful for inducing mystical experiences (James himself had experimented with a variety of narcotics), *The Varieties of Religious Experience* eventually oozed from under the doors of religious studies departments out into the counterculture, becoming a staple for the highbrow stoner — the book is mentioned by name in Huxley's *Brave New World* — and spiritually-minded psychologists alike. When fighting Harvard's ultimately successful campaign to oust him from the university in 1963, Timothy Leary presented himself as flamekeeper of the Jamesian tradition.

Believing that empiricism and mysticism were not antithetical, James was preoccupied with reconciling science and religion through the "correspondences between the accounts of mystical experience documented in sacred texts and reports of drug-induced trance" (Kitchens 2022). Foreshadowing developments in psychedelic science over a century later, James questioned whether it would be possible "to initiate one of these experiences in a lab setting, with all of its 'inner authority and illumination' intact." "If so," he posited, "they might be able to measure and harness its practical fruit: changes in behavior and outlook."

MYSTICAL EXPERIENCES AND PSYCHEDELIC SCIENCE

In 1962, the Good Friday Experiment took place. It has since become legendary in psychedelic circles. The experiment was conducted by Walter Pahnke, a graduate student in theology at Harvard Divinity School. Its purpose was to assess psilocybin's ability to create authentic mystical experiences (Pahnke 1963, 1969). With the approval of Timothy Leary and Richard Alpert, who supervised psychedelic research at Harvard at the time, Pahnke gathered twenty seminary students at Boston University's Marsh Chapel on Good Friday. Ten students were given psilocybin, the other ten received a placebo. After ingesting the substances, the students listened to a Good Friday service. Pahnke's experiment was ostensibly "double-blinded" in that neither the students nor Pahnke knew who received the drug and who received the placebo, though telling the subjects apart was not difficult and speaks to ongoing issues with blinding and expectancy bias in psychedelic research today. In the end, the students who took psilocybin ranked their experiences much higher in mystical qualities than the control group. In the words of Michael Pollan (2015), "Pahnke concluded that the experiences of eight of the subjects who received the psilocybin were 'indistinguishable from, if not identical with,' the classic mystical experiences reported in the literature by William James, Walter Stace, and others." Six months after the experiment, the psilocybin group reported persistent beneficial and life-enhancing impacts.

Decades later, MAPS founder Rick Doblin (1991) published a follow-up study to Pahnke's experiment in which he interviewed most of the original study participants who took psilocybin. He found that their experiences had impacted their lives in profound and enduring ways. However, Doblin also discovered something that Pahnke had failed to mention: a few of the subjects had endured intense anxiety during the original experiment. One student even had to be chased down the streets of Cambridge and given Thorazine because he believed he had been chosen to announce the Second Coming of Christ. Doblin also found that the experiences of some of the original participants had important political implications, inspiring them to work for social change (Doblin 2013). One of these individuals was Mike Young, now a retired Unitarian minister, who believes the experiment helped to transform his political values:

> Before the Experiment, I'd thought it would be fun to get a theology degree, maybe a medical degree, and maybe a law degree. After taking psilocybin, though, I began building a life of social activism … Beginning in the 1960s I was up to my ears in the anti-war movement and the humanist psychology movement. The anti-draft organization for the Bay Area met at my house. I spent 21 days in jail for trying to stop the war, and I worked frequently with the Haight Ashbury Clinic trip-sitting people on bad acid trips … Down in Los Angeles, I worked with juvenile offenders … In Florida, I helped create the Florida Consumer Action Network and then joined a

Black social action movement. I was given the Dr. Martin Luther King Jr. Drum Major for Justice Award by the Black community in Tampa. And so on, for 51 years ... rather than asking about whether psilocybin has a religious or spiritual effect, it might be better to ask whether a psychedelic experience can reframe your values. I think it might have for me. (cited in Coffey 2021a)

While Young's account may not be uncommon among those immersed in the set and setting of the 1960s, some researchers and activists today believe that psychedelic substances can facilitate shifts in political orientation and values, and perhaps even be a catalyst for political action.

In 2006, researchers at Johns Hopkins University published an important scientific paper that helped to catalyze the psychedelic renaissance (Griffiths et al. 2006). These researchers wanted to see if they could replicate the findings of the Good Friday Experiment, this time with thirty-six healthy volunteers who had never taken psilocybin before. The doses were the same in the two experiments, but the new study included multiple psychedelic sessions conducted on an individual basis. Methodologically, this double-blind, placebo-controlled experiment was more rigorous. The researchers concluded that when administered to volunteers under supportive conditions, "psilocybin occasioned experiences similar to spontaneously occurring mystical experiences and which were evaluated by volunteers as having substantial and sustained personal meaning and spiritual significance" (2006, 282). Two-thirds of the subjects rated their participation in the study as among the top five most meaningful experiences of their lives, while a third ranked it as the most meaningful. In a follow-up study fourteen months later, these ratings declined only slightly, with 58 percent of volunteers still ranking it as among the five most meaningful experiences of their lives (Griffiths et al. 2008). Moreover, the strength or "completeness" of the mystical experience closely tracked the reported improvements in life satisfaction, personal well-being and positive behaviour change — reports that relied on self-assessment as well as input from coworkers, friends and family members.

Some may be surprised that most subjects judged the meaningfulness of their psilocybin experience to be comparable with that of "the birth of a first child or death of a parent" (Griffiths et al. 2006, 277). But this kind of description of the experience is not unusual. David Yaden, Brian Earp and Roland Griffiths (2022, 467) point to replicated findings in at least four clinical trials involving psilocybin, noting "*most participants (mean 76%, range 58–94%) rate their psychedelic experiences among the most meaningful experiences of their entire lives 6–14 months after their last session*" (emphasis in original). Michael Pollan also interviewed some of the study's participants: "for most ... their psilocybin journeys had taken place ten or fifteen years earlier, and yet their effects were still keenly felt, in some cases on a daily basis." Pollan has acknowledged that his own psychedelic journeys, undertaken for research purposes, were some of his most meaningful experiences. These kinds of results are not unique to psilocybin and are also found in studies involving LSD, DMT and other compounds (Davis et al. 2020; Schmid and Liechti 2018). As psychedelic science has matured, psychometric instruments for measuring the phenomenology of mystical experiences, like the Mystical Experience Questionnaire (MEQ and MEQ30) and the Hood Mysticism Scale (HMS), have been incorporated into a growing number of research investigations and translated into multiple languages (Hood 1975; MacLean et al. 2012).

The use of mystical language within psychedelic science, as well as efforts to quantify such ineffable phenomena, has drawn criticism from many quarters, including religious scholars (e.g., Taves 2020). There has also been pushback from within the psychedelic community (Jones 2023d). Veteran psychedelic researcher Rick Strassman rails against what he calls "the psychedelic religion of mystical consciousness." "It's a messianic movement," Strassman claims, "they want to bring about a utopia, and in this case, the messiah is the mushroom" (cited in Kitchens 2022). Strassman does not believe psychedelics have any inherent mystical properties or effects, only those created by set and setting, such as filtering the results through quantitative measures like the MEQ and HMS. For Strassman and others, these scales and questionnaires (or even prior knowledge of them) may shape or bias subjects' interpretations of their psychedelic experiences.

Others argue that the subject of mysticism is unscientific because it blurs secular and supernatural concepts, and that psychedelic science should rely on cognitive neuroscientific models to understand mystical phenomena. James Sanders and Josjan Zijlmans (2021), for example, believe mystical language and concepts are the "elephant in the room" of psychedelic research and warn against reliance on non-empirical beliefs. Although they recognize that most psychedelic researchers and therapists do not include supernatural elements in their conception of mysticism, it is too easily misinterpreted as advocating a role for the divine. One of the dangers is that the integration of mysticism into research and clinical practice "risks creating unrealistic and potentially problematic expectations and associations when presented to laypeople, including vulnerable groups pursuing psychedelics as interventions for serious health issues" (2021, 1254). What is needed instead, they claim, is a demystified model of the psychedelic state and greater attention on the part of therapists to how these experiences are interpreted.

Likewise, psychedelic researcher Matthew Johnson (2020) cautions against adopting frameworks drawn from mystical traditions, noting that any association with religion could alienate certain populations from psychedelic therapy. While Johnson believes it is appropriate for researchers to measure these types of experiences, there is a difference, he says, "between measuring something versus pushing it on the participants or making it the default" (cited in Love 2021b). Johnson also expresses concern about the degree to which mystical experiences can shape metaphysical beliefs and even push people into cult-like behaviour:

> Some people really believe they're encountering God ... Even relatively mainstream researchers and clinicians can fall into the trap of playing guru. I've been in over a hundred sessions, and it's humbling to be told you're part of "the most meaningful experience of my life." It can go to your head as a clinician. You can take advantage of that ... the doctor becomes the guru or priest, and they're the access to God. (cited in Evans 2023a)

US researchers have toned down references to mystical experiences in recent years in favour of concepts like personally meaningful experiences. Psychedelic researchers in Europe, in places like Zurich and London, were never much enamoured with mystical experiences to begin with, preferring to use more secular language such as ego death.

It is also important to point out that conceptions of the mystical are social constructs. While psychedelic experiences themselves are ineffable, the available terminology is loaded with culturally laden denotations and connotations. As Willy Pedersen and colleagues

(2021) argue, conceptions of the mystical are conditioned by set and setting and broader cultural tropes and discourses that change over time. How users of psychedelics talk about the mystical in interview narratives reflects these tropes and storylines, rather than being neatly or naturally induced by the experience itself. Bradley Garb and Mitchell Earleywine (2022) suggest that fellow psychedelic researchers should not reify or naturalize the mystical, as it has narrative and even fictional elements that can structure our understanding of psychedelic experiences.

Despite these criticisms, the use and investigation of mystical experiences in psychedelic science and therapy — what researcher Charles Grob describes as "applied mysticism" — is likely here to stay. The scientific and clinical implications of mystical experiences have been demonstrated over time and the methodological tools that were developed to study these experiences continue to have implications for psychedelic-assisted therapy (Breeksema and van Elk 2021). For example, research suggests that positive therapeutic outcomes in biomedical settings tend to correlate with the reporting of mystical-type experiences (Johnson et al. 2019; Weiss et al. 2024) and psychometric instruments like the MEQ and Ego Dissolution Inventory have been shown to predict the effectiveness of psychedelics in treating a range of mental health disorders (e.g., Roseman, Nutt and Carhart-Harris 2018; Strickland, Garcia-Romeu and Johnson 2024). As neuropsychologist Kwonmok Ko and his colleagues (2022) note: "The mystical experience … [has] been closely linked to both symptom reduction and improved quality of life." The same is true in non-clinical settings where the mental health and well-being of otherwise healthy individuals are positively correlated with these experiences (Kangaslampi 2023).

In the end, it may be that a distinct "mystical" state matters less than the subjective psychedelic experience more broadly. Psychedelic-induced mystical experiences are more of an umbrella construct than a singular or fixed state, where more neutral descriptors such as ego dissolution, "peak experience" or profound state of awe can effectively mean or result in the same thing. As philosopher Chris Letheby (2021, 61) has argued, the lasting psychological benefits of psychedelics do not depend on invoking a mystical experience per se, but rather on "some aspect of the psychedelic experience that … correlates fairly reliably with psychometric ratings of mystical-type experience."

CAN PSYCHEDELICS CHANGE YOUR BELIEFS?

Psychedelics have had a lasting influence on philosophy, inspiring important works in epistemology, phenomenology, ethics, sentience, metaphysics and philosophy of mind (Hauskeller and Sjöstedt-Hughes 2022; Letheby 2021; Sjöstedt-Hughes 2021). According to philosopher Peter Sjöstedt-Hughes, "I wouldn't go so far as to say that psychedelics are essential to philosophy generally, but I would say that they are to the philosophy of mind and metaphysics what microscopes are to biology" (cited in Sidhu 2019a).

An interesting set of questions centre around the impact of psychedelics on belief systems. In 2021, a research team led by Christopher Timmermann of the Centre for Psychedelic Research surveyed 866 people from 58 countries (mostly white people in the US and UK) who participated in various psychedelic ceremonies (Timmermann et al. 2021). The research aimed to understand how metaphysical beliefs (the nature of reality, consciousness and free will) might be altered by psychedelic use. Their results suggest not only that psychedelics can change people's belief systems, but also the likely direction of change: a shift away from "hard materialism," or the belief that there is one reality that can be fully explained in materialist terms, and toward fatalism, dualism and panpsychism. Panpsychism, which occupies an important position in metaphysics and philosophy of mind, views consciousness as a fundamental quality of the universe. It is the idea that many or most things have a conscious element to them (such as plants, fungi, animals, insects). Notably, Timmermann and his team advised future researchers to warn participants that their worldviews might be altered by participating in these kinds of studies. Such a warning may be prudent as psychedelic trips can result in something known as "ontological shock," where people's perceptions of reality are so altered that the mind has difficulty adjusting.

A larger and more recent survey of 2,374 people found that psychedelics brought about belief changes that were consistent with those of the previous study: most notably, a rise in non-material and non-physicalist beliefs (Nayak et al. 2023). Higher ratings of mystical experience were associated with greater belief change and these changes endured over time; surveyed an average of 8.4 years after their "reference belief-changing psychedelic experience," many said their shifts in perception remained largely unchanged. The vast majority of participants (87 percent) said the experience changed their fundamental conception of reality. These investigations are supported by a growing number of studies suggesting that psychedelics are associated with a host of belief changes including, once again, those connected to the nature of reality itself (Davis et al. 2020; Griffiths et al. 2019; Nayak and Griffiths 2022). Surveying this literature, it would be a mistake to conclude that psychedelics promote supernatural beliefs. In fact, recent research out of Johns Hopkins University found that psychedelics do not make atheists believe in God (Nayak et al. 2024). Rather, consistent with earlier studies, it revealed significant increases in panpsychism with psychedelic use, which does not necessarily accord with supernatural beliefs (Ritchie 2021).

Broadly speaking, psychedelics facilitate a greater appreciation of the sacred or spiritual dimensions of human life, which can range from supernatural to more secular understandings. Just as "sacred" is sometimes used to denote categories of secular phenomena considered important to human well-being, "spiritual" can also apply to things like community belonging, compassionate attitudes toward others or a sense of personal meaning in one's life. In the words of Stanislav Grof, an early pioneer of transpersonal psychology, "even positivistically oriented scientists, hard-core materialists, skeptics and cynics, uncompromising atheists and anti-religious crusaders such as Marxist philosophers and politicians, suddenly become interested in the spiritual quest" after high-dose psychedelic journeys (cited in Walsh and Grob 2006, 438). According to Professor Jeremy Gilbert (2017), the fact that psychedelics can reliably induce experiences that are similar to mystical experiences found in domains like religion represents a major scientific contribution. It demonstrates that these experiences are not supernatural or fictitious, but "corporeal, material and physical ... a materialist mysticism which acknowledges the complex potentialities of human embodied existence, without tying that recognition to any set of supernatural or theistic beliefs."

Reflecting on his own psychedelic journeys, Michael Pollan (2018, 288), who would likely situate himself within the range of groups outlined by Grof, writes, "I have no problem using the word 'spiritual' to describe elements of what I saw and felt, as long it is not taken in a supernatural sense. For me, 'spiritual' is a good name for some of the powerful mental phenomena that arise when the voice of the ego is muted or silenced." Pollan sees ego dissolution as central to the spiritual dimensions of psychedelics. What emerges in its place, he says, "is invariably a broader, more openhearted and altruistic – that is, more spiritual — idea of what matters in life. One in which a new sense of connection, or love, however defined, seems to figure prominently" (2018, 390). It is remarkable that even devoutly secular and materially grounded individuals often come away from these experiences believing something exists beyond a material understanding of reality, even if they ultimately attribute these insights to molecules flowing through their brains.

When examining the relationship between psychedelics and belief systems, it is worth revisiting one of the central markers of mystical experiences — their noetic quality. William James (1902) argued that mystical states are typically viewed by those who confront them not as subjective phenomena but as legitimate states of knowledge. They contain insights and revelations that are endowed with a profound sense of authority (see Cole-Turner 2021). Such revelations may involve believing in new concepts and generating new insights, or deepening the sense of significance attached to something that was already suspected or believed. Likewise, psychedelic experiences are typically viewed by users as genuine encounters that contain an authority of objective truth, or a form of knowledge that requires no external validation ("more real than real," as some have described it). This shift in beliefs is not something people usually report when using other kinds of drugs, where they are often aware of or embarrassed by the speciousness of their experiences after the fact (Yaden et al. 2017b).

Sometimes, however, psychedelic experiences appear to wildly transgress the boundaries of reality. Ethnobotanist Terence McKenna once referred to the DMT experience as a "100 percent reality channel switch" that catapults users into bizarre realms of complex geometric shapes and off-planet motifs inhabited by intelligent, non-human entities. "These self-transforming machine elf creatures were speaking in a colored language which condensed into rotating machines that were like Fabergé eggs but crafted out of luminescent superconducting ceramics and liquid crystal gels," is how he once described it (McKenna 1987). McKenna is not alone. People encounter "DMT entities" so often that they might be considered universal motifs (Luke and Spowers 2021). According to one study, 94 percent of DMT users (34 of 36) reported encounters with other beings and all recounted emerging into different worlds (Michael, Luke and Robinson 2021). The high frequency of entity encounters is consistent with DMT researcher Peter Meyer's (2010) analysis of 340 DMT trip reports, where two-thirds referenced intelligent and independently existing entities, as well as Rick Strassman's *DMT: The Spirit Molecule* (2001), where roughly half of the participants reported such encounters. The point here is not to claim that psychedelics reveal the existence of other forms of intelligent life, but to underscore the noetic quality of the experience. Of 2,561 DMT users who encountered DMT entities and were surveyed by Johns Hopkins researchers, 81 percent said their encounter felt more real than everyday waking consciousness, 72 percent endorsed believing that the entity continued to exist after their encounter and 80 percent said the experience altered their fundamental conception of reality (Davis et al. 2020). In his book *The Bigger Picture*, Alexander Beiner (2023, 199–200) describes his own encounters with DMT entities during a psychedelic research trial in much the same manner, noting that "any attempt to try and boil down what I was experiencing to 'my brain on drugs' would have felt at odds with my empirical observations."

Reports of DMT entities may lead some to believe that psychedelics promote mass delusion. It is clear that the beliefs and psychological insights generated by psychedelics will not always be "true" in a conventional sense. Like other "aha moments" that have been studied by psychologists over the years, psychedelics can evoke illusory insights that feel real but present a distorted map of reality (McGovern et al. 2024). As Shayla Love (2022a) notes, "false insights can be induced in the lab through some simple tricks, and feelings of insight can spill over in how people regard other worldviews and facts — making untrue facts or extreme beliefs seem more true, a subject highly relevant to psychedelics." Many also expect to glean specific insights or understandings from a psychedelic experience, an important component of set and setting, which may make them more inclined to report them or to accept them as accurate. Although the noetic quality of psychedelic trips is one of their more consistent and fascinating elements, there is no shortage of individuals who come out of these experiences more confused and disoriented than when they went in.

Yet, it can also be argued that what we observe in our everyday waking consciousness is not objective or "true" either, and that, in some instances, psychedelics may elicit a more insightful or accurate picture of reality. In *The Doors of Perception* (1954), Aldous Huxley famously spoke of the mind as a "reducing value" that edits and removes far more information than it admits so that we are not constantly overwhelmed by the enormity of the sensory experience. To make the world comprehensible, our minds must selectively filter what gets in. Ethnopharmacologist Dennis McKenna calls this the "reality hallucination" — the heavily curated and necessarily impoverished version of reality that is constructed by our brains and entrenched in our egos. Viewed in this way, psychedelics may temporarily disable those mechanisms, opening the reducing valve and removing the filter that hides some portion of reality from ordinary consciousness. Philosopher and psychologist Jussi Jylkkä (2024) expands on these ideas, arguing that using psychedelics can provide insight into the fundamental nature of reality by bypassing habitual patterns of thought and perception. In so doing, they can enable us to see our everyday models of reality *as* models — distinct from reality itself — and to acknowledge their limitations. While psychedelics are unlikely to provide a shortcut to universal metaphysical truths, Jylkkä suggests they may offer a more complete picture of reality than is possible within non-altered states of consciousness.

These observations about the psychedelic state are now finding a place within psychedelic science. Neuroscience and brain imaging suggest that psychedelics reduce blood flow to control centres in the brain that filter sensory information (Carhart-Harris et al. 2011). Some researchers have likened Huxley's reducing valve to the brain's "default mode network" (DMN), which shows reduced activity under psychedelics and allows for freer conversations between brain regions that do not normally communicate with one another. Ego dissolution following psychedelic consumption is said to correlate with DMN disintegration and increased functional brain connectivity. How psychedelic-induced mystical experiences differ neurologically from those produced in other ways is not well known (James et al. 2020), but some research suggests there are neural correlates between DMN disintegration and mystical experiences induced by psychedelics and other practices such as deep meditation (Barrett and Griffiths 2018). Disruption of the brain's DMN and experiences of ego dissolution are also posited to be important in a therapeutic context, allowing patients to step outside the confines of rigid, habitual thought patterns and view their situation from a different perspective. In the case of psychedelic-assisted therapy, some suggest it may not matter whether certain insights or breakthroughs accord with something "real" or are merely comforting delusions, so long as people's lives are improved (Letheby 2021; Pollan 2015).

Psychedelic-induced insights or changes in belief can be transformative and even life changing. The knowledge and insights gained through psychedelic use often have social and political implications, such as a greater appreciation of the unity and interconnectedness of all living things or a more honest reckoning with the destructive impacts of human activities. If psychedelics can have a discernible influence on political consciousness, what is it and what are the implications for social change?

05

POWER, POLITICS AND SOCIAL CHANGE

THROUGHOUT HISTORY, SOCIETIES HAVE CONDONED and institutionalized some states of consciousness while vilifying and prohibiting others. Those with power tend to set the frame for what is condoned versus vilified, with the sanctioned states of consciousness often reinforcing the existing social and economic order. Caffeine is an obvious example of an addictive substance that is supported and ritualized in our culture, in part because it helps workers to be more productive and efficient. Dedicated timeouts for the consumption of stimulants — like the coffee break or smoke break — are socially reinforced and institutionally sanctioned. "Add in some booze from time to time and you've got a finely tuned cycle of stimulation-focus-decompression that dovetails with broader economic goals" (Kotler and Wheal 2017, 64). Of course, what is valued or deemed acceptable varies over time. In the sixteenth century, the introduction of coffee into Europe from the Muslim world encountered strong resistance from Catholic authorities, who branded it the "Devil's drink" (Johnstad 2023). Coffee was also outlawed at other points in history when its source or user base was deemed to be politically threatening to the powers that be (Pollan 2021b).

Psychedelics can produce states of consciousness that conflict with dominant norms and values. In the 1960s, part of the motive behind criminalizing psychedelics was due to concerns about their impact on political consciousness. These substances were used by and associated with groups immersed in the counterculture and anti-war movements. Elite fears were only amplified when people like Timothy Leary began announcing to the establishment that young people who took LSD were not going to "join your corporations" or "fight your wars." This was likely part of the reason he was allegedly branded "the most dangerous man in America" by President Richard Nixon. As Terence McKenna once remarked, "Psychedelics are illegal not because a loving government is concerned that you may jump out of a third story window. Psychedelics are illegal because they dissolve opinion structures and culturally laid down models of behaviour and information processing. They open you up to the possibility that everything you know is wrong" (cited in Lin 2014).

Some have singled out the mystical experience as central to the subversive ethos of psychedelics. Roland Griffiths argues that many cultures have been reluctant to condone psychedelics because there is "so much authority that comes out of the primary mystical experience that it can be threatening to existing hierarchical structures" (cited in Pollan 2018, 59). During the 1960s peace movement, philosopher Alan Watts (1968, 82–83) pointed to the association between psychedelics and the challenging of power structures, noting that mystical experiences often result in attitudes that threaten authority: "Unafraid of death and deficient in worldly ambitions, those who have undergone mystical experiences are impervious to threats and promises [and] indifferent to society's traditional rewards and sanctions." Watts' account was overly simplistic, but the point remains that psychedelics can function as catalysts of subversive thought and intellectual dissent.

Today, these claims continue to be exaggerated. If we are to believe modern-day media, psychedelics will not only revolutionize mental health but extinguish political polarization, prevent the rise of fascism, solve the climate crisis and usher in world peace. A growing segment of psychedelic scientists and industry leaders also embrace this narrative, often for self-interested reasons. If psychedelics can save the world, what right does anyone have to criticize medicalization, for-profit drug development or spurious patent claims?

Psychedelics have been famously described by psychiatrist Stanislav Grof as "non-specific amplifiers" that mirror or magnify particular states of mind, rather than inducing specific states of consciousness on a consistent basis. How psychedelics impact states of consciousness and the political landscape is heavily dependent on set and setting, which includes non-pharmacological factors such as personality, preparation, expectations and intentions as well as the physical, social and cultural environments within which the experiences take place. It follows that any shifts in political beliefs precipitated by psychedelics are largely the result of contextual factors and do not result in essentialized outcomes like those suggested by well-worn stereotypes of psychedelics turning people into anti-establishment crusaders. Unlike the 1960s when psychedelics were immersed in countercultural and bottom-up movements for change, today's cultural set and setting primarily entails an individualistic and competitive set of social relations embedded in neoliberal capitalism.

LEFT-WING PSYCHEDELIA

Psychedelic advocates have long asserted that these compounds can inspire progressive values and help foster a more just society. The integration of psychedelics with the political radicalization of the 1960s provides some support for this claim. LSD and other psychedelics played an important role in social movements during this period. They infused the organizing efforts of activist groups like the Diggers, Yippies, Student Nonviolent Coordinating Committee and Students for a Democratic Society (SDS). While members of SDS always drew an important distinction between changing individual consciousness and changing the system, Carl Oglesby, former president of SDS, viewed the psychological impacts of consuming LSD and the tendency to challenge established authority as complementary: "Nothing could stand for that overall sense of going through profound changes so well as the immediate, powerful and explicit transformation that you went through when you dropped acid ... It's not necessarily that the actual content of the LSD experience contributed to politically radical or revolutionary consciousness — it was just that the experience shared the structural characteristics of political rebellion" (cited in Lee and Shlain 1985, 132). More militant organizations, like the Weather Underground, also disseminated psychedelics as consciousness-raising tools.

The late psychologist Ralph Metzner argued that psychedelics had an energizing and amplifying influence on the cultural awakenings of the 1960s. Although he acknowledged no causal link between psychedelic use and cultural transformation, Metzner claimed these movements represented "an expansion of collective consciousness, a transcending of existing limited conventions, attitudes and norms, similar to what is classically associated with psychedelic experiences in the individual" (Metzner

2009, 18; see also Metzner 2008). Journalist David Nickles (2018a) takes a more direct view, stating that "the amount of global suffering stemming from the unchecked systems of American capitalism, imperialism, and militarism would have been far greater without the catalyzing impact of psychedelics on the psyches of those involved in resistance movements." Much has changed since the 1960s, but the optimism surrounding the role of psychedelics in building a better world has not.

Many psychedelic users emphasize the emancipatory potential of these experiences and see them as supporting the transcendence of individualistic notions of liberty and well-being. Other advocates, however, offer a far more utopian view of these potentials, seemingly irrespective of context. Charles Eisenstein (2016, 4) claims that psychedelic mainstreaming would accelerate the transition to a just economy because they facilitate "less quantity and more quality, fewer 'services' and more relationships, fewer 'goods' and more beauty, less competition and more community, less accumulation and more sharing, less work and more play, less extraction and more healing." MAPS founder Rick Doblin (2013) stated that if psychedelic research had not been shut down in the 1970s, the United States would have likely never invaded Iraq. More recently, Doblin is quoted as saying that the psychedelic experience is "the antidote to genocide, to the holocaust, to nuclear destruction, to racism … a tool to bring about mass mental health." He has also suggested that global access to psychedelics could lead to a world of "net-zero trauma" by 2070 through a process of "mass spiritualization" (cited in Devenot 2023, 25). Michael Pollan notes that even those researchers who avoid irrational exuberance around psychedelics often embrace these narratives: "take them out for a drink, and they'll come around to that place, the value of these compounds for the whole civilization" (cited in Ferriss 2018).

Empathy, Openness and Political Beliefs

The relationship between psychedelics, personality and political ideology is a hot topic in today's psychedelic renaissance. Clinical and neuropsychological research suggests that psychedelic use is associated with increased empathy along with pro-social attitudes and behaviour (e.g., Dolder et al. 2016; Griffiths et al. 2018; Mason et al. 2019; Pokorny et al. 2017). One 2020 study found that psychedelic-induced experiences of awe were correlated with increased feelings of connectedness and affective empathetic drive, which in turn were associated with a reduction in maladaptive narcissistic personality traits (van Mulukom, Patterson and van Elk 2020).

Psychedelics have also been associated with increased "openness," one of the Big Five personality traits — a five-factor model of personality that is popular among psychologists (the others are conscientiousness, extraversion, agreeableness and neuroticism). People with a high degree of openness are more likely to be sensitive, imaginative, intellectually curious, adventurous and have a broad-minded tolerance of the viewpoints of others. On the political spectrum, they are more likely to hold liberal views, challenge authority and question traditional values. In both experimental and longitudinal studies, openness has been found to increase following psychedelic administration. In 2011, Johns Hopkins researchers found increases in openness following high-dose psilocybin sessions that were "larger in magnitude than changes in personality typically observed in healthy adults over decades of life experience" (MacLean, Johnson and Griffiths 2011, 1457). In participants who met the criteria for having a "complete" mystical experience, openness levels remained significantly elevated sixteen months after the initial session. Subsequent research has since lent support to these findings, including studies involving psilocybin, LSD, MDMA and ayahuasca (e.g., Barbosa et al. 2016; Erritzoe et al. 2018; Lebedev et al. 2015; Netzband et al. 2020; Wagner et al. 2017; Weiss et al. 2021).

Although the evidence is limited, some have also suggested there is a connection between psychedelic use, trait openness and liberal political values and beliefs. A 2017 study by UK researchers found that lifetime psychedelic use positively predicted liberal political views, openness to experience and "nature relatedness" (Nour, Evans and Carhart-Harris 2017). It also negatively predicted authoritarian political views. The same did not hold for lifetime cocaine use or weekly alcohol consumption. The researchers posited that ego dissolution during the participants' most intense psychedelic experiences was the key explanatory factor. The following year, another UK study involving fourteen patients being treated for depression found that authoritarian political views significantly declined following the administration of psilocybin, though these reductions did not hold at the seven- to twelve-month follow-up point (Lyons and Carhart-Harris 2018). Despite its small sample size and without any suggestion of a causal relationship, the findings led to media headlines such as "scientists find magic mushrooms could help fight fascism" (Ratner 2018) and "magic mushrooms fight authoritarianism" (Smith 2018b).

To our knowledge, these studies represent the only peer-reviewed literature suggesting that psychedelic use can help to predict liberal political values. They have been criticized as methodologically suspect and given the influence of set and setting their conclusions need to be taken cautiously. It is likely that people who experiment with psychedelics already tend to be more open to experience and liberal or left leaning in their views, while less open and more conservative individuals are more likely to self-select out of using psychedelics (Weiss et al. 2023). Psychedelic researchers Matthew Johnson and David Yaden (2020) conclude that the existing evidence does not support the idea that the psychedelic experience results in meaningful changes in political values, beliefs or affiliation.

The idea that psychedelics can facilitate empathy or openness makes intuitive sense to many users and advocates. The replicated finding that psychedelics can, on average, increase openness to experience may be the strongest evidence of their impacts on personality, and perhaps psychedelics are unique in their ability to induce this particular change. However, disentangling the effects of set and setting remains a major challenge. These same concerns hold for research examining other dimensions of "left-wing psychedelia," such as ecology and nature relatedness. Here though, there may be a better evidentiary record to draw upon.

Ecology and Nature Relatedness

For many on the left, the ecological destruction associated with modern capitalism is one of the great tragedies of our age. This destruction has resulted from an acute disconnection between human beings and the natural world where we think of ecosystems and their inhabitants as simply resources for human use. While it is important not to homogenize or romanticize Indigenous cultures, it is likely no coincidence that those areas of the world that have preserved their ecological integrity are often inhabited by Indigenous peoples. A common thread in many of these cultures is a strong connection to nature and a commitment to protecting the environment for future generations. Some have posited a connection between the ecological values of Indigenous communities and their history of psychedelic use (e.g., Reichel-Dolmatoff 1976).

Renowned Swiss chemist Albert Hofmann, who first synthesized LSD in 1938, believed that the capacity of psychedelics to connect human beings with nature was perhaps their most fundamental property. His personal experiences with the drug led him to become an environmental advocate. Shortly before his death at the age of 101, he wrote: "alienation from nature and the loss of the experience of being part of the living creation is the greatest tragedy of our materialist era … I attribute absolute highest importance to consciousness change. I regard psychedelics as catalyzers for this" (Hofmann 2013, 101). Other prominent figures in psychedelia also draw these connections. The late Terence McKenna (1992, 1993) hypothesized that psychedelics provide a gateway to the "Gaian mind" of the planet, allowing us to perceive and appreciate the collective suffering of ecosystems and advance a more symbiotic relationship with the biosphere. Terence's brother, ethnopharmacologist Dennis McKenna, views psychedelics as a catalyst for transforming ecological consciousness. He refers to psychedelics like ayahuasca and magic mushrooms as "ambassadors from Gaia" that are bringing a serious message to our species (cited in Meistere and McKenna 2020).

Sam Gandy (2019), who has studied the relationship between psychedelic use and ecological consciousness, argues that psychedelics are biophilia-enhancing agents; biophilia refers to our innate fondness for nature and our unconscious drive to seek connections with other forms of life. One of the unique powers of psychedelics, Gandy claims, is to increase these connections in people who are otherwise disengaged from the natural world, thereby helping to convert "nature sceptics." Similarly, journalist Alexander Beiner (2023) suggests that the capacity of psychedelics to change our views on consciousness (panpsychism) has important ecological implications. Attributing some form of consciousness to plants, ecosystems and other species, along with corresponding changes in how we view ourselves and our place in the world, can alter our relationship with nature and foster a greater desire to protect it.

Some of the most interesting testimony linking psychedelics with environmental awareness and activism comes from individuals who have had profound or life-changing experiences. For David Nickles, psychedelics and radical politics have been connected since his first experience with psilocybin as a university freshman. Nickles refers to this trip as his first "radical synthesis." The following is his description of the experience at the 2014 Boom Festival:

> I suddenly felt this deep profound sadness knowing that these interconnections exist in ecological systems all over the world, and that these ecological systems are under attack, that they're essentially being decimated by humans. And as this profound sadness enveloped me, I realized that it wasn't just humans, that it was humans organized into corporate hierarchies and that they were engaged in acts of for-profit insanity. Literally poisoning the water we drink, the air we breathe, the ground that we derive sustenance from ... the conclusion that I was left with was to resist, that I needed to find ways of engaging with the world that would not only create a world in which I wanted to be in but that would actively challenge the various systems that were cropping up as problematic during this experience. And for me the experience left me with a very clear message that ecological integrity is perhaps sacrosanct and that given the situation of industrial capitalism, this destruction of ecosystems will be ongoing unless it's forcibly forestalled. (Nickles 2014)

Gail Bradbrook, one of the founders of the climate activist group Extinction Rebellion, embarked on her psychedelic journey with a more specific intention — she wanted to become a more effective social activist. "I wanted answers to how I could bring about social change. What was I missing? What am I not doing? It was a specific prayer for what I called the 'codes for social change'" (Bradbrook 2019). Supported by her use of iboga, kambo and ayahuasca over a two-week period in Costa Rica, Bradbrook felt she was better equipped to face the traumas associated with environmental collapse and more willing to risk her freedom to transform a broken system. Her experiences were a precipitating factor in the formation of Extinction Rebellion.

Psychedelic users often report a deeply felt sense of oneness or unity with the planet and its inhabitants which, for some, has an enduring effect on the way they live their lives. For individuals, one of the strongest predictors of pro-environmental awareness and behaviour is having a personal connection with nature, which is also positively correlated with happiness and other measures of psychological well-being (Capaldi, Dopko and Zelenski 2014; Mackay and Schmitt 2019; Otto and Pensini 2017). Research points to a positive relationship between the use of classical psychedelics and self-reported nature relatedness and pro-environmental behaviour (see Forstmann et al. 2023). Much of this work suggests that psychedelics can increase nature relatedness through experiences of ego dissolution and a heightened sense of external unity or connectedness with the natural world, core elements of psychedelic mystical experiences (Kettner et al. 2019; Nour, Evans and Carhart-Harris 2017; Paterniti, Bright and Gringart 2022).

This research is largely correlation based and relies on self-reports, leaving open the question of whether these associations can be attributed to psychedelic substances or confounding variables such as values, attitudes and personality traits that are positively associated with psychedelic use and/or nature relatedness. Some people who are attracted to psychedelics may already have a deep connection with nature and be more inclined toward environmentalism. However, some research has found that the relationship between psychedelic use and pro-environmental variables remained significant even after controlling for personality traits that could predict psychedelic consumption and an affinity for nature (Forstmann and Sagioglou 2017).

Accounting for predispositions and the influence of set and setting, it is difficult to say what the impacts of widespread ego dissolution would be on communities that are unsympathetic to environmental issues. Nevertheless, some advocates continue to argue that psychedelics can and should be used in a deliberate fashion to broaden ecological awareness and engagement. According to philosophers Nin Kirkham and Chris Letheby (2022), environmental issues are problems of collective action, but there is also a need to change individual behaviour. To meet this need, they propose a program of psychedelic-assisted interventions marked by "the judicious, safe, and controlled administration of 'classic' psychedelic drugs as a form of moral bio-enhancement." Likewise, some medical professionals have suggested that once psychedelics are legally approved for medical conditions, "eco-psychiatrists" should consider using them off-label for what they refer to as "anti-nature pathology," or the imminent threat to planetary health posed by those who routinely abuse the environment (Verma 2018). Gail Bradbrook of the Extinction Rebellion has also called for "mass psychedelic disobedience" in opposition to drug criminalization and to address problems of human "separation" that interfere with climate action. Psychedelic law breaking may not resonate with those who favour medically approved rollouts, but

Bradbook claims we do not have time to wait for the science to tell us these medicines work (cited in Wong 2019).

Hierarchical structures that separate humans from nature have been feeding environmental degradation for centuries. Both collective action and individual change will be necessary to solve these problems. If psychedelics can help facilitate long-term increases in nature relatedness and pro-environmental behaviour among individuals, we support continuing the conversation around how and why this might occur. However, this is very different than claiming that psychedelics can resolve the climate crisis and "save the planet," a prominent media narrative in recent years (e.g., Adams 2020; Schmidt 2021; Sidhu 2019b). Individual actions and behaviours are never going to resolve what are ultimately systemic problems rooted in state and corporate power. This reasoning becomes even more debilitating when we consider the prognosis that our global problems would be solved if only we could get our leaders to trip.

The Allure of Tripping Elites

"Could alt-right assholes be fixed by feeding them shrooms?" was the provocative headline of a 2018 article discussing the relationship between psychedelics and political beliefs (Finster 2018). A related and perhaps more relevant question is whether psychedelics can "fix" our political and economic leaders. Many of today's strongest advocates argue that these drugs have the capacity to inspire empathy and openness, including on the part of politicians, which in turn would facilitate peace, co-operation and mutual understanding. This same argument is applied to the business world, where connections are made between the potential of psychedelic-induced interconnectedness and nature relatedness and helping corporate leaders appreciate and curtail their destructive, extractive practices.

The idea of using psychedelics to modify or correct elite priorities has been circulating since at least the 1960s. Paul McCartney once mused in *Life Magazine* that "if the politicians would take LSD, there wouldn't be any more war, or poverty, or famine" (cited in Thompson 1967). Psychedelic pioneer Al Hubbard believed he would fundamentally change society if he could get psychedelics into the hands of Fortune 500 executives. American poet and writer Allen Ginsberg reacted to one of his own mushroom trips by trying to arrange a phone call between

John F. Kennedy, Soviet leader Nikita Khrushchev and Chairman Mao of China to settle the issue of "the bomb," while Jefferson Airplane's singer Grace Slick devised a scheme to drop acid into President Nixon's tea to convince him to withdraw US troops from Southeast Asia (Hartogsohn 2020). This was all at a time when the CIA was experimenting with LSD for its mind control program MK-Ultra.

Little has changed in this regard. "You do feel that this is a medicine for our moment," remarked Michael Pollan at Big Sur's Esalen Institute in 2019, "if only we could get Trump to trip" (cited in Gunther 2020). Best-selling author and journalist Graham Hancock similarly pronounced that "all politicians should be required to drink ayahuasca 10 times before taking office" (cited in Dahl 2017). While Pollan's remarks were likely in jest, having recently stated that giving Trump psychedelics might make him "more Trumpy" than ever, others take the idea more seriously. Christian Angermayer, prominent psychedelic investor and founder of psychedelic drug company Atai Life Sciences, has claimed that "psychedelics make you a better human being, and that's what we want our politicians to be" (cited in Love 2021c). Ronan Levy, the former CEO of psychedelic company Field Trip Health, has argued that if we can fix those at the top, all of society will be served through something approximating "trickle-down ecstasis," a derivative of trickle-down economics where society's interests are purportedly best served by further enriching the wealthy (Devenot 2023).

Is there any indication this could work? According to Ido Hartogsohn (2022), a professor of science and technology studies at Bar-Ilan University, in the 1950s, a group of government officials and UN ambassadors participated in joint psychedelic sessions, but this little-known episode of "international psychochemical diplomacy" did not lead to world peace and was quickly forgotten. Some years later, in the mid-1980s, MAPS founder Rick Doblin and Carol Rosin, founder of the Institute for Security and Cooperation in Outer Space, reportedly hatched a plan to give MDMA to Soviet scientists and military personnel who were scheduled to negotiate with US President Ronald Reagan, with the goal of injecting "empathy and cross-cultural understanding into the nuclear peace process" (Elder 2021). Roslin claims the drugs were delivered, but whether this happened or what the consequences were remains unknown.

Others point to anecdotal cases from the business world. One bitcoin millionaire known only as "Pine" was so enamoured with ketamine that he apparently donated most of his cryptocurrency wealth to charity (MAPS 2018). Michael Costuros, founder of Entrepreneurs Awakening (EA), a company specializing in ayahuasca retreats and psychedelic-assisted coaching for business leaders and entrepreneurs, claims that psychedelics make CEOs "people-centric, people-focused" individuals, not the kind of "Donald Trump entrepreneurs that are only about extracting value" (cited in Mac 2017). Following an ayahuasca journey with EA, one wealthy arms magnate reportedly left his company to build an arts and music residency program. There is also the case of Roland Kupers, former vice president of sustainable development at Shell. Kupers discovered the psychedelic literature on nature relatedness and subsequently embarked on his own hallucinogenic journey. He now argues that these substances "perform an essential function for climate policy" and that governments need to formally incorporate them into international climate negotiations. "I'm not saying we put psychedelics in the drinking water … but almost," Kupers says (cited in Schmidt 2021). Researchers at the University of Maryland are investigating whether psychedelic experiences can bring about changes in business leaders. Preliminary results from the pilot cohort point to "sustained increases in perceived connectedness to self, others, and the wider world," changes that presumably guide their decision making (Busby 2023a).

Psychedelics can contribute to changing people's values and perspectives, but the argument that "tripping elites" will solve the world's problems is deeply flawed. For one, it is premised on a misunderstanding of institutional power. The ways that for-profit corporations operate have more to do with the structural features of the institutions themselves than the people who run them (Bakan 2004). If the problems we associate with corporate power could be directly traced back to the people involved, then changing the personnel would presumably solve these problems. But "corporate greed" is not simply a by-product of the intentions of corporate executives. It resides in the structural imperatives of profit, market share and economic growth. One only has to imagine what would happen if a fossil-fuel CEO woke up one day (maybe after a psychedelic retreat with EA) and decided to radically scale back oil production in the interests of ecological sustainability. In all likelihood, such a CEO would quickly be forced out and replaced by someone who did not pose a threat to shareholder value. Similar institutional incentives and constraints exist in our state and political systems. While it might make them "nicer" people, tripping elites do nothing to address these institutional realities.

While structural forces are more determinant than individual values or intentions, this does not mean individuals are irrelevant. It is important to consider the kinds of people who are embedded in leadership positions. Individuals who are firmly committed to serving the public interest and uncompromising with respect to their own morals and values do not typically occupy high institutional positions. On the contrary, institutions actively select for "morally flexible" individuals who can compartmentalize their own moral codes and make the "tough" decisions that are demanded by capitalist economic relations. Award-winning journalist Erica Rex (2022) makes the point in her examination of neoliberal power structures. She argues that whereas "traditional" societies tended to select leaders with "life-affirming and alliance-building personality traits," the rise of neoliberalism has created an ideal climate for "dark factor" leadership traits, such as greed, narcissism and grandiosity, to become prominent. These traits are valued and selected for in a society based on competitive, free-market principles. If psychedelics are non-specific amplifiers that tend to magnify existing character traits or states of mind, then psychedelic use might only solidify or amplify these traits. So, can psychedelics fix alt-right assholes? Or would they just make them bigger assholes? In our view, psychedelics would only be likely to positively influence the leaders of today in a cultural and political setting that is radically different.

Anti-Capitalist Perspectives

Left-wing psychedelia includes anti-capitalist perspectives. These perspectives focus on the potential of psychedelics to liberate human consciousness from the norms of capitalist society and to catalyze movements to oppose them. One prominent example is cultural theorist Mark Fisher's (2018) writings on "acid communism." For him, neoliberal capitalism includes manufacturing consciousness and desire in ways that make it unlikely for alternatives to even be contemplated, leading to a sort of "fatalistic acquiescence" that there is no substitute for capitalism. In contrast, Fisher points to the psychedelic experimentalists and political radicals of the 1960s and 1970s as embracing an opportunity to reflect on alternative forms of political economy and move toward something beyond capitalism and state domination. With the widespread adoption of psychedelics in the 1960s, we did see the emergence of new questions and ideas about the nature of human consciousness and democratized access to alternative ways of thinking. For Professor Emma Stamm (2019), Fisher's acid communism makes clear that "psychologically profound experiences — including the use of psychedelic drugs — should be used to galvanize anticapitalist movements." But she cautions that this cannot and should not entail a "presumptive natural link between psychedelic experience and Leftist perspectives."

Scholar Jeremy Gilbert (2017) similarly explores psychedelic socialism. The point of acid communism or psychedelic socialism is to allow for thinking about alternatives. Capitalism and state domination are not only material forms of power; they have the effect of alienation and inundation of the self, resulting in individualization. Under neoliberalism, not only are we taught to behave as isolated, competitive individuals but we are conditioned to believe that problems of poverty, inequality and mental illness simply *happen* to individuals, rather than being a by-product of power and systemic oppression. These forms of individualism are designed, in part, to make us forget that different political realities are possible. A key feature of psychedelic socialism, then, is to generate interest in radical collectivist politics and a "radically different conception of freedom" than the one we have inherited from liberal individualism (Gilbert 2017). For both Gilbert and Fisher, we see the importance of psychedelics not in individualized therapy or "mindfulness," but radical politics and consciousness raising that is collectivist in nature. Just as they did for the counterculture of the 1960s, psychedelics hold the potential to contribute to these alternatives. It is for this reason that preventing psychedelics from being captured by corporations and the medical establishment, both of which disregard (or actively oppose) the radical and collectivist potential of psychedelics, is of utmost importance.

Mateo Sanchez Petrement (2023), a PhD candidate at the University of Amsterdam, further suggests the point of acid communism or psychedelic socialism is to insist on a collectivist and political approach to psychedelics. He underscores that part of what allowed the psychedelic counterculture of the 1960s to emerge was a broader ethos of collectivist political economy. Today's psychedelic renaissance is very different, operating at the tail end of neoliberalism and late modernity, with a myopic focus on individual wellness and the medicalization of distress. The problem with the focus on individual brains and individual health is that it leaves capitalism and state power unchallenged. It also deflects from the countercultural hope that psychedelics can help to change society while embracing "the more tempered, expedient, and de-politicized concern with treating or enhancing individuals with it" (Petrement 2023, 2). This understanding is part of philosopher Christine Hauskeller's (2022) critique of the fetishization of mind health and individualization in psychedelic therapy. For Hauskeller, the individual focus of psychedelic therapy masks societal elements of domination, alienation and distress. From this perspective, psychedelic medicalization may simply represent the latest means of ignoring or bypassing structural problems that lead people to seek (psychedelic) therapy in the first place.

Historian Hallam Roffey (2023) explores some of these ideas in practice, looking at the use of LSD within anarchist movements in Britain and Ireland in the 1970s, a union he refers to as "acid anarchism." As Roffey documents, many of the participants in free communes and similar forms of alternative social organization at that time believed psychedelics could be tools for social and cultural change. By 1970, there were dozens of free communes already established in Britain and "LSD was fundamental to a great number of these communal projects, shared houses, and squats" (Roffey 2023, 320). LSD helped to catalyze the commune movement because of its capacity to shape collective identities and infuse its participants with a "militant anti-materialism." A key figure in these movements was anarchist Bill Dwyer, an LSD advocate who ran the "Island Commune" in Dublin from 1970 to 1972. Dwyer saw LSD as an antidote to the cruelty that pervaded modern society and as one way to liberate the mind from "a world where almost everyone is subjected to authoritarianism and moralistic indoctrination from the very cradle" (Roffey 2023, 321). In a similar vein, other researchers have explored the historical connections between LSD-inspired anarchism and the activists associated with the anti-psychiatry and community mental health movements in Britain in the 1960s and 1970s (e.g., Gallagher 2023). For us, the importance of ideas like acid communism, psychedelic socialism and acid anarchism is in bringing back the political and collectivist dimensions of psychedelics and psychedelic culture as tools for social change.

It is in this context that the work of Psymposia, a non-profit media organization that provides critical perspectives on psychedelic culture, research and politics, is important today. The Psymposia collective has advanced a compelling critique of corporatized psychedelics and processes of medicalization, turning the political economy of psychedelia into popular journalistic and podcast content. Brian Pace and Neşe Devenot (2023), two members of the collective, rightly note that the corporatization and medicalization of psychedelics have at least two serious political effects. The first is to detach psychedelics from countercultural movements and groups. As psychedelics become captured by processes of corporatization and medicalization, the political potential of psychedelia is muted. The second is to constitute anyone using psychedelics (or other drugs) recreationally as problematic and blameworthy. Psymposia's advocacy of non-commodified psychedelia, critiques of medicalization, anti-capitalist stance and support for decriminalization puts them at odds with many advocates of psychedelic mainstreaming.

Lastly, it is important to emphasize the need to carve out space for the psychedelic humanities. Psychedelic humanities once again highlight a (potentially radical) political and collectivist approach to psychedelics. The psychedelic humanities are a safehouse for critical thinking in this area and facilitate cross-disciplinary research on the moral and cultural impacts of these substances (Dyck et al. 2024). Anthropologist Nicolas Langlitz (2023) argues that psychedelics raise cultural and political questions that are not and cannot be answered by medical science. Psychedelic humanities offer a field in which to expand the range of thinking about psychedelic history, ethics and politics at a time when corporatization and medicalization are narrowing the discourse. This narrowing of psychedelic discourse is concerning, as is the prevalence and persistence of right-wing and authoritarian interests in psychedelia today.

RIGHT-WING PSYCHEDELIA

In 2021, Brian Pace and Neşe Devenot published an article in *Frontiers in Psychology* that generated much discussion. They examined historical and contemporary case studies of individuals and movements that embraced psychedelics while also endorsing discriminatory and authoritarian worldviews. Pace and Devenot explained they did not take issue with right-wing people using or promoting psychedelics. Rather, their goal was to counter the false promises of a psychedelic utopia. According to Pace, the article represented "an intervention in a utopian discourse that was playing out with the aid of psychedelic researchers, with the aid of the media, and with the full cooperation of psychedelic advocates and others who stood to profit from psychedelic medicine being approved as quickly as possible" (Psymposia 2022). Devenot added that these utopian narratives are being promoted by "corporadelic" leaders to justify their tactics and ambitions. There is a bait and switch at work where psychedelic capitalists are promising to solve global problems by circulating psychedelics to the masses, when in reality their activities are exacerbating relations of social inequality that are the root cause of these problems in the first place. The fact that psychedelics are commonly perceived as an inherent good provides a useful PR cover for those who want to capitalize on the psychedelic renaissance.

Authoritarianism and the Far Right

Psychedelics can influence openness, empathy, connectedness to nature and participation in progressive movements. As part of these narratives, it is sometimes suggested that psychedelics can act as an antidote to authoritarianism, turning people into caring and open-minded individuals. But psychedelics are not used exclusively by or in support of these values and beliefs. For example, from the 1930s to the 1960s, conservative or reactionary individuals and movements, including aristocrats, the CIA and the Nazis, reported using psychedelics and advocated for psychedelic use (Pace and Devenot 2021). Another example is fascist philosopher Julius Evola, who was described in *The Guardian* as a "staunch LSD advocate" who was admired by "both Adolf Hitler and Steve Bannon" (Ellenhorn and Mugianis 2022a). In his book *Strange Drugs Make for Strange Bedfellows* (2015), psychedelic historian Alan Piper shows that LSD has long been embraced by extreme conservatives, such as author Ernst Jünger, an ardent militarist who denounced democracy and liberal values.

Pace and Devenot (2021) also put forward recent examples of far-right individuals, groups and movements with close ties to psychedelia (see also Love 2021c and Pace 2020). For example, The Base, an international neo-Nazi paramilitary group and training network, used LSD in a "neo-Pagan male-bonding ritual" that involved the beheading of animals (Pace and Devenot 2021, 5). When members of the group were later arrested on drug and weapons charges, they were allegedly attempting to manufacture DMT. The Japanese cult and terrorist organization Aum Shinrikyo, which released sarin (a nerve gas agent) in the Tokyo subway in 1995 killing fourteen people and injuring thousands, was also linked with LSD. Not only did its leaders use the drug in ritualistic practices, but it was administered to new recruits for the purposes of indoctrination. *Stormfront*, a long-running internet hate site imbued with antisemitism and white nationalism, includes extensive material on the scientific and therapeutic impacts of psychedelics.

The list does not end there. Andrew Anglin, founder of the neo-Nazi website *The Daily Stormer*, experimented extensively with both LSD and psilocybin. Gavin McInnis, former leader of the Proud Boys, advised his followers on how to navigate challenging psychedelic experiences. Frederick Brennen, founder of the now defunct "free speech" forum *8chan* (which became a haven for white nationalism) reports he was on mushrooms when he decided to create the platform. Even Jacob Chansley, also known as Jake Angeli, the well-known "QAnon shaman" who participated in the January 6, 2021 attacks on the US Capitol, used psychedelics as part of his exploration of esotericism. "Somehow all those psychedelics failed to turn him into a liberal," writes journalist and author Jules Evans (2021a; see also Pace 2021). According to Pace and Devenot, these examples show that "psychedelics have a place in the cutting edge of the radical right, both digitally and as literal boots on the ground." In addition to the intersections of psychedelics with right-wing activism, "right-wing conspiracy seems more than able to spring from native psychedelic soil" (2021, 5–6).

It has long been argued that psychedelics can enhance suggestibility, increasing the tendency to accept or act on the ideas and attitudes of others (Carhart-Harris et al. 2015; Dupuis and Veissière 2022). When combined with feelings of reverence and revelation, which can arise during psychedelic trips, this is a potentially potent recipe for conspiracy theorizing and cult-like practices. It is widely known that Charles Manson and his followers used psychedelics extensively, which Charles Grob describes as "a telling example of what could happen when these compounds are employed by an unscrupulous, unethical, immoral cult leader" (cited in Ross and Wright 2021). In the US today, there are fears over what might happen if evangelical leaders embraced psychedelics and used them to assert greater control over their tens of millions of followers. The potential of psychedelics to increase the acceptance of dubious truth claims or the machinations of charismatic leaders should not be dismissed.

Today's psychedelic renaissance has also attracted a number of far-right donors and investors. They include billionaire surveillance capitalism magnate and vocal Donald Trump and J.D. Vance supporter Peter Thiel, who is positioned to own a large piece of the psychedelic industry through his investments in Compass Pathways and other firms. Thiel is a staunch proponent of the national security state, having co-founded the surveillance and military intelligence company Palantir. Thiel has donated millions to US Republican senatorial candidates, expressed support for apartheid, decried women getting the vote and railed against the existence of social safety nets and democracy itself (Lythcott-Haims 2016; Plus Three 2020; Thiel 2009). "First Lady of the Alt-Right" Rebekah Mercer also funds research into psychedelic treatments for veterans. The Mercer family is infamous for their support of right-wing causes, from financially backing anti-abortion and climate change denial campaigns to ownership stakes in *Breitbart News* (Swenson 2018). More recently, the Mercers were accused of providing funding to numerous key players who helped incite the 2021 insurrection on Capitol Hill (Hausfeld 2022a).

Summarizing these relationships, Pace (2020) asserts that "the full spectrum of right-wing ideology, from outright Nazism to conservative-leaning centrism, is demonstrably hospitable to psychedelics — not uniquely endangered by them." While it is comforting that the far right has not "embraced psychedelics anywhere near the extent that other subcultures have," a mainstream rollout, he says, could change that overnight.

The CIA and US Military

In the early 1940s, the Office of Strategic Services (OSS), a precursor to the CIA, began testing drugs that had the potential to break down the psychological defences of enemy spies and prisoners of war. After World War Two, the US Navy became interested in mescaline as an interrogation agent after learning of the mind control experiments conducted by Nazi doctors at Dachau concentration camp. Former Nazi scientists involved in these studies were even brought to the US under the auspices of Project Paperclip, a program supervised by the CIA during the early stages of the cold war, to inform US drug experiments (Crim 2018; Jacobsen 2014). In their book *Acid Dreams* (1985, xxiv–xxv), Martin Lee and Bruce Shlain note that "nearly every drug that appeared on the black market during the 1960s — marijuana, cocaine, heroin, PCP, amyl nitrate, mushrooms, DMT, barbiturates, laughing gas, speed, and many others — had previously been scrutinized, tested, and in some cases refined by CIA and army scientists." However, none of these drugs received as much attention as LSD.

The CIA's interest in LSD goes back to at least the early 1950s and Harvard University. Harvard professors Dr. Max Rinkel and Dr. Robert Hyde were interested in "temporary psychotic disturbances" and how much LSD it would take to cause them (Lattin 2010). This was considered respectable research as it was anchored at the Boston Psychopathic Institute and coveted by organizations like the American Psychiatric Association. What Rinkel and Hyde omitted in disseminating their results was that they were funded by the CIA as part of the organization's interest in mind control. The CIA had discovered that Rinkel and Hyde had brought LSD to the US, approached them and later ended up funding their work (Lattin 2010). There was other LSD research at Harvard tied to the military-industrial complex. For example, Dr. Henry Beecher tested the drug on volunteers, including Harvard students, and was funded by the Army Research Council (Ohler 2024). While Harvard-affiliated researchers like Timothy Leary, Richard Alpert (Ram Dass), Huston Smith and Andrew Weil are key figures associated with the LSD counterculture of the 1960s, these links between Harvard and LSD are less well known.

Throughout the 1950s and 1960s, at the same time that the psychedelic counterculture was emerging, the CIA was undertaking multiple secret projects with LSD and other psychedelics. The goal was to discover truth serums and new mechanisms of interrogation and psychological torture. The MK-Ultra program (and its subprojects like Operation Midnight Climax) is now infamous and may represent the most scandalous brainwashing project in US history (Kinzer 2019). With the participation of dozens of colleges, universities, hospitals and pharmaceutical firms, it involved covertly testing LSD on unwitting Americans in cities like San Francisco and New York for over a decade. People from all walks of life were targeted to develop a comprehensive picture of the drug's effects.

The undercover program also included volunteers who were unaware of its seedy underbelly, such as poet Allen Ginsberg, Grateful Dead songwriter Robert Hunter and author Ken Kesey. Ironically, the CIA may have inadvertently helped to catalyze the psychedelic counterculture as all of them became LSD advocates. Kesey and his band of Merry Pranksters proceeded to introduce LSD to thousands of young people with their "acid tests" in the Bay Area and elsewhere (Wolfe 1968).

Author Norman Ohler (2024) is so convinced that the explosion of LSD in the underground was an unintended by-product of CIA experimentation that he characterizes the 1960s counterculture as the "revolt of the guinea pigs." This phrasing is also how Kesey sometimes described his adventures with the Merry Pranksters.

As part of the MK-Ultra program, CIA operatives were also regularly testing LSD on themselves and each other, slipping it into the drinks of unsuspecting colleagues. One victim of these experiments, army scientist Frank Olson, was apparently so troubled by the experience that he committed suicide by jumping out of a hotel window. True to the impacts of set and setting, these CIA self-experimenters were not moved to "trade in their blow darts, shell-fish toxin, and extreme prejudices for flowers, love beads and peace signs" (Lee and Shlain 1985, 148).

Like the Nazis, the CIA conducted drug experiments on vulnerable groups of people, such as ethnic minorities, prisoners and patients in mental health facilities. The Addiction Research Center (ARC), located inside the Federal Medical Center in Lexington Kentucky (known as the Narcotics Farm), was one site where researchers tested psychedelics on prisoners (Campbell, Olsen and Walden 2021). After discovering that people developed a tolerance to LSD after just a few days, researchers decided to test if large doses could break through tolerance or if tolerance dissipated after repeated dosing. Some prisoners in the US penal system were given LSD daily for months. Black prisoners received the worst of it, enduring elevated doses and chronic administration for up to eighty-five days. One "mental patient" at ARC was reportedly dosed with LSD continuously for 174 days (Holloway 2022). This repeated inundation was likely intended to see if LSD might be useful in military and security intelligence in the context of securing confessions. Just like Rinkel and Hyde at Harvard, the ARC research was both linked to and funded by the CIA, which was revealed in US Congressional investigations in the 1970s. Most of the prisoners were people of colour and most of the researchers were white men, raising questions about power and race that continue to resonate in psychedelic research today. These revelations led to the now generally accepted position that prison research is inherently coercive, effectively leading to a ban on biomedical research in prisons.

The CIA was primarily interested in LSD as a tool of clandestine warfare. It was employed as an aid to interrogation on an operational basis from the mid-1950s to the early 1960s. The US Army, on the other hand, was initially interested in psychedelics in the context of seeking out chemical weapons that had the potential to revolutionize combat. To this end, the US Chemical Corps received a large budget increase in the 1950s to develop "nonlethal incapacitants" that could subdue the enemy without causing permanent injury. As part of this research, the army tested LSD on their own soldiers during operational exercises and war game scenarios. By the mid-1960s, "nearly fifteen hundred military personnel had served as guinea pigs in LSD experiments" conducted by the US Chemical Corps (Lee and Shlain 1985, 40). Like the CIA years earlier, the military also began using LSD as an interrogation weapon. However, just as the CIA eventually realized that LSD was not a reliable truth serum or brainwashing drug, the US military was never able to effectively use LSD as a large-scale weapon on the battlefield. LSD was eventually abandoned by the military in favour of a much more potent "super-hallucinogen," known as BZ. BZ rendered those exposed to it with powerful hallucinations, agitation and delirium that could last up to three days. BZ gas was weaponized and used by US troops during the Vietnam War (Lee and Shlain 1985). This sordid history, which remains largely unknown, provides a backdrop for contextualizing some of the recent developments in today's psychedelic renaissance.

US Republicans and the Military-Industrial Complex

One of the obvious examples of right-wing psychedelia in recent years involves US Republican lawmakers, a group widely known for its anti-drug rhetoric and policies. It is also a group that recently provided $2 trillion in tax giveaways to the wealthy while pushing for huge cuts to education, housing, childcare and food aid for the poor. Congressman Matt Gaetz of Florida, former Navy SEAL Dan Crenshaw and Governor Greg Abbott of Texas are but a few examples of prominent Republicans who support psychedelic research and therapy. As well, former Texas governor and presidential candidate Rick Perry, who is known for his radical cuts to environmental regulations, hostility to renewable energy, expansion of gun rights, restrictions on abortion and staunch opposition to LGBTQ rights has been one of the country's most high-profile psychedelic cheerleaders (Hooks 2022). In a bizarre interview at the 2023 Psychedelic Science conference in Denver, Perry described the therapeutic potential of psychedelics as "stunningly positive," while somehow linking the criminalization of psychedelics with the failures of socialized medicine (Gillespie 2023). Though he has never used psychedelics himself, Perry said he is open to trying ibogaine because it has anti-aging properties that can "literally turn back the clock." He also claims that psychedelic therapy enjoys higher support among Republicans than among Democrats because the GOP understands its potential for treating military personnel and veterans.

This last assertion by Perry goes a long way in explaining Republican support for psychedelics, as well as the boosterism of conservative news outlets like *Breitbart* and *Fox News*. According to *The New York Times*, Perry's conversion from "antidrug stalwart to a champion of psychedelic therapies" was inspired by his relationship with combat veterans suffering from PTSD, while Dan Crenshaw, who had consistently opposed drug policy reform in Congress, also changed his position after hearing from fellow veterans (Jacobs 2023). Even the US Department of Defense is getting on board, funding research into psychedelics for veterans through the Defense Advanced Research Projects Agency. The 2024 *National Defense Authorization Act* requires that the Department of Defense establish a process under which military service members with PTSD or traumatic brain injuries can participate in clinical trials involving psilocybin, MDMA, 5-MeO-DMT, ibogaine and other "qualified plant-based alternative therapies," thanks in part to lobbying efforts by Republican members of Congress.

The finding that military veterans suffering from PTSD, addiction and other afflictions may be helped by psychedelics is significant. Conventional interventions are not working for these populations and new forms of treatment are needed (Hooyer, Applbaum and Kasza 2023). That said, the growing relationship between psychedelia and the military-industrial complex is problematic. For one, MAPS and its founder Rick Doblin have made the controversial decision to prioritize veterans and the military in their research, fundraising and advocacy, largely as a political strategy to gain bipartisan support. Doblin has explained his rationale by claiming that "it's a sympathetic patient population." In Doblin's view, the legacy of the 1960s counterculture continues to translate into resistance to psychedelics within the political establishment: "We wouldn't necessarily get over that with cancer patients," he says, "but veterans in particular would help build support" (cited in Siebert 2022, 138). While some may see this as simply tactical maneuvering, it has meant that MAPS has deprioritized other vulnerable populations and helped to promote the idea that the traumas associated with military duty and policing should take precedence over the traumas associated with poverty, police violence, mass incarceration and the war on drugs.

Some of the political figures involved in MAPS' outreach efforts have also raised alarm bells. Retired US Army sergeant Jonathan Lubecky was hired as MAPS' first veterans and governmental affairs liaison. Lubecky has described himself as the organization's "conservative whisperer" with his primary role being to promote the benefits of MDMA within his networks (Hausfeld 2022a). To this end, he lobbied and held meetings with a cadre of questionable figures including Mike Pence, Steve Bannon, Rudy Giuliani, Alex Jones and Donald Trump. Trump is a supporter of psychedelic therapy and even intervened to promote ketamine therapy for military veterans at the request of Rebekah Mercer (Evans 2021a; see also Cary 2019). Trump has also been labeled "the most psychedelic president since JFK" by the Castalia Foundation, a psychedelic organization that dabbles in alt-right conspiracy theories. Although Trump has endorsed draconian drug policies in the past, he has also shown a tendency to embrace psychedelic exceptionalism. Moreover, some of the key figures that will help guide his new administration are psychedelic enthusiasts, including Elon Musk and Robert F. Kennedy Jr., who has criticized the FDA for its "aggressive suppression" of psychedelics.

The Psymposia collective has consistently called out MAPS for its links to right-wing psychedelia. They note that MAPS was publicly and financially supported for decades not by the Pentagon but by a subculture with radically different values. Other psychedelic organizations and start-ups are following MAPS' lead and prioritizing the treatment of military personnel in their pilot projects, advertising and outreach. Even more controversial is that MAPS has promoted the use of MDMA for active-duty soldiers (Hausfeld 2022c; Miller 2013). This application has the potential to turn what some refer to as the "love drug" into a weapon for the military machine, as MDMA has a demonstrated capacity to dampen the biochemical fear response, which could be employed as an asset in military campaigns. In 2024, Doblin went a step further, calling for military recruits to be dosed upon enlistment. He suggested this would help create more efficient soldiers by making them "less reactive" and "more able to handle whatever circumstances come their way" (cited in Hausfeld 2024a). Doblin's position on this matter is eerily similar to that of Timothy Leary, who, when asked about the uses of LSD for young people entering military service by Senator Ted Kennedy in the 1960s, replied: "I should think that in the Army of the future ... LSD will be used to expand consciousness so that these men can do their duties more effectively" (Lee and Shlain 1985, 152). Others suggest that the unsanctioned use of LSD is already common practice among active-duty Marines (Hausfeld 2022b).

Another proposed application of MDMA is treating "moral injury" in soldiers. According to the *MAPS Bulletin*, moral injury can result from complicity in activities that one may find morally objectionable, such as "[storming] into people's homes at night [and] taking fathers away from crying families to military prisons" and participating in "the death of civilians, women, and children" (Lehrner and Yehuda 2021, 15). In some cases, moral injury appears to be a euphemism for participation in war crimes (Hausfeld 2022c). Former Psymposia member David Nickles rejects the idea of providing psychedelic therapy to active-duty soldiers not because he believes the drugs are dangerous to the troops, but because the troops are dangerous to the world. Rather than distributing psychedelics to soldiers who have been tasked with immoral activities, he suggests we should work toward eliminating the causes of trauma, moral injury and military atrocities. "I think it would be preferable to dismantle the drone program," he says, "[rather] than to give drone operators MDMA to cope with the grisly consequences of the choices they make" (cited in Hausfeld 2023a). The fact that psychedelics have the potential to help struggling soldiers and veterans deal with their trauma is important, but so too are concerns that psychedelics will play a role in supporting US militarism.

Similar issues arise when MAPS and other organizations focus on using psychedelic-assisted therapy with police (Nickles 2020b). Police have become interested in psychedelics in recent years to cope with trauma and work-related stress. Pointing to low morale and high attrition rates, some police have expressed an interest in psychedelic assistance (Busby 2024a). One group of officers is calling on the United Nations to lead a campaign to make MDMA-assisted therapy available to their comrades around the world (Busby 2024b). Police have also been incorporated into research on using psychedelics for the treatment of PTSD (Mithoefer et al. 2018; Stevenson 2023).

There is, however, a dark irony in providing psychedelics to those at the frontlines of enforcing the carceral state and the war on drugs. For decades, public police have been working alongside prohibitionists and subjecting drug users to criminalization and violence. While psychedelics may lessen the trauma police experience in exercising their duties, it needs to be acknowledged that these duties continue to include the harassment, arrest and imprisonment of people in possession of or distributing psychedelics and other drugs. In fact, police seizures of some psychedelics, like psilocybin, have sharply increased in recent years (Palamar et al. 2024). At the global level, there has also been an upsurge in arrests for people transporting psychedelics such as ayahuasca, iboga and peyote (Busby 2022). As journalist and Psymposia member Russell Hausfeld (2022a) notes, the starring role played by groups like the police, the military, veterans and right-wing politicians in the current psychedelic renaissance "represents the closing of a long, strange circle: the people and institutions most responsible for enforcing the criminalization of psychedelics are now lauded and prized as ideal treatment demographics."

Transhumanism and the Hallucinogenic Elite

In a 2022 interview on *The Tim Ferriss Show*, drug researcher Hamilton Morris described the history of psychedelics as "profoundly elitist" and Timothy Leary as someone who was more democratically oriented who wanted to break with that tradition of elitism. According to Morris, Leary encouraged widespread psychedelic use because he had faith in the "intelligence of the broader community" and the capacity of the general population to make its own decisions (cited in Ferriss 2022b). While it is true that Leary was something of a psychedelic populist who wanted to turn on the masses to these substances, his legacy is more complicated. Journalist Jules Evans (2023b) positions Leary within the tradition of "evolutionary spirituality," one of the dominant cultural frames for psychedelics over the past century, whose followers believe they are superior to the masses and represent the next step in human evolution. He argues that theories of evolutionary spirituality became popular within the 1960s counterculture thanks to figures like Leary, who suggested that he and his psychedelic inner circle in California were part of an enlightened "genetic elite," while the rest of the world was lower on the evolutionary scale (2023b, 5).

A variant of evolutionary spirituality known as transhumanism is popular in psychedelic circles today and has been for a long time. Transhumanism promotes the enhancement of the human condition through sophisticated technologies that can boost cognition and longevity. Evans describes transhumanism as "effectively a religion for the extremely rich of Silicon Valley" who embrace humanity's capacity to evolve into "superbeings" through the use of artificial intelligence (AI), genetic modification, virtual reality and psychedelics (2023b, 11). Modern transhumanist discourse, according to media theorist Maxim Tvorun-Dunn (2022), is platformed through the think tank Singularity University, co-founded by Ray Kurzweil and prominent psychedelic investor Peter Thiel. The think tank promotes numerous transhumanist endeavors including AI, space travel, biohacking and psychedelia. Just as Timothy Leary's transhumanist vision included an interest in longevity, or humans evolving past their current biological capabilities, many of today's longevity advocates and entrepreneurs view psychedelics as an important part of this transhuman project (Love 2023b).

While employees of Silicon Valley often regard themselves as politically liberal and driven by social justice, the elites who run these industries are more inclined toward a form of transhumanism that is essentialist and undemocratic, often with a healthy dose of narcissism and class privilege. Within this frame, psychedelics are simply another transhumanist tool in support of the vision put forward by enlightened leaders who will use them to advance humanity as they see fit, with little regulatory oversight and no input from the unenlightened masses. As Michael Pollan (2018, 193) points out, "it is one of the many paradoxes of psychedelics that these drugs can sponsor an ego-dissolving experience that in some people quickly leads to massive ego inflation." While Pollan was referencing Timothy Leary, his observation holds for other leaders whose grandiosity appears to be amplified when consuming psychedelics within the frame of transhumanism.

For example, Christian Angermayer, founder of Atai Life Sciences, has spoken at length about his own psychedelic experiences. In recent interviews, Angermayer suggests that "maybe we are *meant* to play God … Maybe we are there to escape the evolutionary velocity, to be gods in our own way." But Angermayer is not talking about everyone. He believes there could be a bifurcation of humanity into two species: the "gods" or evolved superbeings who are willing to "fly to Mars" and biohack their bodies to do so, and the left-behind masses who, for whatever reason, "don't want to merge with machines" (cited in Evans 2023b, 4, 7). Peter Thiel also expresses enthusiasm for space travel and "space manufacturing," but unlike Angermayer he seems content to remain on Earth, ideally in a start-up community that floats on the ocean where he and his fellow "seasteaders" can live unhampered by government regulation (Rushkoff 2023). While Thiel does not hide his contempt for democracy and the masses, Angermayer's elitism includes some concern for those who might have difficulty adjusting to his vision of the transhumanist project. For example, he has stated that robots and AI will render most human workers obsolete over the next decade. To help address this situation, he envisions governments using the "neuroplasticity" of psychedelics to retrain discarded workers into new skills (Wheal 2023). In other words, he sees psychedelics as tools for placating the masses and medicating popular resistance to the inevitable tech-utopian future. According to Neşe Devenot (2023), Angermayer is advocating for a use of psychedelics that approximates the role of "soma" in Aldous Huxley's dystopian novel *Brave New World* (1932), a drug that discourages rebellion and increases complacency on the part of the lower classes.

The transhumanists of Silicon Valley have invested significant capital into the research and commercialization of psychedelics. These substances now form a central part of tech industry culture and identity. Their vision of psychedelia includes a heroic, evolutionary project cemented in a commercialized landscape — one that is both rooted in monopolization and dependent upon growing inequality. It is also one in which the pro-social effects of psychedelics are scooped into a neoliberal system where democracy is subordinated to the machinations of this elite group. Within these circles, the practices of microdosing and psychedelic-assisted therapy have already been recast as tools for capitalist productivity and are being marketed as a way for the general population to extract more work out of their already overworked lives (and to be happy about it in the process).

There are also growing concerns over what scholar Tehseen Noorani (2021a) calls "digital psychedelia" — the expanding infrastructure of digital platforms capitalizing on the revival of medicalized psychedelics and psychedelic-assisted therapy. Its manifestations include predictive analytics, brain-computer interfaces that could replace human therapists, the production of user datasets for commercial use, as well as an assortment of wearable devices and digital apps designed to harvest data, monitor behaviour, record user feedback and provide integration counseling. Considering Big Tech's sordid history with privacy and personal data, it is no stretch to imagine this expanding ensemble of data-gathering technologies and infrastructural platforms being used in nefarious ways. This could include normalizing heightened levels of mass surveillance (Thiel might be interested given his work with Palantir) and the monetization of biomedical data that is not subject to medical privacy laws.

In a similar vein, David Nickles raises the possibility that the marriage of "corporadelia" and information technologies could lead to psychedelic surveillance capitalism (see Pace and Devenot 2023). Surveillance capitalism relies on "smart" and wearable technologies to monitor our desires and bodily functions and creates advertising that responds to changes in our behaviour. Smart fridges, for example, will now send you a prompt when your stock of certain products is getting low. Our daily activities produce data, and these data are harvested by data brokers and surveillance capitalists who then try to sell us more stuff. Such a link is possible with psychedelics too. Nickles points to scenarios in which wearable technology could function as a kind of psychedelic pusher, "knowing" you are depressed before you do. He notes that the social and bioethical implications of digital psychedelia surveillance technologies are significant and underappreciated. Digital monitoring of psychedelic users is one way that today's venture capitalists could get a return on their investments. The psychedelics firm Compass Pathways, for example, advertised an AI data analytics system called "Chanterelle" in a recent pitch to investors. In 2024, Canadian psychedelics company Numinus Wellness advanced into the AI space with its acquisition of MedBright AI, which will be used to leverage and expand its psychedelic-assisted therapy program. As these corporations continue to build the infrastructure for a global psychedelics surveillance industry, they could play a direct role in shaping how users come to understand the nature of their psychedelic experiences. Some company apps already invite users to record their psychedelic experiences in digital "journals," ostensibly for their own good.

For all of these reasons, the integration of modern psychedelia with Big Tech, Silicon Valley elites and their transhuman cosmology of consciousness expansion should be of concern to those who care about the future of the psychedelic renaissance. These relationships also provide further evidence that psychedelics do not have a consistent link with political ideologies and beliefs. As Tvorun-Dunn (2022, 1–2) writes:

> Considering that Silicon Valley has directly contributed to the crystallization of neoliberalism, significant pollution of the environment, disempowerment of labor unions and workers' rights, and development of the surveillance state, the continued prominence of psychedelic drug use by tech executives seems directly incongruous with the pro-social, progressive forming, and environmental attributes which advocates claim psychedelics provide.

PSYCHEDELICS AND SOCIAL CHANGE

Highly dependent on set and setting, the properties of the psychedelic experience are more variable than many would like to believe. Ido Hartogsohn (2013), who has done extensive work on the relationship between set and setting and psychedelic experiences, notes that throughout the 1950s and 1960s, the variety of uses for LSD was wide-ranging. They included use as a "revolutionary molecule" by the counterculture as well as applications as a psychotherapeutic tool, a creativity enhancer, a spiritual sacrament, a mind-control tool by the CIA and a battlefield weapon by the US Chemical Corps. For each of these groups, "LSD represented something different. Each of them created a set and a setting which was distinctly different and which reproduced the effects of the drug in a novel form" (2013, 8). Some researchers have argued that the neoliberal set and setting of advanced capitalism limits the ability of psychedelic users to even imagine the kinds of "collectivist social worlds" that were common in the 1960s (Riley, Thompson and Griffin 2010).

It is important to recognize that even those facets of the psychedelic experience commonly associated with left-wing values and perspectives (openness, interconnection, nature relatedness) can sometimes be expressed alongside competing political or ideological beliefs. While psychedelics may be more likely to enhance a form of openness associated with tolerance and progressive values, under certain circumstances they can facilitate a greater openness to right-wing conspiracy theories. Nature-relatedness has also played an important role in reactionary movements throughout history, such as eco-naturalism and eco-fascism. The same can be said about ego dissolution. Although commonly linked to openness, nature relatedness and the benefits of psychedelic-assisted therapy, the ego-dissolving properties of psychedelics were one of the factors that attracted the CIA and US military to experiment with LSD as a mind-control weapon (Gearin and Devenot 2021). If psychedelics do not have an inherent or directional political basis, then whatever capacities or potentials they may have for social change are very much up for grabs. And if right-wing and corporadelic actors can control the cultural scripts surrounding psychedelic use and deployment, they could become a further lever to entrench their political and economic agendas.

At the same time, the transformative potential of psychedelics and their historical connections to emancipatory movements should not be dismissed. Psychedelics can stimulate meaningful and even radical shifts in individuals. Their boundary-dissolving nature can, for example, serve to counter the barrage of corporate advertising messages informing people that they are deficient and inadequate and that the solution to these voids can be found in consumerism. Under the right circumstances, the insights generated by psychedelics can lead individuals away from alienation, materialism, competitiveness and external validation and toward a more collective and community-oriented set of values, augmented by a heightened sense of intrinsic self-worth (Tempone-Wiltshire and Matthews 2023). Here it is sometimes said that psychedelics are useful for the hallucinations they remove, not the ones they provide. Anecdotal and clinical evidence suggests that psychedelics may be well-suited to help people cope with trauma, including collective traumas arising from systems of colonialism, imperialism, racism and the ongoing destruction of the natural world (e.g., Williams et al. 2021).

Perhaps most importantly, psychedelics can motivate people to challenge these systems directly. David Nickles (2014) refers to this process as "radical psychedelic engagement," or using insights garnered from psychedelic experiences to directly target the root causes of social injustice. He is quick to note, however, that consuming the drugs is not enough. Psychedelics are catalysts, he says, "they can open the door but you must walk through." It may appear as though radical psychedelic engagement is in short supply these days. Timothy Leary's famous plea of "turn on, tune in, drop out" does not resonate the way it used to, and psychedelic movements seem less attuned to social justice than they were in the past. But as writer Bett Williams (2020) reminds us, the underground psychedelic counterculture is still very much alive:

> It's an arena where ayahuasca devotees fight to protect the rainforest and indigenous land rights. Entheogenic herbalists teach the art of rewilding, planting seeds in stricken soils, and helping communities restore traditional farming practices. Radical mycologists tend to fatigued little spots of urban dirt, poisoned by oil and chemical waste, by dropping mushroom spores that grow into mycelium, purifying the soil enough to grow things again. Plant and fungi medicine communities forge alliances with social justice movements, building community gardens and mushroom farms. They support land rights movements that gained momentum at Standing Rock. Native American activists and allies work towards the protection of the endangered peyote cactus. Organizations like The POC Psychedelic Collective fight for safe access to psychedelics in marginalized communities and advocate for radical Drug Policy Reform. Rigorous conversations about decolonization and dismantling structures based on white supremacy are happening in every psychedelic space that matters.

Nevertheless, placing the onus on tripping individuals to enact change will never address the root causes of systemic injustice, something that can only be achieved by sustained, collective action directed against the power systems that govern the planet and its resources. Environmental consultant Rachael Petersen (2020) exposes this flawed line of thinking in relation to the climate crisis. She argues that a mystical experience is no substitute for the education and dedicated work required to mobilize around such a complex issue. One does not emerge from a psychedelic trip knowing right from wrong, Petersen writes, "let alone if a carbon tax is preferable to a cap-and-trade system." Similar problems arise when psychedelic researchers announce they are bringing Israelis and Palestinians together to sort through their respective traumas and facilitate political reconciliation through ayahuasca ceremonies (Roseman and Karkabi 2021; Roseman et al. 2021). Psychedelic-induced empathy or love-ins are no substitute for the difficult work of actively opposing the crimes of the Israeli state and its flagrant violations of international law (International Court of Justice 2024). It is within this context that MAPS made the controversial decision to hold its 2024 Psychedelic Science conference in Tel Aviv. According to Rick Doblin, "a conference about healing trauma in the middle of a hurricane of trauma is a good thing," neglecting to mention that some key backers of the conference had received Israeli government funding (cited in Busby 2024c). Not everyone agreed. Dr. Monnica Williams, a clinical psychologist at the University of Ottawa who was part of the conference organizing committee, decided to boycott the event, stating: "I could not feel good about mingling with colleagues over drinks at a 4-star hotel while less than an hour away, children are having bombs rained on them." For critical issues such as climate change, state violence and many others, the suggestion that psychedelics can usher in a progressive utopia is a dangerous distraction.

06

PSYCHEDELIC MEDICALIZATION

PSYCHEDELICS ENJOYED A RICH TRADITION of therapeutic and medicinal use in Indigenous cultures long before they were embraced by Western researchers. Some traditional healers refer to psychedelics as plant medicines to denote their spiritual and therapeutic benefits. Psilocybin mushrooms, for example, played a role in Aztec healing ceremonies (Nichols 2020; Schultes 1940), while Indigenous peoples in the Amazon have used ayahuasca for centuries to enhance mental and physical health (Schultes 1968). Iboga has long been treated as a sacred medicine by practitioners of the Bwiti religion in West Africa, and Zulu and Xhosa communities in Southern Africa have incorporated a range of psychedelic plants into their healing practices (Sobiecki 2002). Indigenous peoples of Mexico and members of the Native American Church in North America have and continue to use peyote in complex and holistic healing interventions, including for problematic substance use, trauma and physical health ailments (Jones 2007). The thousands of medicinal plant preparations known to Indigenous peoples all over the world is indicative of complex botanical and pharmacological knowledge systems that stretch back centuries.

Western psychedelic medicine and traditional entheogenic healing practices are not absolute or distinct categories and there can be overlap between the two. On the one hand, we see the administration of synthetic or extract-derived compounds to an individual patient in a clinical setting delivered by a clinician whose work is based in classical psychotherapy and/or contemporary neuroscience. On the other is the use of plants or fungi delivered to a group of participants in a ceremonial space by a *curandero* or shaman whose work is rooted in a lineage of traditional knowledge and beliefs. In contrast to biomedical approaches, traditional practices often involve the participation of entire communities to enhance therapeutic benefits and stand in stark contrast to the individualistic framework that dominates psychedelic medicine in the West (Ona, Berrada and Bouso 2022).

Psychedelic medicine owes a debt to Indigenous communities who acted as stewards of these ancient therapeutics, providing some of the historical knowledge upon which the current psychedelic renaissance is based. As a result, the psychedelic renaissance — and the resurgence of psychedelic research within it — has led to concerns about the appropriation and commodification of Indigenous knowledge. While some claim that certain psychedelics being used in therapeutic settings (such as LSD, MDMA or synthetic mescaline) have little to do with Indigenous history or culture, it was often through the observation and study of traditional ceremonies, rituals and shamanistic practices that scientists were introduced to the complex healing properties of psychedelics.

Psychedelic medicalization could occur in different ways, ranging from patient-driven, horizontal and participatory approaches to top-down, profit-driven enterprises constrained by medical gatekeepers. It is the latter approach that dominates today's psychedelic renaissance. This shift translates into medical authorities and pharmaceutical companies controlling decision making around the use of psychedelics in healthcare and their lobby groups pushing for profit-oriented health policies, particularly in the US where private healthcare is commonplace.

KNOWLEDGE CLAIMS AND THE MEDICAL MODEL

Medicalization refers to defining and treating human conditions and problems as medical conditions requiring intervention. The concept has also been used to denote a medical function creep, where an increasing number of physical, mental and developmental conditions become matters for medical experts. The medical descriptions of mental illness, for example, have expanded over the years to encompass more and more domains of adverse human experiences, reframing forms of socially determined distress as in need of psychiatric and psychotropic intervention. Medicalization also has important political and economic implications. Sociologists Peter Conrad and Joseph Schneider (1992, 275) argue that "medicalization increases directly with its economic profitability." In other words, the more something is medicalized, the more the industry cropping up around it expands, creating new and lucrative markets for pharmaceutical companies, specialized groups of physicians and insurance firms. And the more the market and industry expand, the more social issues and forms of social deviance will be subjected to that form of medicalization. We can see this process unfolding in psychedelia today.

The medicalization of psychedelics began in the middle of the twentieth century but slowed in subsequent decades because of prohibition and the tightening of controls over psychiatric research. Today, psychedelics represent a unique case of medicalization for several reasons. For one, these substances are being tested and promoted for a wide range of problems and conditions: from depression, anxiety, bipolar disorder, addiction, eating disorders and PTSD to chronic pain, traumatic brain injury, autism and Alzheimer's disease. Moreover, underground users, researchers and practitioners have informed this medicalization process. During prohibition, these networks of outlaws developed inventories of data and information about psychedelic compounds and experimented with different forms of therapy outside of Western biomedical frameworks. Some of the first medical studies of psilocybin, for example, were initiated because of observations about how underground communities were using it to self-medicate against a variety of conditions, such as depression, anxiety and headaches (Kempner 2024). This continuum — from traditional Indigenous healing practices to underground research and therapeutic practices to today's "above-ground" clinical research — is a unique trajectory in the history of medicalization. According to Professor Johan Söderberg (2022), the medicalization of psychedelics represents a case of "outlaw user innovation," where the knowledge and information collected over decades by a stigmatized psychedelic underground is now being incorporated into medical research, transferred to companies and put under the protection of patent law.

Medicalization is at the forefront of increasing legal access to psychedelics in Canada, the US and elsewhere. Touted as a strategic response to criminalization, legalized medical use is widely viewed as a viable model to destigmatize psychedelics and increase their cultural legitimacy. Most proponents of medicalization see leveraging trust in the medical model as a critical component of psychedelic mainstreaming. In an interview with *The New York Times*, Roland Griffiths argues that (re)synchronizing psychedelics with medical authority will help ensure a smooth rollout. "We need to proceed cautiously," he says, "It's going to be critically important not to threaten existing cultural institutions" (cited in Marchese 2023). Psychiatrist Ben Sessa also believes there is no alternative to working with medical authorities and governments to get these substances approved. Without that cover, he argues they will "remain illegal forever" and "languish in Peruvian jungles," accessible only to "rich trustafarians who can afford to fly out there and enjoy them" (Austin and Sessa 2020). Even many who are critical of the medical model grudgingly accept that in the absence of rational drug policy, the process of taking psychedelics through the medical system is the most strategic option to increasing their legitimacy and availability.

Under such a model, some patients with diagnosed conditions would have legal access to psychedelic therapy. Regulating psychedelics through the medical system could also have benefits, such as reliability of service, consistency of product quality, increased accountability in the case of malpractice and, in select cases, greater affordability. Ibogaine clinics, for example, which are legally operating in many countries primarily to treat addiction, tend to be expensive and out of reach for most people. Ibogaine can also be dangerous, and although many underground practitioners are offering these treatments with harm reduction in mind, medically supervised therapy could potentially save lives (May 2017b).

On the other hand, there are many problems associated with the medical model and the knowledge claims that surround it. Why are psychiatrists, pharmaceutical companies and the medical establishment best suited to bring psychedelics into the mainstream, and why are their knowledge claims privileged over others? As noted above, the clinical promise of psychedelics owes a debt to Indigenous healing practices as well as underground researchers, therapists and guides. Today's medical research is largely confirming what has been well-documented and tested in these communities. Millions of people have consumed psychedelics for therapeutic and other purposes for centuries, with only a tiny fraction having done so under the supervision of a psychiatrist or clinician. This collective human knowledge and experience arguably does and should trump what is coming through the clinical realm.

Similar issues arise when considering knowledge claims around safety. For example, some proponents of medicalization suggest that it is impossible to know whether psychedelics like psilocybin are safe until they have gone through the clinical trial process (Rucker and Young 2021). If they were talking about new chemical entities, this might be true, but psilocybin is a molecule with a well-established track record as a therapeutic tool. Moreover, at least from a pharmacological perspective, psilocybin is one of the safest recreational drugs in the world. There is no reason that Western medicine should sit at the top of a hierarchy of knowledge around defining safety or granting access to psilocybin, or that it should be allowed to function as a gatekeeper of therapeutic approaches. Such claims rely upon an appeal to medical authority — an authority whose track record, at least in the area of mental health, is troublesome. One of the main reasons people are looking for new mental health treatments is that the pharmaceutical industry and medical establishment have failed to adequately treat these conditions. There is also little evidence that psychiatric professionals are better qualified than experienced underground therapists to offer these kinds of treatments. However, under a medical model, it is likely that psychedelic therapists and guides will be pushed out of the field and replaced by credentialed professionals, many of whom have little training in or personal experience with psychedelics.

In addition to these challenges, medicalization in the absence of decriminalization presents a number of problematic scenarios. Confining psychedelic use to a medicalized framework feeds into the prohibitionist narrative that these substances are unsuitable for use outside of a medical setting, where their healing and other potential somehow disappears. This negates (and criminalizes) what psychedelic users have long said about the benefits of taking psychedelics in a safe and supportive environment with people they trust. Psychedelic medicalization threatens to subsume the variety of psychedelic experiences under one dominant epistemology. It also lends support to false dichotomies regarding what qualifies as a "medicine" and what qualifies as a "drug." These contradictions are reflected in systems of bifurcated scheduling, where a drug product is placed in a schedule different from the active ingredient or substance. For example, if the FDA were to approve psilocybin for depression or MDMA for PTSD, what would be rescheduled? If history is any indication, only FDA-approved medicinal psilocybin and MDMA products would be rescheduled, while the substances themselves would remain Schedule 1 drugs and continue to be prosecuted as restricted narcotics. In this way, "the division between the good psychedelic user and the bad psychedelic abuser can be justified as cautiously 'sticking to the science'" (Noorani 2020b, 37).

Medicalization in the absence of decriminalization may also have public health implications. A growing body of non-clinical evidence suggests that the use of classical psychedelics by so-called "healthy normals" (individuals with no diagnosed medical condition) is associated with a range of positive impacts on mental health and well-being, including increased connectedness, greater meaning and purpose in life, as well as improvements in depression, anxiety and problematic substance use (e.g., Bathje et al. 2024; Elsey 2017; Garcia-Romeu et al. 2020; Glynos et al. 2024; Gonzalez et al. 2021; Mans et al. 2021; McCulloch et al. 2022; Raison et al. 2022; Ruffell et al. 2021; van Oorsouw et al. 2021; Wiepking, de Bruin and Ghiță 2023). Likewise, psychedelic researcher Otto Simonsson has co-authored several studies that point to linkages between lifetime psychedelic use and positive markers of physical health (Simonsson et al. 2021a, 2021b; Simonsson, Sexton and Hendricks 2021). Some studies also suggest that psychedelic use may contribute to healthy lifestyle choices and behaviours, including improved diet, increased physical activity and lower consumption of tobacco and alcohol (Garcia-Romeu et al. 2019, 2020; Kohek et al. 2023; Ona et al. 2019; Simonsson et al. 2022; Teixeira et al. 2022). This literature is largely correlational and there are plenty of policy measures that can and should be prioritized before psychedelics to address population health. Nevertheless, these findings point to the potential of preventative public health benefits.

Clinical psychologist Samuli Kangaslampi (2023) found that people tend to report more positive changes in mental health and well-being when they also report having had a psychedelic-induced mystical-type experience (compared with people who do not report such an experience). Moreover, he found "more, and more unequivocal, evidence for this among healthy people than in clinical populations" (2023, 25). Under a medical model, however, there is no provision for the use of psychedelics among healthy individuals. This myopic focus on treating individuals considered to be sick, disturbed or pathological occupies a central place in the history of Western medicine. In the case of psychedelics, this could arguably be detrimental to public health.

There is also no reason to accept Ben Sessa's claim that psychedelics will "remain illegal forever" unless they are medicalized. While medicalization efforts may help to motivate decriminalization initiatives, it is not the goal of these efforts. Jag Davies is the former director of communications strategy at the Drug Policy Alliance and former director of communications at MAPS. He claims that psychedelic researchers and clinicians have a responsibility to support decriminalization. Not only is it unethical to ignore the people who are being harmed by prohibition, but a politically focused movement targeting the harms of criminalization would ultimately benefit psychedelic research moving forward (Austin and Davies 2017). Social scientist Claudia Schwarz-Plaschg (2020) found that many psychedelic researchers are concerned that decriminalization would lead to increased use and a rise in adverse events, which could create a political backlash against the science. For Schwarz-Plaschg, however, it is unclear what, if any, role adverse events played in the backlash against psychedelics in the 1960s. It is also not a given that more people would be drawn to psychedelics if they were decriminalized. In jurisdictions that have legalized cannabis, including Canada, the evidence suggests that its use among young people has remained constant or fallen (Howard 2019; Rosenberg et al. 2024). Likewise, following Portugal's decriminalization initiatives, there was no upsurge in recreational use and problematic drug use declined (Baum 2016). The context of criminalization/prohibition also limits opportunities to disseminate publicly accessible information about safe use that would help avert harmful outcomes, including those that these researchers purport to fear. For these reasons, Schwarz-Plaschg argues that psychedelic researchers should embrace their role as political actors, frame their work with the benefit of all citizens in mind and critically engage with the impacts of draconian drug laws and their associated narratives. Outside of a few critical voices, however, the research community has been silent about or even critical of decriminalization, providing credibility to the idea that medicalization is simply a political project to secure limited legalization.

CLINICAL TRIALS AND METHODOLOGICAL CHALLENGES

Today's cohort of psychedelic researchers is acutely aware that medicalization is equated with respectability. In her book *Acid Revival* (2020), sociologist Danielle Giffort shows that modern researchers and clinicians consciously cultivate the aura of the "sober scientist." They dress and act in ways that are indistinguishable from other pharmacologists. They skillfully frame their research in ways that appeal to academic journals and federal agencies. They reframe vague concepts like ego loss and mystical experience to fit the parameters of biomedical expertise. They know that recruits who are too open or too excited about their own psychedelic experiences are at risk of being filtered out. They are part of the paradigm shift they believe is required to have psychedelics approved as legal medicines. Yet, as Giffort notes, this requires a balancing act, where researchers "feel compelled to distance themselves from the counterculture at the same time that the field's countercultural ties have helped sustain the field, particularly in terms of funding and networking" (2020, 15). The current generation of researchers view themselves as the antithesis of Timothy Leary, she says, whose "impure" science and provocative antics caused the death of the first wave of psychedelic research.

Giffort reframes this narrative, highlighting the inherent difficulties in reconciling the psychedelic experience with new scientific, clinical methodologies and randomized controlled trials (RCTs). Early researchers like Leary, as well as Humphry Osmond and Abram Hoffer, were wary of these methods, which they saw as incompatible with the unique qualities of psychedelic drugs and as ignoring or downplaying the importance of set and setting. They were unable or unwilling to align their psychedelic treatment models with the emerging gold standard of the RCT. Similarly, medical historian Matthew Oram (2018) has argued that the demise of LSD research in the 1970s was related to persistent questions about its therapeutic efficacy, as researchers struggled to integrate RCT standards into psychotherapy (for a Canadian perspective, see Jones 2023b).

The current generation of researchers continues to struggle with many of the same issues (Noorani 2021b). The importance of set and setting is fundamentally at odds with "pharmacologicalism," which is predicated on the belief that a drug's chemical structure determines its action in the body and not the context of the treatment or experience of the patient. Trying to validate the efficacy of psychedelics through the apparatus of RCTs where context is to be controlled and biases eliminated is paradoxical to allowing for and being interested in the role of set and setting in shaping the experience.

Ayahuasca is a good example of a psychedelic that Western medicine struggles to explain or understand. Professor Kenneth Tupper and anthropologist Beatriz Labate (2014, 74) argue that the scientific study of ayahuasca raises challenges to the medical establishment in the terrain of epistemology, noting that it "confounds the simplistic pharmacological reductionism that some authorities would impose on it." Likewise, psychedelic researchers Eduardo Schenberg and Konstantin Gerber (2022) contend that modern biomedicine has no epistemic authority when it comes to ayahuasca. It has been unable to delineate appropriate doses. It disregards the diverse range of preparation and extraction methods and ayahuasca's multifaceted therapeutic properties. Much of the ayahuasca experience falls outside the remit of RCT outcome measures. Instead of identifying a medical problem to be solved in advance, traditional healers claim that ayahuasca encourages the nature of the problem — its sources or root causes — to reveal itself during the experience, which can help guide the healing trajectory. In a simple but revealing example, Schenberg and Gerber (2022) note that early biomedical research tended to classify vomiting as an adverse event and discarded user data on this basis. Yet, traditional practitioners consider it to be a normal part of ayahuasca's effects and sometimes welcome it as a form of physical purification. Drawing attention to the importance of set and setting, Dennis McKenna argues that the only way ayahuasca could be used in Western medicine would be to borrow or learn from shamanic approaches without actually imitating them (Meistere and McKenna 2020). While some attention has been placed on incorporating Indigenous practices into models of how ayahuasca could be used in a clinical setting (e.g., Sloshower 2018), the development of "pharmahuasca" — the biopharmaceutical version of ayahuasca — has often been dismissed for the reasons noted above, as well as the lack of informed consent, reciprocity and benefit sharing with Indigenous communities (Leite 2022). In the case of ayahuasca at least, it may be true that biomedical trials "cannot begin to scratch the surface of what is possible with psychedelic plants when used in an Indigenous setting" (Fotiou 2020, 19).

Accounting for the synergistic pharmacological and contextual effects in psychedelic medicine is likely to become more acute with more and more for-profit companies running clinical trials. As Joseph Dumit and Emilia Sanabria (2022, 296) have shown, "pharmaceutical companies do care about set and setting, precisely in order to prove that they do not matter." As an example, sometimes companies will determine if certain kinds of people are helped more by "context" than others; if so, they will be excluded from clinical trials. Similarly, if therapists or caregivers are suspected to play a role in patient outcomes, the protocols will be sanitized so that the drug is the only form of "care." This is one of the main concerns around psychedelics being brought back into biomedical and capitalist frameworks.

Several features of today's psychedelic clinical trials raise concerns about the generalizability of research findings. First, the research tends to rely on small sample sizes which should not be used to make sweeping claims about efficacy. Most psychedelic clinical trials have also involved carefully selected subject/patient populations, tending to exclude participants with an existing mental condition or family history of mental illness. Very few older adults or patients with serious comorbidities have been included (Bouchet et al. 2024; Johnston et al. 2023). In some trials, disqualification rates are extremely high. Although these selection criteria may be justifiable in terms of optimizing patient safety, they mean that the subjects being tested are not an accurate reflection of the diversity of the population at large.

A second concern is that trial participants often have experience with psychedelics. While this is acceptable or even required in some naturalistic research settings, it can be problematic in psychedelic medicine. A relatively small proportion of the general population reports having used psychedelics. Yet, in many clinical trials, only around half of the samples (and in some cases far less) consist of psychedelic-naïve subjects (Ona, Kohek and Bouso 2022). The inclusion of experienced users is sometimes justified to avoid "bad trips" or other adverse events, but it can result in research bias.

Third, few people of colour are included as research participants in psychedelic studies and clinical trials. One review of eighteen psychedelic medicine studies found that 82 percent of research participants were non-Hispanic white, while only 2.5 percent were Black (Michaels et al. 2018). There are similar disparities in clinical trials involving ketamine (Michaels et al. 2022). These findings suggest both a lack of effective recruitment strategies as well as barriers to research participation, including material inequities and a level of fear and distrust among racialized groups (Chen et al. 2020; George et al. 2020; Natarajan 2021). As Jae Sevelius (2017), professor of medicine at the University of California, explains: "communities of color have long histories of being abused, manipulated, and treated unethically within the context of medical research ... [they] have been devastated by the War on Drugs and subsequent mass incarceration, and thus have much more at stake when asked by researchers to participate in studies that involve illegal substances." This history of abuse includes psychedelic research, such as when Black Americans in prisons and hospital mental wards were exploited by researchers (and the CIA) in the middle of the twentieth century (Holloway 2022; Strauss et al. 2022). Fear forms part of the cultural set and setting within which many people of colour engage with psychedelic use, therapy and research. To paraphrase an anecdote that has been circulating in the media, if a Black man publicly admits to drug use, they get into trouble; when a white man does it (such as Michael Pollan), they get a *New York Times* best seller. The lack of diverse representation informing psychedelic research has limited the generalizability of research findings and hampered the development of culturally informed treatments (Williams, Reed and Aggarwal 2020). These issues become even more important in the context of population studies of lifetime psychedelic use, where race has been found to moderate the association between psychedelic consumption and positive health outcomes (Jones and Nock 2022a; Viña and Stephens 2023).

There are additional methodological challenges to consider. Most clinical research involving psychedelics is "open label," meaning that researchers and participants know what treatment is being administered. However, a small but growing number of trials are attempting to employ a double-blind methodology. Here, neither the subjects nor the researchers are supposed to know which subjects are in the test group (active drug) and which are in the control group (placebo). This methodology is meant to control for the placebo effect as well as reduce potential biases on the part of both subjects and clinicians. The problem is that effective blinding is incredibly difficult because psychedelics have potent subjective and behavioural effects. While trials of most psychoactive medications have issues with blinding, post-study feedback suggests that unblinding rates in psychedelic trials can be extraordinarily high (Mithoefer et al. 2011; Muthukumaraswamy, Forsyth and Lumley 2021; Ross et al. 2016). As an example, a recent study of ten RCTs in psychedelic medicine found that nine of them were considered to have a high risk of bias in the "measurement of the outcome" domain, partly due to unsuccessful blinding or the lack of adequate reporting on blinding (Hovmand et al. 2023). Likewise, a recent review of psychedelic

RCTs found that most studies did not report on the integrity of blinding procedures; in those that did, blinding was unsuccessful (Wen et al. 2024). Psychedelic researchers have proposed some ways to get around this issue. One alternative is the use of active placebos — other drugs that can produce subjective and behavioural effects — but many active placebos function like stimulants, which can trigger feelings of anxiety or, conversely, euphoria. This is problematic in studies on the impacts of psychedelics on mood, as it can skew results.

Another problem related to blinding in psychedelic trials is expectancy bias, where people's expectations about the outcomes of an experiment end up influencing the results. One way this manifests itself in research is that if a patient expects a particular treatment to be effective, they may be more likely to notice or report positive results and/or minimize negative outcomes. Positive expectations can also fuel disappointment when participants believe they have been allocated to the placebo group. In this scenario, participants' symptoms may worsen, amplifying negative outcomes in the placebo group and artificially enhancing the treatment effect. Expectancy bias can also lead researchers to unconsciously interpret results in line with a particular end goal or ignore data that does not conform to it. Given the reputational challenges associated with this type of research and the devotion of many true believers in the field, it is likely that most psychedelic researchers strongly believe in the therapeutic value of these substances to begin with. It has also been suggested that the tendency for these researchers to consume psychedelics themselves may lead to "excess enthusiasm" around the value of these compounds, introducing additional sources of bias (Kious, Schwartz and Lewis 2023).

There is growing evidence that the widespread positive media coverage of today's psychedelic renaissance is influencing the expectations of research participants (Aday et al. 2022). In addition, some participants describe a sense of moral obligation to support these studies and report positive results because they do not want to jeopardize the movement as a whole (even if their symptoms get worse during treatment). As one participant in a MAPS study of MDMA for PTSD recounts: "At the time I felt that if I didn't get better then the FDA was not going to approve it. I was going to fuck up their numbers and then it wasn't going to be legal, and millions of people were not going to have access to it … I really omitted a good number of things that were challenging and difficult" (cited in Dickinson and Mugianis 2021). Expectancy bias can be further enhanced by "dark loops" in the psychedelic ecosystem (Noorani, Bedi and Muthukumaraswamy 2023). These are feedback structures related to participant experiences in RCTs — such as new friendships and community-based networks that form around the trials and the testimonials of former trial participants — which can impact trial outcomes. To help address some of these issues, researchers at the Institute of Psychiatry, Psychology and Neuroscience at King's College London recommend reducing the "excessive hype" surrounding psychedelic trials and the "premature assumptions of their place in clinical psychiatric practice" (Butler, Jelen and Rucker 2022, 3052).

In sum, a good deal of caution needs to be exercised in making assumptions based on the results of psychedelic RCTs. Accordingly, there has been a call for gathering real-world, naturalistic data on legal psychedelic interventions (Carhart-Harris et al. 2022). According to researcher Hannes Kettner, if psychedelics are "conceptualized purely as pharmacological treatments with no regard to context, there is a risk that when adopted in real-world clinical practice they might just be found to be ineffective, or even detrimental" (cited in Seltenrich 2021).

Today's Clinical Research

Despite these wide-ranging methodological challenges and concerns, it would be a mistake to dismiss the clinical evidence that has been accumulated. Building on the research and therapeutic advances of the twentieth century, today's clinical research continues to suggest that psychedelics may be effective in treating mental health conditions (Galvão-Coelho et al. 2021; Irizarry et al. 2022; Luoma et al. 2020; Zafar et al. 2023). Though most clinical trials are in their early stages, many are underway, examining a wide range of indications including depression and anxiety in different population subsets, PTSD, addiction and substance use disorders, obsessive-compulsive disorder and eating disorders. Many physical ailments such as brain injuries, chronic pain and degenerative diseases are also being investigated (Castellanos et al. 2020; Garcia-Romeu et al. 2022; Khan et al. 2021). It is the mental health field, though, where most of the focus remains.

Some psychedelics are being studied more than others. Ibogaine has been used for decades in clinics around the world for medicinal purposes, most often to address opioid and other forms of addiction (dos Santos, Bouso and Hallak 2017; Mash et al. 2018). However, today's clinical research is limited. DemeRx, a subsidiary of Atai Life Sciences, is running an early-stage clinical trial on ibogaine to treat opioid use disorder and there is growing clinical interest in non-hallucinogenic ibogaine derivatives. While it has not been documented why ibogaine has not been studied more systematically, it may be due to its long trip duration, safety concerns and obscure mechanisms of action. Likewise, mescaline has been neglected in clinical research, which may also reflect its long trip duration. There has, however, been some medical research on peyote and it has been widely used as a healing agent in Indigenous communities, including to treat alcoholism and other drug dependence (e.g., Dinis-Oliveira et al. 2019). Pharmaceutical start-up Journey Colab is also conducting a clinical trial on mescaline for the treatment of alcohol use disorder.

Unlike the mid-twentieth century when psychedelic researchers and therapists alike primarily focused on LSD (Krebs and Johansen 2012), it is less popular in clinical circles today. The lack of interest likely reflects the ongoing stigma around LSD and its long-lasting effects (compared with psilocybin, for example). Though limited, there is some recent clinical evidence pointing to LSD's ability to treat anxiety (e.g., Holze et al. 2023), including an ongoing clinical trial by Mind Medicine involving its proprietary drug MM-120, a pharmacologically altered form of LSD, which has shown positive results (LaMotte 2024). There has been a shift, notably among psychedelic companies, to studying compounds with shorter trip durations such as DMT and 5-MeO-DMT. 5-MeO-DMT in particular is a favourite among venture capitalists because it delivers an incredibly powerful experience in only fifteen to twenty minutes. Companies like GH Research, Biomind Labs, Cybin and Beckley Psytech are all running clinical trials with these compounds for the treatment of depression and anxiety, with encouraging early-stage results. While ayahuasca presents unique challenges for Western medicine, clinical researchers in Brazil have been examining its use as a treatment for depression and other ailments, also with positive results (e.g., de L Osório et al. 2015; Palhano-Fontes et al. 2019; Zeifman et al. 2019).

Given its less restricted access as a generic compound and FDA-approved anesthetic, ketamine has been studied more than any other psychedelic in recent years. RCTs on ketamine point to its effectiveness as a fast-acting antidepressant that can be beneficial in addressing suicidal ideation and treatment-resistant depression (e.g., Abbar et al. 2022;

An et al. 2021; Wilkinson et al. 2021). In 2019, the FDA approved esketamine (Spravato), a drug derived from ketamine, for the treatment of depression, and Health Canada did the same in 2020. There is also some evidence of ketamine's effectiveness in treating other mental health conditions (Walsh et al. 2021). As of 2025, Seelos Therapeutics is running a clinical trial on ketamine for the treatment of PTSD and Awakn Life Sciences is investigating ketamine-assisted therapy for the treatment of alcohol use disorder. Despite these findings, research suggests that the effects of ketamine tend to be short-lived and that research bias may be playing a role in the findings (Shamabadi, Ahmadzade and Hasanzadeh 2022; Walsh et al. 2021).

Psilocybin is one compound that has been leading the way in the push for medicalization. Psilocybin has shown encouraging clinical results over the past decade, including for the treatment of substance use disorders (Bogenschutz et al. 2022; Johnson et al. 2014; Johnson, Garcia-Romeu and Griffiths 2017). The evidence also suggests it may be effective in treating depression and anxiety (Watford and Masood 2024). Some of the most notable findings have involved its effects in patients with end-of-life illnesses, in particular the alleviation of depression, anxiety and existential distress (e.g., Agin-Liebes et al. 2020; Griffiths et al. 2016; Ross et al. 2016; Ross et al. 2021). In one of the most well-publicized trials to date evaluating the therapeutic potential of a psychedelic, researchers tested two sessions of psilocybin-assisted therapy against a six-week course of a leading antidepressant, escitalopram (sold under the brand names Lexapro and Cipralex). Although the primary outcome measure indicated no statistically significant difference between the two, the secondary outcome measures did appear to favour psilocybin (Carhart-Harris et al. 2021). Similar results were found in a follow-up study; some secondary measures seemed to favour the psychedelic, but no firm conclusions could be drawn from the data (Erritzoe et al. 2024). Previous research on the use of psilocybin to treat major depressive disorder has produced positive results (e.g., Davis et al. 2021; Gukasyan et al. 2022). Several organizations are conducting clinical trials to further test this relationship, all of which have reported clinically significant reductions in depressive symptoms compared to placebo (Cybin 2024; Goodwin et al. 2022; Raison et al. 2023).

MDMA is the other substance at the forefront of psychedelic medicalization, though some roadblocks have emerged on its pathway to approval. The most advanced psychedelic clinical trials to date are MAPS' Phase 3 trials involving MDMA-assisted therapy for the treatment of PTSD. These trials were administered by MAPS public benefit corporation, a subsidiary of MAPS that was restructured and became Lykos Therapeutics in early 2024. The published results of these trials were significant. In 2021, it was found that 67 percent of the participants in the MDMA group improved to the point where they no longer qualified for a PTSD diagnosis, compared with 32 percent in the placebo group (Mitchell et al. 2021). In the second Phase 3 confirmatory trial, 71 percent of those in the MDMA group no longer met the criteria for PTSD, compared to 48 percent who received the placebo (Mitchell et al. 2023). Despite these results, in August 2024 the FDA rejected Lykos Therapeutics' new drug application for MDMA-assisted therapy. The decision reflected concerns around study design, data quality, adverse events and therapist misconduct, discussed in more detail later in the chapter. Further, the journal *Psychopharmacology* issued retraction notices for three academic papers it previously published related to the Phase 2 trials. While the retractions were primarily related to ethical misconduct in one of the trial sites, they have led to additional questions about this body of research.

Overall, clinical research remains limited with regard to the effects of psychedelics, particularly over a longer term. Recent research also remains relatively concentrated on a sample of these drugs, including ketamine, psilocybin and MDMA. Early evidence suggests that psychedelics may be effective in treating mental health conditions, offering advantages over current drugs and therapeutic regimens. A clearer picture regarding the efficacy of psychedelics should emerge in the years ahead.

MEDICALIZATION AND MENTAL HEALTH

Mental health has become one of the biggest social challenges of the twenty-first century. A growing number of health practitioners, researchers and media commentators suggest there is a global mental health crisis. In its 2022 *World Mental Health Report*, the World Health Organization (2022a) claims that close to a billion people suffer from some form of mental illness. In 2019, the organization estimated that over 300 million people were living with anxiety disorders and 280 million were living with depressive disorders. As well, more than 700,000 people die each year from suicide, with suicide now ranking as the fourth leading cause of death among 15- to 29-year-olds (World Health Organization 2023), leading some to suggest it should be classified as an epidemic (e.g., Menon 2019; Roberts 2018). In 2022, positive self-assessments of mental health in the US were at their lowest point in more than two decades, and a study of a nationally representative sample of US adults found that 90 percent of respondents said the country is experiencing a mental health crisis (Brenan 2022; McPhillips 2022). Reported problematic substance use has also increased significantly over the past few decades, with alcohol issues leading the way (GBD Alcohol and Drug Use Collaborators 2016). According to the United Nations Office on Drugs and Crime (2023), nearly 40 million people suffered from drug use disorders in 2021, a figure that does not include alcohol or tobacco, representing a 45 percent increase over the previous ten years. It has been estimated that mental health conditions account for trillions of dollars in lost "productivity" and additional healthcare and criminal justice costs each year (Isham, Mair and Jackson 2021; Patel et al. 2018).

Further, the World Health Organization (2022a) states that the vast majority of mental health conditions go untreated, and that mental health is one of the most neglected areas of public health worldwide. Even when treatment resources are sought out and available, they are often ineffective. Compared with any other branch of medicine, the treatment of mental illness has an abysmal track record. While the use of commonly prescribed antidepressants, such as SSRIs, has skyrocketed in recent decades, they have also faced considerable backlash due to their side effects and questions about their efficacy (Davies 2021; Moskowitz 2022; Read and Williams 2018; Whitaker 2010).

Psychedelics and the "Mental Health Crisis"

The COVID-19 pandemic exacerbated these trends as government lockdowns, social isolation and economic hardship resulted in large increases in anxiety, depression and problematic substance use worldwide (Ettman et al. 2020; Panchal, Saunders and Rudowitz 2023; World Health Organization 2022b). Research on psychedelic use during the pandemic suggests these substances were perceived by some as providing a level of mental health protection. One survey of 5,618 Argentinians, for example, found that psychedelic use was associated with increased positive affect in the face of pandemic-related stress (Cavanna et al. 2021). Another survey of nearly three thousand people from multiple countries found that psychedelic users reported less psychological and peritraumatic distress during the pandemic period, and that nearly half of these users said that psychedelics had a "large positive impact" on how they coped with the confinement period (Révész et al. 2021). These kinds of studies do not establish causation, so it remains unclear whether the use of psychedelics was itself a protective factor or whether people with certain personality traits or those who engaged in other behaviours that promote mental health are simply more prone to use psychedelics. In any event, a growing number of people around the world are using psychedelics as a DIY mental health treatment.

Are we experiencing a "mental health crisis" or is it more accurately a crisis of modern capitalism? What proportion of diagnosed conditions can be traced to people struggling to cope with financial insecurity, precarious labour or affordable housing? What are the social and psychological impacts of millions of people accepting that they are deficient if they cannot compete or keep their heads above water in a system that is rigged against them? And how are these stressors exacerbated by a trillion-dollar corporate marketing machine that inundates everyone with the message that they are inadequate if they do not own the right products, make enough money or look a certain way?

In the context of medicalization, large numbers of people have been persuaded that their discontent or unhappiness arises from biomedical abnormalities, deficient brain chemistries and/or chemical imbalances, and that a medical intervention is required, usually in the form of a pill taken on a regular basis. This conclusion has been sharply criticized in recent years (Beres 2020; Davies 2021; Davis 2020; Moncrieff et al. 2023). Even if it can be shown that mental illness has a neurological basis, causation is more complicated. Depression, anxiety and problematic substance use can be viewed as predictable reactions to wider societal problems, such as poverty, precarious employment and obscene levels of economic inequality (Tibber et al. 2022). Psychologist Bruce Alexander (2008) explores the mental health impacts of capitalism in his work on the globalization of addiction. For Alexander, the problem of addiction is fundamentally a social phenomenon, anchored in the rise of individualism and competition. These forces have torn people away from vital social bonds. The resulting alienation and social dislocation have contributed to the deterioration of mental health worldwide. Similarly, economists Anne Case and Angus Deaton (2017) draw attention to what they call "deaths of despair" — the increases in drug overdoses, suicide and alcohol-related mortality, particularly among middle-aged white communities in the US, that are associated with widening income inequality and a deterioration in economic and social well-being.

Any serious discussion about improving mental health must address the precarious context in which millions of people live, yet our pharma-dominated system largely denies the possibility of social causation. In the process, it individualizes and depoliticizes mental illness while providing a lucrative market for pharmaceutical companies that profit off the commodification of human distress (Davies, Pace and Devenot 2023; Fisher 2009). This context is important in any discussion of the medicalization of psychedelics. Surveying the growing corporate interest in psychedelic medicine and mental health, author Belén Fernández (2022) writes, "it is no less than mind-bending to argue that the very capitalist system that is responsible for generating vast alienation and mental strife should now be in the business of rectifying the situation with the same profit-over-people approach."

Psychedelics may end up being the best pharmacological option to treat specific mental health conditions, but they alone are not going to "solve" any mental health crisis. Treating individualized emotional and mental suffering, while potentially helpful for many people, does nothing to address the social problems that are contributing to mental illnesses. Without engaging with the socioeconomic determinants of health, psychedelic medicine risks serving as a distraction that offers little more than self-perpetuating cycles of symptom management — maintenance therapies and palliative treatments that help workers get out of bed in the morning and cope with their structural disadvantages. Basic healthcare, living wages and affordable housing would benefit most depressed people more than any drug trip. In fact, some research suggests that for vulnerable populations, such as the unemployed, lifetime psychedelic use is associated with worse mental health outcomes and exacerbates stressful phases of life (e.g., Korman 2023).

Moreover, limiting psychedelics to patients with acute forms of mental illness negates their wider political and cultural potential. Disrupting our current ways of thinking about society, the economy and social change would arguably be more effective in addressing the root causes of mental illness than individualized clinical therapy. The suggestion that a pill is going to fix your problems could easily distract from practices that are potentially more beneficial to mental health, such as various forms of collective struggle where people actively engage in efforts to change the material conditions of their lives.

Questions about Efficacy

The science of how and why psychedelics might work to improve mental health is still in its infancy, but psychedelic neuroscience is starting to shed some light on the neurobiological mechanisms of action (Carhart-Harris and Friston 2019; Vollenweider and Preller 2022). Some researchers are also employing AI in an attempt to "map" psychedelic trips in the brain to optimize their therapeutic use (e.g., Ballentine, Friedman and Bzdok 2022). The dizzying array of terminology used to explain the mental health benefits of psychedelics is confusing to say the least. We are told that psychedelics can "rewire" the brain and repair broken neural networks. Computer analogies are also widespread, such as "code reboot" and "defragmenting our hard drives." The ability of psychedelics to "reset" the brain is one of the most common explanations offered by scientists, psychedelic companies and the media (e.g., Adams 2019; Schraer 2021). For example, pharmacologist and chemist David Nichols, who has been studying psychoactive drugs for over half a century, notes that the psychedelic experience "leads to reset," after which "brain networks go back to a healthier pattern" (cited in Piore 2021).

This assemblage of terminologies is somewhat understandable given the ongoing scientific uncertainty about if and how psychedelics produce mental health benefits, but not everyone is happy about it. Psychedelic commentator Shayla Love (2023a), for instance, is worried that this kind of messaging denotes an "automatic, easy, or fast" fix that can cause unrealistic expectations in potential patients. She also notes disconcerting similarities between the way antidepressants like SSRIs were promoted in the past and the way psychedelics are promoted today. Dr. Rosalind Watts, a former clinical investigator at Imperial College London, has also criticized the reset metaphor because it suggests psychedelic therapy is a magic bullet: "This is a journey into the deepest parts of yourself and potentially might be very challenging. I think the messaging around psychedelics, it would be helpful if that changes a bit" (cited in Love 2020a).

While the reset analogy may not be appropriate for current or potential patients, Watts' former colleague Dr. Robin Carhart-Harris, currently director of the psychedelics program at the University of California, San Francisco, has gone some distance in trying to explain what the "reset mechanism" might be. Carhart-Harris posits that classical psychedelics like psilocybin, LSD and DMT temporarily suppress or deactivate the brain's "default mode network" (DMN), an interconnected group of brain regions that are associated with introspective functions like self-reflection and self-criticism. He describes the DMN as the brain's "orchestra conductor" or "capital city" — the physical counterpart to our ego or sense of self. For people with conditions like anxiety, depression and addiction, he argues that the DMN is overactive, which can lead to rigidly negative or hypercritical thought patterns. Brain imaging suggests that when psychedelics are absorbed, they decrease activity in the DMN and increase connectivity in the rest of the brain, leading to a kind of neural anarchy that enables new connections between brain regions that do not normally communicate with one another (Carhart-Harris et al. 2014; Carhart-Harris and Friston 2019). In lay terms, disrupting the DMN is often explained as "shaking the snow globe," where healthier thought processes have an opportunity to come together as the snow resettles. By disrupting the DMN, psychedelics may loosen the ego's grip on the mind and untether people from well-entrenched, maladaptive thought patterns that contribute to mental illness (Carhart-Harris et al. 2016; Carhart-Harris et al. 2017; Kałużna et al. 2022; Lebedev et al. 2015).

In addition to changes in the DMN and enhanced ego dissolution, another common term that has been used to explain the therapeutic benefits of psychedelics is "neuroplasticity," or the ability of neural networks to change through growth, reorganization and the formation of new connections (Calder and Hasler 2023; De Vos, Mason and Kuypers 2021; Olson 2022). It is theorized that psychedelics can stimulate neuroplasticity leading to long-term improvements in mental health outcomes. Some claim that psychedelic-induced neuroplasticity pushes an adult mind back to a more "childlike state" of learning and flexibility, allowing for new perspectives that can be therapeutic (Gopnik 2018).

These neurobiological theories are typically applied to classical psychedelics. Other substances like ketamine and MDMA are also capable of impacting neuronal structures, but it has been proposed that the mechanisms of action are different. For example, while classical psychedelics are thought to increase connectivity between different parts of the brain, dissociative anesthetics like ketamine may do the opposite — disconnecting neural circuits that regulate consciousness, memory and affective processing (Ionescu et al. 2018). In the case of MDMA, one of the things that sets it apart is its effect on serotonin. MDMA activates serotonin receptors, which increases the amount of serotonin in the brain. It also triggers the release of other neurotransmitters, such as dopamine and norepinephrine. This unique pharmacological cocktail appears conducive to social-emotional learning and cognitive processing. MDMA is also associated with the release of heightened levels of oxytocin, which can decrease activity in the amygdala (the fear and stress centre of the brain) thereby reducing the fear associated with traumatic memories (Furminger 2022; Siebert 2022). Ibogaine also has a broader set of neuropharmacological actions that only partially match those of classical psychedelics. How its biological mechanism of action might impact its ability to treat addiction is not well studied or understood (Underwood, Bright and Lancaster 2021).

It is important not to conflate these neurobiological functions and impacts with psychedelic-assisted psychotherapy (PAP). PAP combines a pharmacological treatment with a psychotherapeutic intervention. Most clinical trials involving psychedelics measure the efficacy of psychedelic-enhanced therapy, not solely the compounds themselves. PAP protocols draw significantly from the first wave of psychedelic research, in particular the work of psychiatrist Stanislav Grof, and much of it remains rooted in pseudo-scientific beliefs. There is also no consensus on what constitutes best practices in the field (Cristea et al. 2022). Despite these significant gaps in the research, it remains an assumption that some form of psychotherapy, alongside psychedelic use, is important for long-term, beneficial outcomes. Instead of seeing psychedelics as simply correcting neurochemical abnormalities, PAP researchers and practitioners tend to emphasize "experiential efficacy," which centres on phenomenological states as key mechanisms for action. These states can include the generation of meaningful or profound insights, an increase in "psychological flexibility," a shift in one's identity and sense of self (I am no longer "a smoker," for example), a shift from experiential avoidance to adaptive acceptance and an increased sense of connectedness to oneself or others (Davis, Barrett and Griffiths 2020; Devenot et al. 2022; Kałużna et al. 2022; Schenberg 2018; Watts and Luoma 2020; Watts et al. 2017; Wolff et al. 2020).

The "integration" component of PAP has received a lot of attention in recent years, though the concept remains vague and protocols vary widely (Bathje, Majeski and Kudowor 2022; Greń et al. 2024). Within the context of PAP, integration usually includes follow-up sessions that help patients make sense of their psychedelic experiences and process or assimilate new insights and perspectives into their everyday lives. This integration is thought to be important because the experience itself can lead to significant psychological changes, such as increased sensitivity and openness, a heightened sense of interconnection and changes in self-perception. When people return to their "old lives" without the necessary support structures in place, it can be destabilizing. Many would argue that integration is the most important component of psychedelic therapy, yet it is costly and therefore likely to be neglected in for-profit contexts.

We have already seen evidence of companies reducing or removing psychotherapy from their protocols for commercial reasons. Psychedelic drug developer Mind Medicine, for example, has attempted to "eliminate" psychotherapeutic intervention in its Phase 2B study of LSD (MM120) for the treatment of generalized anxiety disorder. According to one company spokesperson, "we explicitly prohibit forms of therapy other than the administration of the study drug" (Psychedelic Alpha 2024a). As a result, therapists have been replaced by "dosing session monitors" — staff who monitor safety but do not provide therapy — and follow-up visits are arranged for assessment purposes only. The CEO of Mind Medicine, Robert Barrow, summed up the goal as follows: "Fundamentally, we've tried to really replicate how we would approach development if this was the fourteenth SSRI in development." Similarly, Compass Pathways is increasingly emphasizing "digital support tools" instead of therapy in their research trials. These companies are looking to couch their protocols in ways that make them more attractive to investors and regulators, increasing their commercial viability. While some studies on the impact of psychedelics have found positive results in the absence of psychotherapeutic intervention, most research suggests that psychedelic administration in combination with psychotherapy leads to better outcomes (e.g., Barone et al. 2019; Drozdz et al. 2022; Grabski et al. 2022; Murphy et al. 2022; Schenberg et al. 2014).

Neurobiological explanations of efficacy have generated criticism within the psychedelic field and beyond. Dr. Joanna Moncrieff (2021), a prominent critic of psychopharmacological models of mental illness, asserts that psychedelic researchers are overplaying their hands. Neuropsychologist Andy Mitchell, a psychedelic user and author of *Ten Trips* (2023), is also skeptical. He compares medicalized explanations to "a bowl of cold, half-cooked, semi-digestible" stew filled with ill-defined conceptual ingredients (2023, 74). Thomas Insel, former head of the US National Institute of Mental Health, similarly argues that current explanations around psychedelic efficacy are problematic and should not be taken with a grain of salt but "a whole shaker of salt" (cited in Goldhill 2023). Author and therapist Will Hall (2021a) is more derisive, claiming that the "gee-whiz psychedelic jargon we hear in the media today about 'default mode networks,' 'brain rebooting,' and 'neural connectivity' is just a return of more of the same neurobabble that gave us the last wave of quick-fix faith in SSRI antidepressants." Generally, these and other critics liken neurobiological models in psychedelic medicine to the now-disproven theories that antidepressants work by changing chemical imbalances. Some researchers are responding to the criticism, with the debates becoming more personal and less professional (Love 2022b).

Even though assumptions, methodologies and results are all being challenged, psychedelic researchers remain undeterred. They have their sights set on what Michael Pollan calls the "grand unified theory of mental illness" (cited in Ferriss 2018). The idea is that many different kinds of mental illness, such as depression, anxiety, obsession, addiction and PTSD, are not fundamentally different. The names we give these conditions reflect the arbitrary distinctions of the Diagnostic and Statistical Manual of Mental Disorders and the artificial labels needed for insurance coverage. In other words, they see these as fundamentally similar ailments where people get stuck in repetitive loops of dysfunctional thought and behaviour, reinforced by an over-active and punishing ego. According to psychedelic philanthropist and podcast host Tim Ferriss, this opens up the "tantalizing possibility" that separately labeled conditions could be addressed in a similar way — namely, PAP. For a mental health industry in a legitimacy crisis, this is a tantalizing prospect indeed. If they are correct that PAP works at a fundamental level to address certain root causes of mental illness, this would represent a breakthrough in the mental health field.

However, there are still too many uncertainties to say anything definitive about psychedelic medicine and mental health. Although the research in some areas looks promising, it continues to be limited by small sample sizes and other methodological challenges, as well as a limited evidence base. Another area that remains unresolved is the relative weight that should be given to the efficacy of the drug versus the efficacy of the experience. Are the subjective effects of psychedelics essential to their presumed therapeutic effects? If and how this question is resolved will shape the future of the psychedelic renaissance. In fact, it is already shaping the research agenda and the long-term planning of psychedelic capitalists.

Is the Trip Necessary?

The rationale behind psychedelic medicine can be confusing and contradictory. On the one hand, some claim that psychedelics are a medical intervention that targets underlying brain deficiencies. On the other, psychedelics are promoted as inducing insights and breakthroughs through drug-induced experiences. Clinical researchers have long held that the subjective experience is necessary for mental health benefits. In the middle of the twentieth century, for example, Humphry Osmond and Abram Hoffer argued that the "mind-manifesting" properties of LSD were important in delivering positive outcomes in patients being treated for alcoholism. According to Hoffer, "from the first we considered not the chemical, but the experience as a key factor in therapy — in fact, we used a sort of psychotherapy made possible by the nature of the experience" (cited in Dyck 2006, 317).

In more recent years, psychedelic researchers continue to make claims about experiential efficacy. In their work at Johns Hopkins, David Yaden and Roland Griffiths have tried to demonstrate that subjective effects are necessary for imparting the full and enduring benefits of classical psychedelics. Their arguments largely rely on empirical assessments of psychedelic-induced mystical experiences, which are assumed to mediate the positive therapeutic response in patients with depression, anxiety and addiction (Griffiths et al. 2016; Hendricks 2018; Johnson et al. 2019; Yaden and Griffiths 2021). Their findings are supported by other research where the quality of these experiences is linked to therapeutic efficacy (Dahan et al. 2024; Davis et al. 2019; Ko et al. 2022; Roseman, Nutt and Carhart-Harris 2018; Ross et al. 2016; Weiss et al. 2024). Empathogens like MDMA and dissociatives like ketamine are not reported to produce the same mystical-type experience as classical psychedelics. Yet, the cognitive and emotional impacts of MDMA have long been considered important for MDMA-assisted psychotherapy, and some researchers have argued that extra-pharmacological factors play a key role in the use of ketamine to treat depression (Dore et al. 2019; Lii et al. 2023).

In contrast, other researchers argue that measurable biological processes can better explain the therapeutic benefits of psychedelics. Neuroscientist David Olson (2018, 2020), for example, claims that enhanced neuroplasticity is the most relevant factor in explaining therapeutic outcomes. Some studies of ketamine suggest that its antidepressant benefits are not strictly dependent on the experience (Henderson 2016). The use of psychedelics to treat physical health conditions is also relevant to this debate. For example, there is evidence that psychedelics can provide relief for headaches and migraines, including cluster headaches — a condition so painful they are often referred to as "suicide headaches." This was brought to light by communities of sufferers in underground contexts, including the patient group "Clusterbusters" who developed their own medicines from home-grown psilocybin mushrooms in the absence of effective mainstream treatment interventions (Kempner 2024). These citizen science innovations were subsequently supported by published research (Andersson, Persson and Kjellgren 2017; Schindler et al. 2022). Of note here is that surveys of people suffering from these afflictions reveal that the use of sub-perceptual (micro) doses of psilocybin and LSD, as well as 2-bromo-LSD (which differs only slightly from LSD and is non-hallucinogenic), appear to be at least somewhat effective in treating their conditions (Karst et al. 2010; Schindler et al. 2015, 2022).

Bryan Roth at the University of North Carolina is aiming to discover new chemical compounds that act like tryptamines but do not impart a typical psychedelic experience. His research is funded by a $27 million grant from the Defense Advanced Research Projects Agency (DARPA), a research branch of the US military. Tristan McClure-Begley, who runs DARPA's Focused Pharma program, says the psychedelic experience is an "intolerable, deleterious" side effect that is thwarting the trajectory of psychedelic medicine (cited in Yakowicz 2021). For those looking to capitalize on the psychedelic renaissance, it may also be thwarting future revenue streams.

Biotech entrepreneurs have an interest in maintaining the therapeutic value of psychedelics while reducing or eliminating "the trip." As it stands now, the mind-altering effects of these substances present several obstacles to mainstreaming. PAP is time-consuming and resource intensive. If the experience is a necessary component of treatment, then a complex infrastructure of clinics, clinicians, therapy training programs and integration specialists will be necessary. Moreover, having to provide therapy to a single patient for days, weeks or even months is not viewed favourably by for-profit providers, especially compared with the highly lucrative pill-per-day model offered by the pharmaceutical industry. If, however, effective treatments could be manufactured in the absence of subjective effects, this could increase the efficiency of delivery, patient adoption rates and profit margins. It could also be a big boost to intellectual property portfolios.

The psychedelic industry's incentive to explore the potential of non-hallucinogenic psychedelics has already led to a flurry of research and development initiatives focused on shortening the trip, making it less intense and even engineering out the subjective properties altogether. The biopharmaceutical firm Cybin, for instance, is focused on developing faster onset and shorter duration treatments for depression and addiction using deuterated analogs of existing psychedelics. Many companies are also working to develop non-hallucinogenic therapeutics, such as Bright Minds Biosciences, Delix Therapeutics, Onsero, Enveric Biosciences, Gilgamesh Pharmaceuticals, Psilera Bioscience and Compass Pathways. These companies are anticipating and catering to the perceived interests of Big Pharma, who may be looking to commercialize substances that fit the box of neuroscience but without the subjective effects.

In this vein, scientists and companies are developing new drug discovery and screening technologies in their search for non-subjective treatments. In 2022, the Centre for Addiction and Mental Health was awarded Canada's first federal grant to study the effects of psilocybin on treatment-resistant depression. As part of its work, the institute is exploring whether psilocybin can treat depression without inducing a psychedelic state. Given the potential value for investors and biotech firms in terms of scalability, marketability and profitability, if non-subjective psychedelic treatments are found to be effective, their widespread development is likely inevitable. Shlomi Raz, chief business officer of Beckley Psytech and former CEO of Eleusis, agrees with the direction the field is heading. As he puts it, "the time has come to make psychedelics, once seen as 'out there' substances, mainstream and boring again" (Raz 2020).

However, not everyone is happy with corporate and military efforts to reduce or eliminate the trip. Rick Doblin argues that the idea of a "non-psychedelic, psychedelic compound" is a "bogus pipedream" that distracts from proven treatments that are available right now (cited in Yakowicz 2021). David Yaden, Brian Earp and Roland Griffiths (2022) underscore some of the ethical issues surrounding the development of "non-subjective" psychedelics. While it may reduce costs, they argue this approach detracts from the relational aspects of care. Even if non-subjective psychedelics could bring about the same reductions in clinical symptoms, they would not replicate the less tangible effects on well-being "derived from the human-to-human therapeutic encounter" (2022, 468). They further argue that because traditional psychedelics have been reported to provide positive and meaningful experiences in people's lives, medical providers may have an ethical obligation to provide such an experience or, at the very least, offer classical psychedelics as the default treatment option and standard of care. Law professor Dustin Marlan (2023) also warns of possible legal implications. To the extent that the move to legalize psychedelics depends on their medicalization, the widespread adoption of non-subjective psychedelics could mean that legal access will be limited to synthetic trip-free versions of these drugs, while the "psychedelic experience" remains criminalized.

Non- or less-subjective compounds could be helpful to some patient populations suffering from conditions where the subjective effects are undesirable or who would otherwise not qualify for treatment. These compounds may also lessen the risks of adverse reactions or side effects. For example, non-hallucinogenic ibogaine derivatives such as 18-MC (recently rebranded MM-110) and tabernanthalog (TBG) may be similar to ibogaine in their anti-addictive properties but without the cardiovascular risks (Coffey 2021b; Jaeger 2021). Nevertheless, it should go without saying that the development of next-generation psychedelics is largely driven by profit-generating objectives and not by patient outcomes. The shift away from experiential freedom and efficacy is consistent with the aims of conventional psychiatry and the pharmaceutical industry: "a patient passively takes a pill, hoping that their brain changes its chemistry while every other aspect of reality remains the same, for better or for worse" (Mitchell 2023, 35).

Regardless of the outcomes of the research underway, something valuable has already been lost in these efforts to "make psychedelics boring again" by integrating them into a commodified pharmaceutical context of scalable medicalized technologies. The reduction of psychedelics to neurochemical processes inevitably erodes the value that these substances hold in and of themselves, just as understanding these experiences only in medical terms runs the risk of obscuring other modes of awareness and understanding that may be important in processes of healing and beyond (Ellenhorn and Mugianis 2022b). According to political economist Sandy Hager (2024, 16), the profitability of this enterprise will hinge upon its ability to "tame the unruliness of psychedelics by putting them into a medicalized box." Within that box, writes Alan Piper (2023, 15), psychedelics are little more than a "caged tiger" — one that is amenable and harnessed to the everyday requirements of our consumer culture. It is possible that the current trend may simply represent more of the same near-sighted, reductionist "magic pill" logic that got the mental health industry where it is today.

The Microdosing Debate

Microdosing is one of the hottest trends in psychedelia. Online forums and discussion groups have grown exponentially (Landau 2022). Entire books have been written on microdosing that provide information and coaching (Spotswood 2022). Parents across North America are reportedly microdosing as a way to cope with stress (Lieber 2024). And public figures, from all walks of life, are extolling its benefits for mental health (Waldman 2017). Larry Campbell, former mayor of Vancouver and retired Canadian senator, recently shared his experiences (Hallifax 2022). Campbell had been on antidepressants for two decades, with his struggles with depression and PTSD persisting. During the pandemic, however, Campbell realized he felt better. When he discussed these changes with his wife, she admitted to spiking his coffee with small bits of psilocybin. Tens of thousands of other anecdotal reports from people all over the world are highlighting a catalogue of social, cognitive and health-related benefits related to microdosing (Lea, Amada and Jungaberle 2020). These include but are not limited to: stress relief; increased energy, focus and concentration; enhanced creativity and mood; increased sociability; greater productivity; improved interpersonal relationships; reductions in depression and anxiety; reduced cravings for alcohol and other drugs; and overall improvements in quality of life. Not all accounts are positive, however, with some users reporting irritability, anxiety, mood swings and physiological discomfort.

The term microdosing seems to be one of convenience. A microdose is usually defined as between 1/10 and 1/20 of a recreational or clinical dose. A "correct" microdose is supposed to be sub-perceptual and not yield subjective effects. However, dosing levels vary widely, and optimal dosing intervals have never been empirically validated. According to a 2018 survey, two-thirds of respondents who microdosed were unaware of the dose they were consuming, which limits the conclusions that can be drawn from self-reports (Hutten et al. 2019). Moreover, a systematic review of research on psychedelic microdosing (forty-four studies between 1955 and 2021) found that many research participants are aware of the drugs' effects (Polito and Liknaitzky 2022). The authors therefore caution against describing microdosing as sub-perceptual and suggest a better definition would be "sub-hallucinogenic with no loss of functionality" (2022, 17).

Dr. James Fadiman has been investigating the effects of microdosing since 2010. His book, *The Psychedelic Explorer's Guide* (2011), introduced the topic to large numbers of people and includes anecdotal reports of positive improvements in emotional balance and cognitive functioning. While Fadiman suggests that microdosing does not result in the immediate changes or breakthroughs that higher doses of psychedelics often do, microdosing can produce similar changes over time. He compares the difference between microdosing and macrodosing to "the difference between the FM dial and the AM dial ... there's different things you can do with FM that you can't do with AM, and vice versa" (cited in Austin and Fadiman 2021). Fadiman's research is largely based on "citizen science," which relies heavily on self-reported documentation. One of Fadiman's studies involved more than a thousand volunteers from fifty-nine countries who agreed to microdose once every three days for a month and complete daily evaluations of their emotional state (Fadiman and Korb 2019). These volunteers commonly reported positive effects such as elevated mood, increased productivity and improved interpersonal relationships. Many also found microdosing to be an effective antidepressant, with some discontinuing their use of other medications as a result.

Mycologist Paul Stamets, who has dedicated his life to the study of fungi, is also a microdosing enthusiast who relies on citizen science. One study co-authored by Stamets followed 953 people who self-administered psilocybin and a second group of 180 people who were not microdosing (Rootman et al. 2022). It found small- to medium-sized improvements in mood and mental health that were generally consistent across age, gender and mental health status. This study was the subject of enthusiastic media coverage, with some claiming it represented a breakthrough in the field. It was also included in the information sent to physicians via the medical news website Medscape about recent studies of interest. But it also received some critical commentary (e.g., Sellers and Romach 2023). Writer James Kent (2022b) dubbed it the "microdosing study heard around the world" and pointed to significant methodological issues, including the authors relying on a sample of self-selected microdosers and making no effort to provide a blinded control group or control for dose. He also noted conflicts of interest concerning the researchers' involvement in related commercial activities.

Most studies of microdosing rely on surveys, self-reports and/or analyses of online narratives, without any blinding or dosing controls, making causal inference impossible. While most of these studies may suggest that microdosing is beneficial for a range of indicators and problems, such as mood, creativity and sociability (e.g., Anderson et al. 2019a, 2019b; Petranker et al. 2022; Prochazkova et al. 2018) as well as depression, stress and anxiety (e.g., Cameron, Nazarian and Olson 2020; Lea et al. 2020; Polito and Stevenson 2019; Rootman et al. 2021), the evidence is not strong. In fact, a markedly different picture emerges in research with methodological controls. A defining trend in this literature appears to be that the more scientifically rigorous the evidence, the weaker the results.

Two double-blind, placebo-controlled trials of microdosing were published in 2019. One investigated the effects of LSD on time perception, an aspect of cognitive function (Yanakieva et al. 2019). It found that microdosing was not associated with any robust changes in perception, concentration or consciousness. The second used mood questionnaires and behavioural tasks to assess emotion processing and cognition (Bershad et al. 2019). It found that while LSD did produce measurable subjective and physiological effects (such as increased blood pressure and self-reported ratings of "vigor"), there were no improvements in mood, cognition or emotional processing. While the results of the second study were tentative at best, they were enough for Paul Austin, psychedelic podcaster, "microdosing coach" and CEO of the psychedelics platform *Third Wave*, to conclude they were a "critical step forward in the legitimization of microdosing as a tool for therapy ... We now know, with certainty, that microdosing is not a placebo" (cited in Ginder-Shaw 2019).

More recent studies suggest that Austin may have jumped the gun. In a 2021 placebo-controlled trial of microdosing, researchers found that while participants who microdosed with psilocybin or LSD did experience psychological benefits, those in the placebo group experienced similar improvements and there was no statistically significant difference between the two groups (Szigeti et al. 2021). They also found that participants who believed they were microdosing yielded higher scores on mental health measures regardless of what group they were in. In other words, their guesses about what substance they had taken (microdose or placebo) had a stronger influence on outcomes than the substance itself. These results are in line with three other placebo-controlled studies, which found that microdosing had no significant effect on creativity, depression, anxiety, stress, cognition or emotional processing (de Wit et al. 2022; Marschall et al. 2022; Murphy et al. 2024). Positive expectations around microdosing, it would seem, are significantly predictive of improvements in cognitive function and mental health (Cavanna et al. 2022; Kaertner et al. 2021).

None of this research provides definitive evidence that the benefits of microdosing are simply placebo induced. For one, brain changes (neural complexity) are evident even with small doses of psychedelics, which may help to account for positive self-reports (Murray et al. 2024). In addition, the design of placebo-controlled trials may be insufficient to allow the benefits to take hold and be measured. These trials are short and tend to focus on healthy populations, which means they do not normally allow for the observation of clinical benefits related to particular conditions (see Polito and Liknaitzky 2022, 2024). To understand what is driving the large volume of positive self-reports, controlled longitudinal studies targeting clinical populations are likely necessary. In the end, some contend it does not matter if the effects of microdosing are based on expectation or pharmacology if it is having a positive impact on people's lives.

What does matter is how this research is being framed and interpreted by the media and those who stand to benefit financially. As James Kent (2022b) observes, the media's rush to uncritically report any news that supports the ongoing narrative of the psychedelic renaissance is "creeping uncomfortably close to pro-psychedelic propaganda."

Prominent members of the psychedelic community, like Paul Austin, have a responsibility not to distort this research, especially when their platforms (*Third Wave*) are offering expensive microdosing courses and personalized coaching sessions that promise to "create meaningful life changes," "heal emotional wounds" and "naturally reduce symptoms of anxiety and depression."

In spite of these tensions, the appeal of microdosing continues to grow. Part of the reason is that it is being marketed as a catalyst for better work performance, is well suited to monetization, and more closely aligns with the interests of the pharmaceutical and wellness industries than PAP. Within psychedelic circles, one can find a plethora of voices calling for psychedelics to be marketed as enhancers of creativity, productivity and mood — the next smart drug to boost individualistic pursuits and workplace performance — but few who question the sociopolitical reasons why people might feel understimulated, uninspired and unhappy with their work and lives to begin with.

Don't Believe the Hype?

The surge of positivity around microdosing is but one example of the hype permeating the psychedelic renaissance. Researchers at Johns Hopkins have cautioned that psychedelics are trapped in a hype bubble, which they contend has been driven by media and corporate interests (Yaden, Potash and Griffiths 2022). As psychologist Eiko Fried points out, most media commentators find it "much sexier" to write about the wonders of a miracle drug rather than critically evaluate the boring minutiae of how these drugs may or may not work (cited in MacBride 2023). The corporadelic hype is also not surprising as there are large financial interests at stake. Psychedelic pharmaceutical companies have been "snapping up ailments like hungry hypochondriac hippos" to hedge their bets around possible medical breakthroughs (Siskind 2022). In the process, they are marketing miracle cures and overstating tenuous results from small-scale studies. Even some psychedelic capitalists admit the pendulum has swung too far, such as George Goldsmith, co-founder of Compass Pathways, who says there is "way too much hype, way too much enthusiasm" around psychedelic medicine, a trend that "doesn't help anyone" (cited in Collis 2022).

While some are questioning these media claims, others are drawing on them to bolster public relations and generate excitement among potential investors. In return, the media has been amplifying corporate press releases and framing them as legitimate news stories (Nickles 2020a). As well, most psychedelic media companies (such as Microdose and Psychedelic Invest) are at least partially owned by psychedelic investment firms who stand to benefit when the line between sponsored hype and legitimate news is murky (Evans 2023c). Yet, it is not just the media and corporations that are fueling the hype train. Psychedelic scientists and researchers — who are sometimes in the position of conducting objective research while simultaneously advocating for the legitimacy of the field — are also subject to this criticism.

A few years ago, for example, Ben Sessa, then chief medical officer of Awakn Life Sciences (acquired by Cybin in 2023), misrepresented the results of a small, fourteen-person Phase 2 study of MDMA for alcohol use disorder. These data were collected by researchers at Imperial College London and later acquired by Awakn. When confronted about his statements and presentation of the data, Sessa admitted they were "a bit hyped" as well as highly misleading from a scientific perspective. "But it looks good on twitter" he added (see Hausfeld 2022d). Another example involves one of the trials discussed previously that compared psilocybin and escitalopram for the treatment of depression. Based on pre-defined outcome measures, the results showed no statistically significant differences in efficacy. Although secondary outcome measures appeared to favour psilocybin, the design of the study was such that no firm conclusions could be drawn. Nevertheless, the lead investigator, Robin Carhart-Harris (2021), suggested in *The Guardian* that psilocybin had been proven to be more efficacious.

"I'd like psychedelics to work out," says bioethicist Emma Tumilty, "the idea that there might be something really effective for intractable depression or PTSD is amazing." In Tumilty's view, however, one of the biggest threats to psychedelics "working out" is precisely this pattern of presenting research results in misleading or overhyped ways (cited in Hausfeld 2022d). We have seen this pattern before. The first round of SSRIs was also widely touted as a magic bullet in the mental health field, and the enthusiasm of researchers at the time was almost on par with the optimism we see among many psychedelic researchers today.

To their credit, some psychedelic researchers acknowledge the hype and their role in it. In 2017, Dr. Rosalind Watts gave a TEDx talk on the promise of psilocybin to treat depression, noting that psilocybin had the potential to "revolutionize" mental healthcare. Five years later, Watts expressed regret about her initial unchecked enthusiasm:

> I can't help but feel as if I unknowingly contributed to a simplistic and potentially dangerous narrative around psychedelics; a narrative I'm trying to correct ... So much of my exuberance on that TEDx stage, extolling the powers of psilocybin, was intended to counter a naysaying world which might never allow its true potential to be explored, because of misinformation and misplaced stigma. Little was I to know that my own optimism might prove to become part of the problem rather than the solution. (Watts 2022)

Over the last few years, much of Watts' work has involved establishing support systems and integration services for people who are struggling to cope with the aftermath of their psychedelic experiences.

In addition to bias introduced by researchers and companies having a stake in positive outcomes, most clinical trials have a risk of bias inherent in their methodology, as discussed above (Hovmand et al. 2023; Muthukumaraswamy, Forsyth and Lumley 2021). Like in other areas of medicine (Kirsch and Sapirstein 1999), the importance of the placebo effect in psychedelic research is likely underestimated. According to psychologist Irving Kirsch (2014), associate director of the Program in Placebo Studies and Therapeutic Encounter at Harvard Medical School, analyses of published data and unpublished data hidden by drug companies reveal that the benefits of traditional antidepressants are mainly due to the placebo effect.

To illustrate how powerful the placebo effect can be, in one experiment subjects were given a placebo pill that they were told was a psychedelic and the experiment was designed to maximize their expectations of having a psychedelic experience (Olson et al. 2020). Most participants (61 percent) claimed they experienced psychoactive effects, with some reporting experiences that would be consistent with a high-dose psychedelic trip. In a therapeutic context where psychedelics are actually administered, the interrelated elements of expectation, context and mindset may be an especially powerful combination. Accordingly, some have described psychedelics as "super-placebos" or "placebos on rocket boosters" (e.g., Strassman 2017). When problems of blinding are layered onto substances already sensitive to set and setting, the confounding effects on research outcomes are potentially enormous.

Similar to some microdosing advocates, some medicalization advocates do not think it matters if treatment outcomes are a result of the placebo effect so long as people are benefiting. Speaking at the Psychedelic Science conference in 2023, Ronan Levy, co-founder of Field Trip Health, stated, "almost all of the effect of psychedelic-assisted therapy could be placebo ... Personally I don't have a problem with that. The outcomes are the outcomes, and that's really what matters in my view" (cited in Goldhill 2023). This would make Field Trip Health's $9,255 "Discovery Plus" ketamine-assisted therapy package at their Toronto clinic a very expensive placebo-based treatment. While Levy and others may believe that heightened expectations will enhance whatever placebo-related impacts are responsible for positive outcomes, not everyone has such an experience. Patients who do not respond well to PAP may blame themselves for failure in the face of treatments imbued with so much promise, leading to worse outcomes for treatment-resistant populations. There is also a tendency to blame those who have had negative therapeutic encounters for failing to process or learn from their "challenging experiences." As part of this process, the risks associated with PAP are often downplayed. As the field advances, promoters of psychedelic treatments should be mindful of how they are presenting research results and the potential of these drugs, especially to vulnerable populations who are desperate to find treatments that work. Hyping psychedelic medicines as "cures" or a one-and-done approach to healing is virtually guaranteed to overpromise and underdeliver.

It is possible to be both pro-psychedelic and anti-hype. The psychedelic nature of an enterprise should not be a shield to criticism, just as being devoted to the psychedelic cause is not an excuse to misconstrue research results or make dubious promises. On a positive note, more critical discussions are starting to emerge. A growing number of voices are demanding a more cautious approach to psychedelic discourse, research and therapy. These demands were evident in 2024 when researchers and other concerned citizens pushed back against what they saw as serious research and ethical misconduct in the field of psychedelic medicine.

The FDA Rejects MDMA-Assisted Therapy

In August 2024, the FDA rejected Lykos Therapeutics' new drug application for MDMA-assisted therapy to treat PTSD. While the news came as a shock to many psychedelic advocates, the decision did not happen in a vacuum. In the months leading up to the FDA decision, the data submitted by MAPS/Lykos faced several important tests. The first was in March 2024, when the Institute for Clinical and Economic Review (ICER) — a non-profit organization that evaluates drug costs and clinical trials — released a draft report evaluating the Phase 3 MDMA trials. In its report, ICER acknowledged that MDMA could be an "important addition to treatment options for PTSD." However, it also highlighted a range of concerns. These included functional unblinding and expectancy bias (96 percent and 94 percent of those who received MDMA correctly guessed they were in the treatment arm); ethical and safety violations, including sexual misconduct and pressure on participants to report favourable outcomes; the underreporting of adverse events; problems with the consistency/standardization of psychotherapy protocols; and the possibility that "strong prior beliefs" on the part of researchers and therapists may have biased the results. Overall, ICER concluded there were "substantial concerns about the validity of the results" and that the evidence was insufficient to determine clinical effectiveness (ICER 2024).

The ICER report was followed in April 2024 by a citizen petition to the FDA, submitted by members of Psymposia and other researchers, calling for an advisory meeting on the drug application. The petition reaffirmed many of the issues raised by the ICER report. In June 2024, the FDA convened an advisory committee of independent experts to review the evidence and make a recommendation to the agency. During the hearing, the advisory committee heard testimony from advocates who spoke in favour of the treatment, including veterans, some of whom stated that MDMA-assisted therapy had saved their lives. The committee also heard from more critical voices, such as the ICER, members of Psymposia and other independent investigators. The advisory committee acknowledged that the published data and positive testimonials were compelling. However, they also expressed concerns about the impartiality of therapists and facilitators and how they may have influenced patient outcomes. One former trial participant, Sarah McNamee, told the committee that her therapists suggested she was "helping make history" and was "part of a movement" (Goldhill 2024). McNamee also claimed she was told that her response to the treatment could have implications for FDA approval. Further, the committee reported that another potential source of bias was that 40 percent of trial participants had taken MDMA before (in many pharmacological trials, people with prior exposure are excluded from participation). The panelists also noted that adverse events were likely underreported and that reports of sexual misconduct may be connected to the therapeutic philosophy of MAPS. In the end, nine of the eleven committee members voted that the effectiveness of MDMA-assisted therapy had not been demonstrated, while ten of the eleven voted that the risks outweighed the benefits. Rajesh Narendran, chair of the committee, went so far as to describe the trial data as "meaningless" (Lhooq 2024).

Many had a strong response to the advisory committee decision. Some commentators, such as psychedelic researcher David Yaden, suggested it could have positive implications moving forward: "My hope is that we will start to get a more balanced and nuanced picture of the real risks and benefits of psychedelics ... Maybe the committee hearings will help adjust some people's understanding of the state of the evidence" (cited in Gilbert and Ovalle 2024). Others, however, drew a very different conclusion. MAPS reportedly hired four public relations firms to lobby the FDA and attack the credibility of those who objected to the application. According to Jules Evans (2024a), this campaign included efforts to "rally the veterans, emphasize how many veterans commit suicide every day, and thereby imply that anyone who opposes the legalization of MDMA has blood on their hands." Some veteran groups took up the call, including Heroic Hearts, who wrote an open letter attacking ICER for being in bed with Big Pharma and Psymposia for having an agenda against the military. The letter included a personal attack on Psymposia member Neşe Devenot, who was accused of contributing to "hateful, anti-veteran rhetoric." Although Heroic Hearts eventually retracted this statement, it was not before Devenot received a stream of threatening messages that caused her to fear for her own safety and that of her family. Republican member of Congress Dan Crenshaw also made a video attacking members of ICER and Psymposia, which was recklessly re-tweeted by Elon Musk to his over 200 million followers.

The central claim of these critics was that the interventions by ICER, Psymposia and other detractors were pursued in bad faith and led to the advisory committee's rejection. This perspective ignores the fact that the FDA itself had expressed concerns about the trials long before it made its final decision. As *Psychedelic Alpha* founder and editor Josh Hardman (2024b) points out, "If your drug development process has been entirely derailed by a small, poorly funded group of individuals, you really have to ask yourself whether that's the truth or whether you're looking for a scapegoat ... I agree that the issues unearthed by Psymposia et al. are attractive to journalists and other media folks who look for shock factor stories ... But they're also *true*, at least the most well-publicised incidents" (emphasis in original). A more accurate interpretation would be that these interventions by Psymposia and others represented a principled stance. They were concerned about the direction of the field and the potential harms to vulnerable populations. Indeed, some of the people who spoke out had been harmed themselves during the trials.

The details of the final FDA rejection in August were never made public. However, according to Lykos, the issues raised by the FDA in its response letter echoed those raised by the advisory committee in June. Not only that, but the agency requested an additional Phase 3 study to further test the safety and efficacy of the treatment. It is worth noting that the FDA decision was not so much a rejection of MDMA or MDMA-assisted therapy as it was a statement on the quality of the MAPS/Lykos application. According to journalist Olivia Goldhill (2024), the hype surrounding MDMA and the "evangelist culture" inside MAPS/Lykos regarding its benefits contributed to ethical violations and interfered with rigorous science. It also allowed evidence of harm to go unchallenged. In the long run, the FDA rejection might provide a much-needed course correction for the field, where researchers take issues of ethics, safety and adverse events in psychedelic-assisted therapy more seriously.

SAFETY AND RISKS

Describing the safety and risks of psychedelics is a balancing act. On the one hand, most psychedelics are relatively safe compared with other legal and illegal drugs, and classical psychedelics are among the safest recreational drugs in the world. At the risk of promoting psychedelic exceptionalism, it is important to acknowledge that the safety profiles of most of these compounds contrast sharply with the myths and misconceptions surrounding them. On the other hand, all psychedelics pose some degree of risk and there are indisputable incidences of harm that need to be acknowledged. Some of these risks are being downplayed or ignored by individuals and institutions with a financial and/or professional stake in the psychedelic renaissance.

Ranking of Harms

Before it became controversial in the late 1960s, LSD was the subject of glowing media publicity in mainstream media outlets, such as *Time* and *Life* magazines (Siff 2019). By the late 1960s, however, the coverage shifted to sensationalistic horror stories. LSD became associated with acute insanity (it will cause you to jump out of a tenth-storey window, for example), tumors and leukemia. One of the most widely publicized scares was that LSD caused chromosomal abnormalities, a conclusion that even found its way into mainstream scientific journals (e.g., Cohen, Marinello and Back 1967). While these findings have since been disproven, this coverage affected the trajectory of LSD research (Dahlberg, Mechaneck and Feldstein 1968) and gave credence to a quote commonly attributed to Timothy Leary: "LSD is a psychedelic drug which occasionally causes psychotic behavior in people who have not taken it." Another psychedelic that received widespread negative attention in subsequent decades was MDMA. The media, along with some prominent scientists and the National Institute on Drug Abuse, popularized the narrative that MDMA was a neurotoxin, causing holes in the brain and potentially Parkinson's disease, which is ironic given that MDMA is now being investigated as a treatment for Parkinson's (Jay 2024). In one of neuroscientist George Ricaurte's clinical studies in the early 2000s involving primates, he concluded that recreational doses of MDMA were highly toxic and resulted in permanent brain damage. But there was a catch: the animals had been given methamphetamine, not MDMA. While the journal in which it was published eventually issued a retraction, the reputational damage was done (Barnett and Doblin 2021).

Decades of misinformation about psychedelics have also had an impact on public perceptions as well as the attitudes of mental health professionals. This is in spite of the fact that comparative epidemiological research strongly suggests that classical psychedelics tend to be safer than most other legal and illegal drugs in terms of both physiological toxicity and the risk of dependence (Anthony, Warner and Kessler 1994). In 1958, Dr. Maurice Seevers published addiction liability ratings for a range of drugs, taking into account their ability to produce tolerance, anti-social behaviour, physical deterioration and emotional and physical dependence, along a 24-point scale. Alcohol had the highest score (21 points) while peyote had the lowest (1 point) (Courtwright 2001). In 2006, psychologist Robert Gable conducted a comparative review of psychoactive substances. He found intravenous heroin to be the most dangerous drug as measured by its dependence potential and physiological toxicity. In contrast, psilocybin and LSD were found to have the lowest dependence potential and least acute physiological toxicity (less addictive and toxic than caffeine, for example) (Gable 2006). More recent studies of classical psychedelics also suggest a very low potential for physical dependency, and that they may even have anti-addictive properties (Dinis-Oliveira et al. 2019; Heal, Gosden and Smith 2018; Johnson et al. 2018; Kyzar et al. 2017).

When considering physiological toxicity in isolation, classical psychedelics like psilocybin, LSD and DMT are highly unusual in their safety profiles. According to researcher Matthew Johnson, these substances have "no known lethal overdose. No dose at which there's any observable organ damage, not even a potential mechanism for neurotoxicity … You'd be hard pressed to find anything sold over the counter at CVS, Walgreens that you could say this about" (cited in Ferriss 2019). The fact that common substances like caffeine, aspirin and Tylenol are all more dangerous to the human body than classical psychedelics is striking. Each year, for example, hundreds of Americans die from acetaminophen alone, Tylenol's active ingredient (Schonfeld 2013). Even if one tried, it would be very difficult to die from an overdose of psilocybin or LSD (Hunt 2020; Nichols and Grob 2018).

Neuropsychopharmacologist David Nutt's work has been influential in explaining the comparative risk profiles of psychedelics. Nutt is the former chair of the British Advisory Council on the Misuse of Drugs and author of the bestselling book *Drugs Without the Hot Air* (2012). Part of his responsibilities as Britain's "drug czar" was to assess and rank the harms of various substances. At one point during his tenure, Nutt infuriated the British establishment by claiming (based on epidemiological risk profiles of mortality) that horseback riding was more dangerous than taking MDMA, a drug that was under intense scrutiny at the time. He was fired shortly thereafter.

In 2010, Nutt and his colleagues assessed twenty commonly used psychoactive substances in the UK for different categories of potential harm using multi-criterion decision analysis, a data-driven comparative method that brings together experts from different fields (Nutt, King and Phillips 2010). The assessment included physical, psychological and social impacts of drug consumption, taking into account both harms to users and harms to others (such as family, community and society). Published in *The Lancet*, the results showed that MDMA, LSD and psilocybin mushrooms ranked 17th, 18th and 20th respectively. Alcohol was ranked as the most harmful substance, largely because of its deleterious social impacts, followed by heroin and crack cocaine. Similar analyses (also co-authored by Nutt) conducted in Australia, New Zealand and the European Union led to similar conclusions; alcohol was found to be the most harmful substance while psychedelics ranked near the bottom (Bonomo et al. 2019; Crossin et al. 2023; van Amsterdam et al. 2015). Although none of these studies focused on DMT in their rankings, it is interesting to note that many psychedelic users rank DMT as having the lowest risk of harm compared with other psychedelics (e.g., Winstock, Kaar and Borschmann 2014). As Terence McKenna once suggested, the biggest risk of consuming DMT is "death by astonishment."

Nutt is not without his critics. Some drug experts claim that his risk assessments do not employ standard epidemiologic approaches for assessing population harms. Others suggest they do not accurately account for the prevalence of use (that is, alcohol causes more harm because it is more commonly used). While there may be some truth to this claim, much of this criticism comes from alcohol lobbyists and trade groups and does not change the fact that alcohol consumption contributes to three million deaths a year on average, at least according to the World Health Organization (2022c). Criticism of Nutt has also come from the fact that his organization, Drug Science, purports to be free from commercial influence, yet Nutt himself has occupied positions on the advisory boards of several psychedelic companies, including Compass Pathways, Awakn Life Sciences, Psyched Wellness and Algernon Pharmaceuticals. In this context, he has made public statements about clinical safety that appear to be contradicted by the available evidence (see Evans 2023d).

There is sufficient evidence to conclude that classical psychedelics are relatively safe compared to most other commonly used legal and illegal substances at a population level. While public perceptions may be changing in line with this evidence (Roberts et al. 2020), mental health professionals and governments seem to be lagging. Many US psychologists, for example, tend to judge psychedelics to be comparable to alcohol in terms of safety and less safe than opioids (Davis et al. 2022). Moreover, federal drug classifications of psychedelics in both the US and Canada remain incongruous with the evidence on problematic use, which has hampered research and treatment innovation (Nutt, King and Nichols 2013). The same is true at the international level, where most psychedelics continue to be stigmatized as dangerous and harmful under UN drug control conventions. According to Ruth Dreifuss, former chair of the Global Commission on Drug Policy, global drug scheduling is influenced by "ideology, prejudice and the discrimination of marginalized populations" as well as the financial interests of the pharmaceutical industry. Science is rarely part of the decision-making process, she says, and the recommendations of the scientific community are rarely taken into account (Global Commission on Drug Policy 2019, 3). Similar criticisms have been levelled against the International Narcotics Control Board, the independent body responsible for monitoring the control of substances pursuant to UN drug control conventions (Tupper and Labate 2012).

Not only are there significant differences between psychedelics and other drugs in terms of their comparative risk profiles, but there are important differences between psychedelics themselves. Physiologically, classical psychedelics are the safest, though they are not risk free. Substances like LSD, mescaline, DMT and ayahuasca can cause physiological changes such as increased blood pressure, heart rate and body temperature, which could have health implications, especially for older adults. Given limited research, however, little is known about the precise effects of psychedelics on this segment of the population (Bouchet et al. 2024; Johnston et al. 2023). As well, classical psychedelics have never been formally assessed for cardiovascular safety, but some researchers warn of possible heart risks (McClure-Begley and Roth 2022; Rouaud, Calder and Hasler 2024). These risks might have been at play in the death of 74-year-old California lawyer Richard Burton, whose heart stopped after ingesting a large dose of psilocybin mushrooms in 2018, though no causation was established (Ross and Nickles 2022a). The psychological risks of classical psychedelics, however, can be considerable, especially for people with certain mental illnesses or those at risk for these afflictions (which is why they are screened out of most clinical trials). Although classical psychedelics are not found to cause physical dependency, any mind-altering substance can lead to psychological dependence.

Other psychedelics present somewhat greater dangers. MDMA can cause dehydration and significantly increase body temperature, which has been linked to deaths from heatstroke at raves and other venues

(Saunders and Doblin 1996). Non-pharmaceutical MDMA also has more issues with purity/adulterants than other psychedelics and pairing it with other substances such as alcohol can increase the risks (Furminger 2022). MDMA can also negatively impact the serotonin system at high doses and frequencies of use, and some studies suggest possible deficits in neurocognitive functioning with repeated use, though others have found little difference between users and non-users (Halpern et al. 2011; Siebert 2022; Taurah, Chandler and Sanders 2014). There is still no clear evidence for neurotoxic effects at normal doses.

Ibogaine and ketamine are the two commonly used psychedelics that arguably present the greatest dangers. Chemist Sasha Shulgin once described ibogaine as a "rough trip," physically as well as mentally. There are acute risks associated with ibogaine use, most notably cardiovascular risks. Ibogaine use in the West presents a highly divergent range of outcomes, from people who insist it saved their lives by immediately alleviating their opioid withdrawal symptoms to those who died after ingesting it, usually in settings without medical screening/monitoring or advanced cardiac life support capabilities. Individuals with pre-existing heart conditions and other comorbidities who consume ibogaine in unsafe environments or who combine it with other drugs are at higher risk of adverse reactions (Alper, Stajić and Gill 2012; Koenig and Hilber 2015; Luz and Mash 2021; Noller, Frampton and Yazar-Klosinski 2018; Ona et al. 2022). These risks have increased with the proliferation of pop-up clinics, in Mexico and elsewhere, run by non-specialists looking to capitalize on psychedelic hype. At the same time, some point to the risks of *not* using ibogaine as a treatment in the context of the opioid crisis (May 2017c). However, Jonathan Dickinson, former director of the Global Ibogaine Therapy Alliance, and drug activist Dimitri Mugianis urge caution with respect to ibogaine's role as an addiction treatment. They say there is little evidence that ibogaine leads to long-term abstinence; rather, it primarily plays a "detox" role, which leads to reduced tolerance and therefore an increased risk of death when people use again (Dickinson and Mugianis 2020).

Finally, the risks of ketamine appear to be significantly higher than other psychedelics, with the long-term effects potentially being irreversible. According to Dr. Celia Morgan, professor of psychopharmacology at the University of Exeter, "I've spent quite a bit of my career researching people who struggle with using too much ketamine, and while it's not a big proportion of people, for the people it does effect, it's really serious" (cited in Siebert 2022). Dr. Morgan identifies urinary and bladder damage — sometimes referred to as "ketamine bladder" — as one of the greatest physiological dangers (see also Li et al. 2019; Ma and Chu 2015). Long-term ketamine use may also have neurological and mental health risks (e.g., Fan et al. 2016; Hodgman-Korth 2023; Strous et al. 2022). Long-term use is common because ketamine can lead to serious psychological dependence and addiction (Guzman 2021; Jansen 2004; McConnell 2022). The risks presented by ketamine use can be reduced in clinical settings where dosing is controlled and patients are screened for certain risk factors. Yet, many for-profit ketamine clinics have few controls in place and are neglecting patient safety. As Dr. Morgan states, "I've spoken to people who run ketamine clinics in Canada who confidently tell me that ketamine addiction 'isn't a thing' and they've 'looked at it.' It is definitely a thing, and people are minimizing the risks for corporate gain" (cited in Cormier 2022). Coverage of these risks in the mainstream media has not helped. When actor Matthew Perry died in late 2023 from the "acute effects of ketamine" and a subsequent drowning, the media largely parroted the industry's claim that the drug is safe. On the issue of ketamine's addictiveness, the media was silent (Evans 2023e). Criminal charges have now been brought against some of the individuals who supplied the actor with ketamine, who US prosecutors say was exploited for profit.

Bad Trips and "Challenging Experiences"

Outside of at-risk groups, the use of classical psychedelics is not generally associated with adverse mental health outcomes at a population level. One 2013 study analyzed data from over 130,000 individuals, nearly 22,000 of whom reported at least one experience with LSD, psilocybin or mescaline (Krebs and Johansen 2013). The researchers found no significant association between the use of these substances and mental health problems, such as psychological distress, major depression, general anxiety disorder or psychosis. Interestingly, psychedelic users were found to be at lower risk for some of these ailments (see also Johansen and Krebs 2015). Other studies, in both clinical and non-clinical settings, have similarly found that the use of classical psychedelics is not widely associated with short- or long-term adverse effects, with some pointing to lower levels of psychological distress and impairment among users (e.g., Dos

Santos et al. 2016; Halpern et al. 2005; Hendricks et al. 2015; Holze et al. 2022; Kopra et al. 2022; Schlag et al. 2022; Studerus et al. 2011).

That said, the psychological risks of psychedelic consumption can be serious. A "bad trip" is an unpleasant experience caused by mind-altering drugs. Within the field of psychedelics, the term bad trip is often used synonymously with "challenging experience." Bad trips are often characterized by intense fear, anxiety, paranoia, grief, despair and feelings of existential isolation. Much like "good trips," these experiences can affect people for weeks, months or even years afterward. Such trips are typically influenced by dose as well as set and setting. They are also relatively common. The first documented bad trip on LSD involved Albert Hofmann, the chemist who discovered the drug. In his recounting, the experience included a demon taking possession of his mind and his neighbour transforming into a malevolent witch (Hofmann 1980). In the late 1960s, one survey found that nearly 50 percent of LSD users reported having at least one bad trip. As Martin Lee and Bruce Shlain (1985, 156) point out, this high percentage was partly a consequence of a hostile set and setting, which included increased police repression and the "widespread anxiety that ensued after LSD was declared illegal." By the mid-1970s, however, this "emotionally charged atmosphere had subsided, and the percentage of bad trips dropped accordingly." Even highly experienced users are not immune to bad trips. Psychedelic guru Terence McKenna reportedly had a psilocybin mushroom trip that was so harrowing it led to an existential crisis (McKenna 2012).

People often rate their psychedelic experiences as among the most positive and meaningful of their lives. But when things go wrong, they can also be among the most difficult. One survey asked nearly 2,000 individuals who had at least one bad trip with psilocybin about their most challenging experience (or worst bad trip). Thirty-nine percent rated it as among the five most challenging experiences of their lifetimes, and 11 percent reported putting themselves or others at some risk (Carbonaro et al. 2016). Of those participants whose trip occurred at least one year before the survey, 10 percent reported negative symptoms lasting a year or more, and 7.6 percent sought professional treatment for enduring symptoms.

Some research has explored the duration and impacts of bad trips. In a global survey of nearly 11,000 ayahuasca users, 12 percent of the respondents who experienced adverse mental health effects said they sought out professional support (Bouso et al. 2022). In a US survey of 613 people who reported lifetime use of classical psychedelics, 2.6 percent reported seeking medical, psychological or psychiatric assistance in the days or weeks following their most distressing psychedelic experience (Simonsson et al. 2023). Another global survey of 608 people who reported extended difficulties following a psychedelic trip found that one-third experienced difficulties lasting longer than a year and one-sixth reported difficulties lasting longer than three years (Evans et al. 2023). One of the most commonly reported post-trip difficulties is "existential confusion," where a person's previous model of reality is so disrupted that it impacts their day-to-day functioning. Another is "derealization" — the perception that one is in a dream-like state where normal thoughts and feelings seem unreal. Jules Evans, director of the Challenging Psychedelic Experiences Project, speculates that off-duty pilot Joseph Emerson's attempts to cut the engines of a plane in-flight to San Francisco in October 2023 may have resulted from psychedelic-induced derealization (MacBride 2023). There is also a condition known as "hallucinogen persisting perception disorder" where people can experience persisting perceptual abnormalities lasting months or even years after taking psychedelics (Halpern and Pope 2003; Prideaux 2023a). However, the condition is not well understood and is not exclusively linked to psychedelic use.

While the fact that one can have a bad trip is well known, so too is the idea that these trips can have positive benefits. By the middle of the twentieth century, many psychedelic therapists argued that negative experiences were psychologically meaningful and potentially therapeutic (Walsh and Grob 2006). Today's researchers have also found that negative trips are often associated with increases in reported well-being (e.g., Barrett et al. 2016; Gashi, Sandberg and Pedersen 2020). In one study, 67 percent of respondents regarded the long-term consequences of their worst psychedelic trip to be either positive or mostly positive, whereas only 4 percent reported the long-term consequences to be negative (Johnstad 2021). In a survey of ayahuasca users from more than fifty countries, 88 percent of those who experienced adverse mental health effects in the weeks or months following consumption considered such effects to be part of a positive process of growth or integration (Bouso et al. 2022). According to the Canadian Psychedelic Survey, more than half of respondents who experienced an intensely challenging psychedelic experience reported that "at least some good" came from it, such as overcoming personal fears, addressing longstanding trauma or being able to resolve a challenging situation or emotion (Lake and Lucas 2023). In this way, psychedelics are the opposite of most other drugs; they can make you feel worse when you take them and better when the experience is over.

In a therapeutic context, it is not difficult to see how working through or confronting negative or traumatic emotions might lead to emotional breakthroughs or insights that prove to be beneficial over time. On the other hand, some proponents take this line of reasoning too far, refusing to acknowledge that bad trips can cause serious psychological damage. Some suggest that bad trips do not really exist, only challenging reactions to the lessons that plant medicines are trying to impart (that is, you get the trip you need, not the one you want). Another version of this argument holds that bad trips are the best trips, a position that reflects dogmatic assumptions about the nature of psychedelic healing. It follows that there is a tendency among some advocates to question or even blame individuals who do not respond well to psychedelics. This amounts to "psychedelic gaslighting" — if you had a negative experience, it is because you did not work hard enough, did not "give in" to the experience or did not heed the medicine's wisdom.

When adverse events do occur in the course of psychedelic research, there is also a tendency to rationalize them as not being related to the drug (whereas positive benefits are almost always attributed, at least in part, to the drug). For example, in Compass Pathways' Phase 2B trial of psilocybin for treatment-resistant depression, twelve patients reported serious treatment-emergent adverse events, including suicidal ideation, suicidal behaviour and intentional self-injury. Eleven of these events occurred with patients in the medium- or high-dose psilocybin groups and only one in the placebo group. The company responded by downplaying the possibility of a causal relationship and attributing the results to the specific nature of the condition being treated. It may be the case that suicidal ideation got worse for some participants because of unmet expectations, which could have exacerbated feelings of hopelessness and despair. Or, according to David Nutt, a member of Compass Pathways' scientific advisory board at the time, the incidents of increased suicidality could have been "random events and unrelated to the dose of psilocybin, which would have been fully cleared from the patient's bodies" (cited in

Sample 2022). These conclusions are speculative given that psychedelics can set in motion adverse processes that only emerge weeks or months after the initial session (Breeksema et al. 2022). Not only that, but at least one participant in the trial stated that her post-trip suicidality was directly connected to the psychedelic experience (Evans 2024b). Although she came through it and said she would like to try psilocybin therapy again, she was unhappy with how the company minimized her experience and was disappointed by Nutt's comments on the matter.

There is also evidence that adverse events in psychedelic trials are poorly defined, not systematically assessed and almost certainly underreported (Breeksema et al. 2022; van Elk and Fried 2023). In a review of ten clinical trials involving esketamine, a compound derived from ketamine that has been approved for medical use in North America, researchers found that over 40 percent of serious adverse events were omitted from publication (Taillefer de Laportalière et al. 2023). Of the ten clinical trials included in the analysis, nine were classified as "low quality" with respect to safety. Moreover, in Janssen Pharmaceuticals' clinical trial program involving esketamine (Spravato) for treatment-resistant depression, several people committed suicide (including patients who had previously shown no signs of suicidal ideation), but no connections were made to the drug (Beres 2020; Chen et al. 2023). Some clinical trial participants have also spoken out about the fact that their harmful experiences are not being properly reported or reported at all, including in the MAPS/Lykos MDMA-assisted therapy trials (see Ross and Nickles 2022b, 2022c). As noted earlier, evidence that came to light prior to the FDA rejection of MDMA-assisted therapy pointed to the underreporting of adverse events and their omission from the public record.

The underreporting of adverse events (part of confirmation bias) is not unique to psychedelic research. However, there are some unique qualities of psychedelic research that make these problems more acute. The history of stigma around these substances means that psychedelic researchers may be particularly invested in positive outcomes. If they present uneven or negative results, there is a risk that funding could again become restricted, and the medicalization work underway will be derailed. Moreover, many leading trials are sponsored and run by companies that stand to profit from psychedelic therapy, while others are sponsored by advocates and philanthropists who are emotionally and spiritually invested in psychedelics. Finally, as noted earlier, adverse events are often seen as "part of the process" of psychedelic therapy, effectively normalizing them as a key element of healing. Overall, a survey of the popular and clinical literature suggests that researchers, medical professionals and companies involved in psychedelics do not take patient safety and the impact of adverse events seriously enough. The distinction between population studies suggesting that psychedelics are relatively safe and clinical trials attempting to demonstrate safety and efficacy in vulnerable populations with serious health issues needs to be made clear. Of the billions of dollars being poured into psychedelic research today, almost none of it is dedicated to understanding and preventing adverse events or supporting people after difficult experiences. These important dimensions of psychedelia remain largely in the hands of overtaxed and underfunded harm reduction communities.

The Issue of Therapist Abuse and Related Risks

At least with classical psychedelics and MDMA, the risks of psychedelic use are less a product of the substances themselves (pharmacology) and more about one's mindset and the environment in which they are taken or administered (set and setting). Many of the harms surrounding psychedelic use are interpersonal. The altered states of consciousness induced by psychedelics can leave people more open and vulnerable to suggestion, manipulation and exploitation at the hands of predatory individuals or groups. PAP also provides a unique set of ethical and safety concerns due to the profound changes in identity and beliefs that can accompany a psychedelic experience, as well as the highly vulnerable and suggestible state of subject participants (Dupuis and Veissière 2022). As well, the psychotherapy component of PAP is largely unregulated and neither the FDA nor Health Canada have issued definitive statements as to how this might be done. As a result, some researchers are calling for an enhanced informed consent process for PAP, one that is more comprehensive than is typically required for other psychiatric interventions (Smith and Sisti 2021; Villiger and Trachsel 2023).

In PAP, the power imbalances between subject and therapist — disparities that are amplified by the psychedelic state — can contribute to ethical transgressions and abusive practices. Ethical violations in psychedelic therapy can be traced back to at least the 1950s when UCLA professor Sidney Cohen sounded the alarm that unscrupulous therapists were using LSD to assert power over their clients (Novak 1997). In more recent years, much of the awareness and discussion around these issues was prompted by the podcast *Cover Story: Power Trip*, co-produced by Psymposia and *New York Magazine*. One notable series of incidents involved two MAPS therapists, Donna Dryer and Richard Yensen, who were accused of abusing a clinical trial participant, Meaghan Buisson, at one of the organization's research sites in Vancouver during a Phase 2 MDMA trial (Lindsay 2022; Rosin 2022). Yensen became involved in a sexual relationship with Buisson after the therapy sessions had ended but while she was still part of the trial. Although the original incident occurred in 2015, it was not until Buisson obtained a copy of the video footage of her sessions as a result of a police investigation that the story came to light years later. These exposures led Health Canada to conduct a review of all clinical trials involving MDMA, and they were also a factor in the retraction notices issued by the journal *Psychopharmacology* in 2024. While the therapists involved were eventually condemned for their actions, the events highlighted serious concerns with PAP, including "overly flexible therapy protocols, use of unevaluated and controversial practices, increased suggestibility, vulnerability to abuse, and failures in oversight and regulatory mechanisms" (McNamee, Devenot and Buisson 2023, 412).

Incidents of abuse involving MDMA and other psychedelics have also been documented in underground settings, problems that are made worse by prohibition. As drugs reporter Reilly Capps (2022) writes, "accusations of sexual assaults while the client is tripping ripple through the underground community. Cops are almost always excluded, even in extreme scenarios, because the victim doesn't want to admit to illegal activity, so these crimes rarely end in legal consequences. This leaves clients dangerously exposed and deeply damaged." In one survey of over 1,200 individuals who reported past psychedelic use, 8 percent said they or someone they knew had been the victim of inappropriate sexual contact by a psychedelic guide, sitter or practitioner (Kruger et al. 2024). Fifty-one percent of these incidents involved an underground sitter, guide, doctor or therapist, while 21 percent involved a friend or an acquaintance.

The Buisson case was not the first time that allegations of therapist abuse in MDMA-assisted therapy were made public. Such incidents go back decades to the case of psychiatrist Rick Ingrasci, a high-profile psychedelic therapist accused of sexual violence against multiple women in the 1980s (Diesenhouse 1989; Hausfeld 2019). Some claim the Ingrasci case represented a "huge wake-up call" for the field, evidenced by the introduction of protocols involving a male-female co-therapist team (Passie 2018). Yet, others such as counselor and therapist Will Hall (2021a) assert there were no real consequences for Ingrasci with his colleagues, and little effort was made to investigate the problem in a wider context. Hall (2021b) recently came forward with his own story of abuse at the hands of well-known psychedelic therapists, Aharon Grossbard and Francoise Bourzat, and others have made similar accusations against Grossbard (MacBride 2024). Even though the risks of abuse in MDMA-assisted therapy are well known and have even led to changes in MDMA research protocols, in the context of their own work in this area, MAPS researchers did not warn the FDA or study participants about them until after Buisson's allegations became public (Goldhill 2020).

These issues again came to light in 2024 when it was revealed that psychiatrist Ben Sessa, a leading voice in psychedelic medicine, admitted to discharging one of his patients so that he could pursue a sexual relationship with her (Worthington and Lloyd 2024). She later committed suicide. Sessa's medical licence was suspended for one year. While Sessa's treatment of the patient did not involve psychedelics, the case highlighted the power imbalances that continue to exist in the mental health field — problems that can be made more acute by the enhanced vulnerability of patients under the influence of psychedelics.

Unethical behaviour and abuses of power, including inappropriate sexual contact and sexual assault, have also been reported at psychedelic retreat centres outside of North America (e.g., Hausfeld 2021; Maybin and Casserly 2020). Some of these incidents appear to be related to the commercialization of the psychedelic tourism industry, which has attracted a variety of predators, charlatans and corrupt profit seekers who falsely promote themselves as experienced shamans or healers. One of these cases involved Lily Kay Ross, who was sexually assaulted in the Amazon at the hands of a predatory "shaman" (Monroe 2021). When Ross considered going public with her experiences, some of the most respected voices in the psychedelic community discouraged her from doing so, claiming she would be undermining psychedelic medicine and potentially reinvigorating the war on drugs. In her words: "That shit was dark ... I had been deeply hurt, and the response I got was if I told the story of what had happened to me ... I was going to single-handedly destroy the psychedelic renaissance" (cited in Ross and Wright 2021). Employing the well-worn narrative of "challenging experiences," some even suggested her ordeal provided an opportunity for healing and growth. In the end, Ross did choose to share her experiences publicly and subsequently became one of the hosts of *Cover Story: Power Trip*, providing a platform for other victims to speak out.

The response to Ross' case is not atypical. The psychedelic industry and research community have largely been silent on these issues. Referring to Buisson's experience, David Nickles, co-host of *Cover Story: Power Trip*, writes: "I would like anyone considering understudied psychedelic healthcare interventions for themselves or people they love to consider the deafening silence from both researchers and the industry in the wake of such blatant abuse" (cited in Hausfeld 2023a). Ross (2021) echoes Nickles' concerns, noting that while the response to Will Hall's story did lead to some reflection within psychedelic circles, there is still a long way to go: "I have spoken to many victims of practitioners who use psychedelic drugs to manipulate, exploit, and abuse the people who come to them for help. The chorus of their voices tells the story not just of abuse — its contours and implications — but of silencing, and the psychedelic community's collusion in keeping abuse hidden."

As these therapies continue to scale up with multiple approvals on the horizon, an increased supply of and demand for PAP is almost certain. Without open conversations about these issues and adequate protections in place, the risks to potential users will only increase. It is not simply about identifying and removing bad actors but acknowledging the reasons they are being allowed to operate in psychedelic spaces and the ways their actions are incentivized by an emerging field desperate to avoid negative publicity. Currently, one has the impression that victims are being treated as collateral damage in the fight for medicalization.

07

PSYCHEDELIC CAPITALISM

BY SOME ACCOUNTS, A PSYCHEDELIC "GOLD RUSH" IS UNDERWAY. Wealthy entrepreneurs are investing billions into psychedelic companies, biotechnology start-ups are raising capital and running clinical trials on psychedelic medicines and venture capitalists are strategizing about how best to leverage the prospects of a lucrative mass market. At the same time, companies are racing to capture intellectual property to harness profits from existing compounds and erect legal barriers around new chemicals and their applications. In the process, many companies are beginning to employ the same tactics and strategies of traditional pharmaceutical companies. We also see the psychedelic tourism industry expanding and increasingly resembling other for-profit industries catering to elite clients. Ancillary companies and service providers are growing in anticipation of commercialization. Those at the forefront of this psychedelic gold rush are sending a clear message: they want a seat at the table with other cutting-edge industries, as evidenced, for example, by the establishment of the Psychedelic House of Davos hosted in conjunction with the World Economic Forum meetings (Kary 2022). As *Business Insider* columnist Yeji Lee (2023) writes, "from a grassroots field of self-proclaimed psychonauts and off-beat academics to a crowded arena brimming with venture-capital-backed start-ups and the potential for huge riches," we have entered the era of psychedelic capitalism.

The transformation of psychedelic conferences in recent years is an obvious indicator of growing corporate influence (Murphy-Beiner 2020). In the past, these gatherings had a communal ethos rooted in the psychedelic underground and focused on advancing cultural and academic knowledge. Over the past five years, however, audiences have been increasingly curated, with organizers prioritizing speakers with industry ties and objectives tailored to generating business excitement. Those who hold a critical perspective on the emerging industry are increasingly treated as outsiders. For example, members of Psymposia, drug policy activist Yarelix Estrada and independent journalists Alexander Zaitchik and Sasha Sisko and were all banned from attending the 2022 Wonderland conference, a three-day symposium and trade show, in Miami. A description of the event by Dennis Walker (2022), host of the *Mycopreneur* podcast, helps to explain why critics were unwelcome:

> The psychedelic renaissance has entered its corporate trade show phase … Within 20 minutes of arriving on the first day of the conference, I witnessed psychedelic concierge Zappy Zapolin confidently proclaiming that the psychedelics industry is going to be a trillion dollar market and that we should be healing the world by introducing more celebrities to ketamine … Wonderland is a psychedelics industry event on steroids … Titans of industry and billionaires like Atai Life Sciences founder Christian Angermayer, Godaddy.com founder Bob Parsons, and crypto king Brock Pierce took the stage to share their insights and experiences as psychedelic therapy advocates, which includes elevated set and setting on yachts and private jets … The reality of the 'psychedelic renaissance' is more accurately and unabashedly expressed at Wonderland than anywhere else I've been.

The emergence of psychedelic capitalism has led to bitter divisions in the field. Some psychedelic advocates have argued that there is no choice but to work within a commercial, for-profit model to complete clinical trials, leverage capital to expand therapeutic infrastructure and achieve economies of scale (Paleos 2018). "Capitalism is a good way to scale things up," Michael Pollan remarked at a 2018 psychedelic conference, adding that greed is a powerful force for getting things done (Horizons 2018). In contrast to Pollan's stance, David Nickles (2018a) countered that Pollan was overlooking the risks. For Nickles, capitalism is a great way to scale, only if you "ignore its 'externalities' and don't care about the 'systemic risk' and disasters such externalities create, such as the 2008 global financial crisis or turning the planet into a smoldering wasteland." In an interview with *Time* a few years later, Pollan noted that while he remains excited about psychedelic research, he has become wary of the industry: "I'm a little less excited about the gold rush as capital floods into the space … It seems to me there is more capital than there are good ideas — and there are some really bad ideas. There are attempts to grab territory, with the patent law" (cited in Law 2022).

Returning to the importance of set and setting and the context dependency of psychedelics, it is important to consider the wide-ranging impacts of psychedelic capitalism. For one, the focus on market-driven, individualized healthcare solutions and decontextualized pharmaceutical commodities obscures and devalues other perspectives on these substances and will shape how individuals and society understand psychedelic experiences. Ido Hartogsohn (2023, 138) argues that the new "corporadelic landscape, which reflects and maps onto corporate norms of competitiveness, manipulation, and greed, cannot be conducive for the profound states of ego-dissolving healing [psychedelic medicine] purports to produce." For Hartogsohn and other critics, psychedelic capitalism represents a direct challenge to centuries of communal use as well as the values of the counterculture and psychedelic underground, which have long opposed notions of hierarchy, consumerism and commodification in psychedelia and beyond.

Much like other capitalist industries, the foundations of psychedelic capitalism were largely created by public innovation at the public's expense and are now in the process of being handed over to private capital. The uses of psychedelic plants in Indigenous communities led to extensive historical knowledge about these substances, honed over generations. Pioneering research on psychedelics was also funded by public institutions for decades, including universities and non-profit organizations like MAPS, the Heffter Institute and the Beckley Foundation. There is also a rich tradition of open science and praxis in the underground. This tradition is exemplified by organizations like the DMT-Nexus, which developed repositories of cutting-edge, open-source ethnobotanical information, as well as chemist Sasha Shulgin, who synthesized and self-tested hundreds of new psychedelics and together with his wife Ann Shulgin made these findings public (Shulgin and Shulgin 1991, 1997).

These public stewards helped to generate critical information about safety and risks and lay the scientific groundwork for today's applied research endeavours. The actions of psychedelic capitalists are now threatening to appropriate this vast reservoir of knowledge from "six thousand plus years of R&D of Indigenous, mestizo, countercultural, and contemporary psychonautic culture across the planet" (Devenot, Conner and Doyle 2022, 482). Private players are looking to cash in using the familiar playbook — the socialization of risks and privatization of rewards.

THE PSYCHEDELIC INDUSTRY

While it has accelerated in recent years, the move to commercialize psychedelics is not an entirely new development. Peyote, for example, was introduced into pharmaceutical frameworks in the late nineteenth century. Parke-Davis & Company, one of America's oldest drug makers, produced a tincture made from peyote that was marketed to doctors and the public to treat different ailments (Magnuson, Swan and Richert 2023). In the early-to-mid-twentieth century, large pharmaceutical companies like Merck and Sandoz were marketing psilocybin, LSD and mescaline in the hopes of discovering a profitable use for them. In countries like France, different formulations of ibogaine and mescaline were also available as over-the-counter medications, such as Lambarène, an ibogaine product marketed for the treatment of depression and fatigue, and Le Peyotyl R.D., a mescaline product advertised as a natural tonic to address lack of energy as well as "asthenia, depression, migraines, hysteria and irritating cough" (Hardman 2022). At the same time, psychedelic-assisted therapy became a commercial venture for some North American entrepreneurs, who provided LSD therapy to celebrities at places like the Psychiatric Institute of Beverly Hills in California and the Hollywood Hospital in BC.

Today's psychedelic industry is far greater in scale and scope. In 2024, there were roughly one hundred private and publicly traded psychedelic biotechnology companies, most of which are focused on drug development (Psychedelic Alpha 2024b). The first psychedelic pharmaceutical company to be listed on a public stock exchange was Mind Medicine in March 2020. Before the year was out, roughly two dozen other companies had gone public, some of them in deals underwritten by investment banks like Canaccord Genuity and Eight Capital. Between September

2020 and January 2021 alone, just ten new public companies managed to raise over US$370 million in financing, capital inflows that are almost unheard of in a nascent industry. A smaller number of companies, such as PharmaDrug and Red Light Holland, are beginning to target the recreational side of the industry, which barely exists at the time of this writing. In addition, the number of partnership deals involving psychedelic drugs — such as biopharmaceutical companies linking up with research organizations and universities — grew by 500 percent between 2019 and 2023 (GlobalData 2023).

Venture capital firms, such as the Noetic Fund, JLS Fund, Integrated, Iter Investments, Palo Santo and the Conscious Fund, have established a foothold in psychedelics through their investments in early-stage biotech firms as well as psychedelic media organizations and related businesses (CB Insights 2021, Psychedelic Invest 2021a; Taylor and Gormley 2021). Although venture capital drove much of the early investment in psychedelics, it was soon joined by a "curious coterie" of wealthy individuals, such as "WordPress founder Matt Mullenweg, One Direction's Liam Payne, and the DJ and music producer Diplo" (Hardman 2022). Venture capital investment in psychedelic start-ups reached $2 billion in 2021, a figure that fell to $526 million in 2022 amidst challenging economic conditions (Aday et al. 2023). Capital inflows in the psychedelic sector continued to decline significantly in 2023 (Psychedelic Alpha 2024c). However, according to the *Financial Times*, investments in the psychedelics sector picked up again in early 2024, with January being the second-highest month of fundraising ever recorded. The outlet notes that if these medicines are approved, revenues from psychedelic drugs currently under development could skyrocket over the next five years (Kinder and Barnes 2024).

Recent struggles tied to economic instability have tempered some of the excitement around this industry. Short- and long-term growth projections continue to be highly speculative. According to the *Psychedelic Drugs Market Report: Trends, Forecast and Competitive Analysis to 2030*, the psychedelic market could reach US$10.75 billion by 2027 (GlobeNewswire 2021). Market research firm BrandEssence puts this figure at US$11.8 billion by 2029 (Grind and Bindley 2023), while InsightAce Analytic (2023) predicts US$13.3 billion by 2031. Some financial analysts speculate the industry may eventually exceed US$100 billion globally (Psychedelic News Wire 2020).

Are Psychedelics Like the Cannabis Industry?

The legal cannabis industry and the emerging psychedelic industry offer an obvious point of comparison. Cannabis is associated with a wide spectrum of business structures, including medicinal products, cultivation, processing and recreational products and services, whereas the psychedelic industry lacks a sturdy recreational market and is largely aligned with biotech and pharmaceuticals. Moreover, drug development in cannabis has fallen to the wayside in recent years, but the opposite is true for psychedelics, where drug development is following long-established biotech protocols (such as working alongside the DEA) to create commercially viable products. These differences have implications for investors; the clinical nature of psychedelic medicine makes it more akin to investing in pharmaceuticals or the next disruptor of healthcare delivery, which means the risks and rewards are potentially far greater than for cannabis.

These industries do share some important features. Both groups of substances have long been criminalized and stigmatized for political reasons, and the medical/legal justifications for prohibition have been dubious in both cases. Cannabis is now legal in many US states and, in 2018, Canada legalized cannabis at the federal level. Shortly after it was legalized, over one hundred cannabis companies went public and began offering their shares on Canadian stock exchanges. Likewise in the psychedelic sector, a large proportion of public companies have been incorporated in Canada, in part because Canadian exchanges are littered with failed mining companies that are good candidates for reverse takeovers (RTOs). Going public through an RTO is one of the fastest ways to raise capital as it allows instant access to the stock market and comes with fewer regulatory requirements than an initial public offering (IPO). Psychedelic companies like Mind Medicine, Numinus Wellness and Field Trip Health all emerged through RTOs of failed extractivist firms, just as many new cannabis companies followed a similar made-in-Canada approach years earlier. In addition, a considerable number of early-stage psychedelic investors and executives emerged from the cannabis industry. Some of these include Vic Neufeld, co-founder and former CEO of cannabis producer and distributor Aphria, who became director of the (now defunct) psychedelics company HAVN Life Sciences; Terry Booth, founder of Aurora Cannabis, who became chairman of PharmaDrug's advisory board; Ronan Levy, co-founder of Canadian Cannabis Clinics and CanvasRx and senior vice-president at Aurora Cannabis, who later founded Field Trip Health; and Bruce Linton, co-founder and former CEO of cannabis giant Canopy Growth who subsequently assumed positions at both Mind Medicine and Red Light Holland.

As these examples suggest, another similarity between the two industries, and other industries, is the predominance of white men in executive leadership positions. In cannabis companies across Canada, research has found that women and Black and Indigenous people are significantly underrepresented (Browne 2020a; Maghsoudi et al. 2020). Likewise, Black cannabis entrepreneurs in the US account for less than 2 percent of marijuana businesses (Taylor 2022). What makes these disparities especially relevant is that they involve a previously criminalized substance for which people of colour were (and continue to be) disproportionately targeted (Worthy 2021). Evidence suggests these disparities persist in the psychedelic industry, which represents a continuum in psychedelic history that has glorified white male personalities and a white hippie counterculture while downplaying the important contributions of women and visible minorities in the field (Dyck 2018; Mangini 2024). Women and visible minorities have been and continue to be underrepresented in psychedelic businesses, science and research, advocacy, policy debates and psychedelic conferences (Aldworth 2019; George et al. 2020; Gregoire 2020). In this context, Rachel Harris' recent book *Swimming in the Sacred* (2023), which examines the contributions of women guides in the psychedelic underground, is a unique contribution.

A final alignment between the two industries relates to what attorney Nicole Howell (2020) calls an "unhealthy relationship with profit and investment." In the cannabis field, Howell notes that market consolidation and perverse incentive structures are "driving the lovers and believers out of the game only to be replaced by traditional business fundamentals of 'scale,' 'ROI,' and 'exit strategies.' Legacy operators are increasingly replaced with multistate operators, traditional venture capitalists, and Canadian public company management or ownership." Most of the people who have profited from "cannabis capitalism" are not those who risked their freedom during prohibition to push for criminal justice reform (Halperin 2018). Some long-time underground producers and dispensary owners are now lamenting legalization because of their inability to compete with the major corporate players that dominate the market. Similarly in psychedelics, the influence of the "lovers and believers" is being replaced by those who view these substances as the next profit source. The psychedelic pioneers who chose to leverage the forces of free enterprise to bring psychedelics to the mainstream may soon realize if they have not already, that they basically delivered these substances into the waiting arms of big capital.

The Rise and Fall of the Psychedelic Stock Market

The psychedelic industry, like the cannabis industry before it, has been mired in hype and volatility. The first sector-wide market rally occurred in the latter half of 2020, with many stock prices peaking in late 2020 or early 2021. One notable exception was Mind Medicine, which had an extended "bull run" that ended in April 2021 when it was uplisted to the Nasdaq. In September 2020, shares of UK-based Compass Pathways surged over 70 percent on its first day of trading and its market capitalization spiked to US$1 billion. The early price increases of many psychedelic stocks were remarkable: between August and December 2020, for example, Mind Medicine surged by over 900 percent; Numinus Wellness increased by nearly 700 percent; and Red Light Holland grew by over 400 percent. In June 2021, Atai Life Sciences went public and raised US$225 million during its IPO, having already acquired a major investment stake in Compass Pathways and other firms. This success added to its sizeable cash reserves, secured in part from billionaire investors like Peter Thiel, Mike Novogratz and Thor Björgólfsson. At the time, the company had a market capitalization of roughly US$3.2 billion.

The investment frenzy was short-lived. By late 2021, the stock valuations of many companies had plummeted. It was around this time that Compass Pathways released the results of its Phase 2B trial of psilocybin for treatment-resistant depression. Although the results were generally positive and suggested psilocybin may be effective in treating the condition, some participants experienced adverse events during the trial. The fall of the stock may in part be explained by related safety concerns. But it also reflected the activities of market traders who attempted to strategically profit from scheduled news announcements. Compass Pathways' stock price soared in the lead-up to the news release, but many investors had already decided to employ the familiar "buy the rumour, sell the news" strategy, irrespective of trial results. The psychedelic sector would continue its decline in the months and years that followed. By the middle of 2023, many stock valuations, including powerhouse Atai Life Sciences, had declined by as much as 90 percent, while other companies like HAVN and Mind Cure had collapsed. Mind Cure's failure was indicative of an underdeveloped and overhyped field, as many firms were haphazardly formulating their business strategies. Mind Cure originally focused on the functional mushroom market and then pivoted, first to digital therapeutics and psychedelic therapy centres, then to researching traumatic brain injury, then to manufacturing synthetic ibogaine and finally to treating hypoactive sexual desire disorder in women (Psychedelic Alpha 2022a). It did not help that throughout this period the company was spending inordinate sums on advertising, branding and consulting fees at the expense of business development.

The collapse of the psychedelic stock market reflected macroeconomic conditions. The biotech industry as a whole was faltering during much of this period after a sustained boom in the early years of the COVID-19 pandemic. But psychedelic stocks even underperformed the biotech sector in 2022-23. Many of these companies were grossly overvalued and a market correction, especially in the context of broader market conditions, was likely inevitable. Some of this decline can also be explained, however, by the behaviour of opportunistic company founders who were looking to profit from unrestrained hype. For some, including the word "psychedelic" in a company's name, promotions or marketing materials was all they really had to offer. Some start-ups were able to raise capital with little more than a puffed-up press release. Many of these releases focused on the promise of clinical trials, but investors had ill-informed expectations about drug pipeline costs and timelines to see results. Sabrina Ramkellawan, chief operating officer of Knowde Group, a firm that advises psychedelic companies, says she encountered executives who had no idea how much money it would take to conduct clinical trials (McGovern 2022a). According to *Psychedelic Alpha*'s Josh Hardman (2022), "a cynic might say that many of the earlier stage trials were 'press release trials' … geared towards raising funds." Sa'ad Shah, a managing partner at venture capital firm Noetic Fund, concludes that the "pick a molecule and an indication" strategy that was easily funded back in 2020-21 was no longer recognized as a viable business model past that period (cited in Helm 2023). The high level of retail ownership of psychedelic stocks and the lack of institutional investors only added to their volatility. Wall Street investors have largely steered clear of this sector. For example, while groups like BlackRock and Morgan Stanley were among the top ten shareholders in Atai Life Sciences in 2024, their equity stakes stood at just 1 percent and 1.6 percent respectively (Hager 2024). It is interesting to note that psychedelic stocks rallied significantly in late 2024 following the election of Donald Trump in the US, with investors no doubt hoping that the administration will reduce regulatory barriers for psychedelic firms and expedite the path toward medicalization.

Some observers had predicted how all of this would play out. In early 2020, former hedge fund manager and Goldman Sachs partner Michael Novogratz — an early investor in Compass Pathways and Atai Life Sciences — predicted that the stock prices of psychedelic firms would rise far above their actual value. Speaking at the Context Summits conference, Novogratz told asset managers that psychedelics would be "the next short-term bubble because it's such a positive story" (cited in Berke and Saacks 2020). Even though market bubbles tend to hurt small investors and the fields in which they occur, Novogratz seemed to view this prospect in a positive light. Others were more concerned about how a market bubble and "trend investing" might impact the psychedelic landscape and the people involved. Russell Hausfeld (2020a), for example, drew attention to the collateral damage that could result if the same kinds of speculators who were "wreaking financial havoc throughout the cannabis industry" decided to shift their focus to psychedelics (many cannabis stocks like Tilray, Canopy Growth and Aurora Cannabis lost much of their value in 2019 as speculators abandoned the sector). Hausfeld noted: "These speculators are less concerned about the long-term vision of a mental health company, and more concerned with the investment returns from the next big trend. Presumably, there are more speculators with this mindset entering the space than there are wealthy medical advocates and psychonauts." Hausfeld's assumption turned out to be correct.

An Uncertain Future and the Question of Big Pharma

The implosion of the psychedelic stock market and the stagnating pace of investments over the past few years have led some analysts to question the strength and resilience of the corporadelic project. At the 2022 Horizons: Perspectives on Psychedelics conference in New York, Kevin Balktick (founder of Horizons) questioned whether the term "industry" is even an appropriate descriptor, noting that "the psychedelic industry does not yet exist" (cited in Gunther 2022a). At the same conference, Josh Hardman reminded the audience that the market capitalization of all publicly traded psychedelic companies was just $3.5 billion, a far cry from pharmaceutical giant Pfizer's market value of $250 billion. Speaking in late 2023, Brian Normand of Psymposia suggested we have already seen the "collapse of corporadelia" (Psymposia 2023). MAPS is in financial trouble, he said, and the entire sector is approaching its deathbed. While concerns about the viability of the sector are not without merit, it is premature to write this industry off. Its recent struggles have been tied to market conditions and could shift with the introduction of medical approvals. In fact, it may be just as plausible that the contours of psychedelic capitalism have already been firmly established and that the gravitational pull of venture capital has irrevocably transformed psychedelia across North America.

The future of the industry will undoubtedly be impacted by the "looming elephant in the psychedelic room" — that is, the industry's relationship with Big Pharma (Najum 2022). While large pharmaceutical companies have been hesitant to embrace psychedelic drug development, there are examples to the contrary, such as Danish pharmaceutical company Novo Nordisk's collaboration with the University of Copenhagen; French pharmaceutical giant Sanofi's partnership with Terran Biosciences; AbbVie's option-to-license agreement with Gilgamesh Pharmaceuticals; and the Japanese firm Otsuka's investments and collaborations with Compass Pathways and Atai Life Sciences. Otsuka also purchased Toronto-based psychedelic start-up Mindset Pharma in 2023 (Psychedelic Alpha 2023). As well, Janssen Pharmaceuticals, a division of Johnson & Johnson, has developed and marketed its esketamine drug Spravato for the treatment of depression, one of the company's fastest growing drug products that is expected to achieve "blockbuster" status in the coming years (Kinder and Barnes 2024). According to *The Trip Report* podcast host Zach Haigney (2022), there is a sense among investors that the real validation of the psychedelic industry will come "when a Merck or a Pfizer acquires a MindMed or Compass."

In addition, many executives in leading psychedelic firms have been recruited from some of the top pharmaceutical companies in the world. Beckley Psytech, a private company co-founded by drug policy reformer and founder of the Beckley Foundation, Amanda Fielding, employs several executives who previously worked at Johnson & Johnson and Lilly.

Mind Medicine's executive team is stacked with leadership experience in product development and commercialization from firms like Merck, Roche, Pfizer, AstraZeneca and Johnson & Johnson. The leadership group at Gilgamesh, a company developing and running clinical trials on novel psychedelic compounds, has previous corporate affiliations with Pfizer, Bristol Myers Squibb, Johnson & Johnson, Merck and Lilly. The CEO of Compass Pathways, Kabir Nath, who replaced George Goldsmith in 2022, previously held senior positions at both Otsuka and Bristol Myers Squibb.

In spite of these alliances and research underway, whether psychedelic substances are conducive to the kind of business model favoured by Big Pharma remains to be seen. PAP is time-consuming and resource intensive — a cost-prohibitive barrier. The pharmaceutical industry also has a financial incentive to ensure further treatments are needed or, to put it more bluntly, to keep people sick. These companies are not interested in treatments that are administered once or a handful of times. Their *raison d'être* is making products that people consume daily and ideally for the rest of their lives (this is part of the reason the industry effectively put the brakes on mental health research after developing SSRIs). If, as proponents claim, PAP can offer more lasting solutions by addressing the root causes of mental illness, this would be far less profitable than current drug models. Therefore, should the relationship with pharma giants take hold, there will be pressure to turn psychedelics into maintenance therapies to get patients back in the door. Some company leaders, like Robert Barrow of Mind Medicine, have already stated that they are approaching psychedelic drug development as if they were creating the next round of SSRIs (Psychedelic Alpha 2024a). As it stands, the only form of "treatment" that is well-aligned with broader industry goals would be extended microdosing regimens.

Nevertheless, the pharmaceutical industry is poised to step in more forcefully if conditions shift. These companies know that mental health is an area that requires innovation, reflecting a longstanding crisis of psychopharmacology that goes back decades (Langlitz 2024). If there are profits to be made, these entities will likely assume control of psychedelic medicine and/or partner with psychedelic companies to bring them into their fold. Some psychedelic advocates are waiting patiently for this to happen. For others, the prospect of these substances being used as a profit generator for Big Pharma is the worst possible outcome imaginable.

THE CORPORADELIC SET AND SETTING

A Unique Industry?

A prominent narrative running through the psychedelic renaissance is that the psychedelic industry will be fundamentally different than other capitalist industries. Investors and business leaders speak of a conviction to get these substances into people's hands in a responsible and ethical way. Profits are touted as secondary to improving society. Ronan Levy, co-founder of Field Trip Health, stated in 2020 that he was "excited by the chance to profoundly and positively change the world through psychedelics." He also boldly claimed that his work may allow him to have an impact on humanity that is on par with other corporate visionaries like Elon Musk, Jeff Bezos and Richard Branson (cited in Psychedelic Alpha 2020a). Field Trip Health was one of many companies that ostensibly disavowed business as usual in favour of corporate social responsibility, marked by the adoption of its triple bottom line: "people, planet, and profit" (Shana 2020).

Along these same lines, some suggest that the psychedelic industry was founded by "true believers" who are not only executives but advocates. Indeed, there is no shortage of executives who claim they entered the field because of personally transformative experiences. The former CEO of Mind Medicine, JR Rahn, told *The New Yorker* that psychedelics helped him overcome drug dependence and provided insight into the sources of his depression and anxiety (Heller 2020). Danny Motyka, CEO of Psygen Labs, said he joined the industry because he struggled with depression as a teenager, and that psychedelics improved his mental health and potentially saved his life (Austin and Motyka 2020). Likewise, Payton Nyquvest, co-founder and CEO of Numinus Wellness, experienced chronic pain for decades and subsequently became addicted to opioid painkillers. He credited a series of ayahuasca rituals in Costa Rica with healing his ailments and ultimately saving his life (Brown and Bennett 2022). Lars Wilde, co-founder of Compass Pathways, also revealed that a psilocybin mushrooms trip was pivotal in addressing his treatment-resistant depression. He connected his involvement with Compass Pathways to this life-changing event (Psychedelic Alpha 2020b). Finally, Christian Angermayer, founder and chairman of Atai Life Sciences, said his first experience with psilocybin was "the single most meaningful thing I've ever done and experienced in my whole life, full stop. Nothing comes close to it" (cited in Ferriss 2019). One of Angermayer's drug-induced revelations was that more people should have access to psychedelics, and this impacted his decision to form Atai Life Sciences.

Other executives have been motivated to join the industry because of challenges facing their family members. Timothy Ko, CEO of Entheon Biomedical, started his company after the death of his brother (who struggled with addiction) in the hopes of providing treatment options that worked. Co-founder and CEO of Atai Life Sciences Florian Brand — one of the fifteen highest-paid biopharma CEOs in 2021 — has shared that he and his wife had a transformative healing experience on psilocybin in Amsterdam that helped them deal with the death of a family member (Hausfeld 2020b). One of the most widely circulated stories comes from George Goldsmith, co-founder and former CEO of Compass Pathways. Goldsmith and his wife reported that they discovered psychedelic therapy while searching for a treatment option for their mentally ill son (Lee 2023). They were put in touch with an underground guide who supervised his psilocybin therapy session, leading to dramatic improvements. Not only are industry pioneers motivated by the healing powers of psychedelics, but some claim the psychedelic experience itself has changed the way business is conducted in this sphere. According to Michael Hoyos, co-founder of the Conscious Fund, a venture capital firm specializing in psychedelic medicine, "the interesting thing about these substances is that … on a personal level they have this kind of tremendous capacity to (create) personal development and empathy … I think that's helped a lot of folks that I've spoken to feel almost like a certain responsibility to help this industry flourish and develop in the right way" (cited in McGovern 2020).

Some of these stories are inspiring and we do not doubt the sincerity underpinning most of them. However, the ways that for-profit companies operate have far more to do with the structural features of the institutions than the individual motivations and characteristics of the people who run them. As these substances are thrust into the world of psychedelic capitalism, structural forces will have more influence than personal values or intentions. These institutional realities are currently playing out in debates over decriminalization and drug policy reform. One might expect that the meaningful personal experiences discussed above — all of which occurred in underground or recreational settings — would lead these executives to champion broad, equitable access (that is, make it easier for others to have the experiences they did) and help communities devastated by the war on drugs by supporting decriminalization. Generally speaking, however, this has not been the case.

Psychedelic Capitalists and Decriminalization

Those at the top of the psychedelic industry have a financial stake in medical legalization, wanting to limit legal access to anything outside of the medical-pharma frame. Cheap generic options make it difficult for corporations to wield monopoly power. In this context, recreational psychedelics that are similar to medicalized or patented drug products are seen as competitors, which incentivizes firms to divert people into purchasing proprietary formulations. According to Carlos Plazola, co-founder and former president of Decriminalize Nature, the corporate goal is to "create scarcity to drive up pricing of their materials," incentives that "work directly against our movement" (cited in Farah 2020). To counter this, Decriminalize Nature issued a pledge to psychedelic companies in the hopes of proactively garnering support for decriminalization: "We're hoping that Mindmed and Compass Pathways will issue a public declaration of support for Decrim Nature and Indigenous rights to access plants directly."

Such support has not been forthcoming. In 2020, JR Rahn, then CEO of Mind Medicine, told *Forbes* magazine, "this isn't the 1960s all over again. I want nothing to do with those kinds of folks who want to decriminalize psychedelics" (cited in Yakowicz 2020). Though Rahn does not believe people should go to prison for using drugs, he claims that decriminalization would hinder the field's progress, which presumably includes the progress Mind Medicine has been making in developing intellectual property to secure the company's exclusivity to sell LSD. Rahn's motivations are better reflected in a statement he made shortly after the company began trading on the Nasdaq: "Forty percent of the country is suffering — that's a big, big market" (cited in Cormier 2022). Canadian investor and Shark Tank host Kevin O'Leary also reportedly made his early investments in Mind Medicine contingent on Rahn not supporting broader access. In 2022, when the DEA proposed scheduling five new psychedelic compounds, the chief scientific officer of Field Trip Health, Nathan Bryson, wrote a submission to the DEA that agreed with criminalizing four of the compounds, with the exception of the drug they were working on (Love 2023a).

Executives at Compass Pathways have also been clear about where they stand on decriminalization, as well as other legal pathways that fall outside of a biomedical model. Compass Pathways had no interest in making psychedelics (or even psychedelic therapy) broadly accessible. In the view of its founder George Goldsmith, these substances should be limited to people with serious mental health illnesses and they need to be prescribed by doctors. Compass is no doubt hopeful that its proprietary formulation of psilocybin, COMP360, will be included in these prescriptions. Goldsmith says he supports limiting access to clinical settings because of the possibility of adverse events. "In the wild," he cautions, "God knows what happens" (cited in Piore 2021). Yet, Goldsmith and others are benefiting from the fact that people have been taking psychedelics "in the wild" for thousands of years, providing the foundational knowledge and innovation that companies are now using to develop and market their products.

There is also evidence that Goldsmith intervened to oppose drug policy reform in the US, including Measure 109 in Oregon that legalized psilocybin services. Compass opposed Measure 109 to keep psilocybin therapy within an FDA-approved medical framework. This commitment is reflected in their position statement on psilocybin legalization: "To make sure it is safe and effective in patients, *psilocybin therapy needs to be approved by medical regulators, not legislators*" (Compass Pathways 2020a, emphasis in original). Compass Pathways' position is further reflected in a document submitted to the US Securities and Exchange Commission, stating that "the legalization of psilocybin could also impact our commercial sales if we receive regulatory approval as it would reduce the barrier to entry and could increase competition" (Compass Pathways 2020b, 45). The company is also concerned about the impact of non-profits, as they may be willing to "provide psilocybin-based products at cost or for free, undermining our potential market for COMP360" (2020b, 79). David Bronner (2021) alleges that Goldsmith tried to mobilize opposition against Measure 109 by pressuring researchers at Oregon Health and Science University. While Bronner presents Goldsmith's intervention as a paradigmatic example of "Compass's monopolistic and bullying behavior," other accounts point to a more routine case of corporate lobbying (e.g., Love 2021a). In any event, the materials Goldsmith sent to researchers made his perspectives clear, including that psilocybin therapy must follow the medical route.

While Christian Angermayer's life-changing encounter with psilocybin led him to the realization that more people should have access to psychedelics, he remains adamant that the medical-pharmaceutical route is the only way this should be allowed to happen. Even though his psychedelic trip was not for a medical purpose and took place in a jurisdiction with legal and regulated access, Angermayer told CNBC that "we want to make it legal, but solely for doctors or psychotherapists in a clinical setting … These are not drugs you can take alone" (Rosenbaum 2021). Atai Life Sciences' CEO Florian Brand also believes psychedelics are too powerful to be provided outside of a medical setting. At the Economics of Psychedelic Investing Conference in 2020, he said: "We're focused on getting better treatment for patients, not so much on what could be happening from a policy perspective in 12 years" (cited in Berke and Saacks 2020). Recall that Brand, like Angermayer, claims to have had a healing experience in a jurisdiction where psilocybin is recreationally legal. While taking psychedelics in a medical setting will no doubt be useful for some people,

> The issues arise when — all of a sudden — your 'proper' drug, set, and setting all become dictated *and sold* to you by corporate actors. It seems disingenuous that the people creating this framework have generally either experienced psychedelics outside of a medical model, or traveled to a separate country in order to do so — only to attempt to force everyone else into a medical model they would profit from. (Hausfeld 2020c, emphasis in original)

It is also revealing that Angermayer, who opposes psychedelic use outside of a clinical setting, foresees a dramatic expansion of medical applications. Not only does he want to treat the "more than one billion" people he believes suffer from depression, but also expand Atai's customer base to include diseases that "we don't even have a name for yet," like "being afraid of the future" and "not feeling at home in the world anymore" (cited in Kitchens 2022).

Humane and rational drug policy reform would appear to be bad for business. While psychedelics remain criminalized, there are potential riches to be made in being the only "legitimate" providers of these experiences. According to Brom Rector of venture capital firm Empath Ventures, "it's almost like saying the success of our business depends on us continuing to put people in jail for using drugs, which to me is an unconscionable thing" (cited in Vedantam 2022b). Rector is right. Many of these executives are effectively advocating for a continuation of the war on drugs. As journalist Kelsey Osgood (2021) puts it, "in interview after interview, the bigwigs behind these clinics and research companies talk about taking psychedelics in non-medical settings and/or for reasons that amount to personal growth — they reaped the benefits anyway … You deserve to take drugs on the beach with your friends, just like they did." As these companies continue to expand their intellectual property portfolios, one can only expect more lobbying against decriminalization and support for restricting non-medical access.

Following the Money: From MAPS PBC to Lykos Therapeutics

An example of the new corporadelic set and setting is the recent transformation of the MAPS public benefit corporation (PBC). Rick Doblin founded MAPS in 1986. Its mission was to advance the medicalization of MDMA and broader drug policy reform, including decriminalization. In her book, *I Feel Love* (2023), journalist Rachel Nuwer details the history of how MDMA emerged from the underground to occupy a central place in mainstream medical discourse and practice, in large part due to the advocacy of MAPS and Doblin. As part of its ongoing efforts to advance the medicalization of MDMA, in 2014 MAPS established its PBC as an income-generating instrument for psychedelic research and development. As Doblin explained it, the creation of the PBC was necessary to maintain MAPS' non-profit status and allow it to become "a sustainable non-profit with earned income for further research, education, harm reduction, and advocacy." Doblin went further to say that "MAPS and MAPS PBC must faithfully retain our values against the sometimes diametric values of the systems in which we operate. As the sole shareholder in MAPS PBC, MAPS is able to allocate all proceeds from the sale of pharmaceutical MDMA toward pure public benefit" (Doblin 2023). A few years earlier, MAPS expressed a similar message, claiming that the primary goal of the PBC was to "create a platform for everyone to benefit, unlike companies prioritizing shareholders or the few who are putting up the capital" (Ladou and Lotlikar 2020).

The values-centred approach of MAPS has taken a back seat to other priorities for some time (Silman 2024). MAPS always knew it would need more money. In 2017, the organization experimented with partnership agreements with different psychedelic companies as a way of raising funds. It also operated in close collaboration with Compass Pathways. During this period, critics questioned if the collaborations between MAPS and Compass violated the organization's stated commitment to the "Statement on Open Science and Open Praxis with Psilocybin, MDMA, and Similar Substances" (Nickles 2018b). Some argued that MAPS needed to turn its back on the legacy of underground psychedelic research to succeed, which led to the organization "digging into the hearts (and pocketbooks) of underground psychedelic enthusiasts, while dragging everyone into the garish mainstream light of regulation, big money trials, insurance plans, professional agencies, and a normalizing discourse that requires the marginalization of earlier and more unruly psychedelic authorities, visions, researchers, and community values" (Davis 2018). In fact, Doblin had long defended the entry of for-profit interests — including Compass Pathways but also investors like Peter Thiel and Rebekah Mercer — into the psychedelic field as a positive and inevitable aspect of mainstreaming.

In 2021, MAPS decided it needed to move beyond philanthropy, creating an investment fund with Vine Ventures. Investors in the fund would be awarded a return on their investment that was tied to future revenues from MDMA, though MAPS retained full ownership and control over the PBC (Gunther 2023). Doblin expressed some regret about MAPS coveting investors as the organization had resisted this strategy in the past: "I feel in some ways a sense of massive failure in that I had hoped we would have this bridge to sustainability come through philanthropy. But … now there's all these for-profit companies, and people are saying, 'Why should I donate? Let me just invest'" (cited in Harrison and Jordan 2021).

There were still some indications that MAPS remained committed to its public benefit approach. In late 2021, for example, it placed its "Fully Validated, Multi-Kilogram cGMP Synthesis of MDMA" in the public domain (Nair et al. 2021). The model was validated for commercial synthetic processing for producing large batches of the drug. In some ways, the move aligned MAPS with a group like the Usona Institute, which has published multiple papers on psilocybin manufacturing and put its scalable process for synthesizing psilocybin in the public domain (e.g., Sherwood et al. 2020), and away from the strategies of Compass Pathways, which has attempted to lock up its drug discovery work through intellectual property.

More recent engagement by MAPS, however, has called the organization's motives back into question. To present at the 2023 Psychedelic Science conference in Denver, participants had to sign a thirty-clause contract. One clause asked presenters to limit their speaking engagements that year so that their presentations would be exclusive for MAPS, a move that could curb information sharing among scientists. Another clause stated that MAPS could rescind a presenter's invitation if it determined the presenter (or any organization to which the presenter was associated) "discredits MAPS or tarnishes its reputation and goodwill" (Hausfeld 2023b). These restrictions are similar to provisions found in non-disclosure agreements and non-disparagement clauses that corporations often use to control information and silence their critics.

In April 2023, Doblin indicated that the future of the MAPS PBC was still undecided, stating, "I'm on the knife's edge between capitalism and altruism" (cited in Reardon 2023). Two months later, MAPS decided to open up the PBC to shareholders; it was reported that it was working on an $85 million private share sale to keep its work going until it could start selling MDMA (Wirz 2023). The future of the MAPS PBC was decided a short time later in early 2024. A January 2024 press release announced that the MAPS PBC had closed a Series A financing deal for more than $100 million and that it would be changing its name to Lykos Therapeutics. Amy Emerson, who shifted from CEO of the PBC to CEO of Lykos, explained in the press release that "we are transitioning from a development-stage company to one focused on commercialization." Previously, MAPS was the sole shareholder of the PBC. Once it was dissolved and replaced by Lykos, the entity's ownership structure looked remarkably different. It now included the investment firm Helena as well as Bail Capital, Satori Neuro, Vine Ventures, True Ventures, KittyHawk Ventures and Elizabeth Koch's Unlikely Collaborators Foundation. The move also came with changes to the board structure, with outside interests now in a position to help steer the new entity.

Doblin and other MAPS representatives had long maintained that the primary vehicle for protecting its investments in the PBC would be data exclusivity, not patents. At the same time, there was some indication that the organization had been waffling on its explicit "anti-patent" commitments. In 2023, a spokesperson for the MAPS PBC declined to answer whether MAPS planned to patent its MDMA formulation. Then in early 2024, Lykos CEO Amy Emerson indicated that patenting was "on the table" (cited in Harrison and Jordan 2024). Despite these signs of a shift, many were shocked when it was revealed, in June 2024, that MAPS PBC had already overseen the filing of four provisional patent applications on MDMA, with the first being filed in 2022 (Hardman and Smith 2024). While it is unclear which staff members were privy to the filings, the revelation suggested that MAPS had been deliberately misleading the public. According to *Psychedelic Alpha*'s Josh Hardman and Noah Smith (2024), over the past few years, "sources at the company have repeatedly told Psychedelic Alpha that it had not filed any patents." When asked about intellectual property in June 2023, Michael Mullette, then chief operating officer of MAPS PBC, stated: "We have no patents that we've openly discussed." This statement came months after the company had filed all four of its applications.

While some contend that MAPS had no choice but to work with institutional investors to get their project to the finish line, this is small comfort to those who believed in its public benefit mission. In Hausfeld's (2024b) view, "the decision to accept outside investment in MAPS PBC makes a mockery of a decade of fundraising messaging deployed by the MAPS nonprofit since the PBC's founding in 2014 … After decades of playing both sides, the mask, in other words, has fallen." Doblin appeared as disappointed as anyone: "We're a victim of our own success," he remarked after the establishment of Lykos. "It's heartbreaking because I had hoped to go the whole way with philanthropy, but I was unable to raise the mega millions to do that" (cited in Perrone 2024). "Perhaps, in hindsight, [there] was some naivety, or overoptimism … I really don't think Rick meant any malice or wrongdoing," says Josh Hardman, "but I can see why some people are pissed off" (cited in Busby 2024d).

Things went from bad to worse for Doblin when the FDA rejected MDMA-assisted therapy in August 2024. Following the decision, 75 percent of Lykos staff were laid off, Amy Emerson resigned as CEO and Doblin announced he was leaving the board. Michael Mullette, a long-time pharmaceutical executive who oversaw the commercialization of Moderna's COVID-19 vaccine in North America, was promoted to CEO, and Dr. David Hough, a former vice president at Johnson & Johnson who directed the rollout of the esketamine (Spravato) nasal spray program, was promoted from an advisory role to chief medical officer. Elevating Mullette and Hough represented a pivot toward mainstream pharmaceutical leadership, while the departure of Emerson and Doblin further separated Lykos from its roots in MAPS.

Other psychedelic companies were quick to weigh in on the FDA rejection, distancing themselves from Lykos and casting its failings as unique to the organization. Problems with the psychotherapeutic components of the MDMA trials were a major factor in the FDA's decision. It is therefore likely that for-profit companies like Mind Medicine, Compass Pathways and Atai Life Sciences will use this as an opportunity to further reduce or eliminate psychotherapy from their protocols, regardless of the impacts on patients. As for Doblin and MAPS, this may represent an opportunity to rediscover their roots as advocates for progressive drug policy reform. In a recent interview, Doblin indicated that MAPS would be focused on decriminalization and harm reduction moving forward (Keshavan 2024). He also confirmed that his broader goal remains "net-zero trauma" by 2070.

PSYCHEDELICS AND THE CORPORATE "WELLNESS" INDUSTRY

The corporate sector tends to view psychedelics in much the same way it views other new age health and wellness practices, like yoga and meditation, that are associated with spiritual and/or self-transcendent dimensions. Modern iterations of these practices have formed the basis for a lucrative industry — the corporate wellness industry. They have also come to embody key elements of neoliberal individualism or the neoliberal self.

Professor Patric Plesa and Rotem Petranker, director of the Canadian Centre for Psychedelic Science, examine what they call the neoliberal self-help industry, which is expressed through cultural norms such as individualism, competition and personal responsibility and excludes collectivist approaches to self-improvement (Plesa and Petranker 2022). They draw parallels between the emerging psychedelic therapy industry and this self-help industry, where mental illnesses are framed as individual pathologies and personal moral failings. Other researchers have noted the connections between commercialized "mindfulness" and the growing commercialization of psychedelics (Elf, Isham and Leoni 2023). Mindfulness is a practice that emphasizes the development of cognitive skills that can reduce stress, increase compassion and help people gain insight and awareness into their consciousness (purportedly for the benefit of society at large). Mindfulness has a well-established history in some Eastern traditions, cultivated in practices such as Buddhist meditation. Under neoliberalism, however, mindfulness has been commercialized into "McMindfulness." Whereas Zen Buddhist mindfulness emphasizes selflessness and a culture of community, McMindfulness is centred around individualism, ego-enhancement and workplace productivity. Corporations, governments and the military have co-opted mindfulness as a technique for social control and self-pacification, helping to dissuade individuals from working collectively to change the structural conditions of their lives (Purser 2019).

In this context, McMindfulness and (Mc)psychedelics are similar in that they are being used as tools to increase flexibility and resilience in societies replete with inequality. In the process, their socially oriented, ego-dissolving potentials are subsumed under an individualist/consumerist framework. This shift is evident in the emerging psychedelic therapy industry, which is focused on individual self-improvement and "elite perfectibility" — a trend that "has already shown a remarkable capacity to absorb, defang, and redirect potentially transformative practices like yoga and mindfulness meditation" (Davis 2018). It is also evident in the workplace, where employees are being sold mindfulness (and, in some cases, psychedelics) as a way to cope with stressful work environments and keep them focused on institutional goals. A key driver behind mindfulness in the workplace is that it is more cost-effective for managers to send their employees to mindfulness seminars than to address the root causes of their stress, such as company operations or worker insecurity.

In the case of psychedelics too, employers across numerous industries "from trucking, to software, gaming, financial services, healthcare, and retail" have started to offer psychedelics as part of employee health and wellness packages (Collins 2024). Enthea, a Boston-based start-up, is working to match employers with ketamine providers to speed up the process by which these treatments can be provided to struggling workers (Bannow and Goldhill 2022). Enthea has partnered with natural soap brand Dr. Bronner's, steered by psychedelic enthusiast and leader of the New Approach psychedelic political action committee David Bronner, to provide its employees with coverage for ketamine-assisted therapy. In

The New York Times, writer Zoe Boyer (2021) recounted how ketamine helped to treat her intractable depression. While Boyer described her experience as positive, her article illustrates the role that psychedelics could play in pacifying workers into accepting dead-end jobs: "Though my jobs were poorly paid, ketamine allowed me to utilize the skills I'd learned in therapy to reframe experiences in a positive light. Bleaching gym mats in a martial arts studio and washing buckets in a flower shop became meditative practices, rather than drudgery." In 2022, Ronan Levy, then CEO of Field Trip Health, even took the unusual step of offering a free month of ketamine sessions to thousands of tech workers laid off by companies like Meta, Twitter (X), Apple and Amazon (Mikhail 2022). Rather than trying to placate workers or subdue employee unrest, a better solution to mass layoffs would be labour organizing in the tech industry. In effect, mindfulness and psychedelics are being promoted within capitalist markets and workplaces as a cure for capitalism itself.

Big Tech, Wellness Apps and Surveillance Capitalism

The psychedelic renaissance connects with high-tech capitalism in many ways. Today's capitalist system relies on the granular collection of behavioural and attitudinal data to create micro-targeted advertising for consumers in real time. Business critic Shoshana Zuboff (2015) refers to these practices as "surveillance capitalism." Surveillance capitalism requires that the technologies we use in everyday life operate as surveillance devices. "Smart" devices that feature convenience are harvesting our data and relaying it to data brokers — organizations that buy and sell personal data for profit — and advertisers, who then communicate targeted advertising back to us.

For Zuboff (2015), the first element of surveillance capitalism is that surveillance technologies must be embedded in our daily lives. From smart fridges to wearable monitoring gadgets to Google Home and Amazon Echo, every step we take and decision we make is being translated into data. The second element of surveillance capitalism is that surveillance technologies must be extractive. It is not enough to have traditional consumer surveys. Surveillance must enter the home and become part of the self or body to access granular behavioural data. The third element is the illusion of control. Customization is touted as giving users control of their habits and the uses of these technologies, but in reality these are largely access points for data extraction. The fourth element of surveillance capitalism is that these practices are experimental. Silicon Valley entrepreneurs have been given the green light to experiment with new forms of extraction given the lack of privacy regulation and data protection governing smart technologies and data brokers. There are few legislative limits on how surveillance can be woven into the fabric of daily life, especially in the US. The fifth element of surveillance capitalism is that it is expansive. Just like capitalism itself, new social trends can be commodified and subjected to the logic and practices of surveillance. This is where psychedelics enter the picture. The use of psychedelics can and has become a site of new surveillance practices, the production of personal data to be bought and sold, which can then be translated into advertising and sales for further psychedelic marketing and wellness-industry promotion. For example, an app that is designed for use at different stages of a psychedelic trip may give healthcare professionals and users real-time information about the experience. These data are also likely to be stored and shared with other organizations.

There are a growing number of companies working at the intersection of psychedelia and surveillance capitalism. Bexson Biomedical is creating a wearable ketamine subcutaneous device that allows users to dial in their experiences with ketamine and in the process creates reams of personal data. Individuals will be able to use this smart device to customize their ketamine trip, including its duration and intensity. The device can also be adjusted to be used with other psychedelics and in different settings, such as therapy clinics and retreat centres, again raising questions about third parties who might gain access to the data generated by the device. In 2023, Bexson Biomedical announced that the US military is going to field test the device and that military personnel will receive training in how to use it on the battlefield (Whooley 2023). Apollo Neuroscience also features a wearable device purported to enhance personal well-being. The device has users enter personal data, day and night, about their energy and mood to optimize stress levels, energy and performance. The device has already been advertised to and used by people participating in psychedelic therapy trials, meaning behavioural data coming out of these trials could already be subject to surveillance capitalism and provide a testing ground for further experimentation (Chesak 2023).

Cydelic is a high-tech hardware company that is interested in monitoring the impact of psychedelics on the mind and body. The company has created a wearable biosensor that can be used for gathering precise physiological data. The information streams to a data-gathering console and can be integrated with Fitbit and other devices for further customization. Cydelic is also developing a biometric monitoring program for therapists and patients to examine mental and physical performances and outcomes related to psychedelic use. The technologies created by Cydelic provide biodata for patients undergoing psychedelic therapy. The technologies can be used across patient onboarding, session monitoring and longitudinal growth tracking. Atai Life Sciences is developing an app meant to reduce user reliance on therapists and guides to scale up psychedelic treatments (Psychedelic News Wire 2023). The company will use the app to monitor patient mood and biomarkers for weeks or months after psychedelic therapy sessions to provide content tailored for mindfulness and habit reinforcement. In addition to questions about personal data use, Atai does not seem concerned about whether removing the relational aspects of psychedelic therapy might make these treatments less effective. Other examples include Wesana Solutions, a medical-grade clinical software and cloud platform exploring applications for diagnostic measurements and real-time visualizations of mental and physical responses during and after psychedelic use; and Mind Medicine's digital medicine division, which is working to produce what it calls deep digital diagnoses for in-session monitoring during psychedelic treatments and post-treatment in relation to real-life events. Mind Medicine has also filed patents on technologies to expand session monitoring by synthesizing "continuous passive data collection" from a patient's mobile device and wearables (Psychedelic Alpha 2024a).

Some analysts have an optimistic view of these technologies and their applications, suggesting that ideas like corporate social responsibility (CSR) will help steer companies away from predatory, profit-driven digital applications in the psychedelic space (Shana 2021). Others, however, point to the limitations of CSR and the inherent risks associated with the sharing of these data. Russell Hausfeld (2020d), for one, criticizes the emergence of wellness apps as well as the role of psychedelic companies in their marketing and sales. He draws attention to the relationships between key corporadelic players and the "Calm" app, a mind/body meditation and relaxation app. Calm's co-founders were early investors in Atai Life Sciences and Calm subsequently became a corporate partner of Compass Pathways. Mindstrong is another Compass partner that has focused on creating technologies to monitor digital biomarkers through smart devices. Both Atai Life Science and Compass Pathways have been at the forefront of an aggressive push to dominate psychedelic intellectual property and therapy, so there are reasons to question the implications of these relationships, including privacy concerns, the uses of biomedical data, as well as the possibility that psychedelic integration by trained professionals will be substituted for digital equivalents. Just as importantly, Hausfeld (2020d) asks: "do we want for-profit psychedelic pharmaceutical companies — backed by some of the biggest players in mass surveillance online and in the streets — to stake their paychecks on monitoring and quantifying our digital lives?"

Maxim Tvorun-Dunn (2022) also critiques the integration of surveillance technology, psychedelics and the corporate wellness industry. He notes there is a convergence between the ways technology is developed in Silicon Valley and how the tech industry views psychedelic experimentation and innovation. The extractive, expansionist and experimental elements of surveillance capitalism are key elements of how psychedelic companies approach wellness and user "enlightenment." Similarly, Tehseen Noorani (2021a) has questioned why psychedelic industry players and advocates have dismissed critics of surveillance technologies. One of the critics Noorani refers to is David Nickles, who argues that psychedelic surveillance capitalism is one of the most important and least discussed issues in psychedelia today. In a 2023 interview, Nickles poses a question that nobody in the field seems to be asking: "how might venture capital investors get a return on their investment in a field that may not see widespread FDA approval for years, if ever?" Nickles suggests that the "monetization of granular biomedical data that isn't subject to medical privacy laws offers a literal treasure trove for those unscrupulous individuals who are willing to leverage it" (cited in Pace and Devenot 2023). Building on the work of critics like Nickles, Noorani underscores the importance of drawing attention to technological power and control in the psychedelic industry, including the mining and selling of personal data.

Finally, Neşe Devenot (2023) notes some interesting parallels between the corporate rollout of psychedelics and the corporate rollout of AI. Both are being promoted as tools or technologies that will benefit humanity in multiple ways, such as curing the problems of disease, poverty and climate change. For example, Rick Doblin's promotion of psychedelics in the context of "mass mental health" and "mass spiritualization" mirrors tech industry claims around the social and human-enhancing potential of AI technologies. While social and economic inequality are the primary drivers of these problems, the profit-oriented solutions of tech oligarchs and psychedelic figureheads may end up further entrenching systems of inequality. For Devenot, "any genuinely prosocial applications of either AI or psychedelics will depend on collective resistance to their consumption by neoliberalism and colonialism. The alternative is complicity in their use as technologies of elite persuasion" (2023, 35). In the context of modern capitalism, she says, notions of collective progress and mass healing resulting from the application of psychedelics and AI are little more than elite hallucinations.

The Cautionary Tale of Ketamine Clinics

In the coming years, the lack of experienced therapists and facilitators will be a key challenge for the psychedelic industry. The largest therapy training organization, the California Institute of Integral Studies, only graduates around four hundred people each year (Glastra 2023). Rick Doblin says the goal of MAPS is to train 25,000 therapists in MDMA-assisted therapy for PTSD by 2030, while Michael Pollan suggests that as many as 100,000 new psychedelic facilitators might be needed to meet growing demand (Devine 2022). The lack of trained psychedelic therapists has been described as a "bottleneck" in the field, though the term does not capture the full extent of the problem. There is little vetting or regulation of the organizations offering therapy training, few of these organizations can guarantee that training certifications will receive official recognition, and there are no external bodies to credential most non-clinical programs. Some of the largest therapy-training providers have already gone out of business, including the Synthesis Institute, once considered the "gold standard" in the field (Evans 2023f; Hardman 2023a).

In the context of commercialization, these challenges take on greater significance. With therapist shortages and a largely unregulated environment, the growing demand for psychedelic therapy could translate into large numbers of people entering this field for economic (or more nefarious) reasons. The industry has already faced accusations of neglect and abuse in clinical and other therapeutic settings, and a lack of vetting or oversight will only serve to exacerbate these problems. As psychedelic therapy is integrated into for-profit services and the corporate wellness industry, market pressures will incentivize providers to strip away aspects of in-person care in favour of less costly, depersonalized, do-it-yourself models. In their interviews with psychedelic integration specialists, psychologist Mitch Earleywine and his colleagues found that the most commonly cited concern among these practitioners was the commercialization of psychedelic therapy and providers driven by for-profit objectives (Earleywine et al. 2022).

The growth and operation of ketamine clinics exemplify some of the problems associated with psychedelic therapy in the context of commercialization and corporate wellness. As journalist Ed Prideaux (2023b) puts it, the for-profit ketamine industry "offers a terrifying glimpse at this future of runaway capital." Private ketamine clinics have been operating in Canada since 2018 and in the UK since 2021. In the US, there were a limited number of these clinics operating as late as 2019. By 2023, however, most estimates suggest they had grown to between 600 and 700 at least. Part of the reason for this growth is that ketamine clinics are being treated as placeholders. Many owners believe they will be in a position to seize the market if other substances like psilocybin and MDMA are approved. The industry's growth is also related to the FDA's 2019 approval of esketamine (Spravato) for the treatment of depression (approved by Health Canada in 2020). While Spravato's use is regulated and must be delivered in a certified setting with healthcare professionals, these standards do not apply to generic ketamine. Ketamine is an FDA-approved anesthetic, which means it can be used off-label for other conditions. While the only mental health condition for which there is evidence of ketamine's effectiveness is treatment-resistant depression, ketamine is advertised in clinics across North America as a treatment for depression, anxiety, bipolar disorder, obsessive-compulsive disorder, alcohol use disorder, pain-related ailments, PTSD, autoimmune diseases and more. Ketamine is effectively being pitched as "a cure-all for the struggles of modern existence" (Silman 2023).

Broadening the list of conditions psychedelics can be used for is one way to increase potential customers. Another is to draw them in through advertising and branding, which often involves marketing clinics as high-end luxury spas. Some firms, like Ketamine Media, exist solely to provide marketing advice to providers. This advertising regularly uses tactics that are prohibited in regulated healthcare, such as exaggerated success rates and promises of "cures" (Levine 2021; Ryan and Bennett

2020). Warnings about potential side effects, which can be serious or even dire in the case of ketamine, are virtually non-existent. For example, the antidepressant effects of ketamine often last only days or weeks (Fava et al. 2020). Yet, these short-acting effects are rarely advertised and result in people returning repeatedly for treatment, increasing the risks of dependency and other complications. Off-label ketamine therapy is rarely covered by insurance, and it is expensive. Although a dose of generic ketamine typically costs providers around the price of a cup of coffee, most clients pay anywhere from a few hundred to over a thousand dollars per treatment session, depending on how much clinical or therapeutic supervision is provided.

Concerns have also been raised about the lack of standardized protocols. To date, individual practitioners have typically developed their own treatment protocols, which has led to wide variability in dosing regimens, patient-screening processes and levels of adherence to professional guidelines (Megli 2024; Thielking 2018). Most ketamine providers draw from limited, if any, formal training or experience with mental health. Many clinics do not even have mental health professionals on staff, even though they are often working with people with severe depression and suicidal ideation. Psychiatrist Charles Nemeroff estimates that fewer than five percent of ketamine clinics adhere to appropriate safety standards (Sanacora et al. 2017; Silman 2023). In part, this is because the industry is loaded with entrepreneurs and venture capitalists who have little experience in mental health. As Jules Evans (2023g) points out, the biggest ketamine companies were all founded by individuals who lack any kind of medical background: "Ronan Levy of Field Trip ran a gold company, Dylan Benyon of Mindbloom ran a personal injury lawsuit platform, Mike Stang of Delic sold advertising for High Times, Irwin Naturals sold vitamins. Perhaps they would say that makes them useful disruptors."

These same problems and inconsistencies exist around pairing psychotherapy with ketamine treatments. Some companies, like Field Trip Health in North America and Awakn Life Sciences in the UK, have made an effort to incorporate psychotherapy and integration into their treatment protocols. However, there is no requirement for companies to do so, meaning that many people are left to process the effects of the drug with little guidance or support. In the context of commercialization, therapy is regularly being neglected at every stage to cut costs, which can reduce efficacy, increase dangers for patients and make it more likely that people will seek out or require maintenance dosing. According to Erica Siegal, founder of NEST Harm Reduction,

> The current attitude is 'ramp up your business, get 70 new clients a month.' No one should be doing that — you can't take on 70 new clients and still provide good care. Companies are looking at ketamine treatments from a medicalized treatment lens and not a therapeutic tool on a healing path. It's a pill-mill model. There is inadequate informed consent around risks and harms. A friend of mine rang up a market-leading ketamine company, and after a ten-minute conversation with a sales-person they asked for her credit card details — not a doctor, a salesperson ... If people get dependent on ketamine and can't afford the clinical version, they will go to the black market. This is exactly what happened with Oxycontin and caused the current drug epidemic in the US that has killed more than 760,000 people since 1999. (cited in Evans 2023g)

During the COVID-19 pandemic, the ketamine industry pivoted to telemedicine and at-home delivery as restrictions on prescribing drugs online were lifted. A growing number of companies, such as Mindbloom, Nue Life, KetaMD, Wondermed and Joyous, began providing at-home ketamine delivery to be self-administered by patients, often with some kind of virtual guidance. While some providers did put support systems in place, the level of oversight is generally even less robust than in in-person clinics, as "therapy" is usually provided via video chat or the facilitation of "personalized self-healing protocols." Mindbloom is one company that has been publicly criticized for its lax approach to at-home delivery and therapy. Clients have reported that the company sent them all of their doses at once, increasing the risk of over-consumption, and they were left to do ketamine sessions on their own without meaningful support (Love 2021d). The company's disregard for therapy is also evident in its advertising, where it claims it can provide "five years of therapy in just a few sessions." These practices are in stark contrast to the comments of Dr. Casey Paleos, co-founder and former science director of Mindbloom, who has emphasized the "very, very important distinction" between taking psychedelics and psychedelic-assisted psychotherapy. "These drugs are like any really powerful tool," he states.

"The tool itself has to be handled with a level of training and expertise and knowledge around how to keep a person safe through the process, [and] that shouldn't just be treated trivially" (cited in Wright 2022).

Not all ketamine providers operate the same way, and some practitioners are attempting to do things differently. Dr. Gail Serruya (2022), who opened Voyage Healing in Philadelphia, says their mission is to offer high-quality treatments with a focus on clinical integrity, set and setting and ketamine-assisted psychotherapy. Some reputable providers are likely delivering on their promises as there is evidence that ketamine therapy programs can provide benefits to patients (Hardman 2023b). However, Dr. Serruya is highly critical of broader industry practices, such as prescribing large doses with little medical monitoring and "financial incentives for patients to use more ketamine, such as 'membership' discounts and package deals."

The ketamine craze Dr. Serruya and others critique may be on the decline. In 2023, Ketamine Wellness closed thirteen clinics in the US and Awakn sold off its clinics in the UK. Likewise, Toronto-based Field Trip Health sold or closed multiple clinics across North America and filed for creditor protection. Ronan Levy resigned as CEO and was replaced by a chief restructuring officer. Field Trip Health now operates just a handful of clinics in Canada and the US, a far cry from the seventy-five it had planned to roll out by the end of 2024. This trend paints a pessimistic picture of the commercial viability of ketamine companies, but the way they were rolled out is a cautionary tale for the rest of the industry. In the future, widespread and unregulated off-label use of other psychedelics by for-profit clinics, like psilocybin and MDMA, could result in a similar model that includes a lack of attention to risks, deceptive marketing and little consideration to therapeutic care.

Psychedelic Tourism

In the 1950s, R. Gordon Wasson, an ethnomycologist and vice president of J.P. Morgan, and his wife Valentina Wasson, a pediatrician and ethnomycologist, traveled to Oaxaca, Mexico and ingested psilocybin mushrooms under the guidance of Mazatec *curandera* María Sabina, who lived in Huautla de Jiménez. R. Gordon Wasson (1957) famously wrote about his experiences in *Time* magazine, claiming to be one of the first Westerners to participate in the sacred Mazatec mushroom ritual known as the *velada*. The consequences of the article were far-reaching.

While he initially protected Sabina's identity with a pseudonym and promised not to publish photos, he would later betray her on both accounts. In the subsequent years, hundreds of celebrities, rock stars, hippies and backpackers descended on Huautla to take part in mushroom ceremonies. The area became so popular that government authorities set up a military checkpoint. Once a respected leader in her community, the influx of tourists and their lack of respect for local culture and traditions led to Sabina being ostracized. She was publicly shamed, her house was set on fire, she was surveilled by police and her son was murdered. Sabina died in poverty in 1985. Years later, Wasson expressed regret about what had come to pass: "I have unleashed on lovely Huautla a torrent of commercial exploitation of the vilest kind. Now the mushrooms are exposed to sale everywhere — in every marketplace, in every village doorway" (cited in Love 2020b). Today, t-shirts, keychains, ashtrays and other tourist merchandise with Sabina's image are still sold in marketplaces around Mexico and elsewhere, and international travelers continue to visit the region inspired by Wasson's story. Not only did the episode spark the first wave of psychedelic tourism, but the knowledge that was extracted provided a basis for the medicalization of psilocybin (Gerber et al. 2021).

According to the Global Wellness Institute, the "wellness tourism" market is projected to reach $1.4 trillion by 2027, doubling in size from 2022 (McGroarty 2023). Increasingly, this industry has moved in the direction of "spiritual" tourism, where people travel to foreign destinations for mystical experiences and spiritual growth. Psychedelic tourism and retreats have successfully carved out a niche within this industry. There are several reasons why psychedelic tourism has proliferated, including a greater awareness of the healing properties of psychedelics and a generalized identity crisis in the West — one marked by alienation from materialism and consumerism and the weakening of contemporary forms of religious life. Although psychedelic retreats are becoming popular in Western countries, many Westerners are drawn to nations of the Global South in search of more "authentic" spiritual experiences, which, in the context of commercialization, has become a brand in its own right.

Psychedelic tourism retreats can offer meaningful and powerful communal experiences undertaken in safe environments for healing, personal growth and consciousness expansion. Studies have shown, for example, that retreat attendees often demonstrate improvements in depression and anxiety symptoms following the use of psychedelics in these kinds of settings (Hardman 2023b). Psychedelic tourism can also provide benefits for Indigenous communities. While many Indigenous practitioners have spoken out against the commodification of psychedelics and related tourist activities, others have welcomed the participation of foreigners in their rituals and view it as a way to build partnerships and provide revenues to support community needs. During the COVID-19 pandemic, for example, some groups in the Amazon, like Shipibo-Conibo communities in Peru, were dealt a significant economic blow when they lost support from tourists participating in ayahuasca ceremonies. Some suggest that psychedelic tourism can also help protect Indigenous communities from other extractivist industries, such as logging, agriculture and mining (Vidriales and Ovies 2018). Despite these positive features of the industry, the rise of psychedelic tourism has resulted in a range of negative impacts that are directly connected to its commercialization. We address some of them here by focusing on the expansion of ayahuasca tourism.

Spurred on by romanticized images of Amazonia in the popular imagination, each year tens of thousands of tourists visit retreats in South America to consume ayahuasca under the guidance of Shipibo and other Indigenous healers (Fotiou 2016). One of the central hubs of ayahuasca tourism in the region is Iquitos, Peru. In 2016, thirty ayahuasca retreat centres were serving international clients in Iquitos; by 2019, this number had more than doubled to seventy (Gearin 2022). Before the pandemic shut down international travel in 2020, these retreat centres were serving between fifteen and twenty thousand international travelers annually, representing approximately US$17.5 million in retreat-booking sales. Entrepreneurs Awakening, whose clients include CEOs, banking executives and tech entrepreneurs, offers psychedelic-assisted executive coaching programs that include its signature Amazon Ayahuasca Mastermind Retreat program in Peru. These practices are now so commonplace that they have become a source of parody and amusement in popular culture, typified by a headline article in the satirical news magazine *The Onion*: "Ayahuasca shaman dreading another week of guiding tech CEOs to spiritual oneness."

Anthropologist Daniela Peluso (2017) makes an important distinction between ayahuasca as a contributor to the local economy and ayahuasca as a form of entrepreneurism. She notes that while *ayahuasqueros* (shamans who lead ayahuasca ceremonies) have long been integral to local and regional economies, "systems of reciprocity and tendencies toward egalitarianism" meant that their status did not result in economic stratification (2017, 205). In contrast, ayahuasca entrepreneurialism and processes of commodification have encouraged competitive individualism. The impacts of this shift include local people being unable to access *ayahuasqueros* due to tourist obligations and their inability to afford the increasingly expensive prices these ceremonies demand. Not only are local communities losing access to their own healing traditions, but inequality between and among healers is increasing. Some *ayahuasqueros* are now able to generate large incomes through opportunistic profit-making ventures with foreigners who are willing to shell out thousands of dollars for lodging and ceremonies. These sources of economic stratification are not confined to the Global South, as Indigenous practitioners (and their "gringo" proteges) are increasingly bringing their medicines to the Global North and providing ceremonies in Western countries, often at much higher prices.

Traditional ayahuasca rituals are also being modified or sanitized to cater to tourist markets (de Rios and Rumrrill 2008; Prayag et al. 2016). Aspects of traditional practices that do not accord with Western desires or stereotypes are reduced, while new sets of practices are added, such as a greater emphasis on new-age spirituality. Pre-ritual dietary restrictions have been expanded to match wellness discourses in the West and ayahuasca recipes have been altered to accommodate the desire for more powerful hallucinations. A parallel process can be seen in Mexico, where ceremonies involving psilocybin, peyote, San Pedro and ayahuasca are presided over by what are sometimes called "neo-shamans," or Indigenous practitioners who cater exclusively to tourists and incorporate new-age practices into their ceremonies. While some may view these changes as a rational response to a changing market, some anthropologists and Indigenous groups liken them to a form of colonization (Hay 2020; Peluso 2017). Foreign influence manifests in other ways too. In some countries, like Peru, the majority of ayahuasca tourist centres are owned and operated by Western entrepreneurs and investors. This follows a broader pattern of foreign ownership of tourist enterprises throughout Latin America. Co-founder of Women on Psychedelics, Jessika Lagarde (2021), says there are now more non-Indigenous people in Mexico holding psilocybin ceremonies and profiting off these ventures than Indigenous people, as local communities become estranged from their own traditions. This limits the economic benefits that psychedelic tourism can provide and supports longstanding cycles of economic dependency and wealth transfer from the Global South to the Global North (May 2017a).

The commercialization of ayahuasca also has implications for public health and safety. A growing number of knockoff mystics and pseudo-shamans with little or no training have "picked up the leaf rattle and learned the songs in order to cash in on the explosion of foreign cash" (Highpine 2018). Many established *ayahuasqueros* have expressed concerns about the growth of insufficiently trained practitioners, questioning the efficacy of their healing practices and how it could threaten the reputation of their profession. As Shipibo healer Pedro Tangoa López (2020) notes, "many Shipibo brothers, about my age, became shamans due to the economic boom, not because they were great sages. Some of them become shamans overnight just for the economic benefits." As a result, there is an increase in the number of inexperienced practitioners who may not be prepared to help people through bad trips or handle health emergencies that occasionally arise.

A lack of knowledge as well as stereotypical understandings of Indigenous spirituality can also make it easier for imposters to pass themselves off as experienced and authentic, including in Amazonian communities where ayahuasca is not part of local traditions. Tourists are offered fake ayahuasca on sidewalks and street corners, while unscrupulous shamans perform ceremonies with brews of questionable quality or that are deliberately altered to increase vulnerability and confusion. This has resulted in cases of serious illness and death as well as documented instances of sexual assault (Hearn 2013; Homan 2017; Perryer 2019; Thelwell 2014). Some analysts suggest that romanticized notions of purity and unconditional trust have played a role in the rising tide of sexual violence taking place in this context (Hay 2020). It is important to emphasize that the commercialized set and setting appears to be the main risk factor. According to a recent report by the International Center for Ethnobotanical Education, Research and Service (ICEERS 2023), among the fifty-eight fatalities linked to ayahuasca worldwide between 1994 and 2022, not one autopsy attributed these fatalities to acute ayahuasca intoxication (at least of the traditional brew of *Banisteriopsis caapi* and *Psychotria viridis*). In the few cases where ayahuasca did play a role, they concluded that these deaths could have been prevented if minimum safety standards had been followed.

Finally, the commercialization of ayahuasca tourism has led to concerns about ecological sustainability (Álvarez 2020; Ermakova 2022). It is a common assumption in the West that the only way to have an authentic ayahuasca experience is to travel to its natural habitat and work with an experienced shaman. While this sentiment is understandable and can benefit the parties involved, the sheer volume of tourist traffic has contributed to the overexploitation of wild ayahuasca vines. Ayahuasca tourism is driving deforestation, hastening the destruction of natural reserves and, as some have argued, reducing the quality of the vines and their medicinal properties. The impacts of extractive capitalism are not, however, limited to ayahuasca. The growing popularity of psychedelics and their commodification in both medical and non-medical contexts have resulted in unsustainable harvesting, poaching and other forms of ecological damage. Peyote is an obvious example. Wild peyote populations are in decline because of habitat destruction, unsustainable harvesting, illegal poaching and a growing number of psychedelic tourists traveling to the southern US to seek it out (Virdi 2020). Similar issues have emerged around the extraction of other psychoactive plants, such as *Acacia* subspecies, as well as iboga in Africa. It is not just plants that are at risk. 5-MeO-DMT is commonly extracted from the venom glands of the Sonoran Desert toad. Capturing toads for their venom causes ecological disturbances, displaces these creatures from their natural habitats and reduces their natural defence mechanisms (Villa 2023).

Reflecting on the future of psychedelic tourism, some have proposed that the development of synthetic alternatives could help to address these problems. This proposal is controversial, especially in the case of ayahuasca, since some see it as impossible to pharmacologically replicate ayahuasca's unique properties. It also raises ethical concerns. For instance, when Vancouver-based Filament Health announced plans to develop a medical-grade "pharmahuasca" pill, it was criticized for its lack of attention to informed consent, reciprocity and benefit sharing with Indigenous peoples (Holyanova 2023). At the same time, there is a tendency to glorify and romanticize all naturally occurring plants as the "real thing," while denigrating synthetics as inferior knockoffs. The insistence on using at-risk species when alternatives are available, especially if it risks undermining traditional religious and cultural practices, is a reckless position. Most psychedelics can be easily synthesized. According to Hamilton Morris, "you can take a hundred grams of melatonin and convert that to about a hundred grams of 5-MeO-DMT, which is the equivalent of milking thousands and thousands and thousands of toads" (cited in Ferriss 2021b). As the psychedelic renaissance advances, many naturally occurring psychedelics will not be able to withstand ever-increasing global demand. It is incumbent on those who care about this movement to be cognizant of psychedelic supply chains and their environmental, social and political implications. The potential of ecological collapse is one more reason to limit the exposure of these substances to the logic of capital accumulation.

INTELLECTUAL PROPERTY AND PATENT WARS

Intellectual property (IP) is a key indicator of psychedelic capitalism and one of the most contentious aspects of the psychedelic renaissance. Throughout the twentieth century, IP involving psychedelics was relatively limited. In the US, the first patent on LSD was granted in 1948 to the company Sandoz, naming Albert Hofmann and Arthur Stoll as co-inventors. Several other LSD patents were granted in subsequent decades. In 1997, for example, the Vivus corporation, which was profiled in the Netflix documentary *Orgasm Inc.*, received a patent on methods to treat premature ejaculation with a serotonin agonist, which included LSD (Psychedelic Alpha 2024d). With regard to other psychedelics, the first patents on psilocybin, which also involved chemist Albert Hofmann and his work at Sandoz, were granted in 1958-59. The pharmaceutical company Merck was granted two patents on MDMA in 1914, but the first patents filed for therapeutic purposes were not until the 2000s when several organizations filed applications to use MDMA to treat symptoms of Parkinson's disease. In the 1980s, Howard Lotsof, who first popularized the therapeutic benefits of ibogaine in the 1960s, and his company NDA International secured the first patents on ibogaine to treat various forms of addiction.

To obtain a psychedelic patent one has to convince a patent examiner that the technology or claimed invention is novel, non-obvious, useful and within the scope of patent-eligible subject matter. Many of the psychedelic compounds being researched today, such as psilocybin and DMT, cannot themselves be patented because they are products of nature. Others, like LSD and MDMA, are also ineligible because they were discovered in the early decades of the twentieth century and now exist in the public domain. Part of the reason the pharmaceutical industry has historically shown little interest in psychedelics is because their natural origin and/or established knowledge base makes them ineligible for patent protection. However, patent applicants can use strategies to get around these barriers, such as modifying the structure of psychedelic compounds to create novel formulations, producing or extracting them through new methods, combining them with non-psychoactive substances to alter their effects and/or citing new methods for their use (to treat a particular condition, like weight loss, for example). Even a small modification to a compound (such as adding an extra hydrogen atom) can be enough to make a patent claim, even though these new analogs rarely produce novel effects. Patents can also cover certain aspects of psychedelic administration, such as dosage or applications in a therapeutic context, including the set and setting in which drugs are administered. Taking psilocybin as an example, we have seen a significant rise in patent claims, including around methods of extracting or producing psilocybin, methods of using psilocybin to treat different conditions, dosage-form deliveries, as well as new formulations with a shorter duration of action or faster onset. The sheer number of these claims demonstrates how companies are increasingly attempting to erect legal barriers around substances that have been in the public domain for centuries.

One reason behind the growth in psychedelic IP is the lack of funding for public research and the scheduling of psychedelics as "drugs of abuse," which has made it more difficult to undertake research and has pushed the field in the direction of well-capitalized firms. Other actors, including researchers, non-profits, academic institutions and government bodies are also exploring psychedelic patents, with data being limited as patent applications are not typically published until eighteen months after being filed and they are not always made public. For example, one study found that Mind Medicine had included a reference to patenting or IP in only four of its nearly two hundred press releases. CEO Robert Barrow explained these limited public disclosures by stating there is "enormous commercial value to holding your cards close to your chest" (cited in Pratt and Shams 2024). Nevertheless, we do know enough to confirm that there has been a huge increase in psychedelic IP activity. *Psychedelic Alpha*'s patent tracker database tracks psychedelic-related patent applications and issued patents that were either filed in the US, or that later may be filed in the US. The latter cases involve Patent Cooperation Treaty applications, also known as international applications, where applicants can wait as long as thirty months before converting them into US applications. According to the database, between 2006 and 2015 there were 20 psilocybin-related patent filings listed. This figure grew to 108 between 2016 and 2019, and to over 380 between 2020 and August 2022. Turning to LSD, there were 26 filings listed between 2006 and 2015; 46 from 2016 to 2019; and 144 between 2020 and August 2022. Over these same three time periods, the numbers for MDMA were 25, 40 and 111; for DMT, they were 17, 49 and 147. As these data show, published patent applications increased dramatically from 2020 onwards. Psychedelic researcher Jacob Aday and his colleagues (2023, 17–18) summarize these trends as follows:

> Paralleling the rise of numerous companies formed over the course of just a few years, there has been an enormous increase in the breadth and depth of the patenting landscape. These patents have targeted new molecules, new formulations of existing molecules, new processes for extracting or synthetically producing psychedelics, ways to remove the subjective experience, combinations of psychedelics with adjunct digital therapy, the development of prodrugs, modification of the atomic structure of existing molecules to change their pharmacokinetics, and even aesthetics of the dosing room, among other strategies. This explosion in the number and type of patents in a short period of time has begun to provoke intense competition and litigation to fully secure the freedom to operate — some have described it as a battle to hold and secure the psychedelic space.

Next-Generation Psychedelics

Today, the preferred IP pathway for many industry leaders is the creation of next-generation psychedelics. A number of companies are exploring the potential of non-hallucinogenic compounds focused on shortening the trip or engineering out their subjective properties. Others are eyeing new compounds that may have similar therapeutic properties or advantages over existing formulations. While those involved in this work claim their focus is healing, scalability and access, the ability to secure IP — and thereby control anticipated profits — is front and centre. Generally, patent applications involving novel compounds are more likely to be successful than existing compounds, which has the potential to draw the interest of the pharmaceutical industry. In 2022, the CEO of Mindset Pharma, James Lanthier, said that the business case for next-generation psychedelics is clear: "given that they are 'new,' next generation drugs can enjoy much stronger intellectual property rights, which is essential for the broader pharma industry to make the investments necessary to bring them to market" (cited in Nielson 2022). Shortly thereafter, Mindset Pharma and its novel drug program were purchased by Otsuka. The professional services firm KPMG (2022) has also weighed in on this issue. In its report "Psychedelic Drugs: A Market Poised for Takeoff," the organization notes that to "assuage concerns" of the pharmaceutical industry and make themselves more attractive, psychedelic companies may need to shift their IP focus to "synthetic or deuterated versions that afford them the chance to differentiate their products from naturally occurring substances." Little mention is made of whether these new compounds might offer anything of value, outside of appealing to industry giants.

Atai Life Sciences has focused on expanding IP through novel compounds since its inception. In 2019, the company launched EntheogeniX to pursue new molecules using machine-learning-based drug discovery, and more recently Invyxis, a platform committed to developing new chemical entities. Compass Pathways is also focused on developing new compounds. To this end, they established the Discovery Center under a sponsored research agreement with the University of the Sciences in Philadelphia. The lead chemist, Jason Wallach, is charged with creating "new compounds that differ just a bit from classical psychedelics, like psilocybin or LSD" to fine-tune the contours of a psychedelic trip (Semley 2022). These tweaked molecules, already numbering in the hundreds, can all be patented by Compass Pathways as the lab's discoveries belong to the company, transferred via an "exclusive, royalty-bearing, worldwide license."

In terms of the sheer number of patentable molecules, Enveric Biosciences has its sights set even higher. Enveric acquired the privately held biotechnology firm MagicMed Industries in 2021, thereby gaining control of MagicMed's Psybrary, a vast library of novel drug candidates that elaborate on the chemical scaffolding of natural psychedelics. Enveric also uses artificial intelligence technology to streamline pharmaceutical design by predicting manufacturing capabilities and pharmacological effects. Its "plant to pill" approach is designed to create an endless array of drug candidates that can be licensed to other companies who want to commercialize them. If the broadest claims of the company's patent applications are granted, this could allow them to lock up a huge number of compounds under IP protection. In fact, according to Enveric's CEO Joseph Tucker, "when you take all the patents together and see how many molecules these patents are covering, it's more than one hundred million … If this works out the way we expect, we think we'll have a dominating patented state on the new molecules in the space" (Psychedelic Invest 2021b). While these claims likely overstate what they will actually be able to achieve, this scope of control would no doubt hinder scientific progress (Greenberg and Capps 2021).

Just as interesting as the growth in next-generation psychedelics is the discourse put forward to explain it. In particular, companies and researchers are pointing to the work of open-science advocate Sasha Shulgin. Shulgin discovered, synthesized and self-tested hundreds of new psychedelics and made his findings freely available. Mindset CEO James Lanthier has praised "Shulgin and the other trailblazing psychedelic scientists of the 20th century" as being pivotal in exposing the "undiscovered continent of psychedelics" (cited in Nielson 2022). According to John Semley's (2022) exposé on Jason Wallach and the Discovery Center for *WIRED*, Wallach considers Shulgin to be one of his heroes and has said he taught himself how to make psychedelics by following Shulgin's open-source instructions. Although Wallach is against prohibition and DEA restrictions on psychedelic compounds, he is not similarly critical of the restrictions that Compass Pathways is attempting to assert over the field. "I'm definitely aware of those criticisms," Wallach says. "But I have no reservations." As Semley notes, before leaving the Discovery Center after conducting research for his article, he was "cautioned against stealing away with any proprietary chemical names or structures."

Chemists and other researchers continue to be inspired by the work of Shulgin and others. However, the recent focus on securing IP and corporate control is at odds with the original tenets of his approach to open science. A better illustration of the relationship between Shulgin's legacy and IP-focused drug companies is found in an article by Sean Vandersluis (2021) called "Building on the Shulgin Approach." Vandersluis is a former contract writer for MagicMed Industries who now works for Enveric Biosciences in the same capacity. Although the article offers some perfunctory praise for Shulgin's work, it largely seeks to discredit underground research and open science:

> Companies today such as MagicMed Industries are building on what Shulgin started but in a much larger and more scientifically rigorous way ... Shulgin's sentiment of wanting everyone to benefit from his psychedelics was performed with good intentions but his approach is impossible for most psychedelic companies ... Shulgin himself was not synthesizing his compounds in [good manufacturing practice, or GMP] settings thus exposing anyone who took the drugs to great risk. By not following GMP standards, the compounds cannot be consistently reproduced leading to structure variances due to the lack of quality control. Compounding these risks were the inexperienced chemists who attempted to synthesize these compounds themselves after reading his books ... By publishing his compounds in books, they became public domain, cannot be patented and thus will never attract investors to help develop them into effective medicines ... Contrary to Shulgin's small scale approach that at times lacked scientific rigor, MagicMed is taking a robust, scientific approach to generate many novel analogs in the patented compound library.

Some next-generation drug developers may be interested in optimizing the psychedelic experience for patients, but the focus on producing new molecules rather than building on research to understand the therapeutic efficacy of those that exist remains highly suspect.

Psychedelics in a Broken IP System

In 2022, Shayla Love wrote an article for *VICE* called "Psychedelic Patents Are Broken Because the Patent System is Broken," one of many pieces she has produced on IP in the psychedelic sector (Love 2022c). Love discusses several harmful impacts of the US IP system in the area of pharmaceuticals and drug development, including the production of monopolies, high drug prices and growing economic inequality. "These glaring issues with the patent system," she writes, "should be a concern for the emerging psychedelic industry, which is entering into the world of patenting at scale for the very first time." Some of the same issues discussed by Love were brought to the public's attention during the COVID-19 pandemic. Years after the COVID-19 vaccine had been produced, only a small proportion of people in low-income countries had received a single dose, eliciting strong criticism from academics, international bodies and civil society. These disparities are related to how IP regimes allow high-income countries to hoard knowledge, medications and diagnostics.

In the psychedelics field, the role of IP remains a subject of intense debate (Ferriss 2021c). Proponents argue that drug development is risky and expensive and that, without IP protection, companies would not be able to fund research and development to create new products and move them through the development pipeline. Moreover, proponents claim that patents are crucial for attracting venture capital. In a crowded marketplace, one of the only things that differentiates drug developers is the promise of future returns through IP. IP does not even have to be secured. Even the prospects of obtaining IP rights can make a company more attractive to investors. "It's kind of like an insurance policy," says Gretchen Temelesan, an IP lawyer on the board of psychedelics investment fund Palo Santo Ventures. She argues that patents are vital for attracting investment capital and avoiding the "nightmare scenario" of competitors being able to duplicate and sell the same products (cited in Zarley 2021). These sentiments are echoed by Atai Life Sciences founder Christian Angermayer (2021), who writes, "Without the chance of turning millions into billions, the investors disappear, and without the hundreds of millions of dollars from investors, progress to bring these medicines to patients slows to a glacial pace." For others, the benefits of IP go beyond drug development to include the value of companies as acquisition targets. Sabrina Ramkellawan, chief operating officer with Knowde Group, an organization that provides clinical trial management services for psychedelic firms, predicts that what will attract large pharmaceutical companies to purchase psychedelic start-ups is the strength of their IP portfolios. "They're not going to just come in and (buy) someone who is growing some psilocybin," she adds (cited in McGovern 2022b).

Some proponents also point to public policy justifications for securing IP. From this perspective, the right to exclude competitors can incentivize innovation, directing resources and energy into bringing novel therapies to market. Patents can also encourage investors to disclose their inventions to the public rather than locking them down as trade secrets. One of the most common arguments in support of IP concerns the welfare of potential patients as IP protections are said to speed up the process whereby new drugs can reach those who require new treatments. According to science journalist Marcelo Leite (2021), it is not only "greedy capitalists" who side with this viewpoint but respected psychedelic researchers as well. Neuropsychopharmacologist David Nutt, for example, argues that "patents might be a price we have to pay" to have psychedelics regulated in a timely fashion, while pharmacologist David Nichols believes there is "such a huge need for new therapies for treating depression and addictions that it seems improbable to me that a not-for-profit strategy is sustainable."

Critics counter these claims, especially as they relate to innovation. There are many ways that patents can discourage innovation, hinder competition and hamper research and development. For example, when confronted with a growing number of patents in a given field, start-up inventors tend to reduce their research and development expenditures (Day and Schuster 2019). Not only can patents discourage competitors from entering a field, but they can also force them to divert resources to disputes over ownership. These challenges are especially difficult in the face of patent "thickets" — dense webs of overlapping IP rights that are formed when patent holders make many claims on the same or closely related products. According to the Initiative for Medicines, Access, and Knowledge (2022), who advocate for affordable access to medicine, the US drug industry is rife with anti-competitive patent thickets. They found that, in 2022, an average of seventy-four patents had been granted on each of America's ten best-selling pharmaceutical drugs. Of the 140 average patent applications that were filed on each of these drugs, two-thirds were filed *after* they had already been approved by the FDA, indicating that drugmakers are attempting to extend their exclusivity (and high prices) for as long as possible. There is already evidence of patent thickets emerging in psychedelics; the top psychedelic companies have submitted applications for or own the rights to hundreds of patents (and given delays in publications there are conceivably hundreds more). Patent attorney Graham Pechenik has been sounding the alarm about problematic patents in the psychedelic industry for years. He points to the enormous risk of patents "suppressing research and hindering healthy competition ... History spills over with examples of developing industries consumed by patent wars — from the steam engine and sewing machine, to the lightbulb and radio, up through the smartphone" (cited in McDaniel 2021). According to *The New York Times* (2022):

> Drugmakers for decades have argued that patents are essential to American innovation. For all that lip service to medical advancement, though ... market share is more likely the point. Twelve of the drugs that Medicare spends the most on are protected by more than 600 patents in total ... Many of these patents contain little that's truly new. But the thickets they create have the potential to extend product monopolies for decades. In so doing, they promise to add billions to the nation's soaring health care costs — and to pharmaceutical coffers.

A related issue of concern is "patent trolls," which are companies that are exclusively focused on licensing patents and suing for IP infringement. Patent trolls often buy up patents from struggling companies who want to monetize their remaining assets or acquire liquidated IP from failed firms. Armed with these patents — which are often broad in scope or "low quality" — they can target researchers and small developers with the threat of legal action unless the alleged infringer pays a licensing fee. This practice is often successful, as individuals look to avoid patent litigation, and can inhibit research and innovation. According to lawyer Matt Zorn (2022a), who specializes in patent litigation and describes controlled substances as his "side hustle," it has been estimated that patent trolls cost businesses $29 billion a year in direct expenses, "costs that disproportionately fall on innovative companies." Though it is too early to gauge how these practices might impact psychedelics, Zorn suggests they may be significant. As the industry advances, many start-ups will fail and patents will be picked up by others, potentially leading to a rash of aggressive lawsuits. Graham Pechenik agrees, adding that this could put a damper on the development of future medicalized markets and the applications of psychedelics in legalized markets, and might even have implications in decriminalized settings (Austin and Pechenik 2023).

Critics of IP-related innovation claims also point to the fact that most new drug patents are not associated with new drugs. One investigation found that between 2005 and 2015, 78 percent of the drugs associated with new patents were not actually novel (Feldman 2018). This stems, in part, from a practice known as "evergreening" or "product-hopping," which involves making small modifications to a drug or the process of producing it (often just before a patent expires) in order to refresh the IP with a slightly adapted version. The copycat version, protected by new patents, can be used to extend exclusivity, but it is rarely associated with any demonstrated medicinal or therapeutic advantages. The "innovation" involved here is about manipulating the legal system. As journalist Luke Goldstein (2022) puts it, "gaming patent laws is hardwired into the DNA of every major pharmaceutical giant."

Mason Marks and Glenn Cohen (2021) of the Project on Psychedelics Law and Regulation (POPLAR) at Harvard University point to esketamine as an example of product-hopping in the psychedelic field. Janssen Pharmaceuticals was able to capitalize on ketamine's off-label status and potential efficacy in treating depression by patenting intranasal esketamine at specific dose ranges. Its branded product Stravato — by no means a novel invention — is protected by multiple patents, is expensive and has no proven therapeutic advantage over generic ketamine (Bahji, Vazquez and Zarate 2021; Ramos, Boyd and Alpert 2019; Sagonowsky 2019). The Canadian Federal Court of Appeal recently ruled esketamine is not an "innovative drug" eligible for data exclusivity. Esketamine coming at a higher cost than original compounds is not unique in this context. Patents are often leveraged to reduce competition and obtain market exclusivity, which can result in high prices. Indeed, patents in the pharmaceutical industry tend to go hand-in-hand with drug monopolies and price gouging (Initiative for Medicines, Access, and Knowledge 2022). In the case of psychedelics, the claim that IP and for-profit development expedites the process by which these substances can reach people who need or desire them is highly suspect. To date, psychedelic companies and their executives have delivered these substances to very few people outside of clinical trials, and most approvals are, at best, still years away. Decriminalization and models of regulated legalization that are not restricted to medical diagnoses would be a faster and more equitable route, but they also represent a threat to those companies looking to wield monopoly power over psychedelics.

The biggest problem is that IP regimes expand and entrench systems of social and economic inequality. In his book *Owning the Sun* (2022), Alexander Zaitchik notes that between 2000 and 2018, the world's thirty-five largest drug companies reported gross profits of nearly $9 trillion. Zaitchik argues these astronomical sums were less a product of genuine innovation and more about the ability of these companies to dominate the market through IP. In his words, "The industry's Merlins aren't its scientists and technicians but its patent lawyers and lobbyists … The kind of wealth amassed by the pharmaceutical industry can be created only by the political magic of monopoly" (2022, xi). Economist Dean Baker's work (2016) shows that as IP laws were expanded, the share of income flowing to the pharmaceutical and medical equipment industries sharply increased. He argues this shift was unnecessary, as alternative mechanisms for financing creativity and innovation (such as direct public funding for drug research) have proven effective in the past and would not have resulted in the same upward redistribution (see also Aghion et al. 2019; Chien 2022). Despite the claim that the psychedelic industry represents something fundamentally different than other industries, there is every reason to expect that injustices supported by the race to obtain IP will be replicated here.

"Bad Patents" and the Challenge of Prior Art

In addition to the structural inequities inherent in IP regimes, there is also the more specific problem of low-quality patents, or what are called "bad patents." This designation can result from multiple factors, including trivial variations on inventions, obvious applications of things that are already known and/or patents that are broad in scope and claim ownership of what is already in the public domain. Recent research has documented a surge of overly broad patent applications (and granted patents) on psilocybin, LSD, DMT, 5-MeO DMT and mescaline (Shams et al. 2023). The risk of bad patents may be higher in the psychedelic industry than in most other fields, in part because of the challenges associated with "prior art." Prior art refers to evidence or documentation that is available or has been publicly disclosed that might be relevant to a patent claim. This includes any evidence that an invention is already known or has been used in the past, such as previous patents and patent applications, printed publications and products that already exist in the marketplace. If a patent examiner discovers relevant prior art, it can serve as a basis for rejecting a patent. A patent application on using LSD to treat alcoholism, for example, should be difficult to obtain given the large body of prior art established by Western researchers and therapists in the mid-twentieth century.

The nature of psychedelic prior art is complex and not necessarily accessible to patent examiners. Given the legacy of criminalization and prohibition, public disclosures may be less common, including because of the periods of hiatus on psychedelic research within established institutions. A lot of older research exists in archives, anecdotal stories and case reports, with some underground researchers and practitioners documenting their work in relatively obscure forums, like online forums Bluelight, Shroomery, DMT-Nexus and Erowid. In addition, vast amounts of knowledge rest with Indigenous communities and are shared through oral traditions, which tend not to be well-documented in the West. In some cases, this knowledge has been transmitted this way as a deliberate strategy to protect it (Hauskeller et al. 2022). Patent offices have limited resources and typically lack the time to explore and seek out these and other alternative sources of knowledge and information. The IP system also "prioritizes and biases itself towards a specific form of Western epistemology that gave birth to the patent system in the first place" (Kerdemelidis et al. 2022). These biases were evident, for example, in a patent that was granted to American bio-prospector Loren Miller in the 1980s for his "discovery" of a particular strain of ayahuasca (Press 2022) — a patent case centred around what Kenneth Tupper (2009, 128) calls a "paradigmatic instance of biopiracy." Given that a lot of psychedelic prior art remains elusive, it is easier for companies to secure approvals for "bad patents."

Bad patent applications litter the psychedelic landscape. One application that was heavily criticized came from New York University in 2020, which sought to patent the use of psilocybin to treat depression and anxiety in cancer patients, despite the well-established history of this kind of therapy in clinical research. The details of the application suggest a deliberate effort to deceive the patent office (see Zorn 2022b). Other bad patents have already been granted, some of which would likely never have passed if prior art had been considered. As another example, in 2020, long-time patent attorney and IP expert David Casimir flagged a patent that was granted for a "method for treatment of depression using synaptic pathway training," which is focused on using psychedelics and "cognitive training exercises" to treat depression and other conditions (see Zarley 2021). The patent defines a cognitive training exercise as "an activity relating to or involving conscious intellectual activity, including but not limited to thinking, reasoning, or remembering," which is basically analogous to therapy. Casimir argues that not only are the claims overly broad and obvious, but if psychedelic prior art had been taken into account, the patent would not have been granted.

In 2021, another patent was issued for using LSD to treat food allergies, an area for which there is ample evidence of prior art that called into question whether the claim was novel and non-obvious, including a physician discussing LSD as a treatment for allergies on Joe Rogan's podcast, previous academic publications and considerable online discussion and commentary. At the same time, there is little evidence to support the effectiveness of using psychedelics to treat food or other allergies. While this is by no means the most egregious example of bad patents in the psychedelic field, the case is interesting because it suggests that the bar for showing something actually works before asserting ownership is remarkably low, that applicants can assert ownership claims despite little involvement in or knowledge about what are trying to patent and that evidence of relevant prior art is being neglected.

In 2022, a patent was granted for a DMT vape pen (it also covered vape pens using 5-MeO-DMT and 2C-B), which is an e-cigarette that uses a liquid cartridge containing DMT. The sole "inventor" associated with the claim was a patent lawyer. There were no complicated issues of psychedelic prior art in this case as a quick Google search reveals people selling DMT vape pens all over the internet. However, the patent examiner spent only a few minutes searching for prior art (Psychedelic Alpha 2022b). The vape pen patent exemplifies some of the broader issues in psychedelic capitalism. The "patent land grab" is reaching much further than mental health. It is being folded into all sorts of other inventions that happen to include psychedelics as an optional or potential part of those inventions. One example is a patent application for a device that creates a "personalized scent bubble." The device could be used with perfume and other liquids like insect repellent, but the application also includes psychedelics like LSD and psilocybin (Love 2021e).

One final example concerns a potentially harmful patent granted to Mind Medicine in 2022. The application was filed by Dr. Matthias Liechti, who runs a lab at the University of Basel in Switzerland. Mind Medicine owns the commercial rights to patents filed by Liechti's lab. This patent was granted for a combination of LSD and MDMA, known as "candy flipping" (combining the two drugs in a single psychedelic experience). The practice of ingesting these drugs at the same time is by no means a new invention, as it has been common practice for decades.

The "novel" aspect of the claim, according to Mind Medicine, was that they were using the drugs in the same single dosage oral form, whereas recreational users use them in separate dosage forms. Researcher Matt Baggott disputed this assertion by simply pointing to non-profit psychedelic educational organization Erowid's drug analysis program, which lists twenty examples of people putting LSD and MDMA together in the same oral preparation. Also problematic is that the patent was overly broad and ostensibly gave Mind Medicine the sole right to combine empathogens/entactogens (such as MDMA, MDA, MDEA) with classical psychedelics (such as LSD, DMT, mescaline) into the same single oral dosage form. The patent also covered how these combinations would be used, including for the treatment of numerous psychiatric disorders. This is not the only example of a problematic patent claim associated with Mind Medicine. According to researchers, approximately 90 percent of the company's active patent applications "would do significant damage to the psychedelic field if granted by locking historically utilized therapies behind high paywalls and limiting future research" (Pratt and Shams 2024).

It is important to note that Mind Medicine's patents, and many others that represent a threat to the psychedelic commons, have not gone unchallenged. Porta Sophia — a non-profit organization founded by David Casimir that seeks to protect psychedelic technologies in the public domain — filed third-party submissions to dispute the "candy flipping" patent. Though it was unsuccessful in this case, Porta Sophia continues to challenge similar patents. As of September 2023, the group had filed sixty third-party interventions on applications they found especially egregious (Pratt and Shams 2024). Twelve of these were filed in response to applications submitted by Mind Medicine or its partners at the University of Basel. Porta Sophia has also created a psychedelic prior art library which, at the time of this writing, includes over 1,900 curated pieces of prior art relevant to over fifty different psychedelic compounds. It is meant to be a resource for patent examiners as well as the public and other parties who are interested in challenging applications and making third-party submissions. The database also has the potential to prevent bad patents, because once a group becomes aware of prior art it has a legal obligation (in the US at least) to disclose it to patent examiners ("duty of candor"). As a result of Porta Sophia's interventions, many patent applications have either been abandoned or rejected by the

United States Patent and Trademark Office, citing prior art from Porta Sophia as the reason. One of these included a claim by Yale University and the US Department of Veterans Affairs to patent the use of psychedelics to treat headaches. The drugs claimed as "innovative" treatments in the application included psilocybin, LSD, mescaline and DMT.

Porta Sophia is supported in its efforts by another patent "watchdog" called Freedom to Operate, founded by prominent psychedelic figurehead Carey Turnbull. Freedom to Operate is well financed and has spent millions of dollars challenging bad patents in the psychedelic sector. It has also been using other strategies, such as urging psychedelic companies to agree not to enforce certain patent provisions and "defensive publishing" that puts existing research in the public domain where it can serve as prior art. One company where both groups see little evidence of genuine IP innovation is Compass Pathways. Compass' IP activities have not only put the company in their crosshairs but also invited criticism from a broader segment of the psychedelic community and beyond.

Compass Pathways

Compass Pathways has received a lot of attention both within and outside of psychedelic circles. Its critics often portray it as the arch villain of the psychedelic renaissance. We will not rehash all of the criticism that has been levelled against it here, but the company's backstory is one element worth highlighting. Compass' inauspicious entry into the field was brought to wider attention by Olivia Goldhill (2018) in *Quartz*. Goldhill notes that Compass was first registered as a charitable organization by George Goldsmith and Ekaterina "Katya" Malievskaia in 2015. At the time, the organization was focused on using psilocybin to treat end-of-life anxiety in terminally ill patients. Goldsmith and Malievskaia were also working closely with academics and other researchers with expertise in psilocybin. Some of these researchers were drawn in by the couple's expressed goal of creating a psilocybin hospice on the Isle of Man, where their non-profit entity would conduct clinical trials. Researchers on their team also welcomed the couple's publicly stated interest in open science and data sharing. As George Goldsmith asserted at the Interdisciplinary Conference on Psychedelic Research in Amsterdam in June 2016, "We need open science … And that means that we really need to be sharing data, so that the rising tide lifts all boats. This is not something that I think we can withhold." Just ten days after Goldsmith's comments, however, he and Malievskaia did an about-face, creating the for-profit company Compass Pathways. They also began the process of winding down their non-profit shortly thereafter. According to Goldhill, the timing of the shift raised serious questions "about when Goldsmith and Malievskaia knew that they were planning to switch to a for-profit model, and whether they failed to disclose this to their collaborators while continuing to get valuable information from them under the guise that they were running a charity." Further questions were raised when IP that was owned by the charity was allegedly transferred directly to Goldsmith and Malievskaia.

The abrupt end of the non-profit surprised many of their advisors, with nine of them eventually coming out to suggest that Compass Pathways was deliberately employing tactics that put them in a position to dominate the field, such as blocking the ability of potential rivals to purchase drugs and requiring contracts that gave Compass power over academic research. For example, when Compass signed an exclusive contract with biotech firm Onyx Pharmaceuticals — the only mass producer of pharmaceutical-grade (GMP) psilocybin at the time — to expedite one of its clinical trials, it was able to block the non-profit Usona Institute from accessing GMP psilocybin for its own clinical trial. While this move could be interpreted as a conventional business tactic, "it shocked those who had advised Goldsmith and Malievskaia in the spirit of open science" (Goldhill 2018). At the same time, Compass was asserting control over academic research. While the company did allow independent researchers to access GMP psilocybin, it did so on the condition that it would control any published results and potential IP that emerged from their work. Some of the contracts between Compass and researchers went so far as to stipulate that "Compass can block the public discussion of any study results or the publication of any academic papers if it determines that would interfere with 'interests of secrecy or commercial interests' of the company." According to John Abramson, an expert in healthcare policy at Harvard Medical School, these contracts were restrictive even by pharmaceutical industry standards.

By 2017, Compass' network of associates looked quite different. It now included Peter Thiel, Mike Novogratz and Christian Angermayer, all early investors in the new for-profit entity. In a display of unusual candor (even for him), Angermayer stated that he recalls the 2018 *Quartz* article by Goldhill and believes it positively impacted the company's bottom line. "It was actually a huge boost for Compass fundraising because it stated the obvious" — that Compass did have a monopoly on synthetic psilocybin at the time. "I know George and Katya [didn't] want to say that, and I'm like 'Why not?' ... Biotech is all about having monopoly. That's the whole of biotech" (cited in Lee 2023). Peter Thiel would agree, having penned a piece in *The Wall Street Journal* some years earlier that defended economic monopolies as a positive and liberating force for society (Thiel 2014). Neither of these free-market champions mentioned the fact that monopolies in biotech (and elsewhere) are supported by large public subsidies and granted and enforced by the state through highly protectionist IP mechanisms.

Having secured a cadre of wealthy investors, Compass turned its focus to IP. The company's first set of US patent claims provided some indication of how the company would proceed; that is, using overly broad claims to test the waters of what might be possible in this emerging space. Most of Compass' US claims centred around polymorph A (COMP 360), the company's synthetic crystalline form of psilocybin. As many observers noted at the time, its first US patent application included twenty-seven claims of novelty (Love 2021f; O'Brien 2020). These claims were challenged by Carey Turnbull citing prior art, leading the company to withdraw them all. It then resubmitted its application with ten claims of novelty, which was also challenged by Turnbull, and again, the claims were withdrawn. Compass' application was eventually approved in late 2019 with one independent claim of novelty. In 2020, Turnbull again disputed the patent through patent watchdog Freedom to Operate by submitting a petition to have it invalidated, but this was rejected in August of that year. A month later, Compass launched its IPO. In 2021, Freedom to Operate, working with scientists, launched more rigorous challenges to Compass' patents on synthetic psilocybin, claiming it was not a novel invention. Once again, they were shot down. Others have questioned whether Compass should have been allowed to patent its psilocybin polymorph. Mason Marks and Glenn Cohen (2021), for example, pointed out that some countries do not allow polymorph patents and that the United Nations explicitly recommended that patent examiners should consider polymorphs of existing inventions to be unpatentable. Not to mention the fact that there is no evidence that COMP360 has any clinical advantages over mushrooms growing in one's backyard.

In addition to the controversy surrounding Compass' US patents, its international (PCT) patent applications have also come under heavy scrutiny. In 2020-21, the company filed a series of applications that attempted to patent psilocybin treatments for almost every mental health condition imaginable. These included most disorders the public would be familiar with as well as others that are more obscure, like selective mutism, pyromania, skin-picking and progressive supranuclear ophthalmoplegia. Compass basically copied the Diagnostic and Statistical Manual of Mental Disorders and pasted it into their applications. Although company executives claimed they were only pursuing patents on their own synthetic psilocybin, the international filings suggest that, in fact, the claims were deliberately worded to include blanket coverage. According to Graham Pechenik: "Broadly construed, these cover administering psilocybin in any form — not only polymorph A or hydrate A, not only synthetic, not only purified … [the claims] indeed cover any administration of psilocybin" (cited in McDaniel 2021). Moreover, the claims included treatments with "psilocybin or an *active metabolite* thereof," which would presumably include psilocin and other related compounds (Hausfeld and Nickles 2021, emphasis in original). The company also attempted to patent basic elements of psychedelic-assisted therapy — therapeutic applications that have been rightly described as "cartoonishly generic" (Goldstein 2022). These included the use of soft furnishings, and rooms decorated with "muted colors" or containing a "high-resolution sound system." Other patent claims involved the behaviour of participants, like wearing eye shades, listening to music and laying down on a bed or couch, as well as specifications for patient-therapist interactions, such as holding hands, touching a subject's shoulder and the therapist responding to the subject "if the subject initiates conversation" (Love 2021f; McDaniel 2021). Some of the components in these applications were scaled back after a third-party challenge from Porta Sophia.

While many of these IP claims are clearly a stretch, overly broad patent claims serve several purposes. To start, there is always the off chance that one can slip through a patent office. Many patent examiners do not have much experience with psychedelics and may not be familiar with prior art. Even if a broad claim is rejected, a company can see how a patent office responds and is then in a better position to construct more focused claims with a higher likelihood of success.

Broad patent claims also tend to have a "scorched earth" function that can effectively block research and competition. Once competitors know that certain indications are included in patent applications, it creates an atmosphere of fear and/or uncertainty where they are less likely to conduct their own research or file their own applications. In the case of Compass, those close to the company were complicit in implementing this strategy and well aware of its implications. Christian Angermayer, for instance, has said that the strategy of both Compass and Atai Life Sciences was to direct their lawyers to make patent claims "as broad as possible." He added in a statement to investors that other psychedelic companies "will never be able to bring a product to market, as they will hit the patents of Compass and Atai" (cited in Love 2022c). This kind of direct narrative is not usually relayed to the public. According to John Semley's *WIRED* exposé (2022), Compass executives "exhibit the corporate tendency to stay frustratingly on message. Ask them what they had for breakfast and they'll tell you how excited they are to build a new future for mental health." Compass has also been accused of stealing trade secrets from psychedelic researchers and incorporating this information into its patent applications. In 2024, the University of Maryland joined Professor Scott Thompson and Terran Biosciences in their lawsuit against the company related to these practices (Borchardt 2024). Ultimately, Compass' IP strategy is aimed at building a vertically integrated monopoly to dominate the psilocybin supply chain from synthesis to therapy, using whatever means necessary.

Psychedelic Enclosure

The full implications of corporate ownership and psychedelic IP are not yet known. But it is clear that the psychedelic renaissance is in the early stages of an enclosure movement, where new entrants in the field are attempting to secure as much of the terrain as quickly as they can, and largely to the exclusion of those who served as the stewards of these substances in the past. Corporations are claiming ownership over substances and practices that have been developed over centuries in Indigenous communities, usually without any acknowledgment, consent or compensation. Both national and international IP frameworks disregard collective discoveries and advancements made by early researchers and Indigenous peoples in favour of individual "inventors" in commercial laboratories. The resulting privatization of knowledge is an affront to the norms of open science and research sharing that have long been present in underground, academic and non-profit settings. In the field of IP, patent watchdogs, researchers and activists continue to challenge harmful patents, but this will continue to be difficult in the context of institutional structures that are deeply defective. Psychedelics, it would seem, have been swept up into the well-rehearsed capitalist playbook where private players are incentivized and enabled to fabricate exclusionary rights over what are ultimately the products of collective human struggle and intellectual achievement.

08

LEGAL CHANGE AND PSYCHEDELIC FUTURES

IN THE EARLY TO MID-TWENTIETH CENTURY, researchers studied the benefits of psychedelics like psilocybin, mescaline and LSD. In the 1960s and 1970s, prohibition took hold with Canada, the US and international bodies ratcheting up mechanisms to control psychedelic and other drug use. Today, we see the resumption of psychedelic science and lively debates concerning decriminalization and legalization initiatives. Pharmaceutical consultant David Heal and his colleagues (2023) suggest we are standing on the threshold of a therapeutic "revolution." There has never been more interest in the potential of psychedelics to treat mental health conditions, and clinical research is evolving and informing the approval of psychedelics as medicines. Alongside this shift, the law is beginning to change. However, changes in drug law tend to be narrow in scope, treating psychedelics as if they are merely medicinal in nature. Do we want to limit the potential uses, benefits and applications of psychedelics to the medical realm? Who is included or excluded in this therapeutic "revolution" and who stands to benefit? What kinds of social control and criminalization policies will continue or increase if access is determined by medical and corporate authorities?

The biomedical approach is currently the chief influence on drug law and the primary avenue for psychedelic access in most jurisdictions across North America. The biomedical model may be helpful for some people suffering from particular conditions, but it is also informed by processes of medicalization and corporatization. As a result, virtually any potential benefits that might be gained through the medical realm will be subject to corporate capture in some fashion (Roy 2023). The biomedical model, as it relates to psychedelics and its influence on psychedelic law, will continue to restrict access and allow the corporate-medical complex to direct what drug laws will look like with a focus on financial motives.

Other possible psychedelic futures exist outside of the dominant model of medical access and corporate control, and currently exist to varying degrees in different contexts (Schwarz-Plaschg 2022). Decriminalization allows for these substances to be used in a variety of ways and with a reduced threat of police surveillance, arrest and prosecution. There are many justifications for decriminalizing psychedelics, such as those grounded in public health and cognitive liberty (Boire 2000; Marlan 2019). Legalization can also allow for greater access to be provided through, for example, psychedelic service centres that operate outside of or adjacent to the biomedical system.

While progress has been made in some jurisdictions, it is an open question as to whether psychedelic law is moving forward in a positive way. In both Canada and the US, access to psychedelics remains limited and recreational use continues to be criminalized in most places. As the medical legalization of psychedelics deepens, we could see the continuation and intensification of criminal penalties and enforcement for recreational and other uses. It is in the public interest to move beyond a myopic focus on medical legalization and prohibitionist approaches to a more open model of public access focused on public and community health. This approach would not only serve to mitigate some of the threats associated with the corporate capture of psychedelics, but it could also reduce the harms associated with criminalization and the war on drugs. Moreover, this approach should extend to all drugs and not focus on psychedelics alone.

LEGAL ACCESS TO PSYCHEDELICS IN CANADA

In Canada, legal access to psychedelics is largely limited to a biomedical approach. Although there is currently not much discussion or debate around decriminalization or broader forms of legalization at the federal level, people can legally access psychedelics for medicinal purposes through three main pathways (Doll 2024). The first pathway is via clinical trials. Clinical trials in Canada must receive Health Canada authorization and either an exemption under the *Controlled Drugs and Substances Act* (CDSA) or authorization under the Food and Drug Regulations.

Although most psychedelic trials are being conducted in the US, there are a limited number of ongoing trials in Canada. The second pathway to legally access psychedelics is through section 56(1) of the CDSA. Under this section the Minister of Health can provide an exemption to access a drug for medical, scientific, research or religious purposes. For example, TheraPsil, a non-profit coalition from BC that advocates for medicinal access to psilocybin, has been helping palliative care patients with terminal diagnoses as well as patients with life-threatening diseases obtain approval to use psilocybin under section 56(1). Healthcare professionals can also petition the government for patient access under this provision.

The third legally permitted pathway to medicinal psychedelics is through the Special Access Program (SAP), which exists so that a practitioner can appeal to the Minister of Health for access to drugs at a patient's request. The SAP is outlined in Canada's Food and Drug Regulations (C.08.010 and C.08.011) and Health Canada makes the decision to grant access. A drug must have some officially recognized therapeutic potential for it to be eligible for the SAP. The difference between section 56(1) and the SAP is that the SAP has a defined timeline for ministerial decision making and is restricted to a therapeutic context. In 2022, for example, psychedelic company Numinus Wellness received Health Canada approval for psilocybin treatment under the SAP. The approval allowed Numinus to work with psilocybin in their clinics for patients approved under the protocols. Psilocybin is being provided to Numinus by Psygen, which has also been approved under Health Canada's SAP. Psygen obtained a dealer's licence to create Canada's first dedicated psychedelics manufacturing facility in Calgary. To qualify for the SAP, an applicant must have a serious or life-threatening condition and must have already undergone conventional treatments. Only then can they make applications to a healthcare professional.

There are notable challenges with the SAP pathway. For example, lengthy delays and arbitrary denials led TheraPsil to launch a Charter challenge in 2022 for the legalization of therapeutic psilocybin in Canada. Its basic position is that section 7 of the *Canadian Charter of Rights and Freedoms* (the state cannot infringe on life, liberty and security of the person) is violated when people in medical need are denied. TheraPsil's challenge was supported by a fundraising initiative to take the federal government to court. TheraPsil argues that there are medical grounds for changing the way psilocybin is scheduled in Canada, that psilocybin is legally similar to medical cannabis because it can alleviate suffering with minimal risks and that doctors and patients, not the federal government, should take the lead in determining access as the government lacks the capacity to make such decisions. If successful, the TheraPsil case has the potential to set new legal precedents.

One of the plaintiffs in TheraPsil's Charter challenge was Thomas Hartle, the first person in Canada to legally access psilocybin-assisted therapy. His case exemplifies the problems with Canadian laws. Diagnosed with terminal cancer, Hartle had originally been granted an exemption in 2020 under Health Canada's CDSA, which allowed him to legally grow mushrooms and use them under the care of a professional for a term of one year. When the term was up, he re-applied. While awaiting the decision, Hartle was able to access psilocybin twice through a doctor under the SAP. However, he had to travel to BC for those sessions, which was onerous and expensive. In March 2023, 511 days after reapplying for his second section 56(1) medical exemption, Health Canada rejected his application. The agency cited Hartle's use of the SAP as a justification. The president of TheraPsil, Spencer Hawkswell, said he was appalled by Health Canada's decision and the seventeen months it forced Hartle to wait as his health declined (Spray 2023). Hartle died in August of 2024.

There has also been advocacy in Canada to open up a fourth pathway — psychedelic-assisted therapy under Canada's Medical Assistance in Dying (MAiD) legislation. The MAiD legislation does not currently allow for the "right to try" as an end-of-life care option. In 2020, Field Trip Health submitted a policy brief entitled *Psilocybin-Assisted Therapy & MAiD: A Compassionate Case for Canadians* to the Senate Standing Committee on Justice and Human Rights. The Psychedelic Association of Canada (formerly the Canadian Psychedelic Association) then took over the campaign to push for access to psilocybin-assisted therapy for palliative or terminally ill patients under the MAiD legislation. Proponents argue that the right to try should precede the right to die and this should be written into the legislation. These efforts to amend MAiD and related Canadian laws are supported by public opinion polls indicating that Canadians are highly supportive of the use of psilocybin for therapeutic purposes (TheraPsil 2022; Psychedelic Alpha 2021).

Finally, it is worth noting that TheraPsil has also submitted a detailed proposal to Health Canada for regulating psilocybin-assisted therapy for medical purposes — the Access to Psilocybin for Medical Purposes

Regulations (APMPR). Submitted to the Health Minister in 2021, the APMPR is based on Canada's original medical cannabis law. If adopted, the APMPR would replace the SAP and section 56(1) medical exemption pathways for access to psilocybin with a less restrictive approach.

In addition to these general pathways at the federal level, there have been some developments in Quebec and Alberta. Quebec became the first province to cover the cost of Health Canada-approved psilocybin-assisted psychotherapy in 2022. Also in 2022, the Alberta government became the first province to legalize psychedelic-assisted therapy for the medical use of some psychedelic substances. Access in Alberta is fully medicalized and currently delivered in private clinics, at a high cost. It is also limited to those who have a prescription and requires administration by a licensed psychiatrist. Regulators in Alberta claim these requirements are a matter of safety, but those offering these treatments say it will impede access as few psychiatrists are currently willing to be involved in this type of therapy (Kaufman 2023). In March 2024, Alberta Blue Cross announced it would include psychedelic-assisted therapies as part of its insurance coverage plans, the first insurance company in Canada to do so.

Outside of these legal pathways focused on medicinal use, section 56(1) of the CDSA has been used to allow ayahuasca exemptions for groups associated with the Brazilian religions of Santo Daime and União do Vegetal. Health Canada grants section 56(1) exemptions for ayahuasca on the grounds of religious freedom, which is discussed in greater detail below. It should also be noted that while Canadian legal frameworks largely consist of administratively cumbersome pathways, the reality on the ground is different. It is not generally difficult to obtain recreational psychedelics in Canada and lack of enforcement has reduced the risks associated with purchasing and using them. In addition to an increasing number of storefront dispensaries, large numbers of people can purchase a safe supply of recreational psychedelics through mail-order dispensaries openly and regularly, with little to no concern about criminal justice intervention.

AUSTRALIA: MEDICAL MODEL PAR EXCELLENCE

Throughout 2020 and 2021, Australia's Therapeutic Goods Administration (TGA) was weighing whether to legalize psychedelics for therapy. In late 2021, the TGA rejected a proposal to approve psilocybin and MDMA for therapeutic purposes. The TGA also declined to re-classify these substances from prohibited to controlled, denying their therapeutic value. It was not until early 2023 that Australia shifted, deciding to allow prescription psilocybin and MDMA for therapeutic purposes by moving them from Schedule 9 (a prohibited substance) to Schedule 8 (a controlled substance with some medical value). This federal change applies to all jurisdictions across Australia. This would be akin to Health Canada or the FDA legalizing psychedelic-assisted therapy in their respective countries. Prescriptions are now available for acute medical conditions; MDMA is available for PTSD and psilocybin for treatment-resistant depression. In addition to being restricted to those with specific clinical diagnoses, access is extremely expensive. Without government-approved or regulated products and no insurance coverage of any kind, patients who qualify currently have to pay roughly AU$25,000 out of pocket, or US$17,000, for a treatment regimen. People of limited means continue to have no way to legally access psychedelic-assisted therapy in Australia.

Proponents who were pushing for these legal changes, such as Mind Medicine Australia, saw them as a huge step forward. Arguably most notable was the legalization of MDMA. Most places that are contemplating drug policy liberalization are focused on plant-based psychedelics, whereas the Australian decision put MDMA into the spotlight. While the move was celebrated by many psychedelic enthusiasts around the world, within Australia there has been pushback. Some medical professionals say the policy is a slippery slope in that psilocybin and MDMA could eventually be used in more harmful ways (Lyth 2023). It also drew criticism from some mental health experts for being premature and based on inadequate evidence (see Hardman 2024a).

The Australian model of strictly limiting access to those with acute psychological conditions reinforces our concerns about the biomedical model winning out as the path forward. It is indicative of the corporatized and medicalized orientation of today's psychedelic renaissance. While Australia's reforms might benefit some portion of those who are eligible and can afford treatment, it remains a limited measure that excludes the vast majority of people and thereby reinforces existing health and social inequalities.

THE US: EACH STATE IS A PIECE OF THE PUZZLE

Even though the US is the central hub of the global war on drugs, it is an interesting place with respect to legal reform. Denver, Colorado became the first city to decriminalize psilocybin in May 2019. In November 2020, Oregon became the first state to pass laws decriminalizing psilocybin and legalizing it for supervised use. Many other US states are also exploring decriminalization and legalization options. As of late 2022, twenty-five states had considered seventy-four bills regarding psychedelic decriminalization and legalization. It is predicted that by 2033, most US states will have legalized psychedelics in some fashion (Siegel et al. 2023).

States also have to contend with ongoing restrictions at the federal level in the US. The federal government has long been a barrier to having psychedelics legalized in any way, including as medicines (Marks 2018). One of the main challenges is FDA clinical trials. The FDA trial process can allow a substance to come off the DEA schedule of controlled substances or to be rescheduled. Some psychedelic medicines are currently making their way through FDA trials; however, this is a lengthy, challenging and expensive endeavour. MAPS had been going through the FDA trial process for more than a decade and still had their application for MDMA-assisted therapy denied in 2024.

There are ways to try to expedite the approval process under the FDA. For example, an advocate can petition the FDA for expedited review/approval. A company or organization can also collaborate with the FDA to enhance safety measures and mitigate risk. The other way is to seek a rescheduling of a substance through the DEA. If a company or organization can get a substance moved from Schedule 1 to Schedule 2 or 3, then restrictions are reduced. To reschedule a substance, one has to establish that there is a currently accepted medical use. The problem is, in the eyes of the DEA, there are no clear guidelines around what constitutes a currently accepted medical use, especially given that the DEA largely exists to prohibit the use of psychedelics and other drugs.

Drug scheduling in the US remains a major roadblock because most psychedelics are still classified as Schedule 1 substances. Many advocates have argued that psychedelics should be Schedule 2 substances, which would drop the criteria of "no accepted medical use," though the erroneous distinction of high abuse potential would remain. In 2022, Dr. Sunil Aggarwal of the Advanced Integrative Medical Science Institute petitioned the DEA to move psilocybin into Schedule 2, a request that was denied. Aggarwal is now challenging the DEA in court based on its refusal to permit the use of psilocybin by patients with end-of-life illnesses. Generally, advocates in the US seem to be interested in rescheduling psychedelics somewhere between Schedule 2 and Schedule 4, where Schedule 4 is a drug with little problematic use or dependence potential (Johnson et al. 2018). However, if psychedelic drug rescheduling does come to pass, it could easily take the form of bifurcated scheduling (Zorn 2023a). Bifurcated scheduling allows the DEA and Congress to treat a substance differently from an FDA-approved drug product, meaning that there can be a split in the law between facilitating medical legalization and continuing to uphold mass criminalization. Bifurcated scheduling can also allow private interests to enrich themselves while the general public, especially more vulnerable sectors of the population, continue to suffer at the hands of draconian drug laws. Despite ongoing blocks at the federal level, state law is becoming more liberal. State laws are also beginning to counter stigmatization and change the ways that "drugs" are designated and described. In the following sections, we delve into some of the more significant state-level changes to examine these issues as they play out in specific contexts. As psilocybin and other psychedelics remain Schedule 1 substances, federal law enforcement could step in at any time and disrupt these initiatives but, to date, this has not been the case.

Oregon and Measures 109 and 110

Oregon is one of the states that is leading the way with respect to decriminalizing drugs and was the first to legalize psilocybin. In November 2020, Oregon passed Measure 109, which established the *Oregon Psilocybin Services Act*, and Measure 110, which decriminalized the personal use and possession of illicit drugs. The New Approach political action committee, led in part by David Bronner, bankrolled the Measure 109 campaign. New Approach has also funded initiatives in Colorado as well as decriminalization measures in Washington, DC and elsewhere.

Measure 109 legalizes psilocybin in a limited way, with individuals being able to legally access it under the support of trained facilitators at psychedelic service centres. The architects of the Oregon model wanted to create something different than a purely medicalized approach (Eckert 2022). In keeping with that goal, Measure 109 does not technically include access based on medical or religious grounds. Instead, it adopts a peer support assistance model. Passed in 2020, the law came into effect on January 1, 2023, allowing time for product development, the licensing of sites and the training of facilitators. As part of the act, the

Oregon Health Authority created Oregon Psilocybin Services, the body in charge of managing new products and services, which is steered by the Oregon Psilocybin Advisory Board. There are also five subcommittees, including a products subcommittee, established to regulate access, and dedicated entities to train facilitators to administer psilocybin in centres across the state. Setting up psilocybin service centres involves meeting strict requirements established by these entities and is anchored in state level licensing and supply. The rules for licensing psychedelic service centres include a focus on screening, preparation and integration. There are also rules for the production and manufacturing of psilocybin products. The first operational and legally licensed service provider for psilocybin in Oregon, which navigated these requirements and made connections between mushroom growers, testing labs and facilitators, was the Eugene Psychedelic Integrative Center (EPIC). As of June 2024, twenty-eight psilocybin service centres have been licensed in Oregon. There are also thirty licensed training centres and several hundred licensed facilitators. Many jurisdictions in Oregon, mainly in rural areas of the state, have chosen to opt out of the program and not provide psilocybin services.

While the general parameters of Measure 109 and of EPIC and other centres that followed may represent advances over other models, such as Australia, concerns have been raised about pricing. The cost to set up a psilocybin centre in Oregon is upwards of $60,000, which includes a $10,000 annual fee to the Oregon Health Authority. Some centres offer personalized payment plans including a sliding scale and discounted rates for those who demonstrate financial hardship. However, costs are typically high, ranging from $1,500 to nearly $4,000 for individual high-dose sessions. These prices are influenced by multiple factors, including the requirements for licensing, site quality, product quality and distribution. They are also driven by profit motivations. Andreas Met, chief operating officer of Satya Therapeutics, has said that "costs are too high in general, even our service center ... It's not accessible to people" (cited in Lekhtman 2023a). He suggests that businesses are using high licensing fees as an excuse to gouge clients. It is therefore not surprising that there has been a lack of demand.

Decriminalize Nature has criticized the Oregon model's focus on licensed sites, noting it could open up Oregon to commercialization and corporate capture. Smaller psilocybin growers are underrepresented;

however, the model includes a residency requirement mandating that 50 percent of the ownership interest of any psilocybin provider must be held by one or more residents of the state, which may dissuade outside capital from taking over. The American Psychiatric Association and the Oregon Psychiatric Physicians Association have also expressed concerns with the approach, pointing to a lack of safety measures and oversight (Haigney 2020). The training model involves licensed facilities offering training in psychedelic facilitation. As an example, InnerTrek, outside Portland, trains individuals to guide clients through the psilocybin experience (Anguiano 2024). Reinforcing concerns about oversight, psychiatrist Brian Holoyda (2023) argues that Oregon has "a licensure pathway for 'psilocybin facilitators' without requiring any medical or mental health training … the only education required is a high school diploma; a 120-hour course that includes instruction on irrelevant topics including history and cultural equity; and 40 hours of in-person training." When it comes to screening, protocols require service users to answer only basic questions about potential risk factors, such as history of diagnosis or treatment for psychosis and past/current suicidal ideation. Holoyda asserts this lax approach will likely lead to lawsuits in Oregon, which will put the law in jeopardy.

Other critics have focused on the protection of client data. In 2023, Senate Bill 303 was passed, which requires psychedelic service centres to collect and report client data related to psilocybin services beginning in 2025. Centres are required to share these data not only with the Oregon Health Authority but with other agencies as well. While this information could potentially support monitoring and evaluation efforts, data protection is a real concern in the digital age (Jordan 2023). For example, Bill 303 could make clients vulnerable to social and professional consequences in the case of data leaks.

Building on these critiques, it is clear there has been an unmistakable drift toward medicalization in Oregon. Proponents of Measure 109 tried to avoid language such as "psychedelic therapy" and "therapeutic access" in the provisions, but it is primarily focused on therapy, constituting users as paying clients or customers consistent with the private US healthcare system. As Olivia Goldhill (2022) points out, the narrative of mental health permeates the regulatory language introduced by the Oregon Health Authority and its policies for licensed facilitators.

With the passage of Measure 110 in 2020, which decriminalized the personal use and possession of illicit drugs, Oregon was viewed as a champion of progressive drug policy reform. Measure 110 also inspired decriminalization bills in other US states, such as Massachusetts, Vermont, Maine, Rhode Island, Maryland and Kansas. One of the immediate impacts of decriminalization in Oregon was a significant drop in drug-related arrests, which was not accompanied by an increase in arrests for other types of crimes or a significant increase in 911 service calls related to criminal activity (Davis et al. 2023; RTI International 2022). Contrary to typical moral panic rhetoric about drugs, no crime spree ensued after decriminalization. The reduction in arrests is important for many reasons, including because higher police interactions are associated with lower levels of community health and well-being across a wide range of measures (Cano et al. 2024; Clear 2007). Nonetheless, interviews with law enforcement officers suggest they view these legal changes as an erosion of their authority. Many have expressed frustration that they can no longer "use drug possession as a 'tool' for investigations to pursue and build cases, establish probable cause, and impose what they believed necessary for social order" (Smiley-McDonald et al. 2023).

Of course, decriminalization is no panacea; even with Measure 110, police still have the option to conduct surveillance and impose tickets, fines and referrals, which disproportionately impacts poor and vulnerable people. In fact, research suggests that people who use drugs in Oregon were heavily policed despite drug decriminalization. According to a survey of people who use drugs in eight Oregon counties between March and November of 2023, 74 percent reported criminal justice system involvement in the past year, 67 percent were stopped by police once or multiple times, 33 percent had at least one jail incarceration and 77 percent had their drugs seized at least once by law enforcement after a stop and search (Smiley-McDonald et al. 2024). At the same time, only 14 percent of survey respondents were even aware that drugs had been decriminalized in Oregon.

Furthermore, there has been growing public opposition to the measure. In late 2023, concerns about public drug use and the opioid crisis boiled over. Many politicians and organizations, such as the Coalition to Fix and Improve Measure 110, started pushing back against decriminalization (Kim 2024). Public support for Measure 110 has declined dramatically. According to one poll conducted in August 2023, only 17 percent of Oregon respondents approved of Measure 110 while 43 percent disapproved (41 percent were unsure) (GS Strategy Group/Impact Research 2023). Just 2 percent said Measure 110 had been a success, while 61 percent described it as a failure (27 percent said it needed more time to work). Moreover, roughly three-quarters of respondents supported recriminalizing the personal possession of fentanyl, heroin and methamphetamine, and roughly the same proportion said that people charged with the possession of these substances multiple times should be legally required to undergo addiction treatment. Published research has found no association between decriminalization in Oregon and fatal overdose rates (Joshi et al. 2023; Zoorob et al. 2024). Measure 110 has effectively become a scapegoat for Oregon's rising overdose rate, despite no evidence of a causal relationship between the two.

Oregon has reversed harm reduction measures and moved to ban public drug use. In April 2024, Oregon passed a law undoing key parts of Measure 110. There is a parallel here to what is happening in BC, where the provincial government introduced a similar counter-law in late 2023. Oregon and BC were the first sub-federal jurisdictions in the US and Canada to decriminalize drugs. Both have long been places where harm reduction is relatively well-received. However, in both jurisdictions, we now see moves to re-criminalize the public use of drugs as well as scale back decriminalization and harm reduction. In Oregon, the move to re-criminalize has been criticized by the Health Justice Recovery Alliance, which instead has called for increased funding for safe use sites and detox centres. A key problem in Oregon is that the state decriminalized drugs but did not put enough effort or resources into improving the safety of supply, creating safe use spaces or providing social supports. For example, while Measure 110 did include support for employment, housing and harm reduction services, the funding streams for many of these services were not implemented until a year and a half after decriminalization was enacted. Measure 110 also did not include any training or education for police, who were largely unaware that these services existed (Smiley-McDonald et al. 2023). As the Mayor of Portland put it, the lack of appropriate support services resulted in a "botched implementation" (Rosciglione 2024). Efforts to decriminalize drugs must be accompanied by a boost in wrap-around social and community development initiatives and redistributive social welfare policies to have a chance of succeeding.

Colorado and Proposition 122

In November 2022, Colorado passed Proposition 122, the *Natural Medicine Health Act*. Proposition 122 will provide legalized access to several plant-based psychedelics (psilocybin, DMT, ibogaine and mescaline) and decriminalize individual cultivation, possession, use and sharing for adults aged twenty-one and older. Peyote was excluded from the bill to protect its use in Indigenous communities. To support its implementation of legalized psilocybin, Colorado required a regulatory process to be developed over two years. There have been extensive public consultations concerning site licences, facilitator licences, training and the labelling of products and home cultivation, with the goal of having final drafts of all policies and procedures in place by late 2024 for an expected 2025 rollout. The expected rollout for legalized DMT, ibogaine and mescaline is not until 2026. Regarding licensed facilitators in Colorado, it has been decided that they will require at least 150 hours of coursework, at least forty hours of supervised training and fifty consultation hours. While the regulations prioritize mental health professionals, there are also pathways for other kinds of practitioners. For example, "legacy healers" can receive a license based on two hundred hours of demonstrated field experience with forty or more participants over a minimum of two years.

The Colorado initiative anticipates and is being designed to mitigate some longstanding concerns of drug activists. For example, Proposition 122 is explicitly focused on community engagement and equity. It also states that all licensed entities, such as therapy providers and healing centres, must meet specific environmental, social and governance criteria. Granting industry licences will depend on whether employees can earn a living wage and receive health benefits; whether sustainable agricultural practices, corporate social responsibility and equity/diversity criteria are included; and whether sliding-scale fee models are allowed. From its consultative approach to its inclusion of recreational activities like cultivation and sharing, Colorado appears to represent one of the more progressive models in the US.

To illustrate some of the features of the model and the debates around it, it is useful to look at some of the early exchanges between Sean McAllister — one of the architects of the new law — Matthew Duffy, then a member of the Society for Psychedelic Outreach, Reform and Education (SPORE), an organization affiliated with Decriminalize

Nature — and David Bronner — one of the leaders of New Approach. Duffy (2022) and Decriminalize Nature have been critical of the model, arguing that it will create an industry for psychedelic services and lend itself to corporate capture. According to Duffy, the *Natural Medicine Health Act* puts profit ahead of people and commercialization ahead of community development and access. He also suggests that New Approach, the political action committee that put the bill forward, uses its capital and influence to push for corporate-friendly legalization policies and that the law is a Trojan horse allowing for the corporate takeover of psychedelics in Colorado.

In response, McAllister (2022) argues that the consultation process and community feedback have improved the law, as there will be a focus on encouraging locally owned clinics, as well as providing sliding-scale fees and other financial measures to ensure low-income people can be licensed and are able access psychedelic services. In addition, he argues that limiting individuals from having a business interest in more than five healing centres will help to prevent monopolies, and that the inability of local governments to ban these centres will ensure local clinics will be available in most communities. With respect to the profit structure, he notes that psychedelic distribution will be controlled by licensed providers and a licensed and regulated supply chain. Home cultivation and sharing of psychedelics are allowed, though personal sales are not. In addition, McAllister underscores that the measure includes a focus on BIPOC representation as well as protections against search and seizure. Prior drug convictions cannot be used to ban access to psychedelics in Colorado and current or future use cannot be recorded and used to litigate any cases related to past transgressions. For all of these reasons, he says, the *Natural Medicine Health Act* is tilted toward social justice.

David Bronner (2022) has also responded to Duffy's critique of the Colorado law. Like McAllister, he took issue with the idea that the bill did nothing to prevent corporate capture. Bronner also claims that New Approach was funding and organizing other bills and ballot measures in the early days when these proposals were being introduced in Colorado, such as those put forward by Decriminalize Nature, so it would be disingenuous to suggest New Approach swooped in to steal the show for big business. New Approach has also provided funding for Decriminalize Nature in other states, or at least it did until a falling out between Bronner and the national executive. For Bronner, the ultimate goal should be community advocacy and access alongside medical applications, which the Colorado law allows.

Duffy and Decriminalize Nature raise legitimate concerns about the influence of funders, lobby groups and political action committees (notably New Approach) from outside of the state. The New Approach funding body contributed $3 million in Colorado for Proposition 122, and it is reasonable to assume that they are using their resources to impact the process of legal reform to support business interests. New Approach's strategy of funding lobbyists and political strategists to shape state-level campaigns has drawn criticism from many grassroots organizations who do not feel they have the public's best interests in mind.

In May 2023, a bill was introduced that undermines the original intentions of Proposition 122. Senate Bill 23-290, a bill amending Colorado's Proposition 122 and signed by the state governor, signals a more medicalized and corporatized future for psychedelics in the state. Bill 23-290 is an example of a larger trend of laws being introduced to undermine other laws. It bans community members outside of strict licensing arrangements from gaining income from any activities related to psychedelics (Lekhtman 2023b). It puts further restrictions on the personal cultivation of mushrooms and other natural substances. It also creates further regulations and criminal penalties for unlicensed sales or distribution and for underage and public consumption. Colorado's Bill 23-290 has been criticized for ignoring the voices of stakeholders and introducing these excessive regulations (Jaeger 2023b). It has broadly undermined much of what made the *Natural Medicine Health Act* progressive.

As these legal machinations continue to play out, the Natural Medicine Advisory Board is continuing to steer Colorado's psychedelic legal future and address issues such as access and affordability. Other operators are working outside of current laws to provide access. For example, the Lotus Entheogenic Church partners with non-profits to provide psilocybin to people struggling with substance use, while the Pearl Psychedelic Institute provides access under the guidance of a therapist. Whether these types of initiatives will be allowed to continue under Bill 23-290 is unclear, as it specifies that only state-regulated services and service providers would be allowed to receive financial compensation for delivering psychedelics or psychedelic services. Moreover, with Proposition 122 and Bill 23-290, all synthetic psychedelics and other drugs remain criminalized. In this way, the turn toward plant-based or "natural" medicines is doing little to challenge the architecture of the drug war.

In the lead-up to Proposition 122, dozens of local officials came out against the initiative, suggesting it would lead to rampant crime and drug abuse. According to Greg Ferenstein (2023), however, who has studied crime in Colorado since the loosening of drug laws in the state, this has not been the case. He reports that:

> Less than 3% of drug-related crimes have involved hallucinogens for the past few years in Colorado. There's been no noticeable increase since legalization. Psychedelics represent less than 1% of hospital incidences (like ER visits). Police and hospital representatives corroborate the available Colorado data. Colorado's experience is similar to the Netherlands, where largely unregulated retail sales and therapy services of psilocybin have been legal for years.

The Colorado experience so far suggests no tidal wave of drug-related crime and no spike in health or public safety issues. This is perhaps not surprising given that lifetime psychedelic use is associated with a reduced likelihood of arrest, criminal behaviour and violence (e.g., Hendricks et al. 2018; Jones and Nock 2022b; Tomlinson, Brown and Hoaken 2016). These findings contradict the position of prohibitionists who argue that legal drug use creates the conditions for criminal activity and public health issues to escalate.

California, Bill 58 and TREAT

In June 2023, Bill 58 passed the California State Senate. The law was intended to decriminalize psilocybin, DMT, ibogaine and mescaline (but not peyote). Measures in the bill allowed for the possession of two grams of DMT and psilocybin, fifteen grams of ibogaine, or four ounces of plants/fungi containing these substances. Bill 58 would have legalized the possession, preparation, transfer and purchase of these substances for personal or facilitated use, so access would not be limited to licensed facilities, as in Oregon. Sponsored by Heroic Hearts, which helps military veterans struggling with mental health, Bill 58 was centred around open access to plant-based psychedelics in California.

Bill 58 was a scaled-down version of Bill 519, a deliberate tactic used by its proponents to help it through the Senate. Bill 519 appeared in 2022 and would have decriminalized MDMA, LSD and ketamine, in addition to plant and fungi psychedelics, but was never passed. Bill 58 exclusively focused on natural substances, anticipating concerns that including synthetics would lead to blowback. Senator Scott Weiner was the sponsor of Bill 58 and emphasized the benefits of psychedelics for treating mental health and the need to end drug criminalization. The Assembly Public Safety Committee passed Bill 58, however, the bill still had to pass the General Assembly and the Assembly Health Committee. At the time Bill 58 was being debated, Los Angeles, Oakland, San Francisco and Santa Cruz all had businesses that openly sold psilocybin products. While the municipalities of Oakland, San Francisco and Santa Cruz had decriminalized psilocybin, there is no decriminalization in Los Angeles and police continue to raid dispensaries.

While Bill 58 was working its way through the governance process, TREAT California (which stands for treatments, research, education, access and therapies) emerged in parallel. TREAT was a large public-private partnership initiative pitched by Dr. Jeannie Fontana, an entrepreneur who was involved in the stem cell industry in the 1990s. The stated goal of TREAT was to help psychedelics go from development to the market as efficiently as possible. In July 2023, a ballot initiative measure called the *TREAT California Act* was submitted to the state of California. The TREAT submission noted: drug overdoses are the leading cause of death for citizens aged eighteen to forty-five; every six minutes someone dies from a drug overdose; forty veterans die each day from suicide and self-injury; and many people behind bars have addiction and/or mental health issues. The submission went on to boldly suggest that psychedelics are a remedy for all of these problems. If passed, the initiative would have created the TREAT Institute, a $5 billion combined private and state research and funding agency. It was not interested in (and rejected) decriminalization and instead wanted to reform the medical system to include psychedelics and restrict legalization to therapeutic use, with the ultimate goal of creating a lucrative psychedelic industry in the state. It was ultimately a for-profit model that sought to extract as much as it could from the public purse and enrich private companies. The $5 billion initiative would have made TREAT the biggest player and power broker in psychedelics.

During the summer of 2023, both Bill 58 and the TREAT initiative were being considered in California and it seemed like one or the other would move ahead. By December 2023, however, both Bill 58 and TREAT would be dead. Governor Gavin Newsom vetoed Bill 58, claiming that better regulations and guardrails were needed before psychedelics could be legalized in the state (Herrington 2023). Meanwhile, the leadership at TREAT announced they were withdrawing their ballot initiative and instead would be reallocating their funds into a non-profit entity called TREAT Humanity. This was partly in response to a poll of California voters, which found that 60 percent of Californians opposed state funding for psychedelic therapies (Hu 2023).

In February 2024, Senator Wiener reintroduced legislation under a new name, with language focused on the "supervised consumption" of MDMA, DMT, mescaline and psilocybin. This bill (Bill 1012, which would have established the *Regulated Psychedelics Facilitators Act* and the *Regulated Psychedelic-Assisted Therapy Act*) was singularly focused on psychedelic-assisted therapy, compared to previous iterations (Bill 519, Bill 58) that provided for more open access. Numerous other bills have been brought forward in California, but none have taken hold. For example, a bill focused on psychedelic-assisted psychotherapy for veterans (Bill 941, the *End Veteran Suicide Act*) was introduced in early 2024 but was withdrawn after failing to pass a key policy committee. Another bill introduced in early 2024 that focused on psychedelic-assisted psychotherapy for police and other first responders (Bill 803, the *Heal Our Heroes Act*) also did not receive support to proceed.

The failure of all of these bills means that five major legalization initiatives in California have fallen short (six if one counts the TREAT initiative). While California has long been synonymous with support for psychedelics — from Haight-Ashbury to the Merry Pranksters to the Grateful Dead — it has fallen behind developments in states like Oregon and Colorado. Each time an initiative fails, the likelihood of a further narrowing of the law increases. At the same time, proposals are moving forward to increase criminal penalties for other drugs. For example, Proposition 36, passed in November 2024, will bring back felony charges for possessing certain drugs that were previously treated as misdemeanours. Proposition 36 was supported by companies like Walmart, Target and Home Depot, who collectively donated millions to support the initiative, as well as the California Chamber of Commerce, California Republican Party and multiple police and correctional officer groups.

Other US Initiatives at the Local, State and Federal Levels

The states of Oregon and Colorado have started to pave the way for changes in drug law and policy in other areas of the US. There have been many ballot measures, bills and pilot programs in other states over the past five years, largely focused on medicinal access to psychedelics. An increasing number of states are applying a portion of their opioid settlement funds toward psychedelic research, while others are passing laws to support clinical research or create task forces to explore policy changes. Even highly conservative states have introduced bills that would allow for the use of psilocybin, MDMA and other substances to treat military veterans.

In 2024, for example, the *Compassionate Use and Research of Entheogens (CURE) Act* was introduced in Illinois, which aims to legalize the supervised therapeutic use of psilocybin for adults. However, it also prohibits the sale, use and personal possession of psilocybin. Moved forward by a bipartisan group of politicians, the focus of the law is to provide therapeutic relief to people with mental health issues, with a specific focus on army veterans. Whereas access to psilocybin in Oregon and Colorado occurred under ballot measures (submitted to voters for approval), Illinois would be the first state in the country to pass legislation made by lawmakers. In Massachusetts, a 2024 ballot initiative (the *Natural Psychedelics Substances Act*) aimed to facilitate a legal and regulated psychedelics marketplace. And similar to debates seen elsewhere, this New Approach initiative was opposed by local groups in Massachusetts, such as Bay Staters for Natural Medicine. The proposed law was eventually voted down, with 57 percent of voters rejecting the New Approach ballot measure.

A lot is happening across other states too. In 2023, Maryland passed a bill focusing on access to psychedelics for veterans. In 2024, Utah passed a bill introduced by two Republican senators that authorized a pilot program for hospitals to administer MDMA and psilocybin as an alternative treatment option. Also in 2024, the New Jersey State Senate advanced the *Psilocybin Behavioral Health Access and Services Act* to establish a regulated framework for the production and use of psilocybin as a mental health treatment. Beyond important questions about who is funding these kinds of laws and what their intentions are, most state initiatives have limited their focus to veterans and other population subsets with specific clinical diagnoses, suggesting a highly medicalized future for psychedelics.

While most state initiatives remain limited in scope, dozens of municipalities across the US have partially decriminalized psilocybin in the past five years (Marks 2023a). These include Oakland and Denver in 2019, Santa Cruz, Ann Arbor and the District of Columbia in 2020, several cities in Massachusetts in 2021 and San Francisco in 2022. Other major cities in the US have also partially decriminalized psilocybin and other entheogenic plants, including Seattle, Detroit, Berkeley and Minneapolis. While these initiatives are laudable and reflect a grassroots approach to liberating psychedelic use, they also remain limited, including in the extent to which they can meaningfully influence the ongoing war on drugs. As long as psilocybin is illegal at the state and federal levels, municipal decriminalization means that targeting psilocybin is simply a lower priority for police. Decriminalizing psilocybin also does little to change the ways that other psychedelics and drugs are targeted.

At the federal level in the US, the 2024 *National Defense Authorization Act* includes a section on psychedelic therapy and earmarks funding to study the use of psychedelics to treat brain injuries and trauma among soldiers. Also at the federal level, US Senators Cory Booker and Rand Paul introduced the *Breakthrough Therapies Act* in 2022. The legislation could enable the DEA to transfer therapies involving Schedule 1 substances, such as MDMA and psilocybin, from Schedule 1 to Schedule 2, which has the potential to reduce research barriers and accelerate clinical trials. They updated the act in 2023 to further remove regulatory barriers that inhibit research and compassionate use access to treatments that are restricted under Schedule 1 of the *Controlled Substances Act*. As Russell Hausfeld (2022e) points out, the initiative is interesting because it opens reclassification from Schedule 1 to Schedule 2 to the general substances themselves, not simply specific drug products that receive breakthrough therapy designation. However, he rightly urges caution, noting that rescheduling will not automatically change the penalties for use, possession or trafficking, and that the language of the legislation suggests that once a rescheduled drug makes it through clinical trials and is marketed as a medicine, other versions of that drug may be reclassified back to Schedule 1. In other words, bifurcated scheduling remains a real possibility, which will only guarantee reduced penalties for people who use these substances in medically supervised facilities.

Grassroots activism is also pushing the DEA to consider other contexts in which access should be opened up. In 2022, for example, activists demonstrated and were arrested outside of DEA headquarters in Virginia after demanding the DEA allow terminally ill cancer patients access to psilocybin (Jaeger 2022b). The protest was organized because the DEA continues to obstruct right-to-try laws at federal and state levels. The activists argued that the DEA's ban on psilocybin for terminally ill patients does not accord with legal precedents for access to investigational medications under right-to-try laws. One terminally ill patient, Erinn Baldeschwiler, was arrested at the protest and is suing the DEA over its psilocybin ban.

LAW, RELIGION AND CULTURE: A BACK DOOR FOR ACCESS?

Since the 1980s, the Brazilian government has recognized the religious use of ayahuasca as part of the cultural traditions of Indigenous and African Brazilian populations. In the US and Canada, the legal landscape is more uncertain and calls for access based on religion are multifaceted. For example, a group called Sacred Tribe in Denver has argued that Jewish people should be allowed access to psilocybin distributed by Rabbi Benjamin Gorelick, the self-dubbed Mushroom Rabbi, on the grounds of religious freedom. In Joshua Tree, California, the Hummingbird Church recently began providing its members with ayahuasca on religious grounds. Both groups have been subject to police searches and investigations. The intersection of religious access and the law in the US is a complicated terrain, given the focus on religious freedom and the precedents set by several groups that have established a legal right to psychedelics under the *Religious Freedom Restoration Act*. This Act — signed by President Bill Clinton in 1993 — was brought forward by leaders of the Native American Church, with a focus on authorizing the use of peyote in their ceremonies and cultivating and distributing peyote for ceremonial purposes. Other groups, including those representing Jewish, Christian and other faiths, are now attempting to access and distribute psychedelics under the same law.

In 2006, the US Supreme Court weighed in on religious access to psychedelics. In *Gonzales v O Centro Espirita*, the Supreme Court ruled that access to DMT and ayahuasca for religious purposes should be allowed through the least restrictive means. At the center of the case was Centro Espirita, a group linked to the União do Vegetal religious society, which blends Indigenous Brazilian and Christian sacraments and rituals. The group was importing substances to use in their religious ceremonies and the US Customs agency seized them under the *Controlled Substances Act*. The district court had upheld the seizure, arguing that US Customs was correct to seize these substances because they were not in plant form. However, the US Supreme Court argued this claim was spurious and would lead to an overly broad application of the *Controlled Substances Act*. Further, they maintained that government use of the *Controlled Substances Act* in this case (and similar cases) would violate the *Religious Freedom Restoration Act* as well as the legal precedent found in the use of peyote by the Native American Church. In other words, the Supreme Court ruling maintained that US government agencies should not be using the *Controlled Substances Act* to inhibit religious access to DMT and ayahuasca.

In recent cases involving access to psychedelics on religious grounds, the DEA has intervened in some instances but not others. The Soul Quest Ayahuasca Church of Mother Earth in Orlando, Florida began petitioning the DEA in 2017 for a religious exemption. In 2021, the DEA claimed Soul Quest was not a church but a wellness centre and did not qualify for a religious exemption. Other groups, like the Arizona Yagé Assembly and the Church of the Eagle and the Condor (CEC) in Phoenix, have been challenging the DEA and attempting to establish religious grounds for ayahuasca use. In April 2024, the CEC received the first ayahuasca exemption under the *Controlled Substances Act*, allowing the group to import, manufacture and distribute ayahuasca for religious purposes (Psychedelic Alpha 2024e). The CEC is the first non-Christian church in the US to receive protection for its spiritual use of ayahuasca. With such groups operating across the Global North, it is also important to question to what extent this represents cultural appropriation. For example, several organizations representing Indigenous peoples denounced the 2024 exemption granted to the CEC (and the CEC itself), arguing that the exemption impedes Indigenous self-determination and depreciates the sacred medicine.

Section 56(1) exemptions are a pathway for accessing psychedelics and other drugs that remain illegal in Canada under the CDSA. Section 56(1) exemptions have been granted for supervised injection consumption as well as for clinical research. They can be granted when an application proves access would be in the public interest. These exemptions can also be granted under a claim to religious freedom. Health Canada has granted several section 56(1) exemptions for possession of ayahuasca based on religious grounds. The exemption is important as ayahuasca is a Schedule 3 substance under Canada's CDSA, and possession without an exemption could lead to a three-year prison sentence (Garrod and Blommaert 2023).

There are two religions in Brazil, Santo Daime and União do Vegetal, that blend animism, elements of Christianity and the sacramental use of ayahuasca. Their growing popularity is facilitating the globalization of ayahuasca through the expansion of diasporic chapters of these churches in different countries (Tupper 2017). Further to the adoption of Santo Daime and União do Vegetal in Canada, numerous religious groups have received ayahuasca exemptions (Sheiner 2017). One of these is Céu do Montréal. In 2000, the Céu do Montréal had its ayahuasca seized at the Canada-US border, which was the start of its legal battle to receive a section 56(1) exemption to import ayahuasca for religious purposes. The group argued that this seizure and the ban on importing ayahuasca amounted to an infringement on religious freedoms. In 2006, Health Canada provided the Céu do Montréal with approval "in principle" to import ayahuasca under a section 56(1) exemption. The Harper Conservatives, who came to power shortly thereafter, revoked the approval in 2012. After the election of the Trudeau Liberals, Céu do Montréal received an official exemption in 2017, the first in Canada.

Other exemptions soon followed. In 2019, for example, the Ceu da Divina Luz do Montreal, the Eglise Santo Daime Céu do Vale da Vida in Val-David Quebec, and the Ceu de Toronto all received section 56(1) exemptions to the CDSA allowing them to import and distribute ayahuasca as part of their religious services. In 2020, the Centre for Universal Illumination Luz Divina in Winnipeg, Manitoba received an exemption (Browne 2020b). In 2023, Companionship of the Sacred Vine received the same exemption. These groups generally have to prove the religiosity of their practices and the centrality of ayahuasca to those practices, including by demonstrating their ongoing work with practitioners from Central and South America. Claims related to the medical and healing benefits of traditional plant medicines are not accepted by

Health Canada in this context, so decisions about access are limited to claims around religious ceremonial necessity. All these groups have a connection to Santo Daime or União do Vegetal, with some engaging in outreach and collaboration with First Nations communities across Canada in the spirit of solidarity and religious education (Sheiner 2017).

Some of the disputes over the direction of decriminalization within the psychedelic movement are rooted in differing opinions about access based on religious and cultural grounds. In the US, this includes disagreements between Decriminalize Nature and the Native American Church. Decriminalize Nature continues to insist that peyote should be included in their initiatives, contrary to the position of the Native American Church, who want to see peyote protected (though some local chapters of Decriminalize Nature side with the Church). In 2022, the Native American Church and the Navajo National Council reaffirmed their interest in having peyote protected and controlled. In at least one jurisdiction, Santa Cruz, peyote has been decriminalized and then recriminalized in response to the persuasive arguments of the Native American Church. In Canada, this is not an issue because although mescaline is illegal under the CDSA, peyote is legal to grow, sell and consume, so long as mescaline is not extracted from the cactus.

In some respects, one can understand the position of Decriminalize Nature. The idea of leaving peyote out of their campaigns complicates their position that all natural plants should be legal and freely available to everyone. As Michael Pollan (2021b, 204) points out, to exclude peyote from decriminalization would "foul the beautiful simplicity of the movement's message that there can be no such thing as a 'criminal' plant." Dennis McKenna shares these concerns and has come out against the idea that peyote should remain criminalized (Ferris 2022b). Yet, Pollan, McKenna and organizations like Bay Staters for Natural Medicine argue there may be ways to navigate this impasse. Pollan suggests that non-Indigenous people should pay respect to Indigenous communities by not using their sacrament and by making efforts to obtain mescaline in other ways. San Pedro is another mescaline-containing cactus that, unlike peyote, is legal to grow in the US. While extracting mescaline from the plant is illegal, the extraction process is relatively simple. Likewise, McKenna suggests that instead of keeping peyote criminalized, the psychedelic community should band together to protect its use by Indigenous communities.

While Decriminalize Nature has been and remains an important vehicle for raising awareness about the harms associated with criminalization, its hard-line stance on this issue is problematic as it disregards the concerns of Indigenous communities. Peyote is overharvested and already in danger of extinction in the US (it is also very slow growing). Without protections, decriminalization is likely to exacerbate these problems by increasing demand and threatening availability. The Native American Church fought for decades for legal access and protections for their ceremonial use of peyote, which would be undermined with decriminalization. This debate has not only led to tensions between them and Decriminalize Nature but with others working to advance legal reform (e.g., Bronner 2020b; McGhee 2022), with some accusing the organization of engaging in practices that reflect the legacy of settler colonialism (Labate and Feeney 2022).

A range of church groups and denominations are associated with promoting and/or relying on psychedelic use as part of their practices. Many lack any solid foundations on which to claim religious freedom given that they do not represent actual religions in the eyes of the DEA or other federal bodies (Gunther 2022b). Given the status of decriminalization and legalization at the federal level, these cases continue to be brought forward — and argued — on an ad hoc basis. While some churches are established in good faith, others have been called out as scams. A good example is the Church of Psilomethoxin, rebranded as the Church of the Sacred Synthesis in 2023, which has been laden with suspicion and controversy (Busby 2023b; Nickles 2023). Law enforcement officials have also expressed concern that some groups are using religious grounds to evade drug laws. In 2023, Detroit police raided Soul Tribes International Ministries after city officials alleged it was operating as an "Uber Eats" for illegal narcotics (Londoño 2024).

THE DRUG WAR CONTINUES

Religious use of psychedelics remains a target of the larger drug war. In 2020, Oakland police raided the Zide Door Church of Entheogenic Plants (a branch of the Church of Ambrosia, which now counts more than 115,000 members) and seized $200,000 in cannabis, mushrooms and cash (Roberts 2020). The Church then sued the city and the police department, arguing that the raid was a violation of their constitutional rights and that religious freedoms protect access to psilocybin. This is taking place in a broader context of police repression of psychedelics. While legal reform is progressing, the criminalization of psychedelics continues and by some measures is increasing. Between 2017 and 2022, police seizures of psilocybin mushrooms in the US rose sharply (Palamar et al. 2024). In Europe, governments have been cracking down on organizations that use psychedelics as part of religious and spiritual ceremonies. All over the world, there has been an upsurge in arrests for people transporting ayahuasca, peyote, iboga and other plants (Busby 2022). There are even examples of this in Canada. In 2024, Chad Gillies, a welder from Calgary and an original member of the Companionship of the Sacred Vine, was confronted by a SWAT team after plant ingredients to make ayahuasca had been ordered to his home, apparently without his knowledge. He was injured, arrested and charged with the importation of a scheduled substance (Busby 2024e). While increased criminalization reflects the growing popularity of these substances in today's psychedelic renaissance, it also signals ongoing efforts by state actors to control their use on their own terms.

Mushroom dispensaries in Canada, which are pushing the boundaries of what is legal much like "gray market" cannabis dispensaries did in the 1990s, are one target of the drug war today (Mikhaylova 2023). In 2022, police executed a CDSA search warrant at a mushroom dispensary in Toronto. The drugs were seized, and the owners were charged with possession for the purposes of trafficking and possession of proceeds of a crime. Police in Windsor raided a psilocybin mushroom dispensary three times in 2022-23, with the last raid resulting in the arrest of an employee, an arrest warrant for the business owner and over $36,000 of psilocybin being confiscated (Charlton 2023). In Montreal, a mushroom dispensary was raided three times in three weeks in the summer of 2023, resulting in multiple arrests. The police also cited an injunction to prevent the shop from reopening, though the owners argued they were just getting started and planned to expand into Quebec and Michigan (Adams 2023). That same year, police raided a mushroom dispensary in Winnipeg that had been open for just six days. This raid was particularly aggressive and resulted in multiple arrests and drug trafficking charges. Elton Hall of the Winnipeg Police Service's organized crime division said he initially considered taking a "softer approach," but once the site garnered media attention he changed his position (Macintosh 2023).

It is worth considering the raid of drug activist Dana Larsen's Coca Leaf Café in downtown Vancouver in some detail, given that Larsen's work has received significant media attention. Larsen had been selling more than just mushrooms. Police raided his operations in November 2023 and seized all of the psilocybin, LSD, DMT, 5-MeO-DMT, kratom and coca leaf in his possession. Larsen was arrested but released without charge. This marked a significant departure in police practices since police in Vancouver had been turning a blind eye to these outlets and had not raided dispensaries over the previous three years. The arrest occurred despite the fact Larsen had a municipal licence for his dispensaries. In his view, this was a politically motivated intervention that likely cost taxpayers around $60,000 (based on estimated costs of previous raids).

In December 2023, the City of Vancouver was set to hold a by-law meeting to discuss the Coca Leaf Café and review its licensing, but the hearing was postponed. Larsen questioned the lack of transparency around the postponement and called out individuals on social media, such as prominent politicians like Eleanor Sturko, a former sergeant with the Royal Canadian Mounted Police, who he said were engaging in fearmongering about Coca Leaf Café and similar storefronts. Larsen also sent each Member of the Legislative Assembly (MLA) in BC a coca leaf and a gram of mushrooms, using the politically motivated raids earlier that year as a rationale for the gift. Some of the MLAs did not appreciate the gesture, with the BC Solicitor General Mike Farnworth becoming involved, publicly stating that the act of sending drugs in the mail was "reprehensible" and claiming it disrupted government services. Eleanor Sturko blamed the incident on the NDP government for normalizing drug use in the province. Larsen is a former cannabis activist. To influence public opinion around psychedelics, he advocates using strategies from the movement for cannabis access:

> I feel now we're in a parallel situation when it comes to mushrooms and psychedelics. In the late 90s and early 2000s, we had a lot of court cases in Canada affirming patients' right to use medicinal cannabis and a growing understanding among the public that medicinal marijuana was a valid thing. And it certainly changed people's perceptions around cannabis use. We're kind of using the same strategies now. (cited in Farah 2023)

In August 2024, a BC provincial court decided that Coca Leaf Café did not violate city by-laws. The City of Vancouver had alleged that the business was not a café but a psychedelics shop. The lawyers for Coca Leaf Café argued that a city inspector is in no position to make such a judgement (Chan 2024). The provincial court judge agreed with the defence and dismissed the case for lack of evidence. Despite the ruling and the perception of political policing, Vancouver police raided the café again in October 2024.

Marc Goldgrub (2023), a lawyer and operator of PsychedelicLaw.ca, questions the notion that psilocybin resides in a legal "gray zone" in Canada. He claims this is a source of public confusion and that inconsistent enforcement along with legal waivers for medical purposes are contributing to the problem (similar to what occurred with cannabis years ago). As these stores continue to test the legal waters, Goldgrub says, those involved should be aware of the risks — risks that will be present for some time given Canada's narrow focus on biomedical access. If we look to the US, even in places that have decriminalized psilocybin and legalized its therapeutic use, police repression continues (Busby 2023c; Lekhtman 2022).

In addition to ongoing enforcement tactics, we also see campaigns in North America to make changes at the federal level to expand the reach of criminalization. In the US, the DEA has continued in its efforts to schedule new substances. In December 2023, the DEA proposed placing two psychedelic compounds (DOI and DOC) in Schedule 1 of the *Controlled Substances Act*. Lawyer Matt Zorn (2023b) criticized the move as another indication of tired drug-war thinking, noting that these are substances being used in scientific research and that the DEA's claims about their dangers are weak at best. Zorn's conclusion is not surprising given the DEA's track record in accurately assessing the risks and dangers of psychedelic substances (Labate et al. 2023). There have also been similar moves at the federal level in Canada. In 2023, Canada reaffirmed its commitment to the drug war when it announced new penalties and measures to combat the synthetic drug trade. Global Affairs Canada (2023) issued a Ministerial Declaration that it would take additional measures to fight the production and trafficking of synthetic drugs consistent with its international drug convention obligations. However, social activism has and can make a difference in response to these kinds of policies. In 2016, for example, the DEA announced it would be scheduling kratom as a controlled substance. Extensive public backlash and interventions by members of Congress, including Bernie Sanders, forced the DEA to backtrack on their plan (Shade 2022). Also in 2022, the DEA attempted to schedule five psychedelic compounds (4-OH-DiPT, 5-MeO-AMT, 5-MeO-MiPT, 5-MeO-DET and DiPT). Public pushback and legal activism later led the DEA to abandon the issue, at least for the time being.

We are also seeing a crackdown on grassroots harm reduction and safe supply in Canada, particularly in Vancouver, where there has been significant community mobilization and advocacy around these issues. BC declared a public health emergency in response to drug-related deaths in 2016. Unregulated drug toxicity is the leading cause of death in BC for people aged ten to fifty-nine, accounting for more deaths than suicides, homicides, accidents and natural diseases combined (BC Public Safety and Solicitor General 2024). At the time it declared the emergency, the province began providing a limited amount of safe supply of hydromorphone for people with opioid addiction. As the supply is not enough to meet demand, community activists have organized their own safe supply and safe use options. Beginning in 2021, the Drug User Liberation Front (DULF) started to distribute a safe and tested supply of drugs following the model of compassion clubs that existed before cannabis legalization. In 2023, a man named Jerry Martin opened a safe supply mobile shop selling clean, tested drugs. Vancouver police shut him down after one day and arrested him. Martin had been prepared for the arrest and was ready to move forward with a constitutional challenge for safe drug supply but died of an overdose a month later.

Since 2023, there has been a steady increase in similar crackdowns on harm reduction practices and the sale of psychedelics in Vancouver. These attacks began with a decisive shift in policy when the New Democratic Party of BC brought forward legislation to roll back decriminalization efforts and make public drug use illegal (Bill 34). The bill sought to make it a crime to use drugs within six meters of all building entrances and exits. MLAs in BC, most notably Elenore Sturko, had been highly critical of the government's approach to drug policy and called for this and other changes. She had also claimed that DULF had been using money from the province to buy drugs and guns and that members of both DULF and the Vancouver Area Network of Drug Users (VANDU) were involved in organized crime rings. Shortly after the legislation was brought forward, the police raided DULF, confiscating their supply and arresting their members. DULF co-founders Jeremy Kalicum and Eris Nyx are facing charges of possession for the purposes of trafficking. The arrest of DULF members coincided with the first anniversary of the organization's compassion club and the release of their research findings on their life-saving work. The organization found — based on a sample of self-report data from drug users, including individuals in their compassion club — over the course of one year there were 48 percent fewer police interactions, 57 percent fewer overdoses, 50 percent fewer trips to hospitals, 32 percent fewer uses of Naloxone (which can reverse opioid overdoses), zero deaths and improved health and safety for those using safe supply (Kalicum et al. 2024). Throughout 2024, rallies were organized calling for the charges against the DULF members to be dropped. Despite the increasing number of drug-related deaths in the province, attacks on harm reduction and safe supply continue.

In January 2024, the BC Supreme Court halted Bill 34. In this case, the Harm Reduction Nurses Association won an injunction against the bill, arguing that it violated the *Canadian Charter of Rights and Freedoms* (Gamage 2024a). Lawyers from Pivot Legal Society fought the case on behalf of the Harm Reduction Nurses Association. Their argument was simple: prohibition laws force people to use drugs less safely, which results in harm and death. Supreme Court Chief Justice Christopher Hinkson, who paused Bill 34, cited Chief Coroner Lisa Lapointe's work on safety and toxic drugs. Hinkson ruled that there are not enough safe use sites in the province, so outlawing the public use of drugs is not reasonable and indeed unconstitutional. Around the same time that Bill 34 was put on pause, BC Premier David Eby announced the province would not be moving forward with regulating drugs such as cocaine, heroin and methamphetamine. This announcement was issued despite the fact that numerous legal advocates, harm reduction groups and even the province's Chief Health Officer Bonnie Henry have endorsed safe supply (Office of the Provincial Health Officer 2024). In September 2024, the government announced they would begin involuntarily forcing people into drug treatment in carceral settings, further distancing the province from sensible drug policy.

While these debates around drug policy are most evident in BC, they are happening elsewhere in Canada too. In November 2024, Ontario Premier Doug Ford affirmed that he would be closing nearly half of the province's safe injection sites by introducing the *Community Care and Recovery Act*, prompting criticism from harm reduction advocates, the Canadian Civil Liberties Association, as well as families of those lost to the drug war. In Alberta, where addiction treatment is the focus, there is little interest in evaluation and the companies offering these services typically operate on a for-profit basis. Addiction services provided by for-profit companies may be out of reach financially for many people and they may not always provide an adequate standard of care if it conflicts with their bottom line. Addiction treatment can work, but it has to be part of a larger system of safe supply and safe use, which, given the profit imperative and ideological assumptions around drug use, often is not the case. These kinds of organizations in Alberta are also aligned with the United Conservative Party's stance on drugs, one of prohibition and abstinence. This prohibitionist ideology has material effects. In Red Deer, Alberta, the city council voted to close the city's only overdose prevention site, arguing it needs to follow the "Alberta Model" of becoming free from addiction (Thomson 2024a). The province's decision to close the site left hundreds of people without access to safe use and supply options. Lisa Lapointe commented on this prohibitionist rhetoric emerging among conservative politicians in BC, Alberta and at the federal level:

> We know people who use drugs are people just like us. They're not bad people, they're not villains. Oftentimes they are experiencing trauma and pain and turning to substance use as a means of coping with the place that they find themselves ... As a Coroners Service, we know the people who are dying. We hear from their families. We hear their history and know they are just human beings, some who have struggled and suffered in their lives. To vilify people who use drugs is beyond the pale. (cited in Gamage 2024b)

Research on the effectiveness of harm reduction and safe supply is growing (Global Commission on Drug Policy 2024; Hardill and King 2024; Ledlie et al. 2024; Rammohan et al. 2024; Slaunwhite et al. 2024). According to one study of over 5,000 people in a program in BC, for those who received a safe supply four or more times a week, drug-poisoning deaths were reduced by 89 percent. Even access to a safe supply once a week reduced drug poisoning deaths by 55 percent (Thomson 2024b). These findings are exactly the kinds of benefits that harm reduction advocates have been touting for years. Each untested, tainted bag of drugs that hits the streets increases hospitalizations, overdoses and deaths. These results also underscore that activism for legalizing and decriminalizing psychedelics should be accompanied, as much as possible, by efforts to make all drug use safer. The current momentum around psychedelic use and its benefits cannot and should not ignore these larger issues. In BC and elsewhere, this work to keep people alive is being done by individuals, like Dana Larsen, and by community groups and harm reduction professionals, like those in DULF and VANDU, while politicians and others in positions of institutional power continue to scapegoat people who use drugs for broader social problems and cater to prohibitionist forces on drug law and policy in Canada and beyond.

THE LEGAL LANDSCAPE AND THE FUTURE OF ACCESS

In Australia, a medicalized model has been instituted. Early reports indicate that access is only possible for people with acute clinical diagnoses, and who can afford incredibly expensive treatments. In Canada, there are some additional pathways for medicinal access, but these tend to be limited to those with mental health diagnoses and in the context of end-of-life care. The most significant legal development is the argument, being advanced by TheraPsil, for access to psilocybin under section 7 of the *Canadian Charter of Rights and Freedoms*. The argument for life, liberty and security of the person can and should be pushed to create momentum to bring about safe supply and safe use for all drugs in Canada, not only psychedelics.

In the US, we have started to see examples that go beyond medical models centred around clinical diagnoses. Oregon and Colorado have both laid some groundwork for alternatives. In Oregon, access is limited to psilocybin service centres and largely focused on psychedelic therapy. Like Australia, cost is a major issue. But it is also nested within a somewhat more holistic framework. In Colorado, existing plans would see access to more substances at a larger scale and with safety measures in place, although it remains to be seen what will be implemented in the final regulatory framework. Colorado's model includes some features that, from a social justice perspective, address some longstanding issues raised by advocates, including its focus on community engagement. However, its focus on plant-based psychedelics neglects the concerns of drug users more broadly.

Critics have charged that the bills put forward in Oregon, Colorado, Massachusetts, Illinois and elsewhere are favourable to medicalization and corporatization, despite the rhetoric of equity. Decriminalize Nature has been one of the most vocal critics. They tout the "Grow Gather Gift" model as an alternative, which builds on the peer-mentoring model that has long been a focus of the psychedelic underground (Harder, Steinmetz and Kohek 2023). While these legal initiatives hold some promise, ongoing efforts are needed to expand the scope of both decriminalization and legalization initiatives of this type.

The legal terrain continues to be a site of struggle, and the letter of law matters a great deal for what kind of psychedelic future we end up with. With its overlapping jurisdictions and the significant powers that states have, the US provides a good case study for these struggles. What we see with psychedelics today is competing laws being put in place. For example, Bill 23-290 in Colorado undermines Proposition 122. Oregon passed a law undoing Measure 110. We could soon see the same with Measure 109 in Oregon. Likewise, some local and state initiatives in the US could be on a collision course with the FDA because most psychedelics are still classified under Schedule 1 of the *Controlled Substances Act* (Marks 2023b).

As different jurisdictions move ahead with psychedelic legal reform, it is important to situate these changes in the context of the war on drugs. Psychedelic exceptionalism can be used to reinforce the drug war, intentionally or unintentionally, as well as prohibitionist tropes regarding so-called hard drugs. Decriminalization and legalization should be extended to include safe supply and safe use of all drugs. This extension would signal the beginning of the end of prohibitionist thinking and the scaling of comprehensive approaches to harm reduction.

09

TURN ON, TUNE IN, CASH OUT?

WE BEGAN THIS WORK WITH A SENSE OF ENTHUSIASM, hopeful that the psychedelic renaissance would bring clear benefits to individuals, communities and societies at a time when it is sorely needed. Our perspective changed considerably as we delved into the world behind the media clips and sound bites. These substances continue to hold remarkable potential, but it is important to take a more critical view of some of the interests and actors across psychedelia. At a 2024 psychedelic conference, researcher and activist Neşe Devenot (2024), noted: "when I went into this field, I wanted to study trip reports." However, working in this space has instead led her to adopt a different public stance, "not because I don't love psychedelics," she says, "it's because I love psychedelics, and I think they're so important that we need to get this right." While we come to this field as relative outsiders and with a fraction of the knowledge of Devenot and others, we are also concerned that the psychedelic renaissance is advancing in ways that could not only limit the potential of these substances but also cause significant social harm.

The psychedelic renaissance emerged out of and within the historical and ongoing manifestations of the war on drugs. The drug war has been pervasive in virtually all of North America for more than a century, leading to direct and associated harms through law-enforcement-based harassment, policing and incarceration. After a relatively brief period where psychedelic research and therapy were allowed to flourish, psychedelics were criminalized alongside other drugs in the latter half of the twentieth century. An important part of this history, and a key element of prohibitionist drug laws, has been the targeting of immigrants, people of colour and other groups deemed undesirable and dangerous. The laws and the drug war have been carried out as a form of racialized social control. And the drug war continues today even as psychedelics are decriminalized in certain jurisdictions and partially legalized in others.

Since its inception, psychedelic use has been deeply connected to spirituality, religion and systems of belief. This connection underscores the importance and longstanding influence of psychedelics in these spheres, areas that are increasingly downplayed as the discourse is narrowed in the push for medicalization. In contrast, the relationship between psychedelics and social change has been more nuanced, and at times contradictory. While psychedelics have been and continue to be well-ensconced in progressive social movements, they have also been embraced by various actors on the right, including the police, the military, Silicon Valley elites and Republican politicians. Given these tensions, the transformative potential of psychedelics and claims that these substances can serve as solutions to systemic problems must be approached with extreme caution.

Our examination of medicalization and psychedelic capitalism lies at the heart of our concerns with the psychedelic renaissance. Clinical research on psychedelics is advancing and psychedelic-assisted therapy continues to show promise. However, researchers and activists have also pointed to important risks, and the claims about efficacy remain well ahead of the science. It is not just that the evidence is limited, but that psychedelics, in and of themselves, cannot and should not be seen as a cure for mental health problems rooted in social and structural issues. Without engaging with the socioeconomic determinants of health and the precarious context in which millions of people live, psychedelic medicines may simply serve as maintenance therapies that placate individuals into accepting unjust social conditions. More broadly, it is important to question why Western medicine should sit at the top of a hierarchy of knowledge and access, and whether pharmaceutical companies and the medical establishment are best suited to bring psychedelics into the mainstream.

Crucial aspects of the psychedelic renaissance include the advent of psychedelic capitalism, corporatization and a new "corporadelic" set and setting. With its focus on pharmaceutical commodities and market-driven healthcare solutions, psychedelic capitalism is a direct challenge to the traditions created through centuries of communal use as well as the values of the counterculture and psychedelic underground. Psychedelic capitalism is also threatening to appropriate the knowledge built up by Indigenous communities, public institutions and underground researchers. Those at the top of this industry have a financial stake in medical legalization and, in their narratives and actions, have taken steps to limit legal access to anything outside of the medical-pharma frame. Psychedelic-related surveillance practices and technologies, the growth of psychedelic tourism and for-profit clinics are just some of the threats associated with commercialization. The largest is perhaps the exponential rise in IP activity in the psychedelic field. IP is being leveraged to obtain market exclusivity, restrict research and lock therapies behind paywalls, at the expense of open science and the psychedelic commons. Under psychedelic capitalism, corporations are claiming ownership over substances that have been in the public domain for centuries.

At the same time as medicalization is taking hold, decriminalization initiatives continue to show promise and advance across North America, particularly in the US where dozens of cities have embraced drug policy reform. However, legalization initiatives remain limited. Psychedelic laws generally align with medicalization and corporate objectives. Without a change in direction, the corporate-medical complex will continue to dictate what drug laws will look like in the future, which could lead to the continuation or even the intensification of the broader drug war. For this reason and others, it is in the public interest to move beyond a myopic focus on medical legalization toward more open models of public regulation and access. In contrast to what we see now, a new kind of psychedelic renaissance would not entrench Western power structures but instead be a force for positive social change.

THE THREAT OF CORPORATE CAPTURE

The psychedelic renaissance is still in its infancy, and it will take some time to better understand the full extent of its political, economic and social implications. There are diverse views on what constitutes the greatest threat to a just and equitable psychedelic future. Michael Pollan, for example, suggests the danger lies in "carelessness," which is also what he believed "doomed psychedelics" in the 1960s (cited in Ferriss 2018). Lacking a proper cultural container, Pollan says, reckless psychedelic use in the 1960s created a backlash on the part of dominant institutions, and we need to keep these institutions on board this time around. In contrast, we argue that dominant institutions themselves, especially corporate power, represent the single greatest threat to the psychedelic renaissance. Admittedly, this view reflects our own motivations and biases. As social science researchers, we have examined processes of corporatization and corporate capture in many different social and political spheres, including public education and universities, academic publishing, state regulation, criminal justice and policing and the policy-making process more broadly. The impacts of corporate power go well beyond these areas. Corporate capture in the area of public health has thwarted efforts to promote population health and reduce health inequities. Corporate capture in the food industry has negatively impacted small producers around the world and wreaked havoc on food distribution chains. The corporate capture of environmentalism has spawned hegemonic political narratives that free markets and unfettered growth are the best ways to achieve environmental sustainability. Even some movements for social justice have been largely taken over, such as the fair-trade movement, while countercultural movements and revolutionary figures (such as punk rock music, hip hop culture, Bob Marley and Che Guevara) have been commodified. Psychedelics and their countercultural ethos are now facing exactly these same pressures.

In 2019, David Alder and Kat Conour produced a well-known fictional piece, "We Will Call it Pala." It offered a cautionary tale about the emerging dark side of psychedelics being thrust into the world of corporate capitalism. The story's main character, Learie, had a transformative experience with LSD and subsequently founded a psychedelic company called Gaia Health. After some initial success, the company began to expand across the US. However, other companies were also expanding and undercutting her prices, leading Learie's investors to call for change. Gaia Health shifted therapists to a contract basis. They cut administrative staff. They reduced the duration of treatment. Other companies followed suit by cutting costs in similar ways. Gaia Health investors continued to push for more changes, such as maximizing the number of patients per day and further streamlining treatment protocols. At the same time, one of Gaia's competitors joined in an exclusive partnership with Purdue Pharma to roll out a synthetic DMT nasal spray that could be used without therapy and integration sessions. With

Gaia Health investors looking for an exit strategy and Learie refusing to sell the firm, she was subsequently removed from her position as CEO and replaced by an executive from Goldman Sachs. A year later, Roche Pharmaceuticals bought out Gaia Health. The new corporate entity began to incorporate customized smart devices and digital integration sessions into their therapies. These platforms also generated data that the firm could sell to data brokers. Confronted with the pressures and incentive structures of the corporate marketplace, the story notes that Gaia Health "seemed to have taken on a life of its own."

Five years on, we can see the genesis for this parody playing itself out on multiple fronts. In many jurisdictions, companies are facing the kinds of corporate and market pressures that "Gaia Health" encountered. They are contemplating mergers, buying up smaller ventures to increase market share and tailoring their operations based on future commercial positioning. Executives and managers from the pharmaceutical and financial industries are being brought in to steer psychedelic firms in the "proper" direction. Psychedelic companies are also looking to couch their protocols in ways that make them more attractive to investors, such as aiming for shorter and more marketable approaches to psychedelic therapy while cutting out the more costly elements of patient care. Some companies are looking to eliminate psychotherapeutic intervention altogether. We also see moves toward integrating surveillance capitalism with today's psychedelic industry. Even prominent organizations like MAPS, who once prided themselves on serving the public interest, now claim they are helpless in the face of market pressures. Despite the supposed good intentions of some of the people in this field, the logic of the capitalist system is already and increasingly overwhelming the psychedelic renaissance.

The future of psychedelics cannot be left up to venture capitalists, the pharmaceutical industry and corporate financiers. Many psychedelic users and advocates agree with this sentiment. According to one survey of over 1,200 psychedelic users, most of whom were American, pharmaceutical companies were found to be the least trusted source of knowledge and information about these substances (Kruger et al. 2023a). The survey also found little support for policy models that align with traditional pharmaceutical models, such as those allowing for the patenting of natural or synthetic compounds. Less than 2 percent of the survey sample supported current federal laws, whereas strong support was expressed for policy models that allow people to freely grow, possess and gift psychedelics (Kruger et al. 2023b). To be sure, those who are interested in this movement need to be wary of forging agreements and relationships with institutions whose overriding focus is profit and shareholder value. Canadian psychedelic researchers have recently articulated such concerns in their work in this area, arguing that corporate research sponsorships and financial conflicts of interest are some of the biggest threats to the integrity of psychedelic science moving forward (Buchman and Rosenbaum 2024). As Erik Davis (2018) writes,

> The "psychedelic community" … can no longer pretend that the process of mainstreaming is a purely positive, hope-for-humanity development that is separate from the larger crises of capitalism, militarism, authoritarianism, and the intensification of technological control over subjectivity … The mainstreaming of psychedelics may well be a positive force in this chaotic and collapsing world, but it won't become so by simply smiling and shaking hands with the sharks that are already circling.

THE IMPORTANCE OF PSYCHEDELIC ACTIVISM

At the same time, corporate capture is not inevitable. The future of the psychedelic renaissance will depend, in part, on whether organizations and activists can prevent dominant institutions from taking over. While MAPS may have largely disengaged itself from the battle, there are plenty of people and organizations who continue to fight back. The outcomes will also depend on social movements operating at the borders of or even outside of psychedelia. Psychedelics no longer exist in an insular bubble. If these substances are going to be equitably accessible on a wide scale, activists need to engage with the broader systems and structures within which they have been embedded. Not only is this a valuable course of action in and of itself, but it has the potential to change the political set and setting to one more conducive to what David Nickles calls "radical psychedelic engagement" — using the understandings and insights garnered from psychedelic experiences to target the root causes of social injustice. Psychedelic use in democratic and participatory contexts (as opposed to corporatized or medicalized contexts) opens up possibilities for emancipatory politics, where psychedelics can help to expose structurally alienating conditions and transform hegemonic ideologies (Tempone-Wiltshire and Matthews 2023). The boundary-dissolving nature of psychedelics can, in the right set and setting, lead people and communities away from competitiveness and materialism and help them see alternatives to the status quo.

We maintain that psychedelics are an important tool for human transformation that can play a positive role in community building, political organizing and resistance. There remains value in the socio-psychedelic imaginaries of the 1960s. However, such outcomes are not a guarantee in the current climate of advocating for mainstreaming. Simply getting psychedelics into the hands of more therapists or ramping up the delivery of commercialized services will not deliver the kind of cultural change that many advocates are calling for. Instead, the corporate biomedical paradigm that currently dominates the field may only serve to reproduce the ills of our culture. As neuropsychologist Andy Mitchell (2023, 310) puts it, "We are in danger of taking something we barely understand, something that holds huge promise for changing our perspectives — on mental health, social justice, ecological devastation and general human flourishing — and turning it into a prohibitively expensive, medico-spiritual Disneyland." What is needed is a more grounded approach that goes beyond platitudes that psychedelics are associated with progressive values. If psychedelics are amplifiers of the political set and setting, then the material political reality must be conducive to fostering their transformative potential. This would suggest that grassroots organizing in the form of community-led economic programs, mutual aid projects, local food and environmental campaigns and other concrete strategies to push back against extractive capitalism will be a necessary starting point, where people are actively engaging in efforts to change the material conditions of their lives while also struggling to create the collective context within which real change can materialize. These political conditions could also be supported by fighting for drug policy reform in ways that prioritize decriminalization and harm reduction and pushing back against an elite-driven psychedelic landscape.

ENDING THE WAR ON DRUGS

There are important parallels between what is happening today with tainted drugs and what happened with alcohol during prohibition. During alcohol prohibition, people did not stop drinking alcohol.

Rather, they shifted to bootleg liquor that was often adulterated with methanol. In the US during this period, hundreds of people died each year from toxic alcohol in virtually every major city (Blum 2010). When prohibition ended and a regulated supply was made available, this epidemic ended. The idea that prohibition prevents people from using drugs is an enduring myth that has been dispelled many times over. In the context of prohibition today, fewer people are able to access so-called hard drugs like heroin and instead are turning to substances that often contain fentanyl and other adulterants or to stronger opioids that are too powerful for recreational consumption. The consequences have been staggering. Well over 100,000 people died of drug overdoses/tainted drugs in the US in both 2022 and 2023, with fentanyl and its analogs responsible for the vast majority of these deaths (Centers for Disease Control and Prevention 2023, 2024). This is around one death every five minutes. In BC alone, over 2,500 people lost their lives to toxic drugs in 2023, the largest number of drug-related deaths ever reported to the BC Coroners Service (BC Public Safety and Solicitor General 2024). In the time we have been writing this book, we have had five of our friends or their family members die from accidental drug overdoses. These people did not intend to harm themselves. One has to question whether politicians really care about their citizens if they continue to let thousands of people die each year in this way.

The criminalization of drug use is inhumane and a huge drain on the public purse. As part of our examination of the psychedelic renaissance, we have argued that access to a safe and regulated drug supply is in the public interest. The only real winners with respect to prohibition are organized crime groups, transnational drug cartels and criminal justice agencies that rely on prohibitionist drug policies for their existence. If governments regulated supply and provided safe consumption spaces, not only would drug deaths decline but so too would the health-related costs associated with unsafe use. Police would also have a whole lot less to do. The drug war is one of the main reasons why police powers continue to expand and police budgets continue to grow (Maynard 2022).

Sociologist Akwasi Owusu-Bempah and criminal justice reform advocate Tahira Rehmatullah (2023) offer some ideas about sensible drug policy and legalization in Canada. Although they focus on cannabis, their framework can be extended and applied to other drugs. According to them, equity and social justice following cannabis legalization require three important steps. The first step is amnesty. Everyone who has a criminal record for cannabis possession or sales should receive amnesty and the onus should be on state agencies, not criminalized individuals, to clear these records. Amnesty should also include other charges that stem from cannabis charges or subsequent incarceration. The second step is the redistribution of income for those affected. This could take the form of redistribution of revenue directly from the legal sale of cannabis or other sources, with funds being earmarked to create social and community supports for those most harmed, which are often people of colour. The third step is that people who are released from prison or otherwise impacted by the drug war should be given employment opportunities. They note that Black people were disproportionately criminalized for cannabis and are now the least likely to be included in the legal cannabis industry. This policy framework can be applied to psychedelics and extended to virtually all drug-use charges stemming from the drug war. Criminalization needs to end if policies such as this have a chance of succeeding.

We have advocated throughout the book for the decriminalization of psychedelics. At the same time, we have also cautioned against psychedelic exceptionalism. Decriminalization initiatives that focus solely on plant-based psychedelics or even psychedelics more broadly certainly have their place, but viewing these substances as deserving of special legal protections risks legitimizing the broader classification scheme behind drug criminalization. It also does little to address the criminalization of other substances and the ongoing stigmatization of the people who use them, which are disproportionately the most marginalized in our society. Avoiding psychedelic exceptionalism, decriminalizing all drugs, treating drug use and dependence as a public health issue and incentivizing harm reduction and other support services for at-risk populations would go a long way to mitigating the tragedies of the drug war. We hope this is a vision that a broader segment of the psychedelic community will soon embrace.

REFERENCES

Abbar, Mocrane, Christophe Demattei, Wissam El-Hage, Pierre-Michel Llorca, Ludovic Samalin, Pierre Demaricourt, Raphael Gaillard, Philippe Courtet, Guillaume Vaiva, Philip Gorwood, Pascale Fabbro and Fabrice Jollant. 2022. "Ketamine for the Acute Treatment of Severe Suicidal Ideation: Double Blind, Randomised Placebo Controlled Trial." *BMJ* 376.

Abraham, Ralph. 2008. "Mathematics and the Psychedelic Revolution." *MAPS Bulletin* 18 (1).

Adams, Benjamin. 2023. "Montreal Shroom Shop Raided, Owner Says 'We're Just Getting Started.'" *High Times*, July 14.

Adams, Matthew. 2020. "Could Psychedelics Help Us Resolve the Climate Crisis?" *The Conversation*, January 28.

Adams, Tim. 2019. "Amanda Feilding: 'LSD Can Get Deep Down and Reset the Brain — Like Shaking Up a Snow Globe.'" *The Guardian*, February 10.

Aday, Jacob, Brian Barnett, Dan Grossman, Kevin Murnane, Charles Nichols and Peter Hendricks. 2023. "Psychedelic Commercialization: A Wide-Spanning Overview of the Emerging Psychedelic Industry." *Psychedelic Medicine* 1 (3).

Aday, Jacob, Boris Heifets, Steven Pratscher, Ellen Bradley, Raymond Rosen and Joshua Woolley. 2022. "Great Expectations: Recommendations for Improving the Methodological Rigor of Psychedelic Clinical Trials." *Psychopharmacology* 239 (6): 1989-2010.

Aday, Jacob, Emily Bloesch and Christopher Davoli. 2019. "Beyond LSD: A Broader Psychedelic Zeitgeist During the Early to Mid-20th Century." *Journal of Psychoactive Drugs* 51 (3): 210-217.

Adlin, Ben. 2023. "'Lawmakers Have to Google It': Inside the Struggle to Regulate Kratom." *Filter*, March 28.

Aghion, Philippe, Ufuk Akcigit, Antonin Bergeaud, Richard Blundell and David Hemous. 2019. "Innovation and Top Income Inequality." *The Review of Economic Studies* 86 (1): 1–45.

Agin-Liebes, Gabrielle, Tara Malone, Matthew Yalch, Sarah Mennenga, K Linnae Ponté, Jeffrey Guss, Anthony Bossis, Jim Grigsby, Stacy Fischer and Stephen Ross. 2020. "Long-Term Follow-up of Psilocybin-Assisted Psychotherapy for Psychiatric and Existential Distress in Patients with Life-Threatening Cancer." *Journal of Psychopharmacology* 34 (2): 155–166.

Akers, Brian. Juan Francisco Ruiz, Alan Piper and Carl Ruck. 2011. "A Prehistoric Mural in Spain Depicting Neurotropic *Psilocybe* Mushrooms?" *Economic Botany* 65 (2): 121–128.

Alder, David and Kat Conour. 2019. "We Will Call it Pala." *Here and How Studios*. Hereandnowstudios.com/we-will-call-it-pala

Aldworth, Betty. 2019. "Gender Equity in Cannabis and Psychedelics." *MAPS Bulletin* 29 (1): 54–55.

Alexander, Bruce. 2008. *The Globalization of Addiction: A Study in Poverty of the Spirit*. New York: Oxford University Press.

Alexander, Michelle. 2012. *The New Jim Crow: Mass Incarceration in the Age of Colorblindness*. New York: The New Press.

Alper, Kenneth, Marina Stajić and James Gill. 2012. "Fatalities Temporally Associated with the Ingestion of Ibogaine." *Journal of Forensic Sciences* 57 (2): 398–412.

Altman, Lawrence. 1998. *Who Goes First? The Story of Self-Experimentation in Medicine*. Berkeley: University of California Press.

Álvarez, Carlos Suárez. 2020. "We Are Harvesting the Ayahuasca Vine at an Alarming Rate." *Kahpi*, January 15.

An, Dongjiao, Changwei Wei, Jing Wang and Anshi Wu. 2021. "Intranasal Ketamine for Depression in Adults: A Systematic Review and Meta-Analysis of Randomized, Double-Blind, Placebo-Controlled Trials." *Frontiers in Psychology* 12.

Anderson, Thomas, Rotem Petranker, Adam Christopher, Daniel Rosenbaum, Cory Weissman, Le-Anh Dinh-Williams, Katrina Hui and Emma Hapke. 2019a. "Psychedelic Microdosing Benefits and Challenges: An Empirical Codebook." *Harm Reduction Journal* 16 (1): 43.

Anderson, Thomas, Rotem Petranker, Daniel Rosenbaum, Cory Weissman, Le-Anh Dinh-Williams, Katrina Hui, Emma Hapke and Norman Farb. 2019b. "Microdosing Psychedelics: Personality, Mental Health, and Creativity Differences in Microdosers." *Psychopharmacology* 236 (2): 731–740.

Andersson, Martin, Mari Persson and Anette Kjellgren. 2017. "Psychoactive Substances as a Last Resort – A Qualitative Study of Self-Treatment of Migraine and Cluster Headaches." *Harm Reduction Journal* 14 (1).

Angermayer, Christian. 2021. "An Open Letter to Tim Ferriss About the Value of Patents in the Psychedelic World." *LinkedIn,* March 9. Linkedin.com/pulse/open-letter-tim-ferriss-value-patents-psychedelic-angermayer

Anguiano, Dani. 2024. "Field Trip: Inside America's First Magic Mushroom School." *The Guardian*, January 13.

Anthony, James, Lynn Warner and Ronald Kessler. 1994. "Comparative Epidemiology of Dependence on Tobacco, Alcohol, Controlled Substances, and Inhalants: Basic Findings from the National Comorbidity Survey." *Experimental and Clinical Psychopharmacology* 2 (3): 244–268.

Araújo, Ana Margarida, Félix Carvalho, Maria de Lourdes Bastos, Paula Guedes de Pinho and Márcia Carvalho. 2015. "The Hallucinogenic World of Tryptamines: An Updated Review." *Archives of Toxicology* 89 (8): 1151–1173.

Atkinson, Kate. 2023. "Parkdale Queen West Community Health Centre Safer Opioid Supply Program Evaluation Report." March. pqwchc.org/wp-content/uploads/PQWCHC_SOS_EvaluationReport-Final-2023.pdf

Auerhahn, Kathleen. 1999. "The Split Labor Market and the Origins of
Antidrug Legislation in the United States." *Law and Social Inquiry* 24 (2): 411–440.

Austin, Paul and Graham Pechenik. 2023. "The Psychedelic Patent Puzzle: Unraveling the Impact on Innovation vs. Access." *Third Wave*, May 22.

Austin, Paul and James Fadiman. 2021. "The Genesis of Microdosing: Creativity, Problem-Solving, and Other Feats of Mental Magic." *Third Wave*, February 28.

Austin, Paul and Ben Sessa. 2020. "Dr. Ben Sessa on MDMA, Healing Trauma, and the Future of Psychiatry." *Third Wave*, March 5.

Austin, Paul and Danny Motyka. 2020. "Chemistry, Biosynthetics, and the Promise of Novel Psychedelic Medicines." *Third Wave*, December 20.

Austin, Paul and Jag Davies. 2017. "Why Decriminalization Will Save Lives." *Third Wave*, January 10.
Baer, Drake. 2015. "How Steve Jobs' Acid-Fueled Quest for Enlightenment Made Him the Greatest Product Visionary in History." *Business Insider*, January 29.
Bahji, Anees, Gustavo Vazquez and Carlos Zarate. 2021. "Comparative Efficacy of Racemic Ketamine and Esketamine for Depression: A Systematic Review and Meta-Analysis." *Journal of Affective Disorders* 278: 542–555.
Bakan, Joel. 2004. *The Corporation: The Pathological Pursuit of Profit and Power*. Toronto: Penguin.
Baker, Dean. 2016. *Rigged: How Globalization and the Rules of the Modern Economy Were Structured to Make the Rich Richer*. Washington, DC: Center for Economic and Policy Research.
Balaban, Judy and Cari Beauchamp. 2010. "Cary in the Sky with Diamonds." *Vanity Fair*, July 8.
Ballentine, Galen, Samuel Freesun Friedman and Danilo Bzdok. 2022. "Trips and Neurotransmitters: Discovering Principled Patterns Across 6850 Hallucinogenic Experiences." *Science Advances* 8 (11).
Bannow, Tara and Olivia Goldhill. 2022. "Psychedelic Therapy is Moving to the Next Frontier: Workplace Perk." *STAT*, December 6.
Barber, Patrick Wayne. 2018. *Psychedelic Revolutionaries: LSD and the Birth of Hallucinogenic Research*. Regina: University of Regina Press.
Barbosa, Paulo, Rick Strassman, Dartiu Xavier da Silveira, Kelsy Areco, Robert Hoy, Jessica Pommy, Robert Thoma and Michael Bogenschutz. 2016. "Psychological and Neuropsychological Assessment of Regular Hoasca Users." *Comprehensive Psychiatry* 71: 95–105.
Barnett, Brian, Miranda Arakelian, David Beebe, Jared Ontko, Connor Riegal, Willie Siu, Jeremy Weleff and Harrison Pope. 2024. "American Psychiatrists' Opinions About Classic Hallucinogens and Their Potential Therapeutic Applications: A 7-Year Follow-Up Survey." *Psychedelic Medicine* 2 (1).
Barnett, Brian and Richard Doblin. 2021. "Dissemination of Erroneous Research Findings and Subsequent Retraction in High-Circulation Newspapers: A Case Study of Alleged MDMA-Induced Dopaminergic Neurotoxicity in Primates." *Journal of Psychoactive Drugs* 53 (2): 104–110.
Barnett, Brian, Willie Siu and Harrison Pope. 2018. "A Survey of American Psychiatrists' Attitudes Toward Classic Hallucinogens." *The Journal of Nervous and Mental Disease* 206 (6): 476–480.
Barone, William, Jerome Beck, Michiko Mitsunaga-Whitten and Phillip Perl. 2019. "Perceived Benefits of MDMA-Assisted Psychotherapy beyond Symptom Reduction: Qualitative Follow-Up Study of a Clinical Trial for Individuals with Treatment-Resistant PTSD." *Journal of Psychoactive Drugs* 51 (2): 199–208.
Barrett, Frederick, Matthew Bradstreet, Jeannie-Marie Leoutsakos, Matthew Johnson and Roland Griffiths. 2016. "The Challenging Experience Questionnaire: Characterization of Challenging Experiences with Psilocybin Mushrooms." *Journal of Psychopharmacology* 30 (12): 1279–1295.
Barrett, Frederick and Roland Griffiths. 2018. "Classic Hallucinogens and Mystical Experiences: Phenomenology and Neural Correlates." *Current Topics in Behavioral Neurosciences* 36: 393–430.
Basu, Brishti. 2023. "'A Stable Foundation': Meet the 22-Year-Old Suing Alberta for Safe Supply." *Filter*, March 21.
Bathje, Geoff, Eric Majeski and Mesphina Kudowor. 2022. "Psychedelic Integration: An Analysis of the Concept and its Practice." *Frontiers in Psychology* 13.

Bathje, Geoff, Jonathan Fenton, Daniel Pillersdorf and London Hill. 2024. "A Qualitative Study of Intention and Impact of Ayahuasca Use by Westerners." *Journal of Humanistic Psychology* 64 (4): 653–691.

Baum, Dan. 2016. "Legalize It All." *Harper's Magazine*, March 31.

BC Public Safety and Solicitor General. 2024. "More Than 2,500 Lives Lost to Toxic Drugs in 2023." *BC Coroners Service News*, January 24. www2.gov.bc.ca/assets/gov/birth-adoption-death-marriage-and-divorce/deaths/coroners-service/news/2024/bccs_december_2023_reporting.pdf

BC Coroners Service. 2024. "Unregulated Death Summary — 2023." Reporting released by the BC Coroners Service. app.powerbi.com/view?r=eyJrIjoiZThmOTkxMzgtZWUzN-S00ODk1LWJiZjItYzMyMTFjNmY0MzJiIiwidCI6IjZmZGI1MjAwLTNkMGQtNGE4Y-S1iMDM2LWQzNjg1ZTM1OWFkYyJ9

Beiner, Alexander. 2023. *The Bigger Picture: How Psychedelics Can Help Us Make Sense of the World*. London: Hay House.

Beiner, Alexander. 2021. "Who's in Charge of Psilocybin?" *Chacruna*, May 10.

Beres, Derek. 2020. *Hero's Dose: The Case for Psychedelics in Ritual and Therapy*. Windsor, WI: Outside the Box Publishing.

Berke, Jeremy and Bradley Saacks. 2020. "Famed Investor Michael Novogratz Said Psychedelics Will be the Next 'Short-Term Bubble' After Cannabis – and Predicts Compass Pathways Will Go Public This Year." *Business Insider*, January 20.

Bershad, Anya, Scott Schepers, Michael Bremmer, Royce Lee and Harriet de Wit. 2019. "Acute Subjective and Behavioral Effects of Microdoses of LSD in Healthy Human Volunteers." *Biological Psychiatry* 86 (10): 792–800.

Blum, Deborah. 2010. "The Chemist's War." *Slate*, February 19.

Boehnke, Kevin, Daniel Kruger and Philippe Lucas. 2024. "Changed Substance Use After Psychedelic Experiences Among Individuals in Canada." *International Journal of Mental Health and Addiction* 22: 842–853.

Bogenschutz, Michael, Stephen Ross, Snehal Bhatt, Tara Baron, Alyssa Forcehimes, Eugene Laska, Sarah Mennenga, Kelley O'Donnell, Lindsey Owens, Samantha Podrebarac, John Rotrosen, J. Scott Tonigan and Lindsay Worth. 2022. "Percentage of Heavy Drinking Days Following Psilocybin-Assisted Psychotherapy vs Placebo in the Treatment of Adult Patients with Alcohol Use Disorder: A Randomized Clinical Trial." *JAMA Psychiatry* 79 (10): 953–962.

Boire, Richard. 2000. "On Cognitive Liberty (Part I)." *Journal of Cognitive Liberties* 1 (1): 7–13.

Boldt, Richard. 2010. "Drug Policy in Context: Rhetoric and Practice in the United States and the United Kingdom." *South Carolina Law Review* 62 (2): 261–348.

Bonnie, Richard and Charles Whitebread. 1974. *The Marihuana Conviction: A History of the Marihuana Prohibition in the United States*. Charlottesville: University Press of Virginia.

Bonomo, Yvonne, Amanda Norman, Sam Biondo, Raimondo Bruno, Mark Daglish, Sharon Dawe, Diana Egerton-Warburton, Jonathan Karro, Charles Kim, Simon Lenton, Dan Lubman, Adam Pastor, Jill Rundle, John Ryan, Paul Gordon, Patrick Sharry, David Nutt and David Castle. 2019. "The Australian Drug Harms Ranking Study." *Journal of Psychopharmacology* 33 (7): 759–768.

Borchardt, Debra. 2024. "University of Maryland Joins Lawsuit Against Compass Pathways." *Green Market Report*, March 25.

Bouchet, Lisa, Zachary Sager, Antoine Yrondi, Kabir Nigam, Brian Anderson, Stephen Ross, Petros Petridis and Yvan Beaussant. 2024. "Older Adults in Psychedelic-Assisted Therapy Trials: A Systematic Review." *Journal of Psychopharmacology* 38 (1): 33–48.

Bouso, José Carlos, Óscar Andión, Jerome Sarris, Milan Scheidegger, Luís Fernando Tófoli, Emérita Sátiro Opaleye, Violeta Schubert and Daniel Perkins. 2022. "Adverse Effects of Ayahuasca: Results from the Global Ayahuasca Survey." *PLOS Global Public Health* 2 (11).

Boyd, Susan. 2017. *Busted: An Illustrated History of Drug Prohibition in Canada*. Halifax: Fernwood Publishing.

Boyd, Susan, Connie Carter and Donald MacPherson. 2016. *More Harm Than Good: Drug Policy in Canada*. Halifax: Fernwood.

Boyd, Susan and Donald MacPherson. 2018. "Community Engagement – The Harms of Drug Prohibition: Ongoing Resistance in Vancouver's Downtown Eastside." *BC Studies* 200: 87–96.

Boyer, Zoe. 2021. "I Was Paralyzed by Severe Depression. Then Came Ketamine." *The New York Times*, May 30.

Bradbrook, Gail. 2019. "How Psychedelics Helped to Shape Extinction Rebellion." *Emerge*, March 25.

Brandt, Jaden. 2023. "A Roadmap for Psychedelic Pharmacy in Canada: A Proposed Policy and Operations Approach for Controlled Access to Select Psychedelics for Treatment of Mental Illness." *Drug Science, Policy and Law* 9: 1–11.

Breeksema, Joost, Bouwe Kuin, Jeanine Kamphuis, Wim van den Brink, Eric Vermetten and Robert Schoevers. 2022. "Adverse Events in Clinical Treatments with Serotonergic Psychedelics and MDMA." *Journal of Psychopharmacology* 36 (10): 1100–1117.

Breeksema, Joost and Michiel van Elk. 2021. "Working with Weirdness: A Response to 'Moving Past Mysticism in Psychedelic Science.'" *ACS Pharmacology and Translational Science* 16 (4): 1471–1474.

Brenan, Megan. 2022. "Americans' Reported Mental Health at New Low; More Seek Help." *Gallup*, December 21.

Bronner, David. 2022. "Setting the Record Straight on the Natural Medicines Health Act, New Approach, and PSFC." *Dr. Bronner's All-One Blog*, October 5.

Bronner, David. 2021. "Sounding the Alarm on Compass's Interference with Oregon's Psilocybin Therapy Program." *Dr. Bronner's All-One Blog*, March 31.

Bronner, David. 2020a. "The Unified Field Theory of Psychedelic Integration and Portugal Style Decriminalization." *MAPS Bulletin* 30 (1).

Bronner, David. 2020b. "Clarifying our Support of the Decriminalize Nature Movement and Challenges with its National Leadership." *Dr. Bronner's All-One Blog*, September 28.

Bronskill, Jim. 2020. "Police Chiefs Call for Decriminalization of Personal Drug Use." *CTV News*, July 9.

Brown, Jerry and Julie Brown. 2016. *The Psychedelic Gospels: The Secret History of Hallucinogens in Christianity*. Vermont: Park Street Press.

Brown, Kristen and Drake Bennett. 2022. "Get Ready for the Magic Mushroom Pill." *Bloomberg Businessweek*, August 22.

Browne, Rachel. 2022. "Exclusive Data Shows Canadian Cops Target More Black and Indigenous Folks for Drug Arrests." *VICE*, April 19.

Browne, Rachel. 2020a. "Weed Executives Are (Still) Overwhelmingly White." *VICE*, October 14.

Browne, Rachel. 2020b. "Legal Ayahuasca Churches are Spreading Across Canada." *VICE*, September 17.

Bruhn, Jan, Peter De Smet, Hesham El-Seedi and Olof Beck. 2002. "Mescaline Use for 5700 Years." *The Lancet* 359 (9320): 1866.

Bruno, Tara and Rick Csiernik. 2018. *The Drug Paradox: An Introduction to the Sociology of Psychoactive Substances in Canada*. Toronto: Canadian Scholars.

Buchman, Daniel and Daniel Rosenbaum. 2024. "Psychedelics in PERIL: The Commercial Determinants of Health, Financial Entanglements and Population Health Ethics." *Public Health Ethics* 17 (1–2): 24–39.

Busby, Mattha. 2024a. "Police Officers are Doing Ayahuasca Now." *VICE*, February 9.

Busby, Mattha. 2024b. "Cops Demand the Right for Cops to Do Psychedelic Drugs." *Daily Beast*, March 23.

Busby, Mattha. 2024c. "Psychedelic Community Divided Over Upcoming Conference in Israel." *Filter*, April 15.

Busby, Mattha. 2024d. "Big Money Is Taking Over MDMA-Assisted Therapy." *Jacobin*, February 24.

Busby, Mattha. 2024e. "'Get on Your Knees' — Alberta Cops Raid Home Over Ayahuasca Delivery." *Filter*, March 20.

Busby, Mattha. 2023a. "Unhappy at Work? Maybe Your Boss Just Needs to Trip." *Double Blind*, July 31.

Busby, Mattha. 2023b. "This Veteran-Founded Church Wants to Sell Psychedelics at your Local Drug Store." *Double Blind*, October 16.

Busby, Mattha. 2023c. "Illegal Shroom Dispensaries in the US and Canada are Getting Busted. *Double Blind*, January 4.

Busby, Mattha. 2022. "There's a Worldwide Spike in Arrests of Plant Medicine Practitioners." *Double Blind*, November 21.

Butler, Matt, Luke Jelen and James Rucker. 2022. "Expectancy in Placebo-Controlled Trials of Psychedelics: If So, So What?" *Psychopharmacology* 239 (10): 3047–3055.

Calder, Abigail and Gregor Hasler. 2023. "Towards an Understanding of Psychedelic-induced Neuroplasticity." *Neuropsychopharmacology* 48 (1): 104–112.

Cameron, Lindsay, Angela Nazarian and David Olson. 2020. "Psychedelic Microdosing: Prevalence and Subjective Effects." *Journal of Psychoactive Drugs* 52 (2): 113–122.

Campbell, Nancy, James Olsen and Luke Walden. 2021. *The Narcotic Farm: The Rise and Fall of America's First Prison for Drug Addicts*. Kentucky: University Press of Kentucky.

Cano, Manuel, Patricia Timmons, Madeline Hooten, Kaylin Sweeney and Sehun Oh. 2024. "A Scoping Review of Law Enforcement Drug Seizures and Overdose Mortality in the United States." *International Journal of Drug Policy* 124.

Capaldi, Colin, Raelyne Dopko and John Zelenski. 2014. "The Relationship Between Nature Connectedness and Happiness: A Meta-Analysis." *Frontiers in Psychology* 5: 976.

Capps, Reilly. 2022. "The Advantages of Psychedelic Prohibition." *Double Blind*, May 1.

Carbonaro, Theresa, Matthew Bradstreet, Frederick Barrett, Katherine MacLean, Robert Jesse, Matthew Johnson and Roland Griffiths. 2016. "Survey Study of Challenging Experiences after Ingesting Psilocybin Mushrooms: Acute and Enduring Positive and Negative Consequences." *Journal of Psychopharmacology* 30 (12): 1268–1278.

Carhart-Harris, Robin. 2021. "Psychedelics are Transforming the Way We Understand Depression and its Treatment." *The Guardian*, April 20.

Carhart-Harris, Robin, David Erritzoe, Tim Williams, James Stone, Laurence Reed, Alessandro Colasanti, Robin Tyacke, Robert Leech, Andrea Malizia, Kevin Murphy, Peter Hobden, John Evans, Amanda Feilding, Richard Wise and David Nutt. 2011. "Neural Correlates of the Psychedelic State as Determined by fMRI Studies with Psilocybin." *Proceedings of the National Academy of Sciences* 109: 2138–2143.

Carhart-Harris, Robin and Karl Friston. 2019. "REBUS and the Anarchic Brain: Toward a Unified Model of the Brain Action of Psychedelics." *Pharmacological Reviews* 71 (3): 316–344.

Carhart-Harris, Robin, Bruna Giribaldi, Rosalind Watts, Michelle Baker-Jones, Ashleigh Murphy-Beiner, Roberta Murphy, Jonny Martell, Allan Blemings, David Erritzoe and David Nutt. 2021. "Trial of Psilocybin versus Escitalopram for Depression." *The New England Journal of Medicine* 384 (15): 1402–1411.

Carhart-Harris, Robin, Mendel Kaelen, Matthew Whalley, Mark Bolstridge, Amanda Feilding and David Nutt. 2015. "LSD Enhances Suggestibility in Healthy Volunteers." *Psychopharmacology* 232 (4): 785–794.

Carhart-Harris, Robin, Robert Leech, Peter Hellyer, Murray Shanahan, Amanda Feilding, Enzo Tagliazucchi, Dante Chialvo and David Nutt. 2014. "The Entropic Brain: A Theory of Conscious States Informed by Neuroimaging Research with Psychedelic Drugs." *Frontiers in Human Neuroscience* 8.

Carhart-Harris, Robin, Suresh Muthukumaraswamy, Leor Roseman, Mendel Kaelen, Wouter Droog, Kevin Murphy, Enzo Tagliazucchi, Eduardo Schenberg, Timothy Nest, Csaba Orban, Robert Leech, Luke Williams, Tim Williams, Mark Bolstridge, Ben Sessa, John McGonigle, et al. 2016. "Neural Correlates of the LSD Experience Revealed by Multimodal Neuroimaging." *Proceedings of the National Academy of Sciences of the United States of America* 113 (17): 4853–4858.

Carhart-Harris, Robin, Leor Roseman, Mark Bolstridge, Lysia Demetriou, Justin Nienke Pannekoek, Matthew Wall, Mark Tanner, Mendel Kaelen, John McGonigle, Kevin Murphy, Robert Leech, Helen Valerie Curran and David Nutt. 2017. "Psilocybin for Treatment-Resistant Depression: fMRI-Measured Brain Mechanisms." *Scientific Reports* 7 (1).

Carhart-Harris, Robin, Leor Roseman, Eline Haijen, David Erritzoe, Rosalind Watts, Igor Branchi and Mendel Kaelen. 2018. "Psychedelics and the Essential Importance of Context." *Journal of Psychopharmacology* 32 (7): 725–731.

Carhart-Harris, Robin, Anne Wagner, Manish Agrawal, Hannes Kettner, Jerold Rosenbaum, Adam Gazzaley, David Nutt and David Erritzoe. 2022. "Can Pragmatic Research, Real-World Data and Digital Technologies Aid the Development of Psychedelic Medicine?" *Journal of Psychopharmacology* 36 (1): 6–11.

Carod-Artal, Francisco Javier. 2015. "Hallucinogenic Drugs in Pre-Columbian Mesoamerican Cultures. *Neurologia* 30 (1): 42–49.

Cary, Peter. 2019. "The Controversial Ketamine-Like Drug that Trump is Pushing on Veterans." *The Guardian*, June 18.

Case, Anne, and Angus Deaton. 2017. "Mortality and Morbidity in the 21st Century." *Brookings Papers on Economic Activity* 1: 397–476.

Castellanos, Joel, Chris Woolley, Kelly Bruno, Fadel Zeidan, Adam Halberstadt and Timothy Furnish. 2020. "Chronic Pain and Psychedelics: A Review and Proposed Mechanism of Action." *Regional Anesthesia and Pain Medicine* 45 (7): 486–494.

Cavanna, Federico, Stephanie Muller, Laura Alethia de la Fuente, Federico Zamberlan, Matías Palmucci, Lucie Janeckova, Martin Kuchar, Carla Pallavicini and Enzo Tagliazucchi. 2022. "Microdosing with Psilocybin Mushrooms: A Double-Blind Placebo-Controlled Study." *Translational Psychiatry* 12 (1).

Cavanna, Federico, Carla Pallavicini, Virginia Milano, Juan Cuiule, Rocco Di Tella, Pablo González and Enzo Tagliazucchi. 2021. "Lifetime Use of Psychedelics is Associated with Better Mental Health Indicators During the COVID-19 Pandemic." *Journal of Psychedelic Studies* 5 (2): 83–93.

CB Insights. 2021. "Betting on Magic: Funding for Psychedelics Startups Reaches a Record High." *CB Insights*, November 18.

Centers for Disease Control and Prevention. 2024. "Drug Overdose Deaths in the United States, 2002-2022." *NCHS Data Brief* 491.

Centers for Disease Control and Prevention. 2023. "Provisional Drug Overdose Death Counts." *National Center for Health Statistics*, May 18.

Chambliss, William. 1994. "Don't Confuse Me with Facts: Clinton 'Just Says No.'" *New Left Review*, March/April.

Chan, Cheryl. 2024. "Vancouver Magic Mushroom Dispensary Wins Latest Legal Battle Against City." *Vancouver Sun*, August 29.

Charlton, Lindsay. 2023. "Windsor Police Seize $36k in Drugs Following Raid at Downtown Magic Mushroom Shop." *CTV News*, August 2.

Chen, Xinyuan, Mackenzie Bullard, Christy Duan, Jamilah George, Terence Ching, Stephanie Kilpatrick, Jordan Sloshower and Monnica Williams. 2020. "The Cost of Exclusion in Psychedelic Research." *Bill of Health*, November 6.

Chen, Xu, Xuan Hou, Daisy Bai, Rosanne Lane, Chong Zhang, Carla Canuso, Gang Wang and Dong-Jing Fu. 2023. "Efficacy and Safety of Flexibly Dosed Esketamine Nasal Spray Plus a Newly Initiated Oral Antidepressant in Adult Patients with Treatment-Resistant Depression: A Randomized, Double-Blind, Multicenter, Active-Controlled Study Conducted in China and USA." *Neuropsychiatric Disease and Treatment* 19: 693–707.

Chenevey, Steve. 2022. "Health Watch: Psychedelic Mental Health Therapy." *Fox News*, January 11.

Chesak, Jennifer. 2023. "Can Wearable Tech Ease Anxiety During Psychedelic-Assisted Therapy for PTSD?" *Very Well Health*, October 12.

Chien, Colleen. 2022. "The Inequalities of Innovation." *Emory Law Journal* 72.

Chomsky, Noam. 2002. *Understanding Power*. New York: The New Press.

Chomsky, Noam. 1991. *Deterring Democracy*. New York: Hill and Wang.

Clear, Todd. 2007. *Imprisoning Communities: How Mass Incarceration Makes Disadvantaged Neighborhoods Worse*. New York: Oxford University Press.

Cockburn, Alexander and Jeffrey St. Clair. 1998. *Whiteout: The C.I.A., Drugs and the Press*. London: Verso.

Coffey, Rebecca. 2021a. "Bicycle Day and the 1962 Harvard Experiment that Showed Psilocybin Can Create Lasting, Positive Spiritual Change." *Forbes*, April 19.

Coffey, Rebecca. 2021b. "Move Over, Psilocybin and Ketamine: A New Compound Derived from a Naturally-Growing Hallucinogen May Revolutionize Psychiatry." *Forbes*, June 23.

Cohen, Jonathan and Joanne Csete. 2006. "As Strong as the Weakest Pillar: Harm Reduction, Law Enforcement and Human Rights." *International Journal of Drug Policy* 17 (2): 101–103.

Cohen, Maimon, Michelle Marinello and Nathan Back. 1967. "Chromosomal Damage in Human Leukocytes Induced by Lysergic Acid Diethylamide." *Science* 155 (3768): 1417–1419.

Cole-Turner, Ron. 2022. "Psychedelic Mystical Experience: A New Agenda for Theology." *Religions* 13 (5): 385–401.

Cole-Turner, Ron. 2021. "Psychedelic Epistemology: William James and the 'Noetic Quality' of Mystical Experience." *Religions* 12 (12).

Collins, Sonya. 2024. "Your Employer May be Adding Another Health Benefit to its Roster: Psychedelic Drugs." *Fortune Well*, January 19.

Collis, Helen. 2022. "Navigating the Highs and Lows of Psychedelic Therapies." *Politico*, September 28.

Compass Pathways. 2022. "Two Thirds of Physicians Surveyed Believe Psilocybin Therapy has Potential Benefit for Patients with Treatment-Resistant Depression." *Yahoo Finance*, January 19.

Compass Pathways. 2020a. "Should Psilocybin be Legalised?" January 8. Compasspathways.com/should-psilocybin-be-legalised/

Compass Pathways. 2020b. "Form F-1" August 28. sec.gov/Archives/edgar/data/1816590/000162828020013118/compassf-1.htm

Conrad, Peter and Joseph Schneider. 1992. *Deviance and Medicalization: From Badness to Sickness*. Pennsylvania: Temple University Press.

Cormier, Zoe. 2022. "The Brave New World of Legalized Psychedelics Is Already Here." *The Nation*, March 21.

Courtwright, David. 2001. *Drugs and the Making of the Modern World*. Cambridge: Harvard University Press.

Crim, Brian. 2018. *Our Germans: Project Paperclip and the National Security State*. Baltimore: Johns Hopkins University Press.

Cristea, Ioana, Joar Øveraas Halvorsen, Lisa Cosgrove and Florian Naudet. 2022. "New Treatments for Mental Disorders Should be Routinely Compared to Psychotherapy in Trials Conducted for Regulatory Purposes." *Lancet Psychiatry* 9 (12): 934–936.

Crossin, Rose, Lana Cleland, Chris Wilkins, Marta Rychert, Simon Adamson, Tuari Potiki, Adam Pomerleau, Blair MacDonald, Dwaine Faletanoai, Fiona Hutton, Geoff Noller, Ian Lambie, Jane Sheridan, Jason George, Kali Mercier, Kristen Maynard, et al. 2023. "The New Zealand Drug Harms Ranking Study: A Multi-Criteria Decision Analysis." *Journal of Psychopharmacology* 37 (9): 891–903.

Crowley, Michael. 2019. *Secret Drugs of Buddhism: Psychedelic Sacraments and the Origins of the Vajrayana (2nd ed)*. Santa Fe, New Mexico: Synergetic Press.

Cybin. 2024. "Cybin Reports Positive Phase 2 Data for CYB003, Demonstrating Breakthrough 12-Month Efficacy in Treating Major Depressive Disorder." *Financial Post*, November 18.

Dahan, Jack, David Dadiomov, Tijmen Bostoen and Albert Dahan. 2024. "Meta-Correlation of the Effect of Ketamine and Psilocybin Induced Subjective Effects on Therapeutic Outcome." *NPJ Mental Health Research* 3.

Dahl, Henrik. 2017. "Apolitical Pharmacology: From Altruism to Terrorism in Psychedelic Culture." *The Oak Tree Review*, October 12.

Dahlberg, Charles, Ruth Mechaneck and Stanley Feldstein. 1968. "LSD Research: The Impact of Lay Publicity." *American Journal of Psychiatry* 125 (5): 685–689.

Davies, James. 2021. *Sedated: How Modern Capitalism Created Our Mental Health Crisis*. London: Atlantic Books.

Davies, James, Brian Pace and Neşe Devenot. 2023. "Beyond the Psychedelic Hype: Exploring the Persistence of the Neoliberal Paradigm." *Journal of Psychedelic Studies* 7 (S1): 9–21.

Davis, Alan, Gabrielle Agin-Liebes, Megan España, Brian Pilecki and Jason Luoma. 2022. "Attitudes and Beliefs about the Therapeutic Use of Psychedelic Drugs among Psychologists in the United States." *Journal of Psychoactive Drugs* 54 (4): 309–318.

Davis, Alan, Frederick Barrett and Roland Griffiths. 2020. "Psychological Flexibility Mediates the Relations between Acute Psychedelic Effects and Subjective Decreases in Depression and Anxiety." *Journal of Contextual Behavioral Science* 15: 39–45.

Davis, Alan, Frederick Barrett, Darrick May, Mary Cosimano, Nathan Sepeda, Matthew Johnson, Patrick Finan and Roland Griffiths. 2021. "Effects of Psilocybin-Assisted Therapy on Major Depressive Disorder: A Randomized Clinical Trial." *JAMA Psychiatry* 78 (5): 1–9.

Davis, Alan, John Clifton, Eric Weaver, Ethan Hurwitz, Matthew Johnson and Roland Griffiths. 2020. "Survey of Entity Encounter Experiences Occasioned by Inhaled N,N-Dimethyltryptamine: Phenomenology, Interpretation, and Enduring Effects." *Journal of Psychopharmacology* 34 (9): 1008–1020.

Davis, Alan, Sara So, Rafael Lancelotta, Joseph Barsuglia and Roland Griffiths. 2019. "5-Methoxy-N,N-dimethyltryptamine (5-MeO-DMT) Used in a Naturalistic Group Setting is Associated with Unintended Improvements in Depression and Anxiety." *The American Journal of Drug and Alcohol Abuse* 45 (2): 161–169.

Davis, Corey, Spruha Joshi, Bianca Rivera and Magdalena Cerdá. 2023. "Changes in Arrests Following Decriminalization of Low-Level Drug Possession in Oregon and Washington." *International Journal of Drug Policy* 119.

Davis, Erik. 2022. "The Elephant in the Room is LSD." *Lucid News*, June 14.

Davis, Erik. 2018. "Capitalism on Psychedelics: The Mainstreaming of an Underground." *Chacruna*, September 25.

Davis, Joseph. 2020. *Chemically Imbalanced: Everyday Suffering, Medication, and Our Troubled Quest for Self-Mastery*. Chicago: University of Chicago Press.

Davis, Joshua. 2015. "The Business of Getting High: Head Shops, Countercultural Capitalism, and the Marijuana Legalization Movement." *The Sixties* 8 (1): 27–49.

Daws, Richard, Christopher Timmermann, Bruna Giribaldi, James Sexton, Matthew Wall, David Erritzoe, Leor Roseman, David Nutt and Robin Carhart-Harris. 2022. "Increased Global Integration in the Brain after Psilocybin Therapy for Depression." *Nature Medicine* 28 (4): 844–851.

Day, Greg and W. Michael Schuster. 2019. "Patent Inequality." *Alabama Law Review* 71 (115).

De L Osório, Flávia, Rafael Sanches, Ligia Macedo, Rafael dos Santos, João Maia-de-Oliveira, Lauro Wichert-Ana, Draulio de Araujo, Jordi Riba, José Crippa and Jaime Hallak. 2015. "Antidepressant Effects of a Single Dose of Ayahuasca in Patients with Recurrent Depression: A Preliminary Report." *Brazilian Journal of Psychiatry* 37 (1): 13–20.

De Rios, Marlene and Roger Rumrrill. 2008. *A Hallucinogenic Tea, Laced with Controversy: Ayahuasca in the Amazon and the United States*. Westport, CT: Praeger.

De Vos, Cato, Natasha Mason and Kim Kuypers. 2021. "Psychedelics and Neuroplasticity: A Systematic Review Unraveling the Biological Underpinnings of Psychedelics." *Frontiers in Psychiatry* 12.

De Wit, Harriet, Hanna Molla, Anya Bershad, Michael Bremmer and Royce Lee. 2022. "Repeated Low Doses of LSD in Healthy Adults: A Placebo-Controlled, Dose-Response Study." *Addiction Biology* 27 (2).

Devenot, Neşe 2024. "SXSW Recap: Counter-Narratives for the Psychedelic Status Quo." *Chemical Poetics (Substack)*, March 18.

Devenot, Neşe. 2023. "TESCREAL Hallucinations: Psychedelic and AI Hype as Inequality Engines." *Journal of Psychedelic Studies* 7 (S1): 22–39.

Devenot, Neşe, Trey Conner and Richard Doyle. 2022. "Dark Side of the Shroom: Erasing Indigenous and Counterculture Wisdoms with Psychedelic Capitalism, and the Open Source Alternative." *Anthropology of Consciousness* 33 (2): 476–505.

Devenot, Neşe, Aidan Seale-Feldman, Elyse Smith, Tehseen Noorani, Albert Garcia-Romeu and Matthew Johnson. 2022. "Psychedelic Identity Shift: A Critical Approach to Set and Setting." *Kennedy Institute of Ethics Journal* 32 (4): 359–399.

Devine, Jimi. 2022. "The Need for 100,000 Psychedelic Facilitators is Real." *LA Weekly*, August 3.

Devillaer, Michael. 2024. *Buzz Kill: The Corporatization of Cannabis*. Montreal: Black Rose Books.

Dickinson, Jonathan and Dimitri Mugianis. 2021. "Why Mental Health Researchers are Studying Psychedelics All Wrong." *Salon*, March 6.

Dickinson, Jonathan and Dimitri Mugianis. 2020. "Why Ibogaine is Not the Answer to the Opioid Crisis." *Chacruna*, September 29.

Diesenhouse, Susan. 1989. "Drive Seeks to Make Sex in Therapy a Crime." *The New York Times*, April 6.

Dinis-Oliveira, Ricardo Jorge, Carolina Lança Pereira and Diana Dias da Silva. 2019. "Pharmacokinetic and Pharmacodynamic Aspects of Peyote and Mescaline: Clinical and Forensic Repercussions." *Current Molecular Pharmacology* 12 (3): 184–194.

Doblin, Rick. 2023. "The Balance at MAPS Between Public Benefit and Private Profit." *Psychedelic Alpha*, January 23.

Doblin, Rick. 2013. "'Ask Me Anything' Reddit Interview with Rick Doblin & MAPS." *Psychedelic Frontier*, December 4.

Doblin, Rick. 1991. "Pahnke's 'Good Friday Experiment': A Long-Term Follow-Up and Methodological Critique." *Journal of Transpersonal Psychology* 23 (1): 1–28.

Dolder, Patrick, Yasmin Schmid, Felix Müller, Stefan Borgwardt and Matthias Liechti. 2016. "LSD Acutely Impairs Fear Recognition and Enhances Emotional Empathy and Sociality." *Neuropsychopharmacology* 41 (11): 2638–2646.

Doll, Agnieszka. 2024. "Making 'Medical': How Psychedelics are Becoming Legal in Canada." *Dalhousie Law Journal* 47 (1): 83–119.

Dollar, Cindy Brooks. 2021. "Recreation and Realization: Reported Motivations of Use Among Persons Who Consume Psychedelics in Non-Clinical Settings." *The Journal of Qualitative Criminal Justice and Criminology* 10 (4).

Donaldson, Jesse. 2019. "Hollywood Hospital." *Montecristo Magazine*, April 10.

Donaldson, Jesse and Erika Dyck. 2022. *The Acid Room: The Psychedelic Trials and Tribulations of Hollywood Hospital*. Vancouver: Anvil Press.

Donziger, Steven (ed.). 1996. *The Real War on Crime: The Report of the National Criminal Justice Commission*. New York: HarperCollins.

Dore, Jennifer, Brent Turnipseed, Shannon Dwyer, Andrea Turnipseed, Julane Andries, German Ascani, Celeste Monnette, Angela Huidekoper, Nicole Strauss and Phil Wolfson. 2019. "Ketamine Assisted Psychotherapy (KAP): Patient Demographics, Clinical Data and Outcomes in Three Large Practices Administering Ketamine with Psychotherapy." *Journal of Psychoactive Drugs* 51 (2): 189–198.

Dos Santos, Rafael, Fermanda Balthazar, José Carlos Bouso and Jaime Hallak. 2016. "The Current State of Research on Ayahuasca: A Systematic Review of Human Studies Assessing Psychiatric Symptoms, Neuropsychological Functioning, and Neuroimaging." *Journal of Psychopharmacology* 30 (12): 1230–1247.

Dos Santos, Rafael, José Carlos Bouso and Jaime Hallak. 2017. "The Antiaddictive Effects of Ibogaine: A Systematic Literature Review of Human Studies." *Journal of Psychedelic Studies* 1 (1): 20–28.

Drozdz, Sandra, Akash Goel, Matthew McGarr, Joel Katz, Paul Ritvo, Gabriella Mattina, Venkat Bhat, Calvin Diep and Karim Ladha. 2022. "Ketamine Assisted Psychotherapy: A Systematic Narrative Review of the Literature." *Journal of Pain Research* 15: 1691–1706.

Drug Science. 2021. "Public Attitudes to Psilocybin-Assisted Therapy." ora.ox.ac.uk/objects/uuid:7a09237a-841e-4b63-ae33 a386e417b71d/files/spz50gx41k

Duffy, Matthew. 2022. "Opinion: I Helped Decriminalize Psychedelics in Denver. Here's Why Voters Should Reject the New Psychedelics Proposal." *The Denver Post*, September 8.

Dumit, Joseph and Emilia Sanabria. 2022. "Set, Setting, and Clinical Trials: Colonial Technologies and Psychedelics." In *The Palgrave Handbook of the Anthropology of Technology*, edited by M. Bruun, A. Wahlberg, R. Douglas-Jones, C. Hasse, K. Hoeyer, D. Kristensen and B. Winthereik. Singapore: Palgrave Macmillan.

Dupuis, David and Samuel Veissière. 2022. "Culture, Context, and Ethics in the Therapeutic Use of Hallucinogens: Psychedelics as Active Super-Placebos?" *Transcultural Psychiatry* 59 (5): 571–578.

Dyck, Erika. 2018. "Historian Explains How Women Have been Excluded from the Field of Psychedelic Science." *Chacruna*, October 16.

Dyck, Erika. 2012. *Psychedelic Psychiatry: LSD on the Canadian Prairies*. Winnipeg: University of Manitoba Press.

Dyck, Erika. 2011. "'Just Say Know': Criminalizing LSD and the Politics of Psychedelic Expertise." In *The Real Dope: Historical and Legal Perspectives on the Regulation of Drugs in Canada*, edited by E. Montigny. Toronto: University of Toronto Press.

Dyck, Erika. 2008. *Psychedelic Psychiatry: LSD from Clinic to Campus*. Baltimore: Johns Hopkins University Press.

Dyck, Erika. 2006. "'Hitting Highs at Rock Bottom': LSD Treatment for Alcoholism, 1950-1970." *Social History of Medicine* 19 (2): 313–329.

Dyck, Erika, Tehseen Noorani, Nicolas Langlitz, Alex Dymock, Anne Schlag and Oliver Davis (eds.). 2024. *Psychedelic Humanities*. Lausanne: Frontiers Media SA.

Earleywine, Mitch, Fiona Low, Carmen Lau, Joseph De Leo. 2022. "Integration in Psychedelic-Assisted Treatments: Recurring Themes in Current Providers' Definitions, Challenges, and Concerns." *Journal of Humanistic Psychology*, online first.

Eckert, Thomas. 2022. "The Oregon Model: Origins and Inspirations." *Chacruna*, April 1.

Eisenstein, Charles. 2016. "Psychedelics and Systems Change." *MAPS Bulletin* 26 (1): 4–6.

Elder, Robert. 2021. "Psychedelics: The Newest Tool in Nuclear Negotiations?" *Bulletin of the Atomic Scientists*, December 17.

Elf, Patrick, Amy Isham and Dario Leoni. 2023. "Moving Forward by Looking Back: Critiques of Commercialized Mindfulness and the Future of (Commercialized) Psychedelics." *History of Pharmacy and Pharmaceuticals* 65 (1): 33–62.

Ellenhorn, Ross and Dimitri Mugianis. 2022a. "Why is the American Right Suddenly So Interested in Psychedelic Drugs?" *The Guardian*, October 18.

Ellenhorn, Ross and Dimitri Mugianis. 2022b. "The Corporatization of Psychedelics Would Be a Disaster." *Jacobin*, February 18.

El-Seedi, Hesham, Peter De Smet, Olof Beck, Göran Possnert and Jan Bruhn. 2005. "Prehistoric Peyote Use: Alkaloid Analysis and Radiocarbon Dating of Archaeological Specimens of Lophophora from Texas." *Journal of Ethnopharmacology* 101 (1–3): 238–242.

Elsey, James. 2017. "Psychedelic Drug Use in Healthy Individuals: A Review of Benefits, Costs, and Implications for Drug Policy." *Drug Science, Policy and Law* 3.

Emboden, William. 1981. "Transcultural use of Narcotic Water Lilies in Ancient Egyptian and Maya Drug Ritual." *Journal of Ethnopharmacology* 3 (1): 39–83.

Ens, Andrea. 2019. "'Wish I Would be Normal': LSD and Homosexuality at Hollywood Hospital, 1955–1973" (unpublished PhD dissertation, University of Saskatchewan).

Erickson, Patricia. 1992. "Recent Trends in Canadian Drug Policy: The Decline and Resurgence of Prohibitionism." *Daedalus* 121 (3): 239–267.

Ermakova, Anya. 2022. "The Global Ayahuasca Boom: What About the Conservation of the Ayahuasca Vine?" *Chacruna*, July 15.

Erritzoe, David, Tommaso Barba, Kyle Greenway, Roberta Murphy, Jonny Martell, Bruna Giribaldi, Christopher Timmermann, Ashleigh Murphy-Beiner, Michelle Jones, David Nutta, Brandon Weiss and Robin Carhart-Harris. 2024. "Effect of Psilocybin Versus Escitalopram on Depression Symptom Severity in Patients with Moderate-to-Severe Major Depressive Disorder: Observational 6-Month Follow-Up of Phase 2, Double-Blind, Randomized Controlled Trial." *EClinicalMedicine*, online first.

Erritzoe, David, Leor Roseman, Matthew Nour, Katherine MacLean, Mendel Kaelen, David Nutt and Robin Carhart-Harris. 2018. "Effects of Psilocybin Therapy on Personality Structure." *Acta Psychiatrica Scandinavica* 138 (5): 368–378.

Ettman, Catherine, Salma Abdalla, Gregory Cohen, Laura Sampson, Patrick Vivier and Sandro Galea. 2020. "Prevalence of Depression Symptoms in US Adults Before and During the COVID-19 Pandemic." *JAMA* 3 (9).

Evans, Jules. 2024a. "Lykos Rallies the Troops." *Ecstatic Integration*, June 25.

Evans, Jules. 2024b. "Did Compass Minimize Adverse Experiences in its Psilocybin Trial?" *Ecstatic Integration*, February 23.

Evans, Jules. 2023a. "The Passing of a Psychedelic Prophet." *Ecstatic Integration*, October 24.

Evans, Jules. 2023b. "'More Evolved Than You': Evolutionary Spirituality as a Cultural Frame for Psychedelic Experiences." *Frontiers in Psychology* 14.

Evans, Jules. 2023c. "Who Pays the Piper?" *Ecstatic Integration*, July 14.

Evans, Jules. 2023d. "Does the Medicine Always Give You What We Need?" *Ecstatic Integration*, April 21.

Evans, Jules. 2023e. "Don't Mention Ketamine's Addictiveness." *Ecstatic Integration*, December 19.

Evans, Jules. 2023f. "Synthesis and the Shadow of Psychedelic Capitalism." *Ecstatic Integration*, March 11.

Evans, Jules. 2023g. "Ketamine: the Psychedelic Renaissance Goes Hyper-Capitalist." *Medium*, February 3.

Evans, Jules. 2021a. "Do Psychedelics Make You Liberal? Not Always." *Medium*, February 15.

Evans, Jules. 2021b. "A Closer Look at the 'Qanon Shaman' Leading the Mob." *Medium*, January 7.

Evans, Jules, Oliver Robinson, Eirini Ketzitzidou Argyri, Shayam Suseelan, Ashleigh Murphy-Beiner, Rosalind McAlpine, David Luke, Katrina Michelle and Ed Prideaux. 2023. "Extended Difficulties Following the Use of Psychedelic Drugs: A Mixed Methods Study." *PloS One* 18 (10).

Fadiman, James. 2011. *The Psychedelic Explorer's Guide: Safe, Therapeutic, and Sacred Journeys*. New York: Simon & Schuster.

Fadiman, James and Sophia Korb. 2019. "Might Microdosing Psychedelics Be Safe and Beneficial? An Initial Exploration." *Journal of Psychoactive Drugs* 51 (2): 118–122.

Fan, Ni, Ke Xu, Yuping Ning, Robert Rosenheck, Daping Wang, Xiaoyin Ke, Yi Ding, Bin Sun, Chao Zhou, Xuefeng Deng, Waikwong Tang and Hongbo He. 2016. "Profiling the Psychotic, Depressive and Anxiety Symptoms in Chronic Ketamine Users." *Psychiatry Research* 237: 311–315.

Farah, Troy. 2023. "Meet the 'Magic' Mushroom Shop Salesman Hoping to Demolish Canada's War on Drugs." *Salon*, December 6.

Farah, Troy. 2021. "How PCP Became a Weapon of Police Propaganda [Part 2]." *Psychedelics Today*, August 18.

Farah, Troy. 2020. "Psychedelic Gold Rush? Psilocybin Startup Compass Pathways Goes Public at More than $1B." *Double Blind*, September 29.

Fava, Maurizio, Marlene Freeman, Martina Flynn, Heidi Judge, Bettina Hoeppner, Cristina Cusin, Dawn Ionescu, Sanjay Mathew, Lee Chang, Dan Iosifescu, James Murrough, Charles Debattista, Alan Schatzberg, Madhukar Trivedi, Manish Jha, Gerard Sanacora, et al. 2020. "Double-Blind, Placebo-Controlled, Dose-Ranging Trial of Intravenous Ketamine as Adjunctive Therapy in Treatment-Resistant Depression (TRD)." *Molecular Psychiatry* 25 (7): 1592–1603.

Feldman, Robin. 2018. "May Your Drug Price Be Evergreen." *Journal of Law and the Biosciences* 5 (3): 590–647.

Felker-Kantor, Max. 2024. *DARE to Say No: Policing and the War on Drugs in Schools*. Chapel Hill: UNC Press.

Ferenstein, Greg. 2023. "Legal Psychedelics in Colorado Have Not Increased Public Health Harms." *Microdose*, May 25.

Fernández, Belén. 2022. "The Legal Psychedelics Industry: Capitalism on Drugs." *Al Jazeera*, May 5.

Ferriss, Tim. 2022a. "The Tim Ferriss Show Transcripts: Dennis McKenna – An Ethnopharmacologist on Hallucinogens, Sex-Crazed Cicadas, The Mushrooms of Language, BioGnosis, and Illuminating Obscure Corners (#592)." May 8.

Ferriss, Tim. 2022b. "The Tim Ferriss Show Transcripts: Hamilton Morris and Dr. Mark Plotkin – Exploring the History of Psychoactive Substances, Synthetic vs. Natural Options, Microdosing, 5-MeO-DMT, The 'Drunken Monkey' Hypothesis, Timothy Leary's Legacy, and More (#605)." July 4.

Ferriss, Tim. 2021a. "The Tim Ferriss Show Transcripts: Michael Pollan — This Is Your Mind on Plants (#520)." June 30.

Ferriss, Tim. 2021b. "The Tim Ferriss Show Transcripts: Hamilton Morris on Iboga, 5-MeO-DMT, the Power of Ritual, New Frontiers in Psychedelics, Excellent Problems to Solve, and More (#511)." April 27.

Ferriss, Tim. 2021c. "Some Thoughts on For-Profit Psychedelic Startups and Companies." March 5. tim.blog/2021/03/05/some-thoughts-on-for-profit-psychedelic-startups-and-companies/

Ferriss, Tim. 2019. "The Tim Ferriss Show Transcripts: Psychedelics – Microdosing, Mind-Enhancing Methods, and More (#377)." July 17. tim.blog/2019/07/17/the-tim-ferriss-show-transcripts-psychedelics-microdosing-mind-enhancing-methods-and-more-377/

Ferriss, Tim. 2018. "The Tim Ferriss Show Transcripts: Michael Pollan (#313)." June 26. tim.blog/2018/06/26/the-tim-ferriss-show-transcripts-michael-pollan/

Finster, Tierney. 2018. "Could Alt-Right Assholes Be Fixed by Feeding Them Shrooms?" *Medium*, February 23.

Fisher, Mark. 2018. "Acid Communism." In *K-punk: The Collected and Unpublished Writings of Mark Fisher From 2004–2016*, edited by D. Ambrose. London: Repeater Books.

Fisher, Mark. 2009. *Capitalist Realism: Is There No Alternative?* Zero Books.

Forstmann, Mattias, Hannes Kettner, Christina Sagioglou, Alexander Irvine, Sam Gandy, Robin Carhart-Harris and David Luke. 2023. "Among Psychedelic-Experienced Users, Only Past Use of Psilocybin Reliably Predicts Nature Relatedness." *Journal of Psychopharmacology* 37 (1): 93–106.

Forstmann, Matthias and Christina Sagioglou. 2021. "How Psychedelic Researchers' Self-Admitted Substance Use and their Association with Psychedelic Culture Affect People's Perceptions of their Scientific Integrity and the Quality of their Research." *Public Understanding of Science* 30 (3): 302–318.

Forstmann, Matthias and Christina Sagioglou. 2017. "Lifetime Experience With (Classic) Psychedelics Predicts Pro-Environmental Behavior Through an Increase in Nature Relatedness." *Journal of Psychopharmacology* 31 (8): 975–988.

Foster, Anne. 2023. *The Long War on Drugs*. Durham: Duke University Press.

Fotiou, Evgenia. 2020. "The Role of Indigenous Knowledges in Psychedelic Science." *Journal of Psychedelic Studies* 4 (1): 16–23.

Fotiou, Evgenia. 2016. "The Globalization of Ayahuasca Shamanism and the Erasure of Indigenous Shamanism." *Anthropology of Consciousness* 27 (2): 151–179.

Furminger, Libby. 2022. "Over One Hundred Years of MDMA Research." *Drug Science*, June 29.

Furst, Peter. 1976. *Hallucinogens and Culture*. San Francisco: Chandler and Sharp.

Gable, Robert. 2006. "Acute Toxicity of Drugs Versus Regulatory Status." In *Drugs and Society: U.S. Public Policy*, edited by J. Fish. New York: Rowman & Littlefield.

Gallagher, Mark. 2023. "Did the Master's Tools Dismantle the Master's House? Anti-Psychiatry, Robin Farquharson, and Acid Anarchism." In *Expanding Mindscapes: A Global History of Psychedelics*, edited by E. Dyck and C. Elcock. Cambridge: MIT Press.

Galvão-Coelho, Nicole, Wolfgang Marx, Maria Gonzalez, Justin Sinclair, Michael de Manincor, Daniel Perkins and Jerome Sarris. 2021. "Classic Serotonergic Psychedelics for Mood and Depressive Symptoms: A Meta-Analysis of Mood Disorder Patients and Healthy Participants." *Psychopharmacology* 238 (2): 341–354.

Gamage, Michelle. 2024a. "Retiring Chief Coroner Lisa Lapointe on Staring Death in the Face." *The Tyee*, January 31.

Gamage, Michelle. 2024b. "Advocates Win Injunction Blocking BC's Drug Decriminalization Rollbacks." *The Tyee*, January 3.

Gandy, Sam. 2021. "Predictors and Potentiators of Psychedelic-Occasioned Mystical Experiences." *Journal of Psychedelic Studies* 6 (1): 31–47.

Gandy, Sam. 2019. "Bridging the Divide: Psychedelic Biophilia & Human Nature Connection." *Medium*, August 1.

Gandy, Sam. 2015. "Psychedelic Scientists." *The Nexian*, July 26.

Garb, Bradley and Mitchell Earleywine. 2022. "Mystical Experiences without Mysticism: An Argument for Mystical Fictionalism in Psychedelics." *Journal of Psychedelic Studies* 6 (1): 48–53.

Garcia-Romeu, Albert, Sean Darcy, Hillary Jackson, Toni White and Paul Rosenberg. 2022. "Psychedelics as Novel Therapeutics in Alzheimer's Disease: Rationale and Potential Mechanisms." *Current Topics in Behavioral Neurosciences* 56: 287–317.

Garcia-Romeu, Albert, Alan Davis, Earth Erowid, Fire Erowid, Roland Griffiths and Matthew Johnson. 2020. "Persisting Reductions in Cannabis, Opioid, and Stimulant Misuse after Naturalistic Psychedelic Use: An Online Survey." *Frontiers in Psychiatry* 10.

Garcia-Romeu, Albert, Alan Davis, Fire Erowid, Earth Erowid, Roland Griffiths and Matthew Johnson. 2019. "Cessation and Reduction in Alcohol Consumption and Misuse after Psychedelic Use." *Journal of Psychopharmacology* 33 (9): 1088–1101.

Garrod, Emma and Katrina Blommaert. 2023. "Intersecting Cultures: Exploring Ayahuasca's Legal and Ethical Journey in Canada." In *Religious Freedom and the Global Regulation of Ayahuasca*, edited by B. Labate and C. Cavnar. London: Routledge.

Gashi, Liridona, Sveinung Sandberg and Willy Pedersen. 2020. "Making 'Bad Trips' Good: How Users of Psychedelics Narratively Transform Challenging Trips into Valuable Experiences." *International Journal of Drug Policy* 87.

GBD Alcohol and Drug Use Collaborators. 2016. "The Global Burden of Disease Attributable to Alcohol and Drug Use in 195 Countries and territories, 1990–2016: A Systematic Analysis for the Global Burden of Disease Study 2016." *Lancet Psychiatry* 5 (12): 987–1012.

Gearin, Alex. 2022. "Primitivist Medicine and Capitalist Anxieties in Ayahuasca Tourism Peru." *Journal of the Royal Anthropological Institute* 28 (2): 496–515.

Gearin, Alex and Neşe Devenot. 2021. "Psychedelic Medicalization, Public Discourse, and the Morality of Ego Dissolution." *International Journal of Cultural Studies* 24 (6): 917–935.

George, Jamilah, Timothy Michaels, Jae Sevelius and Monnica Williams. 2020. "The Psychedelic Renaissance and the Limitations of a White-Dominant Medical Framework: A Call for Indigenous and Ethnic Minority Inclusion." *Journal of Psychedelic Studies* 4 (1): 4–15.

Gerber, Konstantin, Inti García Flores, Angela Christina Ruiz, Ismail Ali, Natalie Lyla Ginsberg and Eduardo Schenberg. 2021. "Ethical Concerns about Psilocybin Intellectual Property." *ACS Pharmacology and Translational Science* 4 (2): 573–577.

Gifford, Mary-Elizabeth. 2023. "Powerful D.C. Republicans Drive Psychedelic Research Efforts." *Lucid News*, June 8.

Giffort, Danielle. 2020. *Acid Revival: The Psychedelic Renaissance and the Quest for Medical Legitimacy*. Minnesota: University Of Minnesota Press.

Gilbert, Daniel and David Ovalle. 2024. "After FDA Setback, Psychedelic Drugmakers Distance Themselves from a Pioneer." *The Washington Post*, June 8.

Gilbert, Jeremy. 2017. "Psychedelic Socialism." *Open Democracy*, September 22.

Gillespie, Nick. 2023. "Rick Perry: The Conservative Case for Psychedelic Medicine." *Yahoo News*, August 29.

Gilman, Greg. 2022. "Majority of Mental Health Patients Support Access to Psychedelics, Survey Finds." *Psychedelic Spotlight*, January 19.

Ginder-Shaw, Erin. 2019. "Clinical Research Proves Microdosing LSD is Not a Placebo." *Third Wave*, June 20.

Ginsberg, Merle. 2015. "Ayahuasca, Hollywood's Hip, Heavy Hallucinogen: 'It's Hardly What You Call Partying.'" *The Hollywood Reporter*, September 25.

Girelli, Giada, Marcela Jofré and Ajeng Larasati. 2023. "The Death Penalty for Drug Offences: Global Overview 2023." London: Harm Reduction International.

Glastra, Jazz. 2023. "A Perspective on Providers: Scaling PAT in a Time of Therapist Shortages." *Psychedelic Alpha*, February 1.

Global Affairs Canada. 2023. "Ministerial Declaration on Accelerating and Strengthening the Global Response to Synthetic Drugs." July 7.

Global Commission on Drug Policy. 2024. "Beyond Punishment: From Criminal Justice Responses to Drug Policy Reform." *Global Commission on Drug Policy*. globalcommissionondrugs.org/wp-content/uploads/2024/12/241127-GCDP_Report2024_EN.pdf

Global Commission on Drug Policy. 2019. "Classification of Psychoactive Substances: When Science Was Left Behind." *Global Commission on Drug Policy*. globalcommissionondrugs.org/wp-content/uploads/2019/06/2019Report_EN_web.pdf

GlobalData. 2023. "Partnership Deals for Psychedelic Drugs Take a Trip with 500% Surge in 2023." *Pharmaceutical Technology*, December 1.

Global Drugs Survey. 2021. "GDS 2021 Global Report." *Global Drugs Survey*. globaldrugsurvey.com/wp-content/uploads/2021/12/Report2021_global.pdf

Global Drugs Survey. 2020. "GDS 2020 Psychedelics Key Findings Report." *Global Drugs Survey*. globaldrugsurvey.com/wp-content/uploads/2021/03/GDS2020-Psychedelics-report.pdf

GlobeNewswire. 2021. "Global Psychedelic Drugs Market Report 2020: Market Size is Projected to Reach $10.75 Billion by 2027." *GlobeNewswire*, March 18.

Glynos, Nicolas, Jacob Aday, Daniel Kruger, Kevin Boehnke, Stephanie Lake and Philippe Lucas. 2024. "Psychedelic Substitution: Altered Substance Use Patterns Following Psychedelic Use in a Global Survey." *Frontiers in Psychiatry* 15.

Goldgrub, Marc. 2023. "An Urgent Legal Primer on Toronto's Shroom Shop Explosion." *Psychedelic Spotlight*, May 4.

Goldhill, Olivia. 2024. "What to Watch for in the Crucial FDA Meeting on MDMA Therapy for PTSD." *STAT*, May 31.

Goldhill, Olivia. 2023. "As Psychedelics Near Approval, There's No Consensus on How They Work." *STAT*, July 3.

Goldhill, Olivia. 2022. "'It's Not Medical': Oregon Wrestles with How to Offer Psychedelics Outside the Health Care System." *STAT*, March 10.

Goldhill, Olivia. 2020. "Psychedelic Therapy has a Sexual Abuse Problem." *Quartz*, March 3.

Goldhill, Olivia. 2018. "A Millionaire Couple is Threatening to Create a Magic Mushroom Monopoly." *Quartz*, November 18.

Goldstein, Luke. 2022. "Rollups: The Emerging Magic Mushroom Monopoly." *The American Prospect*, January 10.

Gonzalez, Debora, Jordi Cantillo, Irene Perez, Maria Carvalho, Adam Aronovich, Magi Farre, Amanda Feilding, Jordi Obiols and José Carlos Bouso. 2021. "The Shipibo Ceremonial Use of Ayahuasca to Promote Well-Being: An Observational Study." *Frontiers in Pharmacology* 12.

Goodwin, Guy, Scott Aaronson, Oscar Alvarez, Peter Arden, Annie Baker, James Bennett, Catherine Bird, Renske Blom, Christine Brennan, Donna Brusch, Lisa Burke, Kete Campbell-Coke, Robin Carhart-Harris, Joseph Cattell, Aster Daniel and Charles DeBattista, et al. 2022. "Single-Dose Psilocybin for a Treatment-Resistant Episode of Major Depression." *New England Journal of Medicine* 387 (18): 1637–1648.

Gopnik, Alison. 2018. "For Babies, Life May Be a Trip." *The Wall Street Journal*, July 18.

Gordon, Todd. 2006. "Neoliberalism, Racism, and the War on Drugs in Canada." *Social Justice* 33 (1): 59–78.

Grabski, Meryem, Amy McAndrew, Will Lawn, Beth Marsh, Laura Raymen, Tobias Stevens, Lorna Hardy, Fiona Warren, Michael Bloomfield, Anya Borissova, Emily Maschauer, Rupert Broomby, Robert Price, Rachel Coathup, David Gilhooly, Edward Palmer, et al. 2022. "Adjunctive Ketamine with Relapse Prevention–Based Psychological Therapy in the Treatment of Alcohol Use Disorder." *American Journal of Psychiatry* 179 (2): 152–162.

Graham, Bryan Armen. 2020. "'I'm High as a Georgia Pine': Dock Ellis's No-Hitter on LSD, 50 Years On." *The Guardian*, June 30.

Greenberg, Tony and Reilly Capps. 2021. "There's a Land Grab for Psychedelic Patents: Here's What We Can Do About It." *Psychedelic Times*, April 19.

Gregoire, Carolyn. 2020. "Inside the Movement to Decolonize Psychedelic Pharma." *Proto. Life*, October 29.

Greń, Jakub, Ingmar Gorman, Anastasia Ruban, Filip Tylš, Snehal Bhatt and Marc Aixalà. 2024. "Call for Evidence-Based Psychedelic Integration." *Experimental and Clinical Psychopharmacology* 32 (2): 129–135.

Griffiths, Roland, Ethan Hurwitz, Alan Davis, Matthew Johnson and Robert Jesse. 2019. "Survey of Subjective 'God Encounter Experiences': Comparisons among Naturally Occurring Experiences and Those Occasioned by the Classic Psychedelics Psilocybin, LSD, Ayahuasca, or DMT." *PLoS One* 14 (4).

Griffiths, Roland, Matthew Johnson, Michael Carducci, Annie Umbricht, William Richards, Brian Richards, Mary Cosimano and Margaret Klinedinst. 2016. "Psilocybin Produces Substantial and Sustained Decreases in Depression and Anxiety in Patients with Life-Threatening Cancer: A Randomized Double-Blind Trial." *Journal of Psychopharmacology* 30 (12): 1181–1197.

Griffiths, Roland, Matthew Johnson, William Richards, Brian Richards, Robert Jesse, Katherine MacLean, Frederick Barrett, Mary Cosimano and Maggie Klinedinst. 2018. "Psilocybin-Occasioned Mystical-Type Experience in Combination with Meditation and Other Spiritual Practices Produces Enduring Positive Changes in Psychological Functioning and in Trait Measures of Prosocial Attitudes and Behaviors." *Journal of Psychopharmacology* 32 (1): 49–69.

Griffiths, Roland, William Richards, Matthew Johnson, Una McCann and Robert Jesse. 2008. "Mystical-type Experiences Occasioned by Psilocybin Mediate the Attribution of Personal Meaning and Spiritual Significance 14 Months Later." *Journal of Psychopharmacology* 22 (6): 621–632.

Griffiths, Roland, William Richards, Una McCann and Robert Jesse. 2006. "Psilocybin Can Occasion Mystical-type Experiences Having Substantial and Sustained Personal Meaning and Spiritual Significance." *Psychopharmacology* 187 (3): 268–283.

Grind, Kirsten and Katherine Bindley. 2023. "Magic Mushrooms. LSD. Ketamine. The Drugs That Power Silicon Valley." *The Wall Street Journal*, June 27.

Grinspoon, Lester and James Bakalar. 1979. *Psychedelic Drugs Reconsidered*. New York: Basic Books.

Grof, Stanislav. 1980. *LSD Psychotherapy*. California: Hunter House.

Grof, Stanislav. 1973. "Theoretical and Empirical Basis of Transpersonal Psychology and Psychotherapy: Observations from LSD Research. *Journal of Transpersonal Psychology* 5 (1): 15–53.

GS Strategy Group/Impact Research. 2023. "Ballot Measure 110 Survey Research." August. fixballotmeasure110.com/wp-content/uploads/2023/09/OR-M110-August-2023-Final.pdf

Gukasyan, Natalie, Alan Davis, Frederick Barrett, Mary Cosimano, Nathan Sepeda, Matthew Johnson and Roland Griffiths. 2022. "Efficacy and Safety of Psilocybin-Assisted Treatment for Major Depressive Disorder: Prospective 12-Month Follow-Up." *Journal of Psychopharmacology* 36 (2): 151–158.

Gunther, Marc. 2023. "Shifting Strategy, MAPS Turns to Equity Investment." *Lucid News*, March 28.

Gunther, Marc. 2022a. "At Horizons 2022, A Cloudy Outlook for Psychedelics." *Medium*, October 17.

Gunther, Marc. 2022b. "As Plant-Medicine Churches Grow, Legal Questions Linger." *Lucid News*, August 25.

Gunther, Marc. 2020. "Could Psychedelics Heal the World? *Medium*, January 25.

Guzman, Jose. 2021. "Yes, Ketamine Addiction is a Thing. Here's What You Need to Know." *Double Blind*, May 26.

Hager, Sandy. 2024. "Tracking the Fortunes of Corporate Psychedelia." London: City Political Economy Research Centre.

Haigney, Zach. 2022. "God, Is That You?" *The Trip Report*, April 22.

Haigney, Zach. 2020. "Psychiatrists & Decriminalize Nature Oppose Oregon Ballot Measure." *The Trip Report*, October 2.

Hall, Will. 2021a. "Ending the Silence Around Psychedelic Therapy Abuse." *Mad in America*, September 25.

Hall, Will. 2021b. "Psychedelic Therapy Abuse: My Experience with Aharon Grossbard, Francoise Bourzat … and Their Lawyers." *Medium*, September 18.

Hallifax, James. 2022. "Senator's Wife Secretly Gave Him Psilocybin to Alleviate Depression." *Psychedelic Spotlight*, May 21.

Halperin, Alex. 2018. "Cannabis Capitalism: Who is Making Money in the Marijuana Industry?" *The Guardian*, October 3.

Halpern, John and Harrison Pope. 2003. "Hallucinogen Persisting Perception Disorder: What Do We Know after 50 Years?" *Drug and Alcohol Dependence* 69 (2): 109–119.

Halpern, John, Andrea Sherwood, James Hudson, Staci Gruber, David Kozin and Harrison Pope. 2011. "Residual Neurocognitive Features of Long-Term Ecstasy Users with Minimal Exposure to Other Drugs." *Addiction* 106 (4): 777–786.

Halpern, John, Andrea Sherwood, James Hudson, Deborah Yurgelun-Todd and Harrison Pope. 2005. "Psychological and Cognitive Effects of Long-Term Peyote Use Among Native Americans." *Biological Psychiatry* 58 (8): 624–631.

Harder, Henry, Fabian Steinmetz and Maja Kohek. 2023. "The Psychedelic Social Club: a Regulatory Concept for People who Use Psychedelics?" *Drugs: Education, Prevention and Policy*, online first.

Hardill, Kathy and Carolyn King. 2024. "Embedding a Safer Supply Program in a Small Urban Community: Peterborough 360 Degree Safer Supply Program (SSP) Evaluation May 2022 through December 2023." 360nursepractitionerledclinic.ca/wp-content/uploads/2024/06/EmbeddingSSP_360NPLC.pdf

Hardman, Josh. 2024a. "The Evolving Perceptions of Psychedelics." *reMind*, February.

Hardman, Josh. 2024b. "Pα+ Psychedelic Bulletin #166: Crenshaw and Musk Weigh in on MDMA; Drug Devs Clarify Trial Design in Wake of AdComm; Mini Interview: Joshua Ismin, Psylo." *Psychedelic Alpha*, July 5.

Hardman, Josh. 2023a. "Inside Synthesis Institute's Implosion." *Lucid News*, March 7.

Hardman, Josh. 2023b. "A Market Analysis of Psychedelic Clinics and Retreats." *reMind*, July.

Hardman, Josh. 2022. "Psychedelic Bulletin #121: The State of Psychedelic Economy and Industry; Dispatch from Horizons New York 2022." *Psychedelic Alpha*, October 28.

Hardman, Josh and Noah Smith. 2024. "Lykos Therapeutics Moved to Patent MDMA In Late 2022, Filing Reveals." *Psychedelic Alpha*, June 13.

Harm Reduction International. 2024. "Redirecting Funds to Harm Reduction." hri.global/topics/funding-for-harm-reduction/redirecting-funds/

Harner, Michael. 1973. *Hallucinogens and Shamanism*. New York: Oxford University Press.

Harris, Rachel. 2023. *Swimming in the Sacred: Wisdom from the Psychedelic Underground*. California: New World Library.

Harrison, Ann and Ken Jordan. 2024. "How MAPS PBC Became Lykos Therapeutics and Raised $100M." *Lucid News*, January 12.

Harrison, Ann and Ken Jordan. 2021. "Rick Doblin Explains MAPS' New $70 Million Investment Fund with Vine Ventures." *Lucid News*, December 2.

Hart, Carl. 2022. *Drug Use for Grown-ups: Chasing Liberty in the Land of Fear*. New York: Penguin.

Hart, Carl. 2014. "How the Myth of the 'Negro Cocaine Fiend' Helped Shape American Drug Policy." *The Nation*, January 29.

Hart, Carl. 2013. *High Price: A Neuroscientist's Journey of Self-Discovery That Challenges Everything You Know About Drugs and Society*. New York: HarperCollins.

Hartogsohn, Ido. 2023. "The Corporadelic Set and Setting: On the Consequences of Psychedelic Commodification." *History of Pharmacy and Pharmaceuticals* 65 (1): 131–140.

Hartogsohn, Ido. 2022. "Modalities of the Psychedelic Experience: Microclimates of Set and Setting in Hallucinogen Research and Culture." *Transcultural Psychiatry* 59 (5): 579–591.

Hartogsohn, Ido. 2020. "How Set and Setting Shape Psychedelic Cultures." *Chacruna*, July 30.

Hartogsohn, Ido. 2013. "The American Trip: Set, Setting, and Psychedelics in 20th Century Psychology." *MAPS Bulletin* 23 (1): 6–9.

Hausfeld, Russell. 2024a. "Building Better Killing Machines — With Ecstasy!" *Truthdig*, March 21.

Hausfeld, Russell. 2024b. "Corporadelic: MAPS For-Profit Arm Raises $100 Million." *TruthDig*, January 11.

Hausfeld, Russell. 2023a. "Corporadelia is Knocking at Psychedelia's Door." *Truthdig*, February 8.

Hausfeld, Russell. 2023b. "Psychedelic Science 2023 Contract Muzzles Speakers: Two Clauses Dictate What Presenters Can and Can't Say." *Psymposia*, June 6.

Hausfeld, Russell. 2022a. "A Long Strange Loop." *Truthdig*, November 1.

Hausfeld, Russell. 2022b. "The Few, the Proud ... the Microdosed?" *Truthdig*, December 6.

Hausfeld, Russell. 2022c. "MAPS Advances its Agenda to Treat Active-Duty Soldiers with Psychedelics." *Truthdig*, November 10.

Hausfeld, Russell. 2022d. "How to Open Your Wallet: The Hyped and Distorted Claims of Online Psychedelic Marketing." *Psymposia*, April 28.

Hausfeld, Russell. 2022e. "The Importance of 'Breakthrough' Designation in Drug Policy." *Truthdig*, December 15.

Hausfeld, Russell. 2021. "New Website Details Abuse Allegations Against German Psychedelic Practitioners." *Psymposia*, November 11.

Hausfeld, Russel. 2020a. "Psychedelic Trade Secrets and Get-Rich-Quick Schemes — A Benefit to Investors, a Harm to Progress." *Psymposia*, March 11.

Hausfeld, Russell. 2020b. "Christian Angermayer's ATAI Life Sciences is Positioned to Take the Psychedelic Throne from MAPS." *Psymposia*, March 11.

Hausfeld, Russell. 2020c. "'Making Psychedelics Boring Again' — Unless You're a Privileged Psychedelic Executive, of Course." *Psymposia*, March 11.

Hausfeld, Russell. 2020d. "Calm Down. What's the Worst Thing that the Wellness Industry Could Do to Psychedelics?" *Psymposia*, March 11.

Hausfeld, Russell. 2019. "As Legal Psychedelic Therapy Emerges, Ethicists Urge for More Comprehensive Frameworks to Address Sexual Abuse." *Psymposia*, November 21.

Hausfeld, Russell and David Nickles. 2021. "COMPASS Pathways is Trying to Patent Psilocybin for More Mental Health Conditions Than You Can Name." *Psymposia*, March 18.

Hauskeller, Christine. 2022. "Individualization and Alienation in Psychedelic Psychotherapy." In *Philosophy and Psychedelics: Frameworks for Exceptional Experience*, edited by H. Christine and P. Sjostedt-Hughes. London: Bloomsbury Academic.

Hauskeller, Christine, Taline Artinian, Amelia Fiske, Ernesto Schwarz Marin, Osiris Sinuhé González Romero, Luis Eduardo Luna, Joseph Crickmore and Peter Sjöstedt-Hughes. 2022. "Decolonization is a Metaphor Towards a Different Ethic: The Case from Psychedelic Studies." *Interdisciplinary Science Reviews* 48 (5): 732–751.

Hauskeller, Christine and Peter Sjöstedt-Hughes (eds.). 2022. *Philosophy and Psychedelics: Frameworks for Exceptional Experience*. London: Bloomsbury Academic.

Hay, Mark. 2020. "The Colonization of the Ayahuasca Experience." *JSTOR Daily*, November 4.

Heal, David, Jane Gosden and Sharon Smith. 2018. "Evaluating the Abuse Potential of Psychedelic Drugs as Part of the Safety Pharmacology Assessment for Medical Use in Humans." *Neuropharmacology* 142: 89–115.

Heal, David, Sharon Smith, Sean Belouin and Jack Henningfield. 2023. "Psychedelics: Threshold of a Therapeutic Revolution." *Neuropharmacology* 236.

Healy, David. 2002. *The Creation of Psychopharmacology*. Cambridge: Harvard University Press.

Health Canada. 2023. "Apparent Opioid and Stimulant Toxicity Deaths: Surveillance of Opioid- and Stimulant-Related Harms in Canada." publications.gc.ca/site/eng/9.899667/publication.html

Health Canada. 2019. "Canadian Alcohol and Drugs Survey (CADS): Summary of Results for 2019." canada.ca/en/health-canada/services/canadian-alcohol-drugs-survey/2019-summary.html

Hearn, Kelly. 2013. "Ayahuasca: Fake Shamans and The Divine Vine of Immortality." *Wilderutopia*, July 18.

Heller, Nathan. 2020. "Turn On, Tune In, Get Well." *The New Yorker*, October 5.

Helm, Anna. 2023. "11 Investors Predict a Colorful, If Difficult, Future for Psychedelic Startups." *TechCrunch*, May 12.

Henderson, Theodore. 2016. "Practical Application of the Neuroregenerative Properties of Ketamine: Real World Treatment Experience." *Neural Regeneration Research* 11 (2): 195–200.

Hendricks, Peter. 2018. "Awe: A Putative Mechanism Underlying the Effects of Classic Psychedelic-Assisted Psychotherapy." *International Review of Psychiatry* 30 (4): 331–342.

Hendricks, Peter, Michael Crawford, Karen Cropsey, Heith Copes, N. Wiles Sweat, Zach Walsh and Gregory Pavela. 2018. "The Relationships of Classic Psychedelic Use with Criminal Behavior in the United States Adult Population." *Journal of Psychopharmacology* 32 (1): 37–48.

Hendricks, Peter, Christopher Thorne, Brendan Clark, David Coombs and Matthew Johnson. 2015. "Classic Psychedelic Use is Associated with Reduced Psychological Distress and Suicidality in The United States Adult Population." *Journal of Psychopharmacology* 29 (3): 280–288.

Herrington, Anne. 2023. "California Governor Vetoes Psychedelics Legalization Bill." *Forbes*, October 9.

Highpine, Gayle. 2018. "Is It Cultural Appropriation for White People to Drink Ayahuasca?" *Kahpi*, June 6.

Hodgman-Korth, Madeline. 2023. "Ketamine: Short and Long-Term Effects of Ketamine." *American Addiction Centers*, June 23.

Hofmann, Albert. 2013. *LSD and the Divine Scientist: The Final Thoughts and Reflections of Albert Hofmann*. Vermont: Park Street Press.

Hofmann, Albert. 1980. *LSD: My Problem Child*. New York: McGraw-Hill.

Holloway, Kali. 2022. "The Secret Black History of LSD." *The Nation*, March 22.

Holoyda, Brian. 2023. "Oregon's Sketchy Framework for Psilocybin Program portends a New Implementation Disaster." *The Oregonian*, August 13.

Holyanova, Maria. 2023. "Vancouver Company Creates World's First Ever Ayahuasca Pill." *Psychedelic Spotlight*, February 14.

Holze, Friederike, Toya Caluori, Patrick Vizeli and Matthias Liechti. 2022. "Safety Pharmacology of Acute LSD Administration in Healthy Subjects." *Psychopharmacology* 239 (6): 1893–1905.

Holze, Friederike, Peter Gasser, Felix Müller, Patrick Dolder and Matthias Liechti. 2023. "Lysergic Acid Diethylamide-Assisted Therapy in Patients with Anxiety with and without a Life-Threatening Illness: A Randomized, Double-Blind, Placebo-Controlled Phase II Study." *Biological Psychiatry* 93 (3): 215–223.

Homan, Joshua. 2017. "Disentangling the Ayahuasca Boom: Local Impacts in Western Peruvian Amazonia." In *The World Ayahuasca Diaspora: Reinventions and Controversies*, edited by B. Labate, C. Cavnar and A. Gearin. London: Routledge.

Hood, Ralph. 1975. "The Construction and Preliminary Validation of a Measure of Reported Mystical Experience." *Journal for the Scientific Study of Religion* 14 (1): 29–41.

Hooks, Christopher. 2022. "Rick Perry, Drug Pusher." *Texas Monthly*, May 11.

Hooyer, Katinka, Kalman Applbaum and Daniel Kasza. 2023. "Altered States of Combat: Veteran Trauma and the Quest for Novel Therapeutics in Psychedelic Substances." *Journal of Humanistic Psychology* 63 (6): 744–763.

Horizons. 2018. "Michael Pollan 'How to Change Your Mind.'" *YouTube*, 2018. youtube.com/watch?v=KGSNUyzS1vM&t=1914s

Hovmand, Oliver Rumle, Emil Deleuran Poulsen, Sidse Arnfred and Ole Jakob Storebø. 2023. "Risk of Bias in Randomized Clinical Trials on Psychedelic Medicine: A Systematic Review." *Journal of Psychopharmacology* 37 (7): 649–659.

Howard, Jacqueline. 2019. "Recreational Marijuana Legalization Tied to Decline in Teens Using Pot, Study Says." *CNN*, July 8.

Howell, Nicole. 2020. "How Tripping Can Help Us Reimagine Capitalism Ahead of Psychedelic Commercialization." *Double Blind*, November 18.

Hu, Jane. 2023. "Ten Challenges in Psychedelic Science, TREAT California withdraws Ballot Initiative, and Proposed Changes to Oregon's Psilocybin Services Act." *The Microdose*, November 10.

Hughes, Caitlin and Alex Stevens. 2010. "What Can We Learn from the Portuguese Decriminalization of Illicit Drugs?" *British Journal of Criminology* 50 (6): 999–1022.

Hunt, Katie. 2020. "A Woman Took 550 Times the Usual Dose of LSD, with Surprisingly Positive Consequences." *CTV News*, March 1.

Hutten, Nadia, Natasha Mason, Patrick Dolder and Kim Kuypers. 2019. "Motives and Side-Effects of Microdosing with Psychedelics Among Users." *International Journal of Neuropsychopharmacology* 22 (7): 426–434.

Huxley, Aldous. 1954. *The Doors of Perception*. London: Chatto & Windus.

Huxley, Aldous. 1932. *Brave New World*. London: Chatto & Windus.

Initiative for Medicines, Access, and Knowledge. 2022. "Overpatented, Overpriced — Curbing Patent Abuse: Tackling the Root of the Drug Pricing Crisis." September. i-mak.org/wp-content/uploads/2022/09/Overpatented-Overpriced-2022-FINAL.pdf

InsightAce Analytic. 2023. Global Psychedelic Therapeutics Market Research Report. insightaceanalytic.com/report/global-psychedelic-therapeutics-market/1329.

Institute for Clinical and Economic Review. 2024. "3,4-Methylenedioxymethamphetamine Assisted Psychotherapy for Post-Traumatic Stress Disorder (PTSD): Draft Evidence Report." March 26. icer.org/wp-content/uploads/2024/03/PTSD_Draft-Report_For-Publication_03262024.pdf

International Center for Ethnobotanical Education, Research and Service (ICEERS). 2023. "Ayahuasca Global Consumption & Reported Deaths." June. iceers.org/wp-content/uploads/ICEERS_Ayahuasca_deaths_en.pdf

International Court of Justice. 2024. "Application of the Convention on the Prevention and Punishment of the Crime of Genocide in the Gaza Strip (South Africa v. Israel)." January 26. icj-cij.org/sites/default/files/case-related/192/192-20240126-ord-01-00-en.pdf

International Drug Policy Consortium. 2023. "Off Track: Shadow Report for the Mid-Term Review of the 2019 Ministerial Declaration on Drugs." December. idpc.net/publications/2023/12/idpc-shadow-report-2024

Ionescu, Dawn, Julia Felicione, Aishwarya Gosai, Cristina Cusin, Philip Shin, Benjamin Shapero and Thilo Deckersbach. 2018. "Ketamine-Associated Brain Changes: A Review of the Neuroimaging Literature." *Harvard Review of Psychiatry* 26 (6): 320–339.

Irizarry, Ricardo, Amelia Winczura, Omar Dimassi, Navpreet Dhillon, Annu Minhas and Jeanpaul Larice. 2022. "Psilocybin as a Treatment for Psychiatric Illness: A Meta-Analysis." *Cureus* 14 (11).

Isham, Amy, Simon Mair and Tim Jackson. 2021. "Worker Wellbeing and Productivity in Advanced Economies: Re-examining the Link." *Ecological Economics* 184.

Jacobs, Andrew. 2023. "Veterans Have Become Unlikely Lobbyists in Push to Legalize Psychedelic Drugs." *The New York Times*, June 22.

Jacobsen, Annie. 2014. *Operation Paperclip: The Secret Intelligence Program that Brought Nazi Scientists to America*. New York: Little, Brown and Company.

Jaeger, Alexandria. 2021. "Is 18-MC a Psychedelic Drug?" *Psychedelic Science Review*, March 5.

Jaeger, Kyle. 2023a. "The 'Most Conservative' Massachusetts GOP Lawmaker Files Three Psychedelics Reform Bills, Including Measure to Legalize." *Marijuana Moment*, April 6.

Jaeger, Kyle. 2023b. "New Law Shapes Colorado's Legal Psychedelics Landscape." *Filter*, May 6.

Jaeger, Kyle. 2022a. "Psychedelics Use Increasing Among Adults, but Decreasing for Teens, New Federally Funded Studies Find." *Marijuana Moment*, August 24.

Jaeger, Kyle. 2022b. "Psychedelics Activists Arrested at DEA Headquarters Amid Protest Over Psilocybin Access for Terminal Patients." *Marijuana Moment*, May 9.

James, Edward, Thomas Robertshaw, Mathew Hoskins and Ben Sessa. 2020. "Psilocybin Occasioned Mystical-Type Experiences." *Human Psychopharmacology: Clinical and Experimental* 35 (5).

James, William. 1902. *The Varieties of Religious Experience: A Study in Human Nature*. London: Longmans, Green & Co.

Jansen, Karl. 2004. *Ketamine: Dreams and Realities*. Florida: Multidisciplinary Association for Psychedelic Studies.

Jay, Mike. 2024. "Ecstasy's Odyssey." *The New York Review of Books*, May 23.

Jay, Mike. 2023. *Psychonauts: Drugs and the Making of the Modern Mind*. London: Yale University Press.

Johansen, Pål-Ørjan and Teri Suzanne Krebs. 2015. "Psychedelics not Linked to Mental Health Problems or Suicidal Behavior: A Population Study." *Journal of Psychopharmacology* 29 (3): 270–279.

Johnson, Matthew. 2020. "Consciousness, Religion, and Gurus: Pitfalls of Psychedelic Medicine." *ACS Pharmacology & Translational Science* 4 (2): 578–581.

Johnson, Matthew, Albert Garcia-Romeu, Mary Cosimano and Roland Griffiths. 2014. "Pilot Study of the 5-HT2AR Agonist Psilocybin in the Treatment of Tobacco Addiction." *Journal of Psychopharmacology* 28 (11): 983–992.

Johnson, Matthew, Albert Garcia-Romeu and Roland Griffiths. 2017. "Long-Term Follow-Up of Psilocybin-Facilitated Smoking Cessation." *American Journal of Drug and Alcohol Abuse* 43 (1): 55–60.

Johnson, Matthew, Roland Griffiths, Peter Hendricks and Jack Henningfield. 2018. "The Abuse Potential of Medical Psilocybin According to the 8 Factors of the Controlled Substances Act." *Neuropharmacology* 142: 143–166.

Johnson, Matthew, Peter Hendricks, Frederick Barrett and Roland Griffiths. 2019. "Classic Psychedelics: An Integrative Review of Epidemiology, Therapeutics, Mystical Experience, and Brain Network Function." *Pharmacology & Therapeutics* 197: 83–102.

Johnson, Matthew and David Yaden. 2020. "There's No Good Evidence That Psychedelics Can Change Your Politics or Religion." *Scientific American*, November 5.

Johnstad, Petter. 2023. "Racial and Religious Motives for Drug Criminalization." *Drug Science, Policy and Law* 9: 1–17.

Johnstad, Petter. 2021. "Day Trip to Hell: A Mixed Methods Study of Challenging Psychedelic Experiences." *Journal of Psychedelic Studies* 5 (2): 114–127.

Johnston, Bree, Maria Mangini, Charles Grob and Brian Anderson. 2023. "The Safety and Efficacy of Psychedelic-Assisted Therapies for Older Adults: Knowns and Unknowns." *American Journal of Geriatric Psychiatry* 31 (1): 44–53.

Jones, Andrew. 2023a. "Confronting the Figure of the "Mad Scientist" in Psychedelic History: LSD's Use as a Correctional Tool in the Postwar Period." *Frontiers in Psychology* 14.

Jones, Andrew. 2023b. "The Varieties of Psychedelic Expertise in 1960s Canada: The Psychiatrists behind the Addiction Research Foundation's Study of LSD Therapy." *Canadian Journal of Health History* 40 (1): 33–64.

Jones, Jennifer. 2023c. "Perspectives on the Therapeutic Potential of MDMA: A Nation-Wide Exploratory Survey among Substance Users." *Frontiers in Psychiatry* 14.

Jones, Richard. 2023d. "On the Role of Mysticism in Psychedelic Therapy and Research." *Journal of Psychedelic Psychiatry* 5 (2): 26–47.

Jones, Peter. 2007. "The Native American Church, Peyote, and Health: Expanding Consciousness for Healing Purposes." *Contemporary Justice Review* 10 (4): 411–425.

Jones, Grant and Matthew Nock. 2022a. "Race and Ethnicity Moderate the Associations Between Lifetime Psychedelic Use (MDMA and Psilocybin) and Psychological Distress and Suicidality." *Scientific Reports* 12.

Jones, Grant and Matthew Nock. 2022b. "Psilocybin Use is Associated with Lowered Odds of Crime Arrests in US Adults: A Replication and Extension." *Journal of Psychopharmacology* 36 (1): 66–73.

Jordan, Ken. 2023. "Oregon Bill Would Track Psychedelic Clients." *Lucid News*, January 19.

Joshi, Spruha, Bianca Rivera, Magdalena Cerdá, Gery Guy Jr, Andrea Strahan, Haven Wheelock and Corey Davis. 2023. "One-Year Association of Drug Possession Law Change with Fatal Drug Overdose in Oregon and Washington." *JAMA Psychiatry* 80 (12): 1277–1283.

Jylkkä, Jussi. 2024. "Naturalism and the Hard Problem of Mysticism in Psychedelic Science." *Frontiers in Psychology* 15.

Kaertner, Laura, Michael Steinborn, Hannes Kettner, Meg Spriggs, Leor Roseman, Tobias Buchborn, Maria Balaet, Christopher Timmermann, David Erritzoe and Robin Carhart-Harris. 2021. "Positive Expectations Predict Improved Mental-Health Outcomes Linked to Psychedelic Microdosing." *Scientific Reports* 11.

Kalicum, Jeremy, Eris Nyx, Mary Kennedy and Thomas Kerr. 2024. "The Impact of an Unsanctioned Compassion Club on Non-Fatal Overdose." *International Journal of Drug Policy* 131.

Kałużna, Ada, Marco Schlosser, Emily Craste, Jack Stroud and James Cooke. 2022. "Being No One, Being One: The Role of Ego-Dissolution and Connectedness in the Therapeutic Effects of Psychedelic Experience." *Journal of Psychedelic Studies* 6 (2): 111–136.

Kangaslampi, Samuli. 2023. "Association Between Mystical-Type Experiences under Psychedelics and Improvements in Well-Being or Mental Health — A Comprehensive Review of the Evidence." *Journal of Psychedelic Studies* 7 (1): 18–28.

Karst, Matthias, John Halpern, Michael Bernateck and Torsten Passie. 2010. "The Non-Hallucinogen 2-Bromo-Lysergic Acid Diethylamide as Preventative Treatment for Cluster Headache: An Open, Non-Randomized Case Series." *Cephalalgia* 30 (9): 1140–1144.

Kary, Tiffany. 2022. "Forget Burning Man — Psychedelic Shamans Now Heading to Davos." *Bloomberg*, May 16.

Kaufmann, Bill. 2023. "Psychedelic Therapy Stifled by New Alberta Regulations, Clinic Operators Say." *Calgary Herald*, January 10.

Kavenská, Veronika and Hana Simonová. 2015. "Ayahuasca Tourism: Participants in Shamanic Rituals and their Personality Styles, Motivation, Benefits and Risks." *Journal of Psychoactive Drugs* 47 (5): 351–359.

Kempner, Joanna. 2024. *Psychedelic Outlaws: The Movement Revolutionizing Modern Medicine*. New York: Hachette Books.

Kent, James. 2022a. "Wonderland Miami Exposes Growing Rift in Psychedelic Community." *Psychedelic Spotlight*, November 8.

Kent, James. 2022b. "The Sloppy Science of Psilocybin Microdosing Surveys." *Psychedelic Spotlight*, July 18.

Kerdemelidis, Savva, Celeste Alvarez, Chris Byrnes and Graham Pechenik. 2022. "Pay-For-Success Contracts: An Open Source Alternative to Psychedelic Patents." *Microdose*, August 8.

Kerr, Peter. 1987. "New Violence Seen in Users of Cocaine." *The New York Times*, March 7.

Keshavan, Meghana. 2024. "Rick Doblin, 'Unleashed,' Blasts FDA over Lykos Drug Rejection and Turns to Global Push for MDMA Therapy." *STAT*, August 17.

Kettner, Hannes, Sam Gandy, Eline Haijen and Robin Carhart-Harris. 2019. "From Egoism to Ecoism: Psychedelics Increase Nature Relatedness in a State-Mediated and Context-Dependent Manner." *International Journal of Environmental Research and Public Health* 16 (24).

Kettner, Hannes, Natasha Mason and Kim Kuypers, 2019. "Motives for Classical and Novel Psychoactive Substances Use in Psychedelic Polydrug Users." *Contemporary Drug Problems* 46 (3): 304–320.

Khamsehzadeh, Jahan. 2022. *The Psilocybin Connection: Psychedelics, the Transformation of Consciousness, and Evolution on the Planet*. California: North Atlantic Books.

Khan, Shariq Mansoor, Gregory Carter, Sunil Aggarwal and Julie Holland. 2021. "Psychedelics for Brain Injury: A Mini-Review." *Frontiers in Neurology* 12.

Khenti, Akwatu. 2014. "The Canadian War on Drugs: Structural Violence and Unequal Treatment of Black Canadians." *International Journal of Drug Policy* 25 (2): 190–195.

Killion, Brittany, Audrey Hang Hai, Abdulaziz Alsolami, Michael Vaughn, P. Sehun Oh and Christopher Salas-Wright. 2021. "LSD Use in the United States: Trends, Correlates, and a Typology of Us." *Drug and Alcohol Dependence* 223.

Kim, Tammy. 2024. "A Drug-Decriminalization Fight Erupts in Oregon." *The New Yorker*, January 15.

Kim, Amanda and Joji Suzuki. 2023. "Addiction Specialists' Attitudes Toward Psychedelics: A National Survey." *American Journal on Addictions* 32 (6): 606–609.

Kinder, Tabby and Oliver Barnes. 2024. "Investors Pile into Psychedelic Drug Start-Ups Tackling Mental Health." *Financial Times*, February 10.

Kingsland, James. 2019. "The Shameful History of Psychedelic Gay Conversion Therapy." *Plastic Brain*, May 29.

Kinzer, Stephen. 2019. *Poisoner in Chief: Sidney Gottlieb and the CIA Search for Mind Control*. New York: Henry Holt and Company.

Kious, Brent, Zach Schwartz and Benjamin Lewis. 2023. "Should We Be Leery of Being Leary? Concerns about Psychedelic Use by Psychedelic Researchers." *Journal of Psychopharmacology* 37 (1): 45–48.

Kirkham, Nin and Chris Letheby. 2022. "Psychedelics and Environmental Virtues." *Philosophical Psychology* 37 (2): 371–395.

Kirsch, Irving. 2014. "Antidepressants and the Placebo Effect." *Zeitschrift Für Psychologie* 222 (3): 128–134.

Kirsch, Irving and Guy Sapirstein. 1999. "Listening to Prozac but Hearing Placebo: A Meta-Analysis of Antidepressant Medications." In *How Expectancies Shape Experience*, edited by I. Kirsch. Washington, DC: American Psychological Association.

Kitchens, Travis. 2022. "A Channel for Magic: Ralph Hood's Mysticism Scale and the Occult Roots of the Johns Hopkins Psychedelic Research Program." *Psymposia*, September 9.

Ko, Kwonmok, Gemma Knight, James Rucker and Anthony Cleare. 2022. "Psychedelics, Mystical Experience, and Therapeutic Efficacy: A Systematic Review." *Frontiers in Psychiatry* 13.

Koenig, Xaver and Karlheinz Hilber. 2015. "The Anti-Addiction Drug Ibogaine and the Heart: A Delicate Relation." *Molecules* 20 (2): 2208–2228.

Kohek, Maja, Genís Ona, Michiel van Elk, Rafael Guimarães Dos Santos, Jaime Hallak, Miguel Ángel Alcázar-Córcoles and José Carlos Bouso. 2023. "Ayahuasca and Public Health II: Health Status in a Large Sample of Ayahuasca-Ceremony Participants in the Netherlands." *Journal of Psychoactive Drugs* 55 (3): 247–258.

Kopra, Emma, Jason Ferris, Adam Winstock, Allan Young and James Rucker. 2022. "Adverse Experiences Resulting in Emergency Medical Treatment Seeking Following the Use of Magic Mushrooms." *Journal of Psychopharmacology* 36 (8): 965–973.

Korman, Benjamin. 2023. "Lifetime Classic Psychedelic Use is Associated with Greater Psychological Distress in Unemployed Job Seekers." *Journal of Psychedelic Studies* 7 (2): 90–99.

Korman, Benjamin. 2022. "Recruitment Discrimination of Lifetime Classic Psychedelic Users is Unjustified: Evidence from Employees' Motivation-Based Workplace Absenteeism." *Journal of Psychedelic Studies* 6 (3): 203–210.

Kos-Rabcewicz-Zubkowski, Ludvik. 1975. "Drug Control Laws in Canada." *John Marshall Journal of Practice and Procedure* 9 (1): 99–114.

Kotler, Steven and Jamie Wheal. 2017. *Stealing Fire: How Silicon Valley, the Navy SEALs, and Maverick Scientists are Revolutionizing the Way We Live and Work*. New York: HarperCollins.

KPMG. 2022. "Psychedelic Drugs: A Market Poised for Takeoff." June. kpmg.com/kpmg-us/content/dam/kpmg/pdf/2022/psychedelic-drugs-market-poised-for-takeoff.pdf

Krebs, Teri and Pål-Ørjan Johansen. 2013. "Psychedelics and Mental Health: A Population Study." *PLoS One* 8 (8).

Krebs, Teri and Pål-Ørjan Johansen. 2012. "Lysergic Acid Diethylamide (LSD) for Alcoholism: Meta-Analysis of Randomized Controlled Trials." *Journal of Psychopharmacology* 26 (7): 994–1002.

Kruger, Daniel, Jacob Aday, Christopher Fields, Nicholas Kolbman, Nicolas Glynos, Julie Barron, Moss Herberholz and Kevin Boehnke. 2024. "Psychedelic Therapist Sexual Misconduct and Other Adverse Experiences Among a Sample of Naturalistic Psychedelic Users." *Psychedelic Medicine*, online first.

Kruger, Daniel, Oskar Enghoff, Moss Herberholz, Julie Barron and Kevin Boehnke. 2023a. "'How Do I Learn More About this?': Utilization and Trust of Psychedelic Information Sources Among People Naturalistically Using Psychedelics." *Journal of Psychoactive Drugs* 55 (5): 631–639.

Kruger, Daniel, Julie Barron, Moss Herberholz and Kevin Boehnke. 2023b. "Preferences and Support for Psychedelic Policies and Practices Among Those Using Psychedelics." *Journal of Psychoactive Drugs* 55 (5): 650–659.

Kyzar, Evan, Charles Nichols, Raul Gainetdinov, David Nichols and Allan Kalueff. 2017. "Psychedelic Drugs in Biomedicine." *Trends in Pharmacological Sciences* 38 (11): 992–1005.

La Barre, Weston. 1972. "Hallucinogens and the Shamanistic Origins of Religion." In *Flesh of the Gods: The Ritual Use of Hallucinogens*, edited by P. Furst. London: Allen and Unwin.

Labate, Beatriz, Anna Ermakova, Jordan Sloshower, Nicole Galvão-Coelho, Fernanda Palhano-Fontes, Henrique Antunes, Glauber de Assis, Clancy Cavnar, Draulio de Araújo and Sidarta Ribeiro. 2023. "The DEA Report on Ayahuasca Risks: 'Science' in Service of Prohibition?" *Journal of Psychedelic Studies* 7 (2): 81–89.

Labate, Bia and Kevin Feeney. 2022. "Decriminalize Nature Targets Peyote: Drug Reform or Settler Colonialism?" *Chacruna*, July 1.

Ladou, Ana and Kris Lotlikar. 2020. "A Wholly Public Benefit Model." *MAPS Bulletin* 30 (3): 23–26.

Lagarde, Jessika. 2021. "Spiritual Tourism: The Toxic Impact on Indigenous peoples and Ethical Steps Forward as Psychedelics Boom." *Psychedelic Spotlight*, August 19.

Lake, Stephanie and Philippe Lucas. 2023. "The Canadian Psychedelic Survey: Characteristics, Patterns of Use, and Access in a Large Sample of People Who Use Psychedelic Drugs." *Psychedelic Medicine* 1 (2).

LaMotte, Sandee. 2024. "Single Dose of LSD Provides Immediate and Lasting Relief from Anxiety, Study Says." *CNN*, March 7.

Landau, Meryl Davids. 2022. "Can Microdosing Psychedelics Boost Mental Health? Here's What the Evidence Suggests." *National Geographic*, February 4.

Landau, Meryl Davids. 2021. "Are Psychedelics the Next Big Cure?" *Good Housekeeping*, June 10.

Langlitz, Nicolas. 2024. "Psychedelic Innovations and the Crisis of Psychopharmacology." *BioSocieties* 19: 37–58.

Langlitz, Nicolas. 2023. "What Good are Psychedelic Humanities?" *Frontiers in Psychology* 14.

Laqueur, Hannah. 2015. "Uses and Abuses of Drug Decriminalization in Portugal." *Law & Social Inquiry* 40 (3): 746–781.

Lattin, Don. 2017. *Changing Our Minds: Psychedelic Sacraments and the New Psychotherapy*. New Mexico: Synergetic Press.

Lattin, Don. 2010. *The Harvard Psychedelic Club: How Timothy Leary, Ram Dass, Huston Smith, and Andrew Weil Killed the Fifties and Ushered in a New Age for America*. New York: HarperCollins.

Law, Tara. 2022. "Michael Pollan on the Psychedelic Renaissance and Netflix's New 'How to Change Your Mind' Documentary? *Time*, July 12.

Lea, Toby, Nicole Amada and Henrik Jungaberle. 2020. "Psychedelic Microdosing: A Subreddit Analysis." *Journal of Psychoactive Drugs* 52 (2): 101–112.

Lea, Toby, Nicole Amada, Henrik Jungaberle, Henrike Schecke, Norbert Scherbaum and Michael Klein. 2020. "Perceived Outcomes of Psychedelic Microdosing as Self-Managed Therapies for Mental and Substance Use Disorders." *Psychopharmacology* 237 (5): 1521–1532.

Lebedev, Alexander, Martin Lövdén, Gidon Rosenthal, Amanda Feilding, David Nutt and Robin Carhart-Harris. 2015. "Finding the Self by Losing the Self: Neural Correlates of Ego-Dissolution Under Psilocybin." *Human Brain Mapping* 36 (8): 3137–3153.

Ledlie, Shaleesa, Ria Garg, Clare Cheng, Gillian Kolla, Tony Antoniou, Zachary Bouck and Tara Gomes. 2024. "Prescribed Safer Opioids Supply: A Scoping Review of the Evidence." *International Journal of Drug Policy* 125.

Lee, Yeji. 2023. "How a Family's Struggle to Help their Son Gave Rise to Controversial $400 Million Psychedelics Giant Compass Pathways." *Business Insider*, February 15.

Lee, Martin and Bruce Shlain. 1985. *Acid Dreams: The Complete Social History of LSD: The CIA, the Sixties, and Beyond*. New York: Grove Press.

Lehrner, Amy and Rachel Yehuda. 2021. "Moral Injury and the Promise of MDMA-Assisted Therapy for PTSD." *MAPS Bulletin* 31 (1): 15–19.

Leite, Marcelo. 2022. "Canadian Company Announces Ayahuasca Pills." *Chacruna*, December 22.

Leite, Marcelo. 2021. "Capitalism Goes Rogue with Patent Claims on Psychedelics." *Chacruna*, March 17.

Lekhtman, Alexander. 2023a. "Why Oregon Psilocybin Services Draw Many Clients from Out of State." *Filter*, November 30.

Lekhtman, Alexander. 2023b. "Bill to Drastically Rewrite Colorado's Psychedelics Law Gains Ground." *Filter*, April 27.

Lekhtman, Alexander. 2022. "The Implications of Police Raids on Shops Selling Psilocybin Mushrooms." *Filter*, December 15.

Lekhtman, Alexander. 2019. "How Psychedelic Exceptionalism Harms Drug Users." *Filter*, October 16.

Lekhtman, Alexander. 2018. "After 26 years in Prison for LSD, and Clemency from Obama, Timothy Tyler is a Free Man." *Psymposia*, September 10.

Letheby, Chris. 2021. *Philosophy of Psychedelics*. New York: Oxford University Press.

Levine, Steve. 2021. "Ketamine: A Cautionary Tale." *Psychology Today*, November 30.

Lhooq, Michelle. 2024. "FDA Panel Rejects MDMA Therapy for PTSD." *Double Blind*, June 6.

Li, Chiao-Ching, Sheng-Tang Wu, Tai-Lung Cha, Guang-Huan Sun, Dah-Shyong Yu and En Meng. 2019. "A Survey for Ketamine Abuse and its Relation to the Lower Urinary Tract Symptoms in Taiwan." *Scientific Reports* 9.

Lii, Theresa, Ashleigh Smith, Josephine Flohr, Robin Okada, Cynthia Nyongesa, Lisa Cianfichi, Laura Hack, Alan Schatzberg and Boris Heifets. 2023. "Randomized Trial of Ketamine Masked by Surgical Anesthesia in Patients with Depression." *Nature Mental Health* 1 (11): 876-886.

Lieber, Chavie. 2024. "The Working Woman's Newest Life Hack: Magic Mushrooms." *The Wall Street Journal*, February 6.

Lin, Tao. 2014. "Why Are Psychedelics Illegal?" *VICE*, August 26.

Lindsay, Bethany. 2022. "Footage of Therapists Spooning and Pinning Down Patient in B.C. Trial for MDMA Therapy Prompts Review." *CBC News*, April 9.

Liokaftos, Dimitrios. 2021. "Sociological Investigations of Human Enhancement Drugs: The Case of Microdosing Psychedelics." *International Journal of Drug Policy* 95.

Lippert, Randy and Kevin Walby. 2022. *Police Funding, Dark Money, and the Greedy Institution*. London: Routledge.

Livne, Ofir, Dvora Shmulewitz, Claire Walsh and Deborah Hasin. 2022. "Adolescent and Adult Time Trends in US Hallucinogen Use, 2002-19: Any Use, and Use of Ecstasy, LSD and PCP." *Addiction* 117 (12): 3099–3109.

Londoño, Ernesto. 2024. "Drugs, Sacraments or Medicine? Psychedelic Churches Blur the Line." *The New York Times*, May 12.

López, Pedro Tangoa. 2020. "The Dangers of the Ayahuasca Tourism Boom." *Kahpi*, January 22.

Love, Shayla. 2023a. "'After the Ecstasy, the Laundry' – Shayla Love's Take on Psychedelics in 2022." *Psychedelic Alpha*, January 19.

Love, Shayla. 2023b. "'Long-Lost Best Friends': The Longevity Movement Finds Psychedelics." *The Guardian*, December 8.

Love, Shayla. 2022a. "The Insights Psychedelics Give You Aren't Always True." *VICE*, February 22.

Love, Shayla. 2022b. "Inside the Dispute Over a High-Profile Psychedelic Study." *VICE*, May 16.

Love, Shayla. 2022c. "Psychedelic Patents are Broken Because the Patent System is Broken." *VICE*, May 9.

Love, Shayla. 2021a. "Psychedelics are a Billion-Dollar Business, and No One Can Agree Who Should Control It." *VICE*, September 23.

Love, Shayla. 2021b. "Psychedelic Therapy Needs to Confront the Mystical." *VICE*, February 22.
Love, Shayla. 2021c. "The False Promise of Psychedelic Utopia." *VICE*, November 1.
Love, Shayla. 2021d. "Psychedelic Telemedicine Has Arrived. What Could Possibly Go Wrong?" *VICE*, November 30.
Love, Shayla. 2021e. "The Race to Patent Psychedelics is Just Getting Started." *VICE*, March 5.
Love, Shayla. 2021f. "Can a Company Patent the Basic Components of Psychedelic Therapy?" *VICE*, February 9.
Love, Shayla. 2020a. "I Went to a High-End Psychedelic Retreat to Address My Anxiety." *VICE*, January 29.
Love, Shayla. 2020b. "Get Ready for Pharmaceutical-Grade Magic Mushroom Pills." *VICE*, May 26.
Lowery, Wesley. 2021. "Introducing the Real Will Smith." *GQ*, September 27.
Luke, David and Rory Spowers (eds.). 2021. *DMT Entity Encounters: Dialogues on the Spirit Molecule with Ralph Metzner, Chris Bache, Jeffrey Kripal, Whitley Strieber, Angela Voss, and Others*. Vermont: Park Street Press.
Luoma, Jason, Christina Chwyl, Geoff Bathje, Alan Davis and Rafael Lancelotta. 2020. "A Meta-Analysis of Placebo-Controlled Trials of Psychedelic-Assisted Therapy." *Journal of Psychoactive Drugs* 52 (4): 289–299.
Luz, Matthias and Deborah Mash. 2021. "Evaluating the Toxicity and Therapeutic Potential of Ibogaine in the Treatment of Chronic Opioid Abuse." *Expert Opinion on Drug Metabolism and Toxicity* 17 (9): 1019–1022.
Lyons, Taylor and Robin Carhart-Harris. 2018. "Increased Nature Relatedness and Decreased Authoritarian Political Views after Psilocybin for Treatment-Resistant Depression." *Journal of Psychopharmacology* 32 (7): 811–819.
Lyth, Jaime. 2023. "Australia Legalises Psychedelics for Mental Health, New Zealand Studying Benefits Of MDMA." *New Zealand Herald*, July 1.
Lythcott-Haims, Julie. 2016. "My Conversation with Peter Thiel about Apartheid … And its Unfolding Aftermath." *Medium*, November 2.
Ma, Wai-Kit and Peggy Chu. 2015. "Burden of Ketamine Cystitis in Chinese Society." *Urological Science* 26 (3): 167–173.
Mac, Gabriel. 2017. "The Psychedelic Miracle." *Rolling Stone*, March 9.
MacBride, Katie. 2024. "Aharon Said It Was Healing." *Inverse*, February 20.
MacBride, Katie. 2023. "How Psychedelic Hype is Hurting More People Than We Realize." *Daily Beast*, November 28.
Macedo-Bedoya, Jehoshua and Fatima Calvo-Bellido. 2024. "Hallucinogenic Mushrooms (Psilocybe, Hymenogastraceae) in the Evolutive Development of Man's Consciousness." Fundación Miguel Lillo. lillo.org.ar/journals/index.php/lilloa/article/view/1889
Macintosh, Maggie. 2023. "Police Raid Magic Mushroom Shop, Arrest Two." *Winnipeg Free Press*, May 19.
Mackay, Caroline and Michael Schmitt. 2019. "Do People who Feel Connected to Nature do More to Protect it? A Meta-Analysis." *Journal of Environmental Psychology* 65.
Mackay, Robin. 2018. "The Beginning of Drug Prohibition in Canada: What's Past is Prologue." *Queen's Quarterly* 125 (4): 530–540.
MacLean, Katherine, Jeannie-Marie Leoutsakos, Matthew Johnson and Roland Griffiths. 2012. "Factor Analysis of the Mystical Experience Questionnaire: A Study of Experiences Occasioned by the Hallucinogen Psilocybin." *Journal for the Scientific Study of Religion* 51 (4): 721–737.
MacLean, Katherine, Matthew Johnson and Roland Griffiths. 2011. "Mystical Experiences Occasioned by the Hallucinogen Psilocybin Lead to Increases in the Personality Domain of Openness." *Journal of Psychopharmacology* 25 (11): 1453–1461.

MacLean, J. Ross, Douglas MacDonald, Ultan Byrne and Al Hubbard. 1961. "The Use of LSD-25 in the Treatment of Alcoholism and other Psychiatric Problems." *Quarterly Journal of Studies on Alcohol* 22 (1): 34–45.

Maghsoudi, Nazlee, Indhu Rammohan, Andrea Bowra, Ruby Sniderman, Justine Tanguay, Zachary Bouck, Ayden Scheim, Dan Werb and Akwasi Owusu-Bempah. 2020. "How Diverse is Canada's Legal Cannabis Industry?" *Centre on Drug Policy Evaluation*. https://cdpe.org/wp-content/uploads/dlm_uploads/2020/10/How-Diverse-is-Canada%E2%80%99s-Legal-Cannabis-Industry_CDPE-UofT-Policy-Brief_Final.pdf

Magnuson, Mary, Hannah Swan and Lucas Richert. 2023. "The Introduction of Peyote into Pharmaceutical and Pharmacological Frameworks." *History of Pharmacy and Pharmaceuticals* 65 (1): 169–177.

Mallet, Mark. 2023. "We Must End the Unwitnessed Safe Supply of Opioids." *The Globe and Mail*. September 10.

Mangini, Mariavittoria. 2024. "Unseen Women in Psychedelic History." *Journal of Humanistic Psychology* 64 (4): 635–652.

Mans, Keri, Hannes Kettner, David Erritzoe, Eline Haijen, Mendel Kaelen and Robin Carhart-Harris. 2021. "Sustained, Multifaceted Improvements in Mental Well-Being Following Psychedelic Experiences in a Prospective Opportunity Sample." *Frontiers in Psychiatry* 12.

Marchese, David, 2023. "A Psychedelics Pioneer Takes the Ultimate Trip." *The New York Times Magazine*, April 7.

Marks, Mason. 2023a. "The Varieties of Psychedelic Law." *Neuropharmacology* 226.

Marks, Mason. 2023b. "State-Regulated Psychedelics on a Collision Course With FDA." *JAMA* 330 (24): 2337–2338.

Marks, Mason. 2018. "Psychedelic Medicine for Mental Illness and Substance Use Disorders: Overcoming Social and Legal Obstacles." *NYU Journal of Legislation & Public Policy* 21: 69–140.

Marks, Mason and Glenn Cohen. 2021. "Patents on Psychedelics: The Next Legal Battlefront of Drug Development." *Harvard Law Review Forum* 212.

Marlan, Dustin. 2023. "Psychedelic Capitalism and the Perceptual Threshold." *Boston University Law Review* 103 (2): 643–658.

Marlan, Dustin. 2019. "Beyond Cannabis: Psychedelic Decriminalization and Social Justice." *Lewis & Clark Law Review* 23 (3): 851–892.

Marschall, Josephine, George Fejer, Pascal Lempe, Luisa Prochazkova, Martin Kuchar, Katerina Hajkova and Michiel van Elk. 2022. "Psilocybin Microdosing Does Not Affect Emotion-Related Symptoms and Processing: A Preregistered Field and Lab-Based Study." *Journal of Psychopharmacology* 36 (1): 97–113.

Mash, Deborah, Linda Duque, Bryan Page and Kathleen Allen-Ferdinand. 2018. "Ibogaine Detoxification Transitions Opioid and Cocaine Abusers Between Dependence and Abstinence: Clinical Observations and Treatment Outcomes." *Frontiers in Pharmacology* 9.

Mason, Nathasha, Elisabeth Mischler, Malin Uthaug and Kim Kuypers. 2019. "Sub-Acute Effects of Psilocybin on Empathy, Creative Thinking and Subjective Wellbeing." *Journal of Psychoactive Drugs* 51 (2): 123–134.

May, Jordan. 2017a. "Globalhuasca: A Closer Look at the Global Ayahuasca Movement." *Psymposia*, March 1.

May, Jordan. 2017b. "Patrick Kroupa, Hacker and Ex-Heroin 'Junkie,' on Microdosing and the Medicalization of Ibogaine." *Psymposia*, December 13.

May, Jordan. 2017c. "Talking Ibogaine Research for Opioid Addiction with Thomas Kingsley Brown." *Psymposia*, December 12.

Maybin, Simon and Josephine Casserly. 2020. "I was Sexually Abused by a Shaman at an Ayahuasca Retreat." *BBC*, January 15.

Maynard, Robyn. 2022. "Police Abolition / Black Revolt." In *Disarm, Defund, Dismantle: Police Abolition in Canada*, edited by S. Pasternak, K. Walby and A. Stadnyk. Toronto: BTL Press.
McAllister, Sean. 2022. "Why Colorado's Natural Medicine Health Act is the Right Measure to Access Natural Psychedelic Medicine: Responding to Critics of NMHA." *Chacruna*, September 18.
McAllister, William. 2000. *Drug Diplomacy in the Twentieth Century: An International History*. New York: Routledge.
McClure-Begley, Tristan and Bryan Roth. 2022. "The Promises and Perils of Psychedelic Pharmacology for Psychiatry." *Nature Reviews Drug Discovery* 21 (6): 463–473.
McConnell, Patrick. 2022. "A Deeper Look at Ketamine and its Potential for Addiction." *Microdose*, October 20.
McCulloch, Drummond, Maria Grzywacz, Martin Madsen, Peter Jensen, Brice Ozenne, Sophia Armand, Gitte Knudsen, Patrick Fisher and Dea Stenbæk. 2022. "Psilocybin-Induced Mystical-Type Experiences are Related to Persisting Positive Effects: A Quantitative and Qualitative Report." *Frontiers in Pharmacology* 13.
McDaniel, Piper. 2021. "Is This Peter Thiel-Backed Startup Trying to Monopolize the Astral Plane?" *Mother Jones*, July 6.
McGhee, Ali. 2022. "Decrim Movement Split Over Peyote, Possession Limits, and Tactics." *Lucid News*, April 22.
McGovern, Bryan. 2022a. "What Should Investors Know About Psychedelics Clinical Trials?" *Investing News Network*, February 23.
McGovern, Bryan. 2022b. "What's in a Name? Psychedelics IP Discussion Heats Up." *Investing News Network*, March 14.
McGovern, Bryan. 2020. "Investment Fund Seeks Cultural Reset for Psychedelics." *Investing News Network*, September 3.
McGovern, H.T., Hilary Grimmer, Manoj Doss, Brendan Hutchinson, Christopher Timmermann, Aidan Lyon, Philip Corlett and Ruben Laukkonen. 2024. "An Integrated Theory of False Insights and Beliefs Under Psychedelics." *Communications Psychology* 2 (1).
McGroarty, Beth. 2023. "Wellness Tourism Will Cross the $1 Trillion Mark in 2024." *Global Wellness Institute*, November 28.
McKenna, Dennis. 2012. *The Brotherhood of the Screaming Abyss: My Life with Terence McKenna*. St. Cloud, MN: North Star Press.
McKenna, Terence. 1999. *Food of the Gods: The Search for the Original Tree of Knowledge: A Radical History of Plants, Drugs and Human Evolution*. New York: Random House.
McKenna, Terence. 1993. *History Ends in Green: Gaia, Psychedelics and the Archaic Revival*. Mystic Fire Audio.
McKenna, Terence. 1992. *The Archaic Revival*. San Francisco: HarperOne.
McKenna, Terence. 1987. "Psychedelics Before and After History," presented at San Francisco's California Institute of Integral Studies, October 2. youtube.com/watch?v=hcRGY2Bdk0U.
McNamee, Sarah, Neşe Devenot and Meaghan Buisson. 2023. "Studying Harms is Key to Improving Psychedelic-Assisted Therapy — Participants Call for Changes to Research Landscape." *JAMA Psychiatry* 80 (5): 411–412.
McPhillips, Deidre. 2022. "90% of US Adults Say the United States is Experiencing a Mental Health Crisis, CNN/KFF Poll Finds." *CNN*, October 5.
Megli, Dawn. 2024. "The Ketamine Economy: New Mental Health Clinics are a 'Wild West' with Few Rules." *NPR*, January 30.
Meistere, Una and Dennis McKenna. 2020. "We Need a Transformation of Consciousness on a Global Scale." *Spiriterritory*, November 10.

Menon, Rajan. 2019. "Suicide is Becoming America's Latest Epidemic." *The Nation*, June 18.

Merkur, Dan. 2000. *The Mystery of Manna: The Psychedelic Sacrament of the Bible*. Vermont: Park Street Press.

Merlin, M.D. 2003. "Archaeological Evidence for the Tradition of Psychoactive Plant Use in the Old World." *Economic Botany* 57 (3): 295–323.

Metzner, Ralph. 2009. "Consciousness Expansion and Counterculture in the 1960s and Beyond." *MAPS Bulletin* 19 (1): 16–20.

Metzner, Ralph. 2008. *The Expansion of Consciousness*. California: Regent Press.

Meyer, Peter. 2010. "340 DMT Trip Reports." *Serendipity*, August 20.

Michael, Pascal, David Luke and Oliver Robinson. 2021. "An Encounter with the Other: A Thematic and Content Analysis of DMT Experiences from a Naturalistic Field Study." *Frontiers in Psychology* 12.

Michaels, Timothy, Lebert Lester, Sara de la Salle and Monnica Williams. 2022. "Ethnoracial Inclusion in Clinical Trials of Ketamine in the Treatment of Mental Health Disorders." *Journal of Studies on Alcohol and Drugs* 83 (4): 596–607.

Michaels, Timothy, Jennifer Purdon, Alexis Collins and Monnica Williams. 2018. "Inclusion of People of Color in Psychedelic-Assisted Psychotherapy: A Review of the Literature." *BMC Psychiatry* 18 (1): 245.

Michaud, Liam, Gillian Kolla, Katherine Rudzinski and Adrian Guta. 2024. "Mapping a Moral Panic: News Media Narratives and Medical Expertise in Public Debates on Safer Supply, Diversion, and Youth Drug Use in Canada." *International Journal of Drug Policy* 127.

Mikhail, Alexa. 2022. "Laid-off Workers Can Now Get a Free Month of Ketamine-Assisted Therapy Services to Help with their Mental Health." *Fortune*, November 30.

Mikhaylova, Sofie. 2023. "An Updated (Living) List of North American Psychedelic Dispensaries." *Psychedelic Spotlight*, June 19.

Miller, Greg. 2013. "A Psychedelic-Science Advocate Takes His Case to the Pentagon." *WIRED*, May 3.

Millière, Raphaël. 2017. "Looking for the Self: Phenomenology, Neurophysiology and Philosophical Significance of Drug-induced Ego Dissolution." *Frontiers in Human Neuroscience* 11.

Mitchell, Andy. 2023. *Ten Trips: The New Reality of Psychedelics*. New York: Harper Wave.

Mitchell, Jennifer, Michael Bogenschutz, Alia Lilienstein, Charlotte Harrison, Sarah Kleiman, Kelly Parker-Guilbert, Marcela Ot'alora G., Wael Garas, Casey Paleos, Ingmar Gorman, Christopher Nicholas, Michael Mithoefer, Shannon Carlin, Bruce Poulter, Ann Mithoefer, et al. 2021. "MDMA-Assisted Therapy for Severe PTSD: A Randomized, Double-Blind, Placebo-Controlled Phase 3 Study." *Nature Medicine* 27: 1025–1033.

Mitchell, Jennifer, Marcela Ot'alora G., Bessel van der Kolk, Scott Shannon, Michael Bogenschutz, Yevgeniy Gelfand, Casey Paleos, Christopher Nicholas, Sylvestre Quevedo, Brooke Balliett, Scott Hamilton, Michael Mithoefer, Sarah Kleiman, Kelly Parker-Guilbert, Keren Tzarfaty, et al. 2023. "MDMA-Assisted Therapy for Moderate to Severe PTSD: A Randomized, Placebo-Controlled Phase 3 Trial." *Nature Medicine* 29 (10): 2473–2480.

Mithoefer, Michael, Ann Mithoefer, Allison Feduccia, Lisa Jerome, Mark Wagner, Joy Wymer, Julie Holland, Scott Hamilton, Berra Yazar-Klosinski, Amy Emerson and Rick Doblin. 2018. "3,4-methylenedioxymethamphetamine (MDMA)-assisted Psychotherapy for Post-Traumatic Stress Disorder in Military Veterans, Firefighters, and Police Officers." *The Lancet Psychiatry* 5 (6): 486–497.

Mithoefer, Michael, Mark Wagner, Ann Mithoefer, Lisa Jerome and Rick Doblin. 2011. "The Safety and Efficacy of {+/-}3,4-Methylenedioxymethamphetamine-Assisted Psychotherapy in Subjects with Chronic, Treatment-Resistant Posttraumatic Stress

Disorder: The First Randomized Controlled Pilot Study." *Journal of Psychopharmacology* 25 (4): 439–452.

Mohr, Ian. 2021. "Lil Nas X Took Psychedelic Mushrooms for Album Inspiration." *Page Six*, November 1.

Moncrieff, Joanna. 2021. "Psychedelics — The New Psychiatric Craze." *Mad in America*, September 2.

Moncrieff, Joanna, Ruth Cooper, Tom Stockmann, Simone Amendola, Michael Hengartner and Mark Horowitz. 2023. "The Serotonin Theory of Depression: A Systematic Umbrella Review of the Evidence." *Molecular Psychiatry* 28 (8): 3243–3256.

Monroe, Rachel. 2021. "Sexual Assault in the Amazon." *The Cut*, November 30.

MorningConsult. 2023. "U.S. Adults, Especially Millennials, Are Interested in Psychedelics as Mental Health Treatment." September 21.

Móró, Levente, Katalin Simon, Imre Bárd and József Rácz. 2011. "Voice of the Psychonauts: Coping, Life Purpose, and Spirituality in Psychedelic Drug Users." *Journal of Psychoactive Drugs* 43 (3): 188–198.

Moskowitz, P.E. 2022. "Breaking Off My Chemical Romance." *The Nation*, March 23.

Multidisciplinary Association for Psychedelic Studies (MAPS). 2018. "Bitcoin, Ketamine, And Pineapples: Why I Donated $5 Million in Bitcoin to MAPS." *MAPS Bulletin* 28 (3): 36–37.

Muraresku, Brian. 2020. *The Immortality Key: The Secret History of the Religion with No Name*. New York: St. Martin's Press.

Murphy, Roberta, Hannes Kettner, Rick Zeifman, Bruna Giribaldi, Laura Kartner, Jonny Martell, Tim Read, Ashleigh Murphy-Beiner, Michelle Baker-Jones, David Nutt, David Erritzoe, Rosalind Watts and Robin Carhart-Harris. 2022. "Therapeutic Alliance and Rapport Modulate Responses to Psilocybin Assisted Therapy for Depression." *Frontiers in Pharmacology* 12.

Murphy, Robin, Rachael Sumner, Kate Godfrey, Acima Mabidikama, Reece Roberts, Frederick Sundram and Suresh Muthukumaraswamy. 2024. "Multimodal Creativity Assessments Following Acute and Sustained Microdosing of Lysergic Acid Diethylamide." *Psychopharmacology*, online first.

Murphy-Beiner, Ashleigh. 2020. "Profitdelic: A New Psychedelic Conference Trend." *Chacruna*, July 20.

Murray, Conor, Joel Frohlich, Connor Haggarty, Ilaria Tare, Royce Lee and Harriet de Wit. 2024. "Neural Complexity is Increased After Low Doses of LSD, But Not Moderate to High Doses of Oral THC or Methamphetamine." *Neuropsychopharmacology* 49: 1120–1128.

Muthukumaraswamy, Suresh, Anna Forsyth and Thomas Lumley. 2021. "Blinding and Expectancy Confounds in Psychedelic Randomised Controlled Trials." *Expert Review of Clinical Pharmacology* 14 (9): 1133–1152.

Nadelmann, Ethan. 1989. "Drug Prohibition in the United States: Costs, Consequences, and Alternatives." *Science* 245 (4921): 939–947.

Nair, Jay, Linda Hakes, Berra Yazar-Klosinski and Kathryn Paisner. 2021. "Fully Validated, Multi-Kilogram cGMP Synthesis of MDMA." *ACS Omega* 7 (1): 900–907.

Najum, Jason. 2022. "Big Pharma Gets into Psychedelics With $5M Mindset Deal." *Microdose*, January 10.

Natarajan, Madison. 2021. "Researchers Concerned About Whitewashing of Psychedelic-Assisted Mental Health Research." *Mad in America*, August 5.

Nayak, Sandeep and Roland Griffiths. 2022. "A Single Belief-Changing Psychedelic Experience is Associated with Increased Attribution of Consciousness to Living and Non-living Entities." *Frontiers in Psychology* 13.

Nayak, Sandeep, Manvir Singh, David Yaden and Roland Griffiths. 2023. "Belief Changes Associated with Psychedelic Use." *Journal of Psychopharmacology* 37 (1): 80–92.

Nayak, Sandeep, Sydney White, Samantha Hilbert, Matthew Lowe, Heather Jackson, Roland Griffiths, Albert Garcia-Romeu and David Yaden. 2024. "Psychedelic Experiences Increase Mind Perception but do not Change Atheist-Believer Status: A Prospective Longitudinal Study." *Journal of Psychoactive Drugs*, online first.

Nemu, Danny. 2019. "Getting High with the Most High: Entheogens in the Old Testament." *Journal of Psychedelic Studies* 3 (2): 117–132.

Netzband, Nige, Simon Ruffell, Samuel Linton, Wai Fung Tsang and Tom Wolff. 2020. "Modulatory Effects of Ayahuasca on Personality Structure in a Traditional Framework." *Psychopharmacology* 237 (10): 3161–3171.

New York Times (Editorial Board). 2022. "Save America's Patent System." *The New York Times*, April 16.

Nichols, David. 2022. "Entactogens: How the Name for a Novel Class of Psychoactive Agents Originated." *Frontiers in Psychiatry* 13.

Nichols, David. 2020. "Psilocybin: From Ancient Magic to Modern Medicine." *The Journal of Antibiotics* 73 (10): 679–686.

Nichols, David. 2016. "Psychedelics." *Pharmacological Reviews* 68 (2): 264–355.

Nichols, David and Charles Grob. 2018. "Is LSD Toxic?" *Forensic Science International* 284: 141–145.

Nickles, David. 2023. "The Church of Psilomethoxin Part 2: Unraveling the Sacred Chemistry." *Psymposia*, May 3

Nickles, David. 2020a. "Psychedelic Media Should Stop Parroting Corporate Press Releases." *Psymposia*, October 12.

Nickles, David. 2020b. "We Need to Talk About MAPS Supporting the Police, the Military, and Violent White Supremacism." *Psymposia*, July 17.

Nickles, David. 2018a. "It's time to Debunk Prohibitionist Narratives and Calls for Monopolies within Psychedelic Science." *Psymposia*, October 25.

Nickles, David. 2018b. "An Open Letter Regarding the Statement on Open Science and Open Praxis." *The Nexian*, August 15.

Nickles, David. 2014. "Boom 2014: DMT — Turn On, Tune In, Rise Up!" *YouTube*, August 20. youtube.com/watch?v=F-dI76jjcNY

Nielson, Jeff. 2022. "Psychedelic Drug Patenting: Still Only Scratching the Surface." *Dynamic Wealth Research*, April 25.

Nolfi, Joey. 2022. "Will Smith Saw His Career Destroyed in 'Hellish' Ayahuasca Trip Before Oscars Slap. *Entertainment Weekly*, May 24.

Noller, Geoffrey, Chris Frampton and Berra Yazar-Klosinski. 2018. "Ibogaine Treatment Outcomes for Opioid Dependence from a Twelve-Month Follow-Up Observational Study." *American Journal of Drug and Alcohol Abuse* 44 (1): 37–46.

Noorani, Tehseen. 2021a. "Digital Psychedelia: Hidden Experience and the Challenge of Paranoia." *Somatosphere*, September 15.

Noorani, Tehseen. 2021b. "Containment Matters: Set and Setting in Contemporary Psychedelic Psychiatry." *Philosophy, Psychiatry, & Psychology* 28 (3): 201–216.

Noorani, Tehseen. 2020a. "The Pollan Effect: Psychedelic Research between World and Word." *Society for Cultural Anthropology*, July 21.

Noorani, Tehseen. 2020b. "Making Psychedelics into Medicines: The Politics and Paradoxes of Medicalization." *Journal of Psychedelic Studies* 4 (1): 34–39.

Noorani, Tehseen, Gillinder Bedi and Suresh Muthukumaraswamy. 2023. "Dark Loops: Contagion Effects, Consistency and Chemosocial Matrices in Psychedelic-Assisted Therapy Trials." *Psychological Medicine* 53 (13): 5892–5901.

Nour, Matthew, Lisa Evans and Robin Carhart-Harris. 2017. "Psychedelics, Personality and Political Perspectives." *Journal of Psychoactive Drugs* 49 (3): 182–191.

Novak, Steven. 1997. "LSD before Leary: Sidney Cohen's Critique of 1950s Psychedelic Drug Research." *Isis* 88 (1): 87–110.
Nutt, David. 2012. *Drugs Without the Hot Air: Minimizing the Harms of Legal and Illegal Drugs.* Cambridge: UIT Cambridge Ltd.
Nutt, David, Leslie King and David Nichols. 2013. "Effects of Schedule I Drug Laws on Neuroscience Research and Treatment Innovation." *Nature Reviews Neuroscience* 14 (8): 577–585.
Nutt, David, Leslie King and Lawrence Phillips. 2010. "Drug Harms in the UK: A Multicriteria Decision Analysis." *The Lancet* 376 (9752): 1558–1565.
Nuwer, Rachel. 2023. *I Feel Love: MDMA and the Quest for Connection in a Fractured World.* New York: Bloomsbury.
Nuwer, Rachel. 2021. "A Psychedelic Drug Passes a Big Test for PTSD Treatment." *The New York Times*, May 3.
Nyberg, Harri. 1992. "Religious Use of Hallucinogenic Fungi: A Comparison Between Siberian and Mesoamerican Cultures." *Karstenia* 32 (2): 71–80.
O'Brien, Jeffrey. 2020. "Business Gets Ready to Trip: How Psychedelic Drugs May Revolutionize Mental Health Care." *Fortune*, February 17.
Office of the Provincial Health Officer. 2024. *Alternatives to Unregulated Drugs: Another Step in Saving Lives.* Victoria, BC. https://www2.gov.bc.ca/assets/gov/health/about-bc-s-health-care-system/office-of-the-provincial-health-officer/reports-publications/special-reports/alternatives_to_unregulated_drugs.pdf
Ohler, Norman. 2024. *Tripped: Nazi Germany, the CIA, and the Dawn of the Psychedelic Age.* New York: Mariner Books.
Okrent, Daniel. 2011. *Last Call: The Rise and Fall of Prohibition.* New York: Scribner.
Olson, David. 2022. "Biochemical Mechanisms Underlying Psychedelic-Induced Neuroplasticity." *Biochemistry* 61 (3): 127–136.
Olson, David. 2020. "The Subjective Effects of Psychedelics May Not Be Necessary for Their Enduring Therapeutic Effects." *ACS Pharmacology and Translational Science* 4 (2): 563–567.
Olson, David. 2018. "Psychoplastogens: A Promising Class of Plasticity-Promoting Neurotherapeutics." *Journal of Experimental Neuroscience* 12.
Olson, Jay, Léah Suissa-Rocheleau, Michael Lifshitz, Amir Raz and Samuel Veissière. 2020. "Tripping on Nothing: Placebo Psychedelics and Contextual Factors." *Psychopharmacology* 237 (5): 1371–1382.
Ona, Genís, Ali Berrada and José Carlos Bouso. 2022. "Communalistic Use of Psychoactive Plants as a Bridge between Traditional Healing Practices and Western Medicine: A New Path for the Global Mental Health Movement." *Transcultural Psychiatry* 59 (5): 638–651.
Ona, Genís, Maja Kohek and José Carlos Bouso. 2022. "The Illusion of Knowledge in the Emerging Field of Psychedelic Research." *New Ideas in Psychology* 67.
Ona, Genís, Maja Kohek, Tomàs Massaguer, Alfred Gomariz, Daniel Jiménez, Rafael Dos Santos, Jaime Hallak, Miguel Ángel Alcázar-Córcoles and José Carlos Bouso. 2019. "Ayahuasca and Public Health: Health Status, Psychosocial Well-Being, Lifestyle and Coping Strategies in a Large Sample of Ritual Ayahuasca Users." *Journal of Psychoactive Drugs* 51 (2): 135–145.
Ona, Genís, Juliana Rocha, José Carlos Bouso, Jaime Hallak, Tre Borràs, Maria Teresa Colomina and Rafael Dos Santos. 2022. "The Adverse Events of Ibogaine in Humans: An Updated Systematic Review of the Literature (2015–2020)." *Psychopharmacology* 239 (6): 1977–1987.
Oram, Matthew. 2018. *The Trials of Psychedelic Therapy: LSD Psychotherapy in America.* Baltimore: Johns Hopkins University Press.

Orth, Taylor. 2022. "One in Four Americans Say They've Tried At Least One Psychedelic Drug." *YouGov*, July 28.
Osgood, Kelsey. 2021. "Big Tech's Psychedelics Grift." *WIRED*, November 7.
Ostrow, Ronald. 1990. "Casual Drug Users Should Be Shot, Gates Says." *Los Angeles Times*, September 6.
Ott, Jonathan. 1996. *Pharmacotheon: Entheogenic Drugs, Their Plant Sources and History*. Kennewick, WA: Natural Products Company.
Otto, Siegmar and Pamela Pensini. 2017. "Nature-Based Environmental Education of Children: Environmental Knowledge and Connectedness to Nature, Together, are Related to Ecological Behaviour." *Global Environmental Change* 47: 88–94.
Owusu-Bempah, Akwasi and Alex Luscombe. 2021. "Race, Cannabis and the Canadian War on Drugs: An Examination of Cannabis Arrest Data by Race in Five Cities." *International Journal of Drug Policy* 91: 102937.
Owusu-Bempah, Akwasi and Tahira Rehmatullah. 2023. *Waiting to Inhale: Cannabis Legalization and the Fight for Racial Justice*. Boston: MIT Press.
Pace, Brian. 2021. "Jake Angeli: The Psychedelic Guru Who Stormed the Capitol." *Psymposia*, January 7.
Pace, Brian. 2020. "Lucy in The Sky with Nazis: Psychedelics and the Right Wing." *Psymposia*, February 3.
Pace, Brian and Neşe Devenot. 2023. "Blowing Glass at Stone Houses: An Interview with Psychedelic Anticapitalist David Nickles." *History of Pharmacy and Pharmaceuticals* 65 (1): 141–159.
Pace, Brian and Neşe Devenot. 2021. "Right-Wing Psychedelia: Case Studies in Cultural Plasticity and Political Pluripotency." *Frontiers in Psychology* 12.
Pahnke, Walter. 1969. "Psychedelic Drugs and Mystical Experience." *International Psychiatry Clinics* 5 (4): 149–162.
Pahnke, Walter. 1963. "Drugs and Mysticism: An Analysis of the Relationship between Psychedelic Drugs and the Mystical Consciousness." Doctoral dissertation, Harvard University.
Palamar, Joseph, Nicole Fitzgerald, Thomas Carr, Caroline Rutherford, Katherine Keyes and Linda Cottler. 2024. "National and Regional Trends in Seizures of Shrooms (Psilocybin) in the United States, 2017–2022." *Drug and Alcohol Dependence*, January 29.
Paleos, Casey. 2018. "On Treading Lightly Through the Lion's Den: The Path to Psychedelic Legitimacy." *Chacruna*, October 18.
Paley, Dawn. 2014. *Drug War Capitalism*. California: AK Press.
Palhano-Fontes, Fernanda, Dayanna Barreto, Heloisa Onias, Katia Andrade, Morgana Novaes, Jessica Pessoa, Sergio Mota-Rolim, Flávia Osório, Rafael Sanches, Rafael dos Santos, Luís Tófoli, Gabriela de Oliveira Silveira, Mauricio Yonamine, Jordi Riba, Francisco Santos, et al. 2019. "Rapid Antidepressant Effects of the Psychedelic Ayahuasca in Treatment-Resistant Depression: A Randomized Placebo-Controlled Trial." *Psychological Medicine* 49 (4): 655–663.
Panchal, Nirmita, Heather Saunders, Robin Rudowitz and Cynthia Cox. 2023. "The Implications of COVID-19 for Mental Health and Substance Use." *KFF*, March 20.
Passie, Torsten. 2018. "The Early Use of MDMA ('Ecstasy') in Psychotherapy (1977-1985)." *Drug Science, Policy and Law* 4.
Passie, Torsten and Udo Benzenhöfer. 2016. "The History of MDMA as an Underground Drug in the United States, 1960-1979." *Journal of Psychoactive Drugs* 48 (2): 67–75.
Patel, Vikram, Shekhar Saxena, Crick Lund, Graham Thornicroft, Florence Baingana, Paul Bolton, Dan Chisholm, Pamela Collins, Janice Cooper, Julian Eaton, Helen Herrman, Mohammad Herzallah, Yueqin Huang, Mark Jordans, Arthur Kleinman, Maria Elena Medina-Mora, et al. 2018. "The Lancet Commission on Global Mental Health and Sustainable Development." *Lancet* 392 (10157): 1553–1598.

Paterniti, Kelly, Stephen Bright and Eyal Gringart. 2022. "The Relationship Between Psychedelic Use, Mystical Experiences, and Pro-Environmental Behaviors." *Journal of Humanistic Psychology*, online first.

Patrick, Megan, Richard Miech, Lloyd Johnston and Patrick O'Malley. 2023. "Monitoring the Future Panel Study Annual Report: National Data on Substance Use Among Adults Ages 19 to 60, 1976-2022." *Monitoring the Future Monograph Series*. Ann Arbor, MI: University of Michigan Institute for Social Research.

Pedersen, Willy, Heith Copes, and Liridona Gashi. 2021. "Narratives of the Mystical Among Users of Psychedelics." *Acta Sociologica* 64 (2): 230–246.

Peluso, Daniela. 2017. "Global Ayahuasca: An Entrepreneurial Ecosystem." In *The World Ayahuasca Diaspora: Reinventions and Controversies*, edited by B. Labate, C. Cavnar and A. Gearin. London: Routledge.

Perrone, Matthew. 2024. "As Investors Pile into Psychedelics, Idealism Gives Way to Pharma Economics." *The Independent*, February 3.

Perryer, Sophie. 2019. "Tourists are Having a Bad Trip on Counterfeit Ayahuasca." *Business Destinations*, September 11.

Petersen, Rachael. 2020. "Magical (Psychedelic) Thinking in the Era of Climate Change and COVID-19." *Psymposia*, July 11.

Petranker, Rotem, Thomas Anderson, Larissa Maier, Monica Barratt, Jason Ferris and Adam Winstock. 2022. "Microdosing Psychedelics: Subjective Benefits and Challenges, Substance Testing Behavior, and the Relevance of Intention." *Journal of Psychopharmacology* 36 (1): 85–96.

Petrement, Mateo Sanchez. 2023. "Historicizing Psychedelics: Counterculture, Renaissance, and the Neoliberal Matrix." *Frontiers in Sociology* 8.

Pettigrew, Jack. 2011. "Iconography in Bradshaw Rock Art: Breaking the Circularity." *Clinical & Experimental Optometry* 94 (5): 403–417.

Pew Charitable Trusts. 2022. "Drug Arrests Stayed High Even as Imprisonment Fell from 2009 to 2019." February.

Piore, Adam. 2021. "Magic Mushrooms May Be the Biggest Advance in Treating Depression Since Prozac." *Newsweek Magazine*, September 22.

Piper, Alan. 2023. *Bicycle Day and other Psychedelic Essays*. London: Psychedelic Press.

Piper, Alan. 2015. *Strange Drugs Make for Strange Bedfellows: Ernst Jünger, Albert Hofmann and the Politics of Psychedelics*. Oregon: Invisible College Publishing.

Plesa, Patric and Rotem Petranker. 2022. "Manifest Your Desires: Psychedelics and the Self-Help Industry." *International Journal of Drug Policy* 105.

Plus Three. 2020. "Dear Psychedelic Researchers." *Psymposia*, April 4.

Pokorny, Thomas, Katrin Preller, Michael Kometer, Isabel Dziobek and Franz Vollenweider. 2017. "Effect of Psilocybin on Empathy and Moral Decision-Making." *The International Journal of Neuropsychopharmacology* 20 (9): 747–757.

Polito, Vince and Paul Liknaitzky. 2024. "Is Microdosing a Placebo? A Rapid Review of Low-Dose LSD and Psilocybin Research." *Journal of Psychopharmacology* 38 (8): 701–711.

Polito, Vince and Paul Liknaitzky. 2022. "The Emerging Science of Microdosing: A Systematic Review of Research on Low Dose Psychedelics (1955–2021) and Recommendations for the Field." *Neuroscience and Biobehavioral Reviews* 139.

Polito, Vince and Richard Stevenson. 2019. "A Systematic Study of Microdosing Psychedelics." *PLoS One* 14 (2).

Pollan, Michael. 2021a. "How Should We Do Drugs Now?" *The New York Times*, July 13.

Pollan, Michael. 2021b. *This is Your Mind on Plants*. New York: Penguin.

Pollan, Michael. 2019. "Not So Fast on Psychedelic Mushrooms." *The New York Times*, May 10.

Pollan, Michael. 2018. *How to Change Your Mind: What the New Science of Psychedelics Teaches Us About Consciousness, Dying, Addiction, Depression, and Transcendence.* London: Penguin.

Pollan, Michael. 2015. "The Trip Treatment." *The New Yorker,* February 2.

Porta, Carolyn, Madison Weirick, Anna Graefe, Scott Harpin and Caroline Dorsen. 2024. "Nurses' Perceptions of Psychedelics to Address Mental Health Problems in the United States." *Psychedelic Medicine* 2 (3): 178–183.

Pratt, Amanda and Shahin Shams. 2024. "Beyond the Psychedelic Competitive Moat: Chasing the Patent Dragon." *Bill of Health,* February 24.

Prayag, Girish, Paolo Mura, Colin Hall and Julien Fontaine. 2016. "Spirituality, Drugs, and Tourism: Tourists' and Shamans' Experiences of Ayahuasca in Iquitos, Peru." *Tourism Recreation Research* 41 (3): 314–325.

Press, Sara. 2022. "Ayahuasca on Trial: Biocolonialism, Biopiracy, and the Commodification of the Sacred." *History of Pharmacy and Pharmaceuticals* 63 (2): 328–353.

Prideaux, Ed. 2023a. "Living with Hallucinogen Persisting Perception Disorder (HPPD)." *Ecstatic Integration,* February 13.

Prideaux, Ed. 2023b. "Is the Psychedelic Industrial Complex Evil?" *UnHerd,* January 25.

Prochazkova, Luisa, Dominique Lippelt, Lorenza Colzato, Martin Kuchar, Zsuzsika Sjoerds and Bernhard Hommel. 2018. "Exploring the Effect of Microdosing Psychedelics on Creativity in an Open-Label Natural Setting." *Psychopharmacology* 235 (12): 3401–3413.

Provine, Doris Marie. 2008. *Unequal under Law: Race in the War on Drugs.* Chicago: University of Chicago Press.

Psychedelic Alpha. 2024a. "MindMed's 'Total Elimination' of Psychotherapy in LSD Study Stokes Debate Around its Role in Psychedelic Therapies." *Psychedelic Alpha,* April 5.

Psychedelic Alpha. 2024b. "Psychedelic Stocks & Companies." *Psychedelic Alpha,* psychedelicalpha.com/psilocybin-stocks-shroom-stocks

Psychedelic Alpha. 2024c. "Psychedelic Funding & Public Markets in 2023." *Psychedelic Alpha,* January 18.

Psychedelic Alpha. 2024d. "Psychedelic Patent Trackers." *Psychedelic Alpha,* psychedelicalpha.com/data.

Psychedelic Alpha. 2024e. "The Church of the Eagle and the Condor Settles with Federal Agencies, Can Continue Importing and Using Ayahuasca." *Psychedelic Alpha,* March 8.

Psychedelic Alpha. 2023. "Big Pharma Company Otsuka to Acquire Mindset Pharma for CAD $80m." *Psychedelic Alpha,* August 31.

Psychedelic Alpha. 2022a. "Psychedelic Bulletin: MINDCURE – A Canary in the Psychedelic Coal Mine?" *Psychedelic Bulletin,* March 18.

Psychedelic Alpha. 2022b. "Psychedelic Bulletin: Patent Granted Covering DMT Vapes; Microdosing Produces "Negligible" Effects." *Psychedelic Bulletin,* February 6.

Psychedelic Alpha. 2021. "Canadians Overwhelmingly Support Legal Access to Psilocybin-Assisted Therapy, Poll Reveals." *Psychedelic Alpha,* August 4.

Psychedelic Alpha. 2020a. "Interview with Ronan Levy, Founder of Field Trip Health." *Psychedelic Alpha,* April 16.

Psychedelic Alpha. 2020b. "Lars Wilde, Co-founder of COMPASS Pathways." *Psychedelic Alpha,* December 13.

Psychedelic Invest. 2021a. "Visualizing the Psychedelics Investment Ecosystem." *Psychedelic Invest,* April 9.

Psychedelic Invest. 2021b. "MagicMed: Finding the Derivative with Dr. Joseph Tucker." *Psychedelic Invest,* May 24.

Psychedelic News Wire. 2023. "Debate Over the Use of Apps in Psychedelic Therapy Grows." *Psychedelic News Wire,* January 20.

Psychedelic News Wire. 2020. "Psychedelic Medicines May Develop Into $100 Billion Business Opportunity." *Psychedelic News Wire*, December 29.
Psymposia. 2023. "Talking Psychedelic Hype with Journalist Katie MacBride." *YouTube*, December 14, 2023. youtube.com/watch?v=7wf4WOpi_2Y&t=3181s
Psymposia. 2022. "[Live] #Wonderbanned at Wonderland (Psymposia Reacts to Hamilton Morris)." *YouTube*, November 15. youtube.com/watch?v=ckxKJQedx1c
Purser, Ronald. 2019. *McMindfulness: How Mindfulness Became the New Capitalist Spirituality*. London: Repeater Books.
Raison, Charles, Gerard Sanacora, Joshua Woolley, Keith Heinzerling, Boadie Dunlop, Randall Brown, Rishi Kakar, Michael Hassman, Rupal Trivedi, Reid Robison, Natalie Gukasyan, Sandeep Nayak, Xiaojue Hu, Kelley O'Donnell, Benjamin Kelmendi, Jordan Sloshower, et al. 2023. "Single-Dose Psilocybin Treatment for Major Depressive Disorder: A Randomized Clinical Trial." *JAMA* 330 (9): 843–853.
Raison, Charles, Rakesh Jain, Andrew Penn, Steven Cole and Saundra Jain. 2022. "Effects of Naturalistic Psychedelic Use on Depression, Anxiety, and Well-Being: Associations with Patterns of Use, Reported Harms, and Transformative Mental States." *Frontiers in Psychiatry* 13.
Rammohan, Indhu, Tommi Gaines, Ayden Scheim, Ahmed Bayoumi and Dan Werb. 2024. "Overdose Mortality Incidence and Supervised Consumption Services in Toronto, Canada: An Ecological Study and Spatial Analysis." *The Lancet Public Health* 9 (2): e79–e87.
Ramos, Marco, J. Wesley Boyd and Michael Alpert. 2019. "The New Ketamine-Based Antidepressant is a Rip-Off." *VICE*, May 17.
Ramsay, George. 2023. "NFL Star Aaron Rodgers Credits Psychedelics for Improving His Performance on the Football Field." *CNN*, June 23.
Ratner, Paul. 2018. "Scientists Find Magic Mushrooms Could Help Fight Fascism." *Big Think*, January 28.
Ray, Bradley, Steven Korzeniewski, George Mohler, Jennifer Carroll, Brandon Del Pozo, Grant Victor, Philip Huynh and Bethany Hedden. 2023. "Spatiotemporal Analysis Exploring the Effect of Law Enforcement Drug Market Disruptions on Overdose, Indianapolis, Indiana, 2020-2021." *American Journal of Public Health* 113 (7): 750–758.
Raz, Shlomi. 2020. "Transforming Psychedelics into Mainstream Medicines." *STAT*, January 7.
Read, John and James Williams. 2018. "Adverse Effects of Antidepressants Reported by a Large International Cohort: Emotional Blunting, Suicidality, and Withdrawal Effects." *Current Drug Safety* 13 (3): 176–186.
Reardon, Sara. 2023. "US Could Soon Approve MDMA Therapy — Opening an Era of Psychedelic Medicine." *Nature*, April 19.
Reichel, Chloe. 2021. "A Q&A with Mason Marks on New Psychedelics Law and Regulation Initiative." *Harvard Law Today*, July 7.
Reichel-Dolmatoff, Gerardo. 1976. "Cosmology as Ecological Analysis: A View from the Rainforest." *Man* 11: 307–318.
Reinarman, Craig and Harry Levine. 2004. "Crack in the Rearview Mirror: Deconstructing Drug War Mythology." *Social Justice* 31 (1/2): 182–199.
Reinarman, Craig and Harry Levine (eds.). 1997. *Crack in America: Demon Drugs and Social Justice*. Berkeley: University of California Press.
Reinarman, Craig and Harry Levine. 1989. "Crack in Context: Politics and Media in the Making of a Drug Scare." *Contemporary Drug Problems* 16: 535–577.
Révész, Dóra, Genís Ona, Giordano Rossi, Juliana Rocha, Rafael Dos Santos, Jaime Hallak, Miguel Alcázar-Córcoles and José Carlos Bouso. 2021. "Cross-Sectional Associations Between Lifetime Use of Psychedelic Drugs and Psychometric Measures During the COVID-19 Confinement: A Transcultural Study." *Frontiers in Psychiatry* 12.

Rex, Erica. 2022. "The Culture is the Poison: Why Psychedelics are Dangerous Medicine in a Neoliberal Society." *Mad in America*, September 8.
Richards, William. 2015. *Sacred Knowledge: Psychedelics and Religious Experiences*. New York: Columbia University Press.
Riley, Chris. 2021. "Perceptions of Marijuana and Psychedelics." *Medium*, January 19.
Riley, Sarah, James Thompson and Christine Griffin. 2010. "Turn On, Tune In, but Don't Drop Out: The Impact of Neo-Liberalism on Magic Mushroom Users' (In)ability to Imagine Collectivist Social Worlds." *International Journal of Drug Policy* 21 (6): 445–451.
Ritchie, Sarah. 2021. "Panpsychism and Spiritual Flourishing: Constructive Engagement with the New Science of Psychedelics." *Journal of Consciousness Studies* 28 (9–10): 268–288.
Roberts, Carl, Isaac Osborne-Miller, Jon Cole, Suzanne Gage and Paul Christiansen. 2020. "Perceived Harm, Motivations for Use and Subjective Experiences of Recreational Psychedelic 'Magic' Mushroom Use." *Journal of Psychopharmacology* 34 (9): 999–1007.
Roberts, Chris. 2020. "Cops Raided and Shut Down the Only Magic Mushroom 'Church' in the U.S." *VICE*, August 20.
Roberts, Nicole. 2018. "Suicide Isn't a U.S. Problem. It's a Global Health Epidemic." *Forbes*, June 15.
Roffey, Hallam. 2023. "Psychedelics, Political Radicalism, and Transnational Acid-Anarchism in the 1970s. In *Expanding Mindscapes: A Global History of Psychedelics*, edited by E. Dyck and C. Elcock. Cambridge: MIT Press.
Rootman, Joseph, Maggie Kiraga, Pamela Kryskow, Kalin Harvey, Paul Stamets, Eesmyal Santos-Brault, Kim Kuypers and Zach Walsh. 2022. "Psilocybin Microdosers Demonstrate Greater Observed Improvements in Mood and Mental Health at One Month Relative to Non-Microdosing Controls." *Scientific Reports* 12 (1).
Rootman, Joseph, Pamela Kryskow, Kalin Harvey, Paul Stamets, Eesmyal Santos-Brault, Kim Kuypers, Vince Polito, Francoise Bourzat and Zach Walsh. 2021. "Adults Who Microdose Psychedelics Report Health Related Motivations and Lower Levels of Anxiety and Depression Compared to Non-Microdosers." *Scientific Reports* 11 (1).
Rosciglione, Annabella. 2024. "Oregon Recriminalizes Drugs after State's 'Huge Mistake.'" *Washington Examiner*, April 2.
Roseman, Leor and Nadeem Karkabi. 2021. "On Revelations and Revolutions: Drinking Ayahuasca Among Palestinians Under Israeli Occupation." *Frontiers in Psychology* 12.
Roseman, Leor, David Nutt and Robin Carhart-Harris. 2018. "Quality of Acute Psychedelic Experience Predicts Therapeutic Efficacy of Psilocybin for Treatment-Resistant Depression." *Frontiers in Pharmacology* 8.
Roseman, Leor, Yiftach Ron, Antwan Saca, Natalie Ginsberg, Lisa Luan, Nadeem Karkabi, Rick Doblin and Robin Carhart-Harris. 2021. "Relational Processes in Ayahuasca Groups of Palestinians and Israelis." *Frontiers in Pharmacology* 12.
Rosenbaum, Eric. 2021. "A Psychedelic Drug Boom in Mental Health Treatment Comes Closer to Reality." *CNBC*, May 10.
Rosenberg, Morris, Oyedeji Ayonrinde, Patricia Conrod, Lynda Levesque and Peter Selby. 2024. "Legislative Review of the Cannabis Act: Final Report of the Expert Panel." *Health Canada*, March.
Rosin, Hanna. 2022. "You Won't Feel High After Watching This Video." *The Cut*, March 22.
Ross, Lily Kay. 2021. "The Masters of Bad Trips." *Psymposia*, November 11.
Ross, Lily Kay and David Nickles. 2022a. "Who Am I Fooling?" *The Cut*, March 15.
Ross, Lily Kay and David Nickles. 2022b. "Political Science." *The Cut*, March 8.
Ross, Lily Kay and David Nickles. 2022c. "Open-Heart Surgery." *The Cut*, March 2.
Ross, Lily Kay and iO Tillett Wright. 2021. "That's an Old Story." *The Cut*, December 7.
Ross, Stephen, Gabrielle Agin-Liebes, Sharon Lo, Richard Zeifman, Leila Ghazal, Julia Benville, Silvia Franco Corso, Christian Real, Jeffrey Guss, Anthony Bossis and Sarah

Mennenga. 2021. "Acute and Sustained Reductions in Loss of Meaning and Suicidal Ideation Following Psilocybin-Assisted Psychotherapy for Psychiatric and Existential Distress in Life-Threatening Cancer." *ACS Pharmacology & Translational Science* 4 (2): 553–562.

Ross, Stephen, Anthony Bossis, Jeffrey Guss, Gabrielle Agin-Liebes, Tara Malone, Barry Cohen, Sarah Mennenga, Alexander Belser, Krystallia Kalliontzi, James Babb, Zhe Su, Patricia Corby and Brian Schmidt. 2016. "Rapid and Sustained Symptom Reduction Following Psilocybin Treatment for Anxiety and Depression in Patients with Life-Threatening Cancer: A Randomized Controlled Trial." *Journal of Psychopharmacology* 30 (12): 1165–1180.

Rouaud, Antonin, Abigail Calder and Gregor Hasler. 2024. "Microdosing Psychedelics and the Risk of Cardiac Fibrosis and Valvulopathy: Comparison to Known Cardiotoxins." *Journal of Psychopharmacology* 38 (3): 217–224.

Roy, Victor. 2023. *Capitalizing a Cure: How Finance Controls the Price and Value of Medicines.* Los Angeles: University of California Press.

RTI International. 2022. "Building the Evidence: Understanding the Impacts of Drug Decriminalization in Oregon." October 11.

Ruck, Carl, Jeremy Bigwood, Danny Staples, Jonathan Ott and Robert Gordon Wasson. 1979. "Entheogens." *Journal of Psychedelic Drugs* 11 (1–2): 145–146.

Rucker, James and Allan Young. 2021. "Psilocybin: From Serendipity to Credibility?" *Frontiers in Psychiatry* 12.

Ruffell, Simon, Nige Netzband, WaiFung Tsang, Merlin Davies, Antonio Inserra, Matthew Butler, James Rucker, Luís Tófoli, Emma Dempster, Allan Young and Celia Morgan. 2021. "Ceremonial Ayahuasca in Amazonian Retreats — Mental Health and Epigenetic Outcomes from a Six-Month Naturalistic Study." *Frontiers in Psychiatry* 12.

Ryan, Wesley and Raquel Bennett. 2020. "Ethical Guidelines for Ketamine Clinicians." *Journal of Psychedelic Psychiatry* 2 (4): 19–23.

Sagonowsky, Eric. 2019. "Cost Watchdogs Scold J&J for 'Overpricing' its New Ketamine-Like Antidepressant." *Fierce Pharma*, May 10.

Samorini, Giorgio. 2019. "The Oldest Archaeological Data Evidencing the Relationship of Homo Sapiens with Psychoactive Plants: A Worldwide Overview." *Journal of Psychedelic Studies* 3 (2): 63–80.

Sample, Ian. 2022. "Magic Mushrooms' Psilocybin Can Alleviate Severe Depression When Used with Therapy." *The Guardian*, November 2.

Sanacora, Gerard, Mark Frye, William McDonald, Sanjay Mathew, Mason Turner, Alan Schatzberg, Paul Summergrad and Charles Nemeroff. 2017. "A Consensus Statement on the Use of Ketamine in the Treatment of Mood Disorders." *JAMA Psychiatry* 74 (4): 399–405.

Sanders, James and Josjan Zijlmans. 2021. "Moving Past Mysticism in Psychedelic Science." *ACS Pharmacology & Translational Science* ACS 4 (3): 1253–1255.

Sants, Arthur. 2022. "The Promise of Psychedelics." *Investors' Chronicle*, July 14.

Saunders, Nicholas and Rick Doblin. 1996. *Ecstasy: Dance, Trance and Transformation.* California: Quick American Archives.

Schenberg, Eduardo. 2018. "Psychedelic-Assisted Psychotherapy: A Paradigm Shift in Psychiatric Research and Development." *Frontiers in Pharmacology* 9.

Schenberg, Eduardo, Maria de Castro Comis, Bruno Chaves and Dartiu da Silveira. 2014. "Treating Drug Dependence with the Aid of Ibogaine: A Retrospective Study." *Journal of Psychopharmacology* 28 (11): 993–1000.

Schenberg, Eduardo and Konstantin Gerber. 2022. "Overcoming Epistemic Injustices in the Biomedical Study of Ayahuasca: Towards Ethical and Sustainable Regulation." *Transcultural Psychiatry* 59 (5): 610–624.

Schindler, Emmanuelle, Christopher Gottschalk, Marsha Weil, Robert Shapiro, Douglas Wright and Richard Andrew Sewell. 2015. "Indoleamine Hallucinogens in Cluster Headache: Results of the Clusterbusters Medication Use Survey." *Journal of Psychoactive Drugs* 47 (5): 372–381.

Schindler, Emmanuelle, Andrew Sewell, Christopher Gottschalk, Christina Luddy, Taylor Flynn, Yutong Zhu, Hayley Lindsey, Brian Pittman, Nicholas Cozzi and Deepak D'Souza. 2022. "Exploratory Investigation of a Patient-Informed Low-Dose Psilocybin Pulse Regimen in the Suppression of Cluster Headache: Results from a Randomized, Double-Blind, Placebo-Controlled Trial." *Headache* 62 (10): 1383–1394.

Schlag, Anne, Jacob Aday, Iram Salam, Jo Neill and David Nutt. 2022. "Adverse Effects of Psychedelics: From Anecdotes and Misinformation to Systematic Science." *Journal of Psychopharmacology* 36 (3): 258–272.

Schmidt, Elena. 2021. "How the Psychedelic Revolution Might Just Save The Planet." *Third Wave*, October 21.

Schonfeld, Zach. 2013. "150 Americans Die Each Year from Tylenol's Most Active Ingredient." *The Atlantic*, September 20.

Schraer, Rachel. 2021. "Psychedelic Therapy Could 'Reset' Depressed Brain." *BBC*, March 14.

Schultes, Richard Evans. 1968. "Some Impacts of Spruce's Amazon Explorations on Modern Phytochemical Research." *Rhodora* 70: 313–339.

Schultes, Richard Evans. 1940. "Teonanacatl: The Narcotic Mushroom of the Aztecs." *American Anthropologist* 42 (3): 429–443.

Schultes, Richard Evans, Albert Hofmann and Christian Rätsch. 2001. *Plants of the Gods: Their Sacred, Healing, and Hallucinogenic Powers*. Vermont: Healing Arts Press.

Schwarz-Plaschg, Claudia. 2022. "Socio-Psychedelic Imaginaries: Envisioning and Building Legal Psychedelic Worlds in The United States." *European Journal of Futures Research* 10 (1): 1–16.

Schwarz-Plaschg, Claudia. 2020. "Why Psychedelic Researchers Should Not Push Back Against Decriminalization." *Chacruna*, May 22.

Sellers, Edward and Myroslava Romach. 2023. "Psychedelics: Science Sabotaged by Social Media." *Neuropharmacology* 227.

Seltenrich, Nate. 2021. "Real-World Research in Psychedelic Science." *Psychedelic Science Review*, July 6.

Semley, John. 2022. "The High-Stakes Race to Engineer New Psychedelic Drugs." *WIRED*, July 26.

Serruya, Gail. 2022. "The Potential Dangers of Ketamine Telehealth Services." *Psychology Today*, May 13.

Sessa, Ben. 2012. *The Psychedelic Renaissance: Reassessing the Role of Psychedelic Drugs in 21st Century Psychiatry and Society*. London: Muswell Hill Press.

Sevelius, Jae. 2017. "How Psychedelic Science Privileges Some, Neglects Others, and Limits Us All." *Psymposia*, September 20.

Shade, Soren. 2022. "The Intertwined Prohibitionist Histories of Psychedelics and Kratom." *Psychedelics Today*, June 3.

Shamabadi, Ahmad, Ali Ahmadzade and Alireza Hasanzadeh. 2022. "Ketamine for Suicidality: An Umbrella Review." *British Journal of Clinical Pharmacology* 88 (9): 3990–4018.

Shams, Shahin, Amanda Pratt, Sisi Li and Tom Isenbarger. 2023. "The Evolving Role of History in the Past, Present, and Future of Psychedelic Patenting." *History of Pharmacy and Pharmaceuticals* 65 (1): 117–130.

Shana, Ali. 2021. "Psychedelic CSR: Building Ethical Frameworks for Psychedelic Tech." *Microdose*, September 29.

Shana, Ali. 2020. "Corporate Social Responsibility in the Emerging Psychedelic Industry." *Microdose*, August 6.

Sharir, Moran. 2020. "The Dutch Psychiatrist Who Treated Traumatized Holocaust Survivors With LSD." *Haaretz*, March 14.

Sheffield, Rob. 2019. "The Eternal Sunshine of Harry Styles." *Rolling Stone*, August 26.

Sheiner, Eli. 2017. "Culling the Spirits: An Exploration of Santo Daime's Adaptation in Canada." In *The World Ayahuasca Diaspora: Reinventions and Controversies*, edited by B. Labate, C. Cavnar and A. Gearin. London: Routledge.

Sherwood, Alexander, Poncho Meisenheimer, Gary Tarpley and Robert Kargbo. 2020. "An Improved, Practical, and Scalable Five-Step Synthesis of Psilocybin." *Synthesis* 52: 688–694.

Shulgin, Alexander and Ann Shulgin. 1997. *TiHKAL: The Continuation*. Berkeley: Transform Press.

Shulgin, Alexander and Ann Shulgin. 1991. *PiHKAL: A Chemical Love Story*. Berkeley: Transform Press.

Sidhu, Kiran. 2019a. "What Psychedelics Reveal About the Nature of Consciousness." *Filter*, May 20.

Sidhu, Kiran. 2019b. "How Psychedelic Drugs Could Help Save the Planet." *Filter*, October 10.

Siebert, Amanda. 2022. *Psyched: Seven Cutting-Edge Psychedelics Changing the World*. Vancouver: Greystone Books.

Siegel, Joshua, James Daily, Demetrius Perry and Ginger Nicol. 2023. "Psychedelic Drug Legislative Reform and Legalization in the US." *JAMA Psychiatry* 80 (1): 77–83.

Siff, Stephen. 2019. "Henry Luce's Strange Trip: Coverage of LSD is Time and Life, 1954-68." *Journalism History* 34 (3): 126–134.

Silman, Anna. 2024. "MDMA Therapy Could be Legal by Summer. Why Are So Many Advocates Sounding the Alarm?" *Business Insider*, May 13.

Silman, Anna. 2023. "Ketamine is Being Sold as a Depression Wonder Drug. For Some, It's Making Everything Worse." *Business Insider*, January 25.

Simonsson, Otto, Peter Hendricks, Robin Carhart-Harris, Hannes Kettner and Walter Osika. 2021a. "Association Between Lifetime Classic Psychedelic Use and Hypertension in the Past Year." *Hypertension* 77 (5): 1510–1516.

Simonsson, Otto, Walter Osika, Robin Carhart-Harris and Peter Hendricks. 2021b. "Associations Between Lifetime Classic Psychedelic Use and Cardiometabolic Diseases." *Scientific Reports* 11 (1).

Simonsson, Otto, Peter Hendricks, Richard Chambers, Walter Osika and Simon Goldberg. 2023. "Prevalence and Associations of Challenging, Difficult or Distressing Experiences Using Classic Psychedelics." *Journal of Affective Disorders* 326: 105–110.

Simonsson, Otto, Peter Hendricks, Richard Chambers, Walter Osika and Simon Goldberg. 2022. "Classic Psychedelics, Health Behavior, and Physical Health." *Therapeutic Advances in Psychopharmacology* 12.

Simonsson, Otto, James Sexton and Peter Hendricks. 2021. "Associations between Lifetime Classic Psychedelic Use and Markers of Physical Health." *Journal of Psychopharmacology* 35 (4): 447–452.

Siskind, Sarah Rose. 2022. "Is the Hype Around Psychedelics Bursting?" *Psychology Today*, February 23.

Sjöstedt-Hughes, Peter. 2021. *Modes of Sentience: Psychedelics, Metaphysics, Panpsychism*. London: Psychedelic Press.

Slade, Harvey. 2021. "Drug Decriminalization in Portugal: Setting the Record Straight." Bristol: Transform Drug Policy Foundation. transformdrugs.org/assets/files/PDFs/Drug-decriminalisation-in-Portugal-setting-the-record-straight.pdf

Slaunwhite, Amanda, Jeong Min, Heather Palis, Karen Urbanoski, Bernie Pauly, Brittany Barker, Alexis Crabtree, Paxton Bach, Emmanuel Krebs, Laura Dale, Louise Meilleur and Bohdan Nosyk. 2024. "Effect of Risk Mitigation Guidance for Opioid and Stimulant Dispensations on Mortality and Acute Care Visits During Dual Public Health Emergencies: Retrospective Cohort Study." *BMJ* 384.

Sloshower, Jordan. 2018. "Integrating Psychedelic Medicines and Psychiatry: Theory and Methods of a Model Clinic." In *Plant Medicines, Healing and Psychedelic Science*, edited by B. Labate and C. Cavnar. New York: Springer.

Smiley-McDonald, Hope, Peyton Attaway, Lynn Wenger, Kathryn Greenwell, Barrot Lambdin and Alex Kral. 2023. "'All Carrots and No Stick': Perceived Impacts, Changes in Practices, and Attitudes among Law Enforcement Following Drug Decriminalization in Oregon State, USA." *International Journal of Drug Policy* 118.

Smiley-McDonald, Hope, Esther Chung, Lynn Wenger, Morgan Godvin, Danielle Good, Gillian Leichtling, Erica Browne, Barrot Lambdin, and Alex Kral. 2024. "Criminal Legal System Engagement among People Who Use Drugs in Oregon following Decriminalization of Drug Possession." *Drug and Alcohol Dependence* 264.

Smith, Huston. 2000. *Cleansing the Doors of Perception: The Religious Significance of Entheogenic Plants and Chemicals*. New York: Putnam.

Smith, Matthew. 2018a. "One in Five Brits Think It's Ok for MPs and CEOs to Smoke Cannabis." *YouGov*, September 20.

Smith, Phillip. 2018b. "Magic Mushrooms Fight Authoritarianism." *AlterNet*, January 26.

Smith, William and Dominic Sisti. 2021. "Ethics and Ego Dissolution: The Case of Psilocybin." *Journal of Medical Ethics* 47 (12): 807–814.

Sobiecki, Jean. 2002. "A Preliminary Inventory of Plants Used for Psychoactive Purposes in Southern African Healing Traditions." *Transactions of the Royal Society of South Africa* 57 (1): 1–24.

Söderberg, Johan. 2022. "The Psychedelic Renaissance: A Case of Outlaw User Innovation in the Pharmaceutical Industry." *Prometheus* 38 (4): 385–398.

Spiers, Nicholas, Beatriz Labate, Anna Ermakova, Patrick Farrell, Osiris Sinuhé González Romero, Ibrahim Gabriell and Nidia Olvera. 2024. "Indigenous Psilocybin Mushroom Practices: An Annotated Bibliography." *Journal of Psychedelic Studies* 8 (1): 3–25.

Spotswood, C.J. 2022. *The Microdosing Guidebook: A Step-by-Step Manual to Improve Your Physical and Mental Health through Psychedelic Medicine*. California: Ulysses Press.

Spray, Hannah. 2023. "Health Canada Denies Terminally Ill Sask. Man Permission to Continue Magic Mushroom Therapy." *CBC News*, March 2.

Srinivasan, Arun. 2022. "Mark Messier Recounts Transformative Experience with Magic Mushrooms: 'The Light Bulb Came on For Me.'" *Yahoo Life*, December 23.

Stace, Walter. 1960. *Mysticism and Philosophy*. Pennsylvania: Lippincott.

Stamm, Emma. 2019. "Turn on, Tune In, Rise Up." *Commune*, September 7.

Stein, Diana, Sarah Costello and Karen Foster (eds.). 2021. *The Routledge Companion to Ecstatic Experience in the Ancient World*. New York: Routledge.

Stevenson, Renae. 2023. "Psychonautical Engineering: Synergizing the Magic of Mindfulness, Mushrooms, and Mindsets for Police Officer Well-Being." *Journal of Community Safety and Well-Being* 6 (3): 103–108.

Strassman, Rick. 2022. *The Psychedelic Handbook: A Practical Guide to Psilocybin, LSD, Ketamine, MDMA, and DMT/Ayahuasca*. Berkeley: Ulysses Press.

Strassman, Rick. 2001. *DMT: The Spirit Molecule: A Doctor's Revolutionary Research into the Biology of Near-Death and Mystical Experiences*. Vermont: Park Street Press.

Strassman, Rick. 2017. "The Political Correction of Psychedelics. Part 3. Psychedelics as Super-Placebos." rickstrassman.com/the-political-correction-of-psychedelics-part-3-psychedelics-as-super-placebos/

Strauss, Dana, Sara de la Salle, Jordan Sloshower and Monnica Williams. 2022. "Research Abuses Against People of Colour and Other Vulnerable Groups in Early Psychedelic Research." *Journal of Medical Ethics* 48: 728–737.

Strickland, Justin, Albert Garcia-Romeu and Matthew Johnson. 2024. "The Mystical Experience Questionnaire 4-Item and Challenging Experience Questionnaire 7-Item." *Psychedelic Medicine* 2 (1).

Strous, Jurriaan, Cees Weeland, Femke van der Draai, Joost Daams, Damiaan Denys, Anja Lok, Robert Schoevers and Martijn Figee. 2022. "Brain Changes Associated with Long-Term Ketamine Abuse, A Systematic Review." *Frontiers in Neuroanatomy* 16.

Studerus, Erich, Michael Kometer, Felix Hasler and Franz Vollenweider. 2011. "Acute, Subacute and Long-Term Subjective Effects of Psilocybin in Healthy Humans: A Pooled Analysis of Experimental Studies." *Journal of Psychopharmacology* 25 (11): 1434–1452.

Substance Abuse and Mental Health Services Administration. 2022. "Key Substance Use and Mental Health Indicators in the United States: Results from the 2021 National Survey on Drug Use and Health." Center for Behavioral Health Statistics and Quality, Substance Abuse and Mental Health Services Administration. samhsa.gov/data/report/2021-nsduh-annual-national-report

Sweeney, Mary, Sandeep Nayak, Ethan Hurwitz, Lisa Mitchell, Thomas Cody Swift and Roland Griffiths. 2022. "Comparison of Psychedelic and Near-Death or other Non-Ordinary Experiences in Changing Attitudes about Death and Dying." *PLoS One* 17 (8).

Swenson, Kyle. 2018. "Rebekah Mercer, the Billionaire Backer of Bannon and Trump, Chooses Sides." *The Washington Post*, January 5.

Szigeti, Balázs, Laura Kartner, Allan Blemings, Fernando Rosas, Amanda Feilding, David Nutt, Robin Carhart-Harris and David Erritzoe. 2021. "Self-Blinding Citizen Science to Explore Psychedelic Microdosing." *eLife* 10.

Taillefer de Laportalière, Tanguy, Adeline Jullien, Antoine Yrondi, Philippe Cestac and François Montastruc. 2023. "Reporting of Harms in Clinical Trials of Esketamine in Depression: A Systematic Review." *Psychological Medicine* 53 (10): 4305–4315.

Tanne, Janice. 2004. "Humphry Osmond." *British Medical Journal* 328 (7441).

Taurah, Lynn, Chris Chandler and Geoff Sanders. 2014. "Depression, Impulsiveness, Sleep, and Memory in Past and Present Polydrug Users of 3,4-Methylenedioxymethamphetamine (MDMA, Ecstasy)." *Psychopharmacology* 231 (4): 737–751.

Taves, Ann. 2020. "Mystical and Other Alterations in Sense of Self: An Expanded Framework for Studying Nonordinary Experiences." *Perspectives on Psychological Science* 15 (3): 669–690.

Taylor, Amiah. 2022. "Black Cannabis Entrepreneurs Account for Less than 2% of the Nation's Marijuana Businesses." *Fortune*, April 26.

Taylor, Jonathan. 2015. "The Stimulants of Prohibition: Illegality and New Synthetic Drugs." *Territory, Politics, Governance* 3 (4): 407–427.

Taylor, Isaac and Brian Gormley. 2021. "New Venture Firm Adds to Surge in Psychedelic Investments." *The Wall Street Journal*, April 29.

Teixeira, Pedro, Matthew Johnson, Christopher Timmermann, Rosalind Watts, David Erritzoe, Hannah Douglass, Hannes Kettner and Robin Carhart-Harris. 2022. "Psychedelics and Health Behaviour Change." *Journal of Psychopharmacology* 36 (1): 12–19.

Tempone-Wiltshire, Julien and Floren Matthews. 2023. "Evaluating the Role of Psychedelic Psychotherapy in Addressing Societal Alienation: Imaginaries of Liberation." *Journal of Psychedelic Studies* 7 (3): 238–252.

Terris, Ben. 2023. "AOC, Dan Crenshaw and the Mellow Struggle for Psychedelic Drug Access." *The Washington Post*, July 6.

Thelwell, Emma. 2014. "Why Do People Take Ayahuasca?" *BBC News*, April 29.

TheraPsil. 2022. "Public Opinion on Psilocybin Regulations in Canada." January. therapsil.ca/wp-content/uploads/2024/04/Public-Perception-Poll.pdf

Thiel, Peter. 2014. "Competition is for Losers." *The Wall Street Journal*, September 12.

Thiel, Peter. 2009. "The Education of a Libertarian." *Cato Unbound*, April 13.

Thielking, Megan. 2018. "Ketamine Gives Hope to Patients with Severe Depression. But Some Clinics Stray from the Science and Hype its Benefits." *STAT*, September 24.

Thompson, Thomas. 1967. "The New Far-Out Beatles." *Life Magazine*, June 16. the-paulmccartney-project.com/interview/interview-for-life-magazine/

Thomson, Euan. 2024a. "City of Recovery." *Drug Data Decoded*, February 18.

Thomson, Euan. 2024b. "Up Next … 'Experts' Debate the Ethics of Reducing Drug Poisoning Deaths." *Drug Data Decoded*, January 11.

Tibber, Marc, Fahreen Walji, James Kirkbride and Vyv Huddy. 2022. "The Association Between Income Inequality and Adult Mental Health at the Subnational Level — A Systematic Review." *Social Psychiatry and Psychiatric Epidemiology* 57 (1): 1–24.

Timmermann, Christopher, Hannes Kettner, Chris Letheby, Leor Roseman, Fernando Rosas and Robin Carhart-Harris. 2021. "Psychedelics Alter Metaphysical Beliefs." *Scientific Reports* 11.

Tomlinson, Monica, Matthew Brown and Peter Hoaken. 2016. "Recreational Drug Use and Human Aggressive Behavior: A Comprehensive Review Since 2003." *Aggression and Violent Behavior* 27: 9–29.

Toro, Gianluca, Benjamin Thomas and Jonathan Ott. 2007. *Drugs of the Dreaming*. Vermont: Park Street Press.

Tupper, Kenneth. 2017. "The Economics of Ayahuasca: Money, Markets, and the Value of the Vine." In *The World Ayahuasca Diaspora: Reinventions and Controversies*, edited by B. Labate, C. Cavnar and A. Gearin. London: Routledge.

Tupper, Kenneth. 2012. "Psychoactive Substances and the English Language: 'Drugs,' Discourses, and Public Policy." *Contemporary Drug Problems* 39 (3): 461–492.

Tupper, Kenneth. 2009. "Ayahuasca Healing Beyond the Amazon: The Globalization of a Traditional Indigenous Entheogenic Practice." *Global Networks* 9 (1): 117–136.

Tupper, Kenneth and Beatriz Labate. 2014. "Ayahuasca, Psychedelic Studies and Health Sciences: The Politics of Knowledge and Inquiry into an Amazonian Plant Brew." *Current Drug Abuse Reviews* 7 (2): 71–80.

Tupper, Kenneth and Beatriz Labate. 2012. "Plants, Psychoactive Substances and the International Narcotics Control Board: The Control of Nature and the Nature of Control." *Human Rights and Drugs* 2 (1): 17–28.

Tvorun-Dunn, Maxim. 2022. "Acid Liberalism: Silicon Valley's Enlightened Technocrats, and the Legalization of Psychedelics." *International Journal of Drug Policy* 110.

Tymoczko, Dmitri. 1996. "The Nitrous Oxide Philosopher." *The Atlantic*, May 1.

UC Berkeley Center for the Science of Psychedelics. 2023. "New National Poll: More Than 60 Percent of U.S. Voters Support Legalizing Psychedelic Therapy." June 20. psychedelics.berkeley.edu/berkeley-psychedelics-survey-2023/

Underwood, Martie, Stephen Bright and Brian Les Lancaster. 2021. "A Narrative Review of the Pharmacological, Cultural and Psychological Literature on Ibogaine." *Journal of Psychedelic Studies* 5 (1): 44–54.

United Nations Office on Drugs and Crime. 2023. "World Drug Report 2023." June. unodc.org/res/WDR-2023/WDR23_Exsum_fin_DP.pdf

van Amsterdam, Jan, David Nutt, Lawrence Phillips and Wim van den Brink. 2015. "European Rating of Drug Harms." *Journal of Psychopharmacology* 29 (6): 655–660.

van Elk, Michiel and Eiko Fried. 2023. "History Repeating: Guidelines to Address Common Problems in Psychedelic Science." *Therapeutic Advances in Psychopharmacology* 13.

van Mulukom, Valerie, Ruairi Patterson and Michiel van Elk. 2020. "Broadening Your Mind to Include Others: The Relationship between Serotonergic Psychedelic Experiences and Maladaptive Narcissism." *Psychopharmacology* 237 (9): 2725–2737.

van Oorsouw, Kim, Malin Uthaug, Natasha Mason, Nick Broers and Johannes Ramaekers. 2021. "Sub-Acute and Long-Term Effects of Ayahuasca on Mental Health and Well-Being in Healthy Ceremony Attendants: A Replication Study." *Journal of Psychedelic Studies* 5 (2): 103–113.

Vandersluis, Sean. 2021. "Building on the Shulgin Approach." *Microdose*, April 22.

Vedantam, Keerthi. 2022a. "Therapy, Music and Spas: The Non-Drug Startups in Psychedelics." *Crunchbase*, September 20.

Vedantam, Keerthi. 2022b. "Psychedelics Provide New Frontier for Venture Funding, But Nuances Prevail." *Crunchbase*, July 19.

Verma, Shawn. 2018. "Can Psilocybin Make People Feel More Empathy to Nature?" *Chacruna*, August 23.

Vidriales Arturo and Diego Ovies. 2018. "Psychedelic Tourism in Mexico, a Thriving Trend." *PASOS* 16 (4): 1037–1050.

Villa, Robert. 2023. "Toad in the Road: Biocultural History and Conservation Challenges of the Sonoran Desert Toad." *Journal of Psychedelic Studies* 7 (S1): 68–79.

Villiger, Daniel and Manuel Trachsel. 2023. "With Great Power Comes Great Vulnerability: An Ethical Analysis of Psychedelics' Therapeutic Mechanisms Proposed by the REBUS Hypothesis." *Journal of Medical Ethics* 49 (12): 826–832.

Virdi, Jasmine. 2020. "Indigenous Voices in Peyote Conservation: Preserving Medicine for Future Generations." *Psychedelics Today*, September 16.

Vollenweider, Franz and Katrin Preller. 2022. "Psychedelic Drugs: Neurobiology and Potential for treatment of Psychiatric Disorders." *Nature Reviews Neuroscience* 21 (11): 611–624.

Wagner, Mark, Michael Mithoefer, Ann Mithoefer, Rebecca MacAulay, Lisa Jerome, Berra Yazar-Klosinski and Rick Doblin. 2017. "Therapeutic Effect of Increased Openness: Investigating Mechanism of Action in MDMA-Assisted Psychotherapy." *Journal of Psychopharmacology* 31 (8): 967–974.

Waldman, Ayelet. 2017. *A Really Good Day: How Microdosing Made a Mega Difference in My Mood, My Marriage, and My Life*. New York: Knopf.

Walker, Dennis. 2022. "Spiraling Down Wonderland's Psychedelic Corporate Rabbit Hole." *Lucid News*, November 15.

Walsh, Charlotte. 2016. "Psychedelics and Cognitive Liberty: Reimagining Drug Policy Through the Prism of Human Rights." *International Journal of Drug Policy* 29: 80–87.

Walsh, Claire, Ofir Livne, Dvora Shmulewitz, Malki Stohl and Deborah Hasin. 2022. "Use of Plant-Based Hallucinogens and Dissociative Agents: U.S. Time Trends, 2002–2019." *Addictive Behaviors Reports* 16.

Walsh, Roger and Charles Grob. 2006. "Early Psychedelic Investigators Reflect on the Psychological and Social Implications of their Research." *Journal of Humanistic Psychology* 46 (4): 432–448.

Walsh, Zach, Ozden Mollaahmetoglu, Joseph Rootman, Shannon Golsof, Johanna Keeler, Beth Marsh, David Nutt, Celia Morgan. 2021. "Ketamine for the Treatment of Mental Health and Substance Use Disorders: Comprehensive Systematic Review." *British Journal of Psychiatry Open* 8 (1).

Wasson, Robert Gordon. 1957. "Seeking the Magic Mushroom." *Life* 49 (19).

Wasson, Robert Gordon. 1968. *Soma: Divine Mushroom of Immortality*. New York: Harcourt Brace Jovanovich.

Wasson, Robert Gordon. 1986. *Persephone's Quest: Entheogens and the Origins of Religion*. Connecticut: Yale University Press.

Wasson, Robert Gordon, Albert Hofmann and Carl Ruck. 2008. *The Road to Eleusis: Unveiling the Secrets of the Mysteries*. California: North Atlantic Books.

Watford, Tessa and Naqash Masood. 2024. "Psilocybin, an Effective Treatment for Major Depressive Disorder in Adults — A Systematic Review." *Clinical Psychopharmacology and Neuroscience* 22 (1): 2–12.

Watts, Alan. 1968. "Psychedelics and Religious Experience." *California Law Review* 56: 74–85.

Watts, Rosalind. 2022. "Can Magic Mushrooms Unlock Depression? What I've Learned in the Five Years Since My TEDx Talk." *Medium*, February 28.

Watts, Rosalind, Camilla Day, Jacob Krzanowski, David Nutt and Robin Carhart-Harris. 2017. "Patients' Accounts of Increased 'Connectedness' and 'Acceptance' after Psilocybin for Treatment-Resistant Depression." *Journal of Humanistic Psychology* 57 (5): 520–564.

Watts, Rosalind and Jason Luoma. 2020. "The Use of the Psychological Flexibility Model to Support Psychedelic Assisted Therapy." *Journal of Contextual Behavioral Science* 15: 92–102.

Webb, Megan, Heith Copes and Peter Hendricks. 2019. "Narrative Identity, Rationality, and Microdosing Classic Psychedelics." *International Journal of Drug Policy* 70: 33–39.

Weiss, Brandon, Joshua Miller, Nathan Carter and William Keith Campbell. 2021. "Examining Changes in Personality Following Shamanic Ceremonial Use of Ayahuasca." *Scientific Reports* 11 (1).

Weiss, Brandon, Leor Roseman, Bruna Giribaldi, David Nutt, Robin Carhart-Harris and David Erritzoe. 2024. "Unique Psychological Mechanisms Underlying Psilocybin Therapy Versus Escitalopram Treatment in the Treatment of Major Depressive Disorder." *International Journal of Mental Health and Addiction* 22: 806–841.

Weiss, Brandon, Chelsea Sleep, Nicholas Beller, David Erritzoe and W. Keith Campbell. 2023. "Perceptions of Psychedelic Personality Change, Determinants of Use, Setting and Drug Moderation: Toward a Holistic Model." *Journal of Psychedelic Studies* 7 (3): 200–226.

Wen, Alexander, Nikhita Singhal, Brett Jones, Richard Zeifman, Shobha Mehta, Mohammad Shenasa, Daniel Blumberger, Zafiris Daskalakis and Cory Weissman. 2024. "A Systematic Review of Study Design and Placebo Controls in Psychedelic Research." *Psychedelic Medicine* 2 (1): 15–24.

Wheal, Jamie. 2023. "Psychedelic Fascism: Too Big to Fail?" *Substack*, July 23.

Whitaker, Robert. 2010. *Anatomy of an Epidemic: Magic Bullets, Psychiatric Drugs, and the Astonishing Rise of Mental Illness in America*. New York: Crown.

Whitelaw, Mallory. 2017. "A Path to Peace in the US Drug War: Why California Should Implement the Portuguese Model for Drug Decriminalization." *Loyola of Los Angeles International and Comparative Law Review* 40 (1).

Whooley, Sean. 2023. "US Military to Test Bexson Biomedical Ketamine Delivery Device." *Drug Delivery*, July 28.

Wiepking, Lennart, Ed de Bruin and Alexandra Ghiță. 2023. "The Potential of Psilocybin Use to Enhance Well-Being in Healthy Individuals — A Scoping Review." *Journal of Psychedelic Studies* 7 (3): 184–199.

Wilkinson, Samuel, Taeho Rhee, Jutta Joormann, Ryan Webler, Mayra Lopez, Brandon Kitay, Madonna Fasula, Christina Elder, Lisa Fenton and Gerard Sanacora. 2021. "Cognitive Behavioral Therapy to Sustain the Antidepressant Effects of Ketamine in Treatment-Resistant Depression: A Randomized Clinical Trial." *Psychotherapy and Psychosomatics* 90 (5): 318–327.

Williams, Bett. 2020. "Psychedelics Won the Election — Except the Psychedelic that is Donald Trump." *Double Blind*, May 26.

Williams, Keith and Suzanne Brant. 2023. "Tending a Vibrant World: Gift Logic and Sacred Plant Medicines. *History of Pharmacy and Pharmaceuticals* 65 (1): 8–32.

Williams, Monnica, Alan Davis, Yitong Xin, Nathan Sepeda, Pamela Colón Grigas, Sinead Sinnott and Angela Haeny. 2021. "People of Color in North America Report Improvements in Racial Trauma and Mental Health Symptoms Following Psychedelic Experiences." *Drugs: Education, Prevention and Policy* 28 (3): 215–226.

Williams, Monnica, Sara Reed and Ritika Aggarwal. 2020. "Culturally Informed Research Design Issues in a Study for MDMA-Assisted Psychotherapy for Posttraumatic Stress Disorder." *Journal of Psychedelic Studies* 4 (1): 40–50.

Williams, Sophie. 2021. "Meet the Women who Regularly Microdose Psychedelics." *Cosmopolitan*, August 27.

Winkelman, Michael. 2019. "Introduction: Evidence for Entheogen Use in Prehistory and World Religions." *Journal of Psychedelic Studies* 3 (2): 43–62.

Winstock, Adam, Stephen Kaar and Rohan Borschmann. 2014. "Dimethyltryptamine (DMT): Prevalence, User Characteristics and Abuse Liability in a Large Global Sample." *Journal of Psychopharmacology* 28 (1): 49–54.

Wirz, Matt. 2023. "Ecstasy-for-Medicine Advocate MAPS looks for Cash Lifeline." *The Wall Street Journal*, June 28.

Wolff, Max, Ricarda Evens, Lea Mertens, Michael Koslowski, Felix Betzler, Gerhard Gründer and Henrik Jungaberle. 2020. "Learning to Let Go: A Cognitive-Behavioral Model of How Psychedelic Therapy Promotes Acceptance." *Frontiers in Psychiatry* 11.

Wong, Sam. 2019. "Extinction Rebellion Founder Calls for Mass Psychedelic Disobedience." *New Scientist*, August 19.

World Health Organization. 2023. "Fact Sheets — Depressive Disorder (Depression)." March 31. who.int/news-room/fact-sheets/detail/depression

World Health Organization. 2022a. *World Mental Health Report: Transforming Mental Health for All.* Geneva. iris.who.int/bitstream/handle/10665/356119/9789240049338-eng.pdf?sequence=1

World Health Organization. 2022b. "COVID-19 Pandemic Triggers 25% Increase in Prevalence of Anxiety and Depression Worldwide." March 2. who.int/news/item/02-03-2022-covid-19-pandemic-triggers-25-increase-in-prevalence-of-anxiety-and-depression-worldwide

World Health Organization. 2022c. "Fact Sheets — Alcohol." May 9. who.int/news-room/fact-sheets/detail/alcohol

Worthington, Elise and Mary Lloyd. 2024. "Leading Psychedelic Trainer Ben Sessa Suspended over Relationship with Vulnerable Former Patient." *Australian Broadcasting Corporation*, March 6.

Worthy, Patrice. 2021. "The Cannabis Industry is Booming, but for Many Black Americans the Price of Entry is Steep." *The Guardian*, September 7.

Wozniak, Antal, Hartmut Wessler and Julia Lück. 2017. "Who Prevails in the Visual Framing Contest about the United Nations Climate Change Conferences?" *Journalism Studies* 18 (11): 1433–1452.

Wright, Webb. 2022. "The Psychedelic Gold Rush: Marketing the Future of Mental Healthcare to the Masses." *The Drum*, May 2.

Xavier, Jessica, Jennifer McDermid, Jane Buxton, Iesha Henderson, Amber Streukens, Jessica Lamb and Alissa Greer. 2024. "People Who Use Drugs' Prioritization of Regulation Amid Decriminalization Reforms in British Columbia, Canada: A Qualitative Study." *International Journal of Drug Policy* 125.

Yaden, David, Brian Earp and Roland Griffiths. 2022. "Ethical Issues Regarding Nonsubjective Psychedelics as Standard of Care." *Cambridge Quarterly of Healthcare Ethics* 31 (4): 464–471.

Yaden, David, James Potash and Roland Griffiths. 2022. "Preparing for the Bursting of the Psychedelic Hype Bubble." *JAMA Psychiatry* 79 (10): 943–944.

Yaden, David, Khoa Le Nguyen, Margaret Kern, Alexander Belser, Johannes Eichstaedt, Jonathan Iwry, Mary Smith, Nancy Wintering, Ralph Hood and Andrew Newberg. 2017a. "Of Roots and Fruits: A Comparison of Psychedelic and Nonpsychedelic Mystical Experiences." *Journal of Humanistic Psychology* 57 (4): 338–353.

Yaden, David, Khoa Le Nguyen, Margaret Kern, Nancy Wintering, Johannes Eichstaedt, H. Andrew Schwartz, Anneke Buffone, Laura Smith, Mark Waldman, Ralph Hood and Andrew Newberg. 2017b. "The Noetic Quality: A Multimethod Exploratory Study." *Psychology of Consciousness: Theory, Research, and Practice* 4 (1): 54–62.

Yaden, David and Roland Griffiths. 2021. "The Subjective Effects of Psychedelics Are Necessary for Their Enduring Therapeutic Effects." *ACS Pharmacology & Translational Science* 4 (2): 568–572.

Yakowicz, Will. 2021. "The Future of Psychedelic Medicine Might Skip the Trip." *Forbes*, June 23.

Yakowicz, Will. 2020. "This New York City Pharma Startup Wants to Turn LSD Into an FDA-Approved Medicine for Anxiety Disorder." *Forbes*, April 1.

Yanakieva, Steliana, Naya Polychroni, Neiloufar Family, Luke Williams, David Luke and Devin Terhune. 2019. "The Effects of Microdose LSD on Time Perception: A Randomised, Double-Blind, Placebo-Controlled Trial." *Psychopharmacology* 236 (4): 1159–1170.

Yaremko, Jeff and Kevin Walby. 2023. "Slow Panic? The Regulation of Salvia Divinorum in Canada, 1991–2019." *Deviant Behavior* 44 (8): 1179–1193.

YouGov. 2022. "Daily Survey: Psychedelics." *YouGov,* July 27. docs.cdn.yougov.com/tt7pb-cho6l/tabs_Psychedelics_20220722%20%281%29.pdf

Zafar, Rayyan, Maxim Siegel, Rebecca Harding, Tommaso Barba, Claudio Agnorelli, Shayam Suseelan, Leor Roseman, Matthew Wall, David Nutt and David Erritzoe. 2023. "Psychedelic Therapy in the Treatment of Addiction: The Past, Present and Future." *Frontiers in Psychiatry* 14.

Zaitchik, Alexander. 2022. *Owning the Sun: A People's History of Monopoly Medicine from Aspirin to Covid-19 Vaccines.* Berkeley, CA: Counterpoint.

Zarley, B. David. 2021. "Should Psychedelics be Patented?" *Freethink*, December 29.

Zeifman, Richard, Fernanda Palhano-Fontes, Jaime Hallak, Emerson Arcoverde, João Paulo Maia-Oliveira and Draulio Araujo. 2019. "The Impact of Ayahuasca on Suicidality: Results from a Randomized Controlled Trial." *Frontiers in Pharmacology* 10.

Zemon, Matt. 2022. *Psychedelics For Everyone: A Beginner's Guide to these Powerful Medicines for Anxiety, Depression, Addiction, PTSD, and Expanding Consciousness.* North Carolina: Psyched Publishing.

Zibbell, Jon, Sarah Clarke, Alex Kral, Nicholas Richardson, Dennis Cauchon and Arnie Aldridge. 2022. "Association Between Law Enforcement Seizures of Illicit Drugs and Drug Overdose Deaths Involving Cocaine and Nethamphetamine, Ohio, 2014–2019." *Drug and Alcohol Dependence* 232.

Zimonjic, Peter. 2023. "Poilievre-Backed Motion Calls for an End to Safe Drug Policies and More Cash for Treatment." *CBC News.* May 29.

Zoorob, Michael, Ju Park, Alex Kral, Barrot Lambdin and Brandon del Pozo. 2024. "Drug Decriminalization, Fentanyl, and Fatal Overdoses in Oregon." *JAMA* 7 (9).

Zorn, Matt. 2023a. "Bifurcated (Re)Scheduling." *On Drugs*, May 5.

Zorn, Matt. 2023b. "Groundhog Day: DOI/DOC —> Schedule I?" *On Drugs*, December 21.

Zorn, Matt. 2022a. "Do Bad Psychedelic Patents Matter?" *Lucid News*, June 28.

Zorn, Matt. 2022b. "Hot Psilocybin Patent Garbage." *On Drugs*, May 23.

Zuboff, Shoshana. 2015. "Big Other: Surveillance Capitalism and the Prospects of an Information Civilization." *Journal of Information Technology* 30 (1): 75–89.

INDEX

2C-B, 9, 212
5-MeO-DMT, 9, 12, 99, 123, 199–200, 210, 212, 246, 248

abstinence, 36, 40–41, 47, 54, 56, 153, 250
acid, 66, 79, 87, 89–91, 95–96, 116
   acid anarchism, 91
   acid communism, 89–91
   see also LSD
activism/activists, 1–2, 5, 9–10, 24, 27, 33, 43, 46, 53–54, 60, 66–67, 79, 83–84, 91, 94, 108, 153, 164, 219, 232, 240, 246–249, 251, 253–254, 258–259
   harm reduction activism, 33, 53–54, 164, 248–249, 251
   psychedelic-related activism, 1–2, 9–10, 24, 27, 33, 66–67, 79, 83–84, 91, 94, 108, 219, 232, 240, 246–248, 251, 253–254, 258–259
addiction, 12–13, 17, 22, 30, 35–36, 39–40, 47, 49–51, 55–57, 77, 97, 99, 112–113, 122, 127, 130–131, 133–134, 136–137, 149–150, 153–154, 175–176, 200, 207, 231, 236, 248, 250
   psychedelics for the treatment of, 12–13, 17, 22, 39–40, 50, 99, 112–113, 122, 130–131, 133–134, 136–137, 153, 176, 200, 207, 236
   see also drug dependency; substance use disorders
advertising, 1, 28, 51, 100, 105, 107, 166, 171, 186–187, 191–193
   see also marketing
alcohol, 16, 18–20, 30, 35–36, 39–41, 51, 77, 81, 115, 123–124, 126, 128, 134, 138, 143, 149, 151, 153, 191, 210, 259–260

alcoholism, 39–41, 123, 134, 210
alcohol use disorder, 16, 123–124, 143, 191
   psychedelics for the treatment of, 16, 39–41, 123–124, 134, 143, 191, 210
   see also substance use disorders
alienation, 4, 69, 83, 90–91, 107, 127–128, 195, 259
Amazon (forest), 7, 61, 110, 161, 196, 198
Angermayer, Christian, 23, 87, 103–104, 164, 175–176, 179, 206, 215, 218
antidepressants, 123–124, 126, 129, 133, 138, 144
   SSRIs, 126, 129, 132–133, 143, 174
   see also psychiatry
anxiety (psychedelics for the treatment of), 13, 16, 19, 40, 46, 112, 115, 122–124, 132–134, 138, 140–142, 175, 191, 196, 211, 214
artificial intelligence (AI), 21, 103–105, 129, 189–190, 204
Atai Life Sciences, 21, 23, 87, 103, 123, 164, 170–173, 175–176, 179, 184, 188, 203, 206, 218
Australia, 21, 23, 61, 151, 224–225, 228, 251
authoritarian/authoritarianism, 81–82, 91–93, 258
Awakn Life Sciences, 124, 143, 151, 192, 194
ayahuasca, 7, 9, 11–12, 25, 61, 81, 83–84, 87–88, 102, 108, 110, 117–118, 123, 152, 155–156, 161, 175, 196–199, 211, 224, 240–242, 245
   ayahuasca ceremonies/rituals, 7, 11, 61, 84, 108, 110, 118, 175, 196–199, 240–242
   ayahuasca tourism, 12, 25, 88, 161, 195–199
   ayahuasqueros, 197–198

bad trips/challenging experiences, 119, 145, 154–159, 162, 198
barbiturates, 38, 43, 95
Barrow, Robert, 132, 174, 201
Bay Staters for Natural Medicine, 238, 243
Beckley Foundation, 20, 165, 173
Beckley Psytech, 123, 136, 173
Big Pharma, 136, 147, 172–174
  see also pharmaceutical industry
biomedicine, 15, 21, 29, 70, 97, 105, 111–112, 117–119, 127, 176, 178, 187, 189, 220–221, 225, 247, 259
  see also medical model; medicalization; psychedelic medicine; Western medicine
biotechnology, 3, 25, 135–136, 163, 166–168, 171, 203, 215–216
Black people, 31, 33, 37–39, 45–50, 52, 67, 97, 107, 119–120, 169, 254, 261
  and psychedelic research/experimentation, 97, 107, 119–120
  and the war on drugs, 33, 37–39, 45–50, 52, 169, 254, 261
Brave New World, 5, 65, 104
  see also Aldous Huxley
Bronner, David, 27, 178, 185, 227, 233
Burning Man, 12, 23–24

caffeine/coffee, 50, 77, 138, 150, 192
California, 20, 44, 102, 119, 130, 152, 166, 190, 235–238, 240
Canadian Charter of Rights and Freedoms, 54, 222, 249, 251
cancer, 24, 41, 99, 211, 223, 240
cannabis/marijuana, 16–17, 19, 25, 33–34, 38–39, 45–46, 52, 58–59, 95, 116, 168–170, 172, 223–224, 244–248, 260–261
  cannabis industry, 25, 33, 59, 168–170, 172, 261
  legalization of, 33, 52, 58–59, 116, 168, 223–224, 247–248, 260–261
capitalism/capitalists, 2–5, 23, 25, 28–29, 60, 79–80, 84, 89–91, 93, 95, 105, 123, 127, 134, 142, 163–166, 169, 173, 176–177, 182, 186–190, 192, 199–200, 207, 212, 254–255, 257–258
  see also psychedelic industry
Carhart-Harris, Robin, 13, 129–130, 143
celebrities, 1, 11–14, 164, 166, 195
Central Intelligence Agency (CIA), 48, 87, 93, 95–98, 106–107
  MK-Ultra, 87, 96–97

Christianity, 64, 66, 240–242
classical psychedelics, 9–10, 17, 19, 30, 63, 85, 115, 130–131, 134, 137, 148–152, 154, 156, 159, 203, 213
climate change, 14–15, 78, 84–86, 88, 95, 108–109, 189
  see also ecology/nature; environment
clinical trials, 2–3, 21–22, 24, 40, 68, 74, 99, 114, 116–125, 131–132, 140–141, 143–144, 146–148, 152, 157–160, 163–164, 170–171, 174, 181, 184, 187, 206, 209, 214–215, 221, 226, 239
  adverse events in, 118–119, 125, 146–148, 157–159, 170
  blinding in, 66–67, 120–121, 140, 144, 146
  randomized controlled trials (RCTs), 117–118, 120–123
  see also psychedelic medicine
Clusterbusters, 135
coca, 1, 30, 33, 37, 50, 54, 246–247
Coca Leaf Café, 33, 54, 246–247
cocaine, 18, 30, 34, 37, 47, 59, 81, 95, 151, 249
  crack cocaine, 32, 47–48, 151
colonialism, 7, 34, 107, 190, 244
commercialization, 4, 25, 104, 132, 136, 140, 161, 163, 166, 168, 174, 178, 182–185, 190–192, 194–196, 198–199, 201, 204, 212, 215, 218, 228, 233, 255, 257, 259
commodification, 1, 4, 30, 92, 111, 128, 138, 165, 187, 196–197, 199, 254, 256
Compass Pathways, 21, 28, 95, 105, 132, 136, 142, 151, 157, 170, 172–178, 181–182, 184, 188–189, 203–204, 214–218
  COMP360, 178, 216
  intellectual property (IP)/patents, 28, 177–178, 182, 189, 203–204, 214–218
compassion clubs, 248–249
consciousness, 3, 6, 7, 11, 13–14, 19–20, 28, 30, 32, 35, 41, 61–64, 68, 71, 74–79, 83, 89–90, 101, 105, 131, 140, 159, 185, 195
Conservative Party of Canada, 49–51, 57, 242
  see also politicians
conspiracy theories, 94, 100, 106
consumerism, 4, 107, 138, 165, 185–186, 195
Controlled Drugs and Substances Act (CDSA), 23, 50–51, 54, 59, 221–224, 241–243, 245
Controlled Substances Act, 44, 46, 239, 241, 247, 252
corporadelia/corporadelic, 2, 8, 93, 105, 107, 142, 165, 172–173, 175, 180, 188, 254

corporate capture/ownership, 25, 90, 92, 169, 182, 197, 210, 218, 221, 228–229, 233, 255–258
corporatization, 4–5, 15, 17, 27, 33, 62, 91–92, 220, 225, 234, 252, 254, 256, 258
counterculture, 8–10, 13, 22–23, 33, 42, 45–46, 65, 77, 79, 90–92, 96–97, 99, 102, 106, 108, 117, 165–166, 169, 255–256
Cover Story: Power Trip, 160, 162
COVID-19 pandemic, 126, 171, 183, 193, 196, 206
creativity, 7, 41, 106, 138, 140–142, 210
crime, 31, 47, 49, 51–53, 59, 101, 109, 126, 160, 230, 235, 245, 248, 260
criminal justice, 9, 20, 26, 47, 49, 51, 53, 57, 59, 126, 169, 224, 230, 256, 260
criminalization, 17, 22, 30–33, 35, 38–39, 43, 45–47, 51–54, 56–57, 77, 85, 99, 102, 112, 114, 116, 137, 168–169, 178–179, 211, 220–221, 227, 231, 235–236, 243–245, 247, 253, 260–261
  of psychedelics, 17, 22, 32–33, 38–39, 57, 85, 99, 102, 114, 137, 168–169, 178, 211, 221, 227, 235, 243–245, 247, 261
Cybin, 21, 123, 136, 143

decriminalization, 2–4, 9, 17, 23–24, 26–27, 32–33, 51, 54–60, 92, 114–116, 176–178, 180, 184, 208–209, 220–221, 226–228, 230–236, 239, 243–244, 247–249, 251–252, 254–255, 259, 261
  in British Columbia, 54, 57, 59, 231, 248–249
  in Colorado, 24, 226–227, 232–235, 238–239, 252
  in Oregon, 226–227, 230–231, 252
  in Portugal, 58, 116
  of psychedelics, 2–4, 9, 17, 23–24, 26–27, 32–33, 59–60, 92, 114–116, 176–178, 180, 184, 208–209, 220–221, 226–228, 230–236, 239, 243–244, 247, 251–252, 254–255, 259, 261
Decriminalize Nature, 9, 24, 177, 228, 233–234, 243–244, 252
default mode network (DMN), 75, 130, 133
democracy, 2, 90, 93, 95, 102–104, 258
depression, 12, 15–17, 19, 22, 37, 40–41, 81, 105, 112, 114–115, 122–130, 133–136, 138–144, 154, 157–158, 166, 170, 173, 175, 179, 186, 191–192, 196, 207, 209, 211, 225

psychedelics for the treatment of, 11, 15–17, 19, 22, 40–41, 81, 112, 114–115, 122–124, 126–128, 130, 133–136, 138–143, 157–158, 166, 170, 173, 175, 179, 186, 191–192, 196, 207, 209, 211, 225
Devenot, Neşe, 2, 92–94, 104, 147, 189–190, 253
Diagnostic and Statistical Manual of Mental Disorders, 133, 217
digital psychedelia, 104–105, 132, 171, 188–189, 202, 257
  see also surveillance capitalism
dispensaries, 21, 169, 224, 236, 245–246
dissociatives, 10, 31, 131, 134
DMT, 9–10, 12, 18, 20, 25, 42–43, 50, 63, 68, 73–74, 93, 95, 99, 123, 130, 150–152, 165, 199–200, 202, 210–214, 232, 235, 237, 240–241, 246, 256
  DMT entities, 73–74
DMT-Nexus, 20, 165, 211
Doblin, Rick, 1–2, 53, 66, 80, 87, 99–101, 109, 137, 180–184, 189–190
Drug Abuse Control Amendments, 44–45
drug deaths, 33, 51, 54–58, 151–152, 176, 248–251, 260
  see also overdoses; tainted drugs
drug dependency, 50, 123, 149–150, 152, 154, 175, 192, 227, 261
  see also addiction; substance use disorders
Drug Enforcement Administration (DEA), 23, 28, 38, 46, 49–50, 168, 177, 204, 226–227, 239–241, 244, 247–248
drug possession, 16, 23–24, 36, 42–44, 46–47, 50–52, 54, 58–59, 102, 155, 227, 230–232, 235, 237–239, 242, 245–246, 249, 258, 261
drug safety/risks, 14, 16–19, 35, 49–51, 54–56, 58–59, 113–114, 119, 123, 128, 137, 146–162, 158–162, 166, 170, 192–193, 198–199, 224, 226, 229, 231, 235, 247, 249, 251
  comparative risk profiles, 16–18, 148–154
drug scheduling/classifications, 23–24, 27–28, 31, 35, 43–46, 50, 114, 152, 177, 201, 222, 225–227, 239, 242, 245, 247–248, 252, 261
  bifurcated scheduling, 27, 114, 227, 239
  Canadian drug scheduling, 23, 42–44, 46, 50, 151, 222, 242

international drug scheduling, 23, 43–44, 152, 224–225, 247
US drug scheduling, 23–24, 27–28, 35, 44–46, 50, 114, 151, 177, 226–227, 239, 247–248, 252
drug seizures, 51, 102, 230, 233, 241–242, 244–246
drug trafficking, 43, 48–50, 52, 239, 245, 247, 249
Drug User Liberation Front (DULF), 54, 248–249, 251

ecology/nature, 4, 7, 9, 14, 19, 22, 30, 78, 81–86, 88, 93, 106–109, 189, 199–200, 259
see also climate change; environment
ego death/dissolution, 62, 69–70, 72, 75, 81, 85, 103, 107, 117, 130, 165, 185
empathogens, 10, 134, 213
empathy, 10, 80–82, 86–87, 93, 108, 134, 176, 213
end-of-life illness/care, 15, 24, 124, 214, 222–223, 240, 251
entheogens, 9, 19, 45, 108, 110, 203, 234, 238–239, 244
entrepreneurs, 25, 38, 53, 88, 103, 135, 163, 166, 169, 187, 192, 196–197, 236
Enveric Biosciences, 136, 203–205
environment, 22, 82–86, 98, 106, 108, 200, 232, 256, 259
see also climate change; ecology/nature
Erowid, 20, 211, 213
esketamine, 124, 158, 173, 184, 191, 209
see also ketamine; Spravato
Evans, Jules, 94, 102–103, 147, 156, 192

fascism, 14, 78, 82, 93, 107
Federal Bureau of Investigation (FBI), 17, 46
Federal Bureau of Narcotics (FBN), 38
fentanyl, 49, 55, 231, 260
Ferriss, Tim, 12–13, 102, 133
Field Trip Health, 87, 145, 168–169, 175, 177, 186, 192, 194, 223
Food and Drug Administration (FDA), 27, 50, 100, 114, 121, 123–125, 145–148, 158–159, 161, 178, 183–184, 189, 191, 207, 225–227, 252
Food and Drugs Act, 42–43, 46, 50
Freedom to Operate, 214, 216

Gandy, Sam, 41, 62, 83
God, 64, 69, 72, 103, 178
see also religion

Goldsmith, George, 142, 174, 176, 178–179, 214–215
Good Friday Experiment, 65–67
Griffiths, Roland, 13, 53, 68, 78, 112, 134, 137
Grof, Stanislav, 7, 40, 72, 78, 131

hallucinations, 10, 39, 42, 75, 98, 107, 190, 197
hallucinogens, 9, 11–12, 22, 43–44, 62, 88, 98, 102, 123, 135–137, 139, 156, 202, 235
Hardman, Josh, 147, 171, 173, 183
harm reduction, 4–5, 20, 26, 32–33, 51, 53–57, 59, 113, 159, 180, 184, 193, 231, 248–252, 259, 261
in Vancouver, 53–54, 248–251
see also activism/activists; safe supply; safe use
Hart, Carl, 30–31, 54
Hartogsohn, Ido, 87, 106, 165
Hausfeld, Russell, 102, 172, 183, 188–189, 239
head shops, 33
Health Canada, 23, 51, 55, 58, 124, 159–160, 191, 221–225, 242–243
healthy normals, 32, 115
Heroic Hearts, 147, 235
heroin, 30, 34, 40, 45, 55, 95, 150–151, 231, 249, 260
Hoffer, Abram, 39–40, 42, 117, 134
Hofmann, Albert, 83, 155, 200
Hollywood Hospital, 39–41, 166
Huxley, Aldous, 5, 8, 65, 74–75, 104

iboga, 62, 84, 102, 110, 199, 245
ibogaine, 9–10, 51, 99, 113, 122–123, 131, 137, 153, 166, 171, 200, 232, 235
for the treatment of addiction/opioid use disorder, 113, 122–123, 137, 153, 200
dangers of, 113, 137, 153
immigrants, 35–36, 38, 254
imperialism, 80, 107
incarceration, 48–49, 52, 100, 120, 230, 253, 261
mass incarceration, 49, 100, 120
racial disparities in incarceration, 36, 47–49, 120
see also prisons; prisoners
Indigenous peoples/cultures, 1, 4–7, 11, 28, 40, 52, 59, 61, 64, 82, 108, 110–113, 118, 123, 165–166, 169, 177, 196–199, 211, 218, 232, 240–241, 243–244, 255

Indigenous knowledge, 4, 19, 21, 110–113, 118, 165–166, 178, 195, 211, 218, 255
Indigenous healers, 5, 11, 29–30, 61, 110–113, 118, 123, 196–197
see also ayahuasca; shamans
individualism/individualized therapy, 29, 56–57, 79–80, 86, 90–91, 108, 110–111, 115, 127–128, 142, 165, 184–185, 197, 254
inequality, 3, 29, 49, 90, 93, 104, 127–128, 185, 190, 197, 205, 209
informed consent, 118, 159, 193, 199
Institute for Clinical and Economic Review (ICER), 146–147
insurance (coverage for psychedelics), 181, 192, 224–225
intellectual property (IP), 2, 4, 14, 25, 136, 163, 177, 180, 182–183, 189, 200–219, 255
see also patents

James, William, 63–66, 73
Janssen Pharmaceuticals, 158, 173, 209
Johns Hopkins University, 13–14, 20, 63, 67, 72, 74, 81, 134, 142
Johnson, Matthew, 13, 69, 82, 150

ketamine, 10, 12, 18, 30–31, 50, 87, 100, 119, 123–125, 130–131, 134–135, 145, 153–154, 158, 164, 185–187, 190–194, 209, 236
for the treatment of depression, 123–124, 135, 158, 173, 186, 191–192, 209
dangers of, 153–154, 192–194
ketamine-assisted therapy, 31, 100, 123–124, 135, 145, 185, 191–194
see also esketamine
ketamine clinics, 154, 190–194, 255
kratom, 50, 246, 248
kykeon, 7, 61

Larsen, Dana, 246, 251
see also Coca Leaf Café
law enforcement, 47, 49–51, 54–55, 57–58, 227, 230, 244, 253
see also police/policing
Leary, Timothy, 21, 42, 65, 77, 96, 101–103, 107, 117, 149
legalization, 3, 16, 22–24, 26, 32–33, 36, 52, 58–59, 60, 112, 116, 137, 147, 168–169, 177–178, 208–209, 220–222, 224–229, 232–238, 244, 247–248, 251–252, 254–255, 260–261

in Colorado, 232–235, 237–238, 251–252
in Oregon, 24, 178, 226–229, 235, 237–238, 251–252
of cannabis, 25, 33, 52, 58–59, 116, 168–169, 223–224, 246–248, 260–261
of psychedelics, 3, 16, 22–24, 26, 32–33, 59–60, 112, 137, 147, 177–178, 208–209, 220–222, 224–229, 232–238, 244, 247, 251–252, 254–255, 260–261
Levy, Ronan, 87, 145, 168, 175, 186, 192, 194
lobbying/lobbyists, 99, 111, 147, 151, 178, 180, 210, 234
Love, Shayla, 2, 23, 26–27, 74, 129, 205–206
LSD, 7, 9–12, 17–18, 21, 25, 35, 39–45, 50–51, 66, 68, 78–79, 81, 83, 86–87, 89–91, 93–98, 101, 106–107, 111, 116–117, 123, 130, 132, 134–135, 140–141, 149–152, 154–155, 159, 166, 177, 200–203, 210, 212–214, 220, 236, 246, 256
LSD-assisted therapy, 10, 39–41, 106, 117, 123, 132, 134, 159, 166
Lykos Therapeutics, 125, 145–146, 148, 158, 180, 182–184
see also Multidisciplinary Association for Psychedelic Studies (MAPS)

magic mushrooms, 11, 13, 17, 82–83
see also psilocybin; psilocybin mushrooms
MagicMed Industries, 203, 205
marketing, 45, 49, 127, 142, 166, 171, 187–188, 191, 194
see also advertising
McKenna, Dennis, 75, 83, 118, 243
McKenna, Terence, 7, 73, 78, 83, 151, 155
MDA, 50, 213
MDMA, 2, 9–11, 15–18, 23–25, 31, 46, 50, 59, 81, 87, 99–101, 111, 114, 121, 124–125, 130–131, 134–135, 143, 145–153, 158–161, 180–184, 190–191, 194, 200–202, 212–213, 224–226, 236–239
for the treatment of post-traumatic stress disorder (PTSD), 2, 15, 23, 114, 121, 125, 145–148, 158, 160–161, 190, 225
in clinical trials, 2, 99, 121, 125, 143, 145–148, 158, 160–161, 183–184, 226
MDMA-assisted therapy, 16, 23, 46, 101, 111, 125, 135, 145–148, 158, 160–161, 183–184, 190, 224–226

media, 3–4, 13–15, 19, 23, 31, 36–37, 48, 55, 78, 81–82, 86, 91–92, 103, 120–121, 125, 129, 133, 140–143, 148–149, 154, 167, 191, 245–246, 253
   coverage of psychedelics, 3–4, 13–15, 19, 78, 81–82, 86, 121, 129, 133, 140–143, 149, 154
   role in psychedelic hype, 4, 13–14, 78, 81–82, 86, 92, 121, 140–143
   psychedelic media companies, 14, 143, 167
Medical Assistance in Dying (MAiD), 16, 223
medical establishment, 1, 4, 19, 22, 49, 90, 113–114, 118, 254
medical model (of psychedelic access and mainstreaming), 111–115, 178–179, 220–221, 224–225, 251
medicalization, 2, 4–5, 15, 17, 20, 22, 26–29, 32–33, 53, 60, 62, 78, 90–92, 104, 110–116, 124–125, 127–128, 133, 137–138, 145, 158, 162, 172, 177, 180, 193, 195, 208, 220, 224–225, 227, 229, 234, 239, 251–252, 254–255, 258
meditation, 62, 75, 184–185, 188
mental health, 14, 16, 19–22, 24, 39–40, 53, 63, 70, 78, 80, 91, 97, 114–115, 122, 124–130, 133–134, 136, 138, 140–141, 143–144, 149, 151, 154–156, 161, 172, 174–175, 178, 190–192, 212, 217–218, 220, 225, 229, 232, 235–236, 238, 251, 254, 259
   mental health crisis, 125–128
mental illness, 35, 90, 111, 119, 125–128, 130, 133, 152, 174, 184–185
   socioeconomic determinants of, 29, 90, 127–128, 185
   see also psychiatry
Merck, 166, 173–174, 200
Merry Pranksters, 96–97, 237
mescaline, 9–11, 18, 40–42, 50, 61, 95, 111, 123, 152, 154, 166, 210, 213–214, 220, 232, 235, 237, 243
methamphetamine, 30–31, 59, 149, 231, 249
microdosing, 18–19, 32, 104, 138–142, 145, 174
military, 4, 21–22, 24, 53, 87, 93, 95–102, 107, 135, 137, 147, 185, 187, 195, 235, 238, 254
   militarism, 4, 80, 101, 258
   military-industrial complex, 4, 96, 98–99
   soldiers/veterans, 21–22, 95, 98–102, 146–147, 214, 235–239

mind control, 87, 95–96, 106–107
   see also Central Intelligence Agency (CIA)
Mind Medicine (MindMed), 21, 123, 132, 166, 168–170, 173–175, 177, 184, 188, 201, 212–213
Mindbloom, 192–193
mindfulness, 90, 184–186, 188
Mindset Pharma, 173, 203–204
monopolies, 28, 33, 104, 177–178, 205, 208–210, 216, 218, 233
   in the drug industry, 177, 205, 208–210, 216
   in the psychedelic industry, 28, 33, 104, 177–178, 209, 216, 218, 233
   see also psychedelic industry
moral panic, 20, 42, 49, 55–56, 230
Morris, Hamilton, 2, 102, 200
Multidisciplinary Association for Psychedelic Studies (MAPS), 1–2, 20, 66, 80, 87, 99–101, 109, 116, 121, 125, 146–148, 158, 160–161, 165, 173, 180–184, 190, 226, 257–258
   MAPS Public Benefit Corporation (PBC), 125, 180–183
   see also Lykos Therapeutics
Musk, Elon, 12, 100, 147, 175
mystical experiences, 61–73, 75, 78, 81, 85, 108, 115, 117, 134, 195
   and religion, 63–65, 68–69, 72
   in psychedelic research and science, 65–73, 75, 81, 85, 115, 117, 134
   Mystical Experience Questionnaire (MEQ), 68, 70
mysticism, 12, 40, 63–66, 68–70, 72, 198

narcotics, 37–40, 42–44, 50, 65, 97, 114, 152, 244
National Defense Authorization Act, 24, 99, 239
Native American Church, 40, 64, 110, 240–241, 243–244
Nazis/Nazism, 93–95, 97
neoliberalism, 29, 49, 79, 89–90, 104, 106, 184–185, 190
neuroplasticity, 104, 130, 135
neuroscience, 3, 7, 20, 22, 28, 30, 41, 68, 75, 110, 122, 129, 135–136, 149, 187
   see also psychedelic science
New Approach, 185, 227, 233–234, 238
next-generation psychedelics, 22, 137, 174, 202–205

see also non-hallucinogenic/non-subjective psychedelics
Nichols, David, 41, 129, 207
Nickles, David, 3, 80, 83–84, 101, 105, 107, 162, 164, 189, 258
Nixon, Richard, 45–46, 78, 87
noetic, 62, 73–74
non-hallucinogenic/non-subjective psychedelics, 123, 134–137, 202
  see also next-generation psychedelics
non-profit organizations, 2, 16, 20–21, 25, 91, 146, 165, 178, 180, 201, 213–215, 222, 234, 237
non-specific amplifiers, 7, 78, 89
  see also set and setting
Noorani, Tehseen, 104, 189
Numinus Wellness, 105, 168, 170, 175, 222
Nutt, David, 45, 150–151, 157–158, 207

obsessive-compulsive disorder, 41, 122, 191
openness, 10, 80–82, 86, 93, 106–107, 132
opioids, 18, 30, 49–50, 55–57, 59, 122–123, 151, 153, 175, 230, 238, 248–249, 260
  opioid addiction/opioid use disorder, 49–50, 55–56, 122–123, 153, 175, 248
  opioid crisis, 30, 49, 153, 230, 248
opium, 35–37, 43, 49, 53
Osmond, Humphry, 5, 39–40, 42, 117, 134
Otsuka, 173–174, 203
overdoses, 51, 55–57, 59, 128, 150, 231, 236, 248–251, 260
  overdose deaths, 55–57, 59, 150, 231, 236, 248–249, 260
  see also drug deaths; tainted drugs
OxyContin, 49, 193

panpsychism, 71–72, 83
patents, 25, 28, 78, 112, 165, 177, 182–183, 188, 200–214, 216–219, 257
  bad patents, 25, 208, 210–214
  patent applications, 25, 183, 188, 200–204, 207, 210–214, 216–218
  patent examiners, 210–213, 216–217
  prior art, 210–214, 216–217
  see also intellectual property (IP)
PCP, 10, 30–31, 95
personality, 8, 78, 80–82, 85, 89, 127, 169
peyote, 7, 9, 18, 40, 61, 64, 102, 108, 110, 123, 149, 166, 197, 199, 232, 235, 240–241, 243–245

pharmaceutical companies, 4, 15, 28–29, 31, 33, 44, 49, 96, 111–113, 118, 128, 142, 163, 166–168, 173, 189, 200, 206–207, 209–210, 254, 257
pharmaceutical industry, 5, 19, 22, 114, 136–138, 142, 152, 166, 168, 173–174, 184, 201, 203, 205, 207–210, 215, 257
  see also Big Pharma
pharmacology, 3, 7–8, 17, 22, 29–30, 41, 75, 78, 83, 110, 114, 116–118, 122–123, 128–129, 131, 135, 141, 146, 159, 199, 204, 207
  see also psychopharmacology
pharmahuasca, 118, 199
philanthropy, 12, 20, 133, 158, 181, 183
philosophy, 7, 61–64, 70–71, 75, 78, 85, 91, 93, 147
plant medicines, 1, 8, 110, 157, 242
police/policing, 31, 36–37, 40, 43, 45–47, 49–57, 59, 100–102, 155, 160, 195, 221, 230–231, 235–240, 244–249, 253–254, 256, 260
  drug-related arrests, 33, 45–49, 51–52, 55, 58, 102, 221, 230, 235, 240, 245–246, 248–249
  police raids, 45, 236, 244–247, 249
  police surveillance, 33, 40, 195, 221, 230
  see also law enforcement
political economy, 3, 26, 89–90, 92
politicians, 1, 3, 17, 22–24, 32, 37, 41–42, 51, 53–54, 56–57, 60, 72, 86–87, 95, 98–102, 147, 230, 236–239, 242, 246, 250–251, 254, 260
  conservative politicians, 9, 22–24, 32, 45, 51, 53–54, 56–57, 60, 100, 102, 242, 246, 250
  Republican politicians, 22–24, 95, 98–100, 102, 147, 238, 254
Pollan, Michael, 11, 14, 26, 41, 46, 62, 66, 68, 72–73, 80, 87, 103, 120, 133, 164–165, 190, 243, 255
  Pollan effect, 14
polymorph, 216–217
popular culture, 9–11, 13, 39, 196
Porta Sophia, 213–214, 217
post-traumatic stress disorder (PTSD), 15–16, 22, 40, 46, 99, 101, 112, 114, 121–122, 124–125, 133, 138, 143, 145–146, 190–191, 225
poverty, 29, 31, 49, 53, 86, 90, 100, 127, 189, 195
prisons, 36, 41, 43, 47, 52, 58, 97, 101–102, 120, 177, 242, 261

prisoners, 41, 48, 52, 58, 95, 97, 102, 261
see also incarceration
prohibition, 3, 13, 23, 26, 29, 34–39, 43–46, 50–53, 57–58, 102, 112, 114, 116, 160, 168–169, 204, 211, 220–221, 235, 249–252, 254, 259–260
see also war on drugs
psilocin, 9, 217
psilocybin, 7, 9–12, 15–18, 21, 23–25, 28, 42, 44, 50, 61, 65–68, 81, 83, 94, 99, 102, 110, 112–114, 123–125, 130, 135–136, 138–139, 141, 143–144, 150–152, 154–155, 157–158, 166, 170, 175–176, 178–179, 181–182, 191, 194–195, 197–198, 200–203, 206, 210–212, 214–218, 220, 222–229, 232, 234–240, 244–247, 251
    for the treatment of depression, 12, 15–17, 112, 114, 124, 130, 136, 143, 157–158, 170, 175, 211, 225
    in clinical trials, 68, 99, 124–125, 143, 157–158, 170, 211, 215
    psilocybin-assisted therapy, 15–16, 24, 124, 143, 176, 178, 222–225, 229, 247, 251
psilocybin mushrooms, 7, 12, 42, 61, 64, 68, 86, 94–95, 108, 110, 135, 151–152, 155, 175, 194–195, 216, 223, 228, 234, 240, 244–246
see also magic mushrooms
Psychedelic Alpha, 147, 171, 183, 201
psychedelic commons, 4, 28, 213, 255
psychedelic exceptionalism, 29–30, 100, 148, 252, 261
psychedelic hype, 4, 14–15, 28, 122, 142–143, 145, 148, 153, 170–171
see also media
psychedelic industry, 2, 4, 14, 25, 27–28, 59, 78, 95, 136, 154, 161–170, 172–177, 184–185, 189–196, 202–203, 206–208, 210, 233, 236, 255, 257
    investments/investors, 1, 3, 12, 21–22, 87, 94–95, 103–105, 132, 136, 143, 163, 166–173, 175, 177, 179, 181–183, 188–189, 197, 203, 205–207, 215–216, 218, 256–257
    venture capital/capitalists, 3–5, 14, 22–23, 25, 28, 60, 105, 123, 163, 167, 169, 171, 173, 176, 180–182, 189, 192, 206, 257

see also capitalism/capitalists; intellectual property (IP); ketamine clinics; monopolies; psychedelic tourism, start-ups, stock market
psychedelic mainstreaming, 2, 4, 11, 13, 23, 26, 29, 33, 53, 80, 92, 95, 112–113, 136, 170, 180–181, 254, 258–259
psychedelic medicine, 1–5, 7–8, 13, 15–16, 18, 21–24, 26–30, 32–33, 35, 44, 53, 60, 70, 85–86, 92, 110–120, 122–125, 128–138, 142–148, 158–159, 161, 163, 165, 167–168, 173–174, 176–180, 188, 199, 205–206, 208–209, 220–227, 232–236, 238–240, 247, 251, 254–255
    expectancy bias in psychedelic research/medicine, 14, 66, 69, 121, 141, 144, 146
    neurobiological models/mechanisms of action, 9–10, 22, 129–135
    patients, 8, 14, 16–17, 22, 24, 40–41, 75, 81, 97, 99, 110–111, 113, 117, 119, 121, 124, 128–129, 132, 134–137, 145–146, 154, 157–159, 161, 174, 178–179, 184, 188, 192–194, 205–207, 211, 214, 217, 222–223, 225–226, 240, 246, 256–257
    placebo-controlled experiments/trials, 66–67, 120–121, 124–125, 140–141, 157
    placebo effect, 120, 144–145
see also biomedicine; clinical trials; medicalization; psychedelic science; psychiatry; Western medicine
psychedelic renaissance, 2–6, 10, 15, 18, 23, 26–28, 62, 67, 80, 90, 93–94, 98, 102, 106, 111, 121, 134–135, 141–142, 148, 162, 164, 175, 186, 200, 214, 218, 225, 245, 253–258, 260
psychedelic retreats, 11–12, 25, 88, 161, 187, 195–196
psychedelic science, 1–2, 9, 12–14, 16, 20–22, 26–29, 39–42, 45, 65, 68, 70, 75, 78, 82, 86, 92, 98, 109–111, 115–117, 129, 135–136, 139, 143, 145, 148–149, 165, 169, 181–182, 184, 203–205, 214–215, 219–220, 254–255, 258
    open science, 165, 181, 204–205, 214–215, 219, 255
    psychedelic science conferences, 1–2, 12, 98, 109, 145, 182
see also neuroscience; psychedelic medicine
psychedelic socialism, 90–91

psychedelic therapy, 1–2, 4–5, 8, 10, 15–18, 20–24, 26, 28–31, 39–42, 46, 63, 69–70, 75, 90–91, 98–101, 104–107, 110–114, 117, 120, 122–125, 128–137, 141, 144–148, 156–162, 164, 166, 171, 176, 178–179, 183–185, 187–194, 200–202, 205, 210–211, 217, 220, 222–226, 229, 232, 236–239, 251, 253–257, 259
   facilitators and guides, 29, 113–114, 146, 160, 169, 176, 188, 190, 227–229, 232, 235, 237
   integration component of, 105, 132, 136, 144, 188–189, 191–192, 228, 256–257
   in the mid-twentieth century, 10, 20, 39–42, 106, 110, 117, 122–123, 134, 156, 159, 166, 210
   psychedelic-assisted therapy, 15–16, 24, 28, 39–42, 70, 75, 101, 104–105, 107, 124–125, 145–148, 158, 160, 166, 183, 185, 190, 217, 223–226, 237, 254
   psychedelic-assisted psychotherapy (PAP), 24, 39, 131–133, 135–136, 142, 145, 159–160, 162, 174, 192–194, 224, 237
   therapist misconduct/abuse, 2, 4, 125, 145–148, 158–162, 190
   therapy training, 26, 114, 136, 190, 192, 194, 227–229, 232
   see also individualism/individualized therapy; military (soldiers/veterans); psychedelic medicine; psychedelic underground; psychotherapy
psychedelic tourism, 12, 25, 88, 161, 163, 194–199, 255
   see also ayahuasca
psychedelic underground, 2, 5, 13, 17, 20, 28–29, 41, 45–46, 97, 108, 112–114, 135, 160, 164–165, 169, 176, 180–181, 205, 211, 219, 252, 255
   underground researchers, therapists and guides, 5, 20, 29, 41, 45, 108, 112–114, 160, 164–165, 169, 176, 181, 205, 211, 219, 255
psychiatry, 4, 7–8, 17–20, 22, 27, 39–41, 46, 78, 85, 91, 96, 111–114, 122, 131, 137, 156, 159–161, 166, 192, 213, 224, 229
   psychiatrists, 4, 7–8, 18–20, 27, 39–40, 46, 78, 85, 113–114, 131, 160–161, 192, 224, 229
   see also antidepressants; mental illness
psychonauts, 34, 163, 166, 172

psychopharmacology, 41, 45, 133, 150, 153, 174, 207
   see also pharmacology
Psychopharmacology (journal), 125, 160
psychotherapy, 10, 15, 21, 24, 39, 42, 46, 106, 110, 117, 131–132, 134–135, 146, 159, 179, 185, 192–194, 224, 237, 257
   see also psychedelic therapy
Psymposia, 2, 91–92, 100–102, 146–148, 160, 164, 173
Purdue Pharma, 49, 256

race/racism, 31, 35, 37, 45, 47–49, 52, 80, 97, 107, 119–120, 254
Reagan, Ronald, 46–48, 87
recreational drug use, 8, 18, 31–33, 35–36, 46–47, 53, 58, 60, 92, 114, 116, 139, 148–149, 167–168, 177, 179, 213, 221, 224, 232, 260
Red Light Holland, 167, 169–170
religion, 4, 6–9, 35, 40, 62–65, 67–69, 72, 103, 110, 195, 200, 222, 224, 227, 240–245, 254
   psychedelics and religious freedom, 224, 240–244
   psychedelics and religious practice, 4, 6–9, 35, 40, 62–65, 68–69, 72, 103, 106, 110, 240–241, 254
   psychedelic churches, 224, 234, 240–244
   Santo Daime, 224, 242–243
   União do Vegetal, 224, 241–243
   see also mystical experiences; spiritual/spirituality
Republican Party, 22–23, 95, 98–100, 147, 238, 254
   see also politicians
Royal Canadian Mounted Police (RCMP), 37, 39–40, 246

sacred, 7, 62, 64–65, 72, 110, 169, 194, 240–242, 244–245
   see also religion; spiritual/spirituality
safe supply, 33, 51, 55–57, 59, 224, 231, 248–252, 260
safe use, 26, 54–55, 57, 59, 116, 231, 241, 248–252, 260
   safe injection sites, 54–55, 241, 250
salvia divinorum, 10, 18, 50
San Pedro, 9, 61, 197, 243
Sandoz, 45, 166, 200
serotonin/serotonergic system, 8–10, 22, 41, 131, 153, 200

Sessa, Ben, 27, 113, 115, 143, 161
set and setting, 7–9, 67–68, 70, 74, 78–79, 82, 85, 97, 106–107, 117–118, 120, 144, 155, 159, 164–165, 175, 179–180, 194, 198, 201, 254, 258–259
    and politics, 77–79, 82, 89, 106–107, 165, 258–259
    in clinical research, 8, 117–118, 120, 144, 194
    of the 1960s, 8, 10, 22, 33, 65–67, 77–79, 89–90, 97, 99, 106, 155, 255–256, 259
    corporadelic/neoliberal, 2, 8, 79, 106, 164–165, 175–177, 179–180, 198, 254
sexual misconduct/assault 146–147, 160–161, 198
    see also psychedelic tourism; psychedelic therapy
shamans, 9, 11, 23–24, 94, 111, 118, 161, 197–199
Shulgin, Alexander (Sasha), 45, 153, 165, 204–205
Silicon Valley, 11, 23, 103–107, 187, 189, 254
    see also technology industry
social change, 4–5, 8, 29, 66, 76–77, 79–80, 84, 86, 89–91, 106–108, 128–129, 254–255, 259
    see also activism
social control, 36–38, 48–49, 51, 185, 220, 254
social justice, 5, 32, 103, 107–108, 233, 251, 256, 258–260
social movements, 1–5, 8, 13, 22–23, 35–36, 46, 53–55, 66–67, 77–80, 89–93, 107–108, 121, 177, 243, 246, 254, 256, 258
    see also activism; social change
Soma, 61, 64, 104
Special Access Program (SAP), 222–224
spiritual/spirituality, 3–4, 7, 9, 19–21, 41, 61–63, 65, 67, 72–73, 80, 102–103, 106, 110, 158, 184, 190, 195–198, 241, 245, 254, 259
    evolutionary spirituality, 102–103
    see also mystical experiences; sacred
Spravato, 124, 158, 173, 184, 191
    see also esketamine
start-ups, 3, 25–26, 100, 123, 163, 167, 171, 173, 206, 208
    see also psychedelic industry
stigma/stigmatization, 3, 9, 14–15, 20, 22, 26, 30–31, 33, 35, 39, 45, 112, 123, 144, 152, 158, 168, 227, 261

around/of psychedelics, 3, 9, 14–15, 20, 22, 45, 112, 123, 144, 152, 158, 168, 227
stimulants, 34, 50, 77, 121
stock market, 25, 166, 168, 170–172
    see also psychedelic industry
Strassman, Rick, 9, 63, 68, 74
substance use disorders, 16–17, 39, 55–56, 110, 122–124, 126–127, 143, 191, 234
    psychedelics for the treatment of, 16–17, 39, 110, 122–124, 143, 191, 234
    see also addiction, drug dependency
suicide, 44, 97, 125, 128, 135, 147, 157–158, 161, 236–237, 248
    suicidal ideation, 123, 157–158, 192, 229
supernatural, 68–69, 72
surveillance capitalism, 94–95, 105–106, 186–189, 255, 257
    see also digital psychedelia
synthetic drugs, 9, 43, 52, 110–111, 137, 171, 181, 199, 202–203, 216–217, 234, 236, 247, 256–257
synthetic psychedelics, 9, 110–111, 137, 171, 181, 199, 202–203, 216–217, 234, 236, 256–257

tainted drugs, 33, 49, 54–56, 58, 153, 251, 259–260
technology industry, 3, 11–12, 23, 25–26, 104–106, 135–136, 163, 166–168, 171, 186–190, 196, 215–216
    see also biotechnology, Silicon Valley
TheraPsil, 16, 222–223, 251
Thiel, Peter, 23, 95, 103–105, 170, 181, 215–216
tobacco, 1, 30, 51, 77, 115, 131, 126
transhumanism, 102–105
trauma, 7, 13, 22, 80, 84, 99–102, 107–110, 112, 127, 131, 157, 171, 184, 239, 250
    see also post-traumatic stress disorder
TREAT California, 235–237
Trump, Donald, 87–88, 95, 100, 172
tryptamines, 9, 135
Turnbull, Carey, 214, 216

United Nations (UN), 23, 43–44, 101, 126, 152, 216
US Congress, 24, 39, 97–99, 147, 227, 248
Usona Institute, 21, 181, 215
utopia, 68, 80, 92–93, 104, 109

Vancouver, 21, 33, 37, 42, 44, 53–54, 138, 160, 199, 246–248

Vancouver Area Network of Drug Users (VANDU), 54, 248, 251

war, 6, 45–49, 51–53, 66, 77–78, 80, 86, 95, 97–98, 101
    anti-war movement, 22, 45–46, 66, 77–78
    see also military
war on drugs, 1–2, 26, 28, 31–34, 41–43, 45–49, 51–53, 100, 102, 120, 161, 177, 180, 221, 225, 235, 239, 244–245, 247–248, 250, 252–255, 259–261
    and psychedelics, 1–2, 26, 28, 33, 42, 47, 53, 102, 120, 161, 180, 221, 225, 235, 239, 244–245, 247, 252–253, 255, 259–261
    and racialized communities, 31, 45, 47–49, 52, 100, 102, 120, 177, 254, 260–261
Wasson, R. Gordon, 64, 194–195
Watts, Alan, 63, 78
Watts, Rosalind, 129, 143–144
wellness industry, 4, 13, 142, 184–189, 191, 195
Western medicine, 21, 29, 110–112, 114–118, 123, 254
    see also biomedicine, medical model; medicalization; psychedelic medicine
World Health Organization (WHO), 125–126, 151

Yaden, David, 63, 68, 82, 134, 137, 147
yoga, 62, 184–185